CARING FOR YOUR PARENTS

A Sourcebook of Options and Solutions
for Both Generations

Also by Helene MacLean

Author: THERE'S NO PLACE LIKE PARIS

Coeditor: CITY LIFE

Major Contributor to:
THE MODERN ENCYCLOPEDIA OF BABY AND CHILD CARE
THE COMPLETE BOOK OF BETTER HEALTH
EVERYWOMAN'S HEALTH

Contributing Editor:
THE DOUBLEDAY DICTIONARY
THE DOUBLEDAY ROGET'S THESAURUS

CARING
FOR YOUR PARENTS

A Sourcebook of Options and Solutions
for Both Generations

Helene MacLean

A DOLPHIN BOOK

Doubleday & Company, Inc., Garden City, New York

1987

306.87
m22

To the memory of my parents

ACKNOWLEDGMENTS

I would like to express my gratitude to:
  my agent, Barbara Lowenstein, for her unflagging confidence in me;
  my editor, Lisa Wager, for her enthusiastic support;
  my friend, Dr. Richard Wagman, for his professional suggestions;
  my daughter, Rebecca MacLean, for her perceptive comments;
  and to the many people in public and private agencies nationwide
    who provided essential information by phone and by mail.
Special thanks are due Betty Ransom, Coordinator,
  National Institute on Adult Daycare of the
    National Council on the Aging; and
  Herman Janiger, Consumer Affairs Officer, New York
    District Office of the U.S. Food and Drug Administration.

Library of Congress Cataloging-in-Publication Data

MacLean, Helene.
Caring for your parents.

"A Dolphin book."
Includes index.
1. Parents, Aged—Care and hygiene—United States.   2.
Parents, Aged—United States—Family relationships.   3.
Adult children—United States.   I. Title.
HQ1063.6.M33   1987   306.8'7   86-16816
ISBN 0-385-24148-8
ISBN 0-385-23314-0 (pbk.)

CONTENTS

PREFACE

Most people's parents are still pretty competent about looking after themselves during their sixties and early seventies. If you were to ask them whether they want more help from their children, they'd be likely to tell you in no uncertain terms that they prefer to be in charge of their own lives for as long as possible.

Whatever the state of your parents' health and their avowed intentions, their strength will inevitably decline with advancing age, and for some, their emotional health and mental competence may deteriorate too. Whether this decline occurs almost imperceptibly over many years or within a brief span, adult children can have a sense of genuine accomplishment when they help a parent of advanced age function independently for as long as they're able.

The most effective way to do this is to be alert to your parents' health needs, to be informed about community resources, alternative living arrangements, government programs established for their benefit and yours, and a wide variety of support groups. Above all, try to anticipate problems before they become crises.

The purpose of this book is to help you help them live their later years comfortably, productively, and with unimpaired self-esteem.

Public policy in health and human services should recognize that it is the family and not the government that provides most of the care to older people in this country. In this respect, government should see its caregiving role as being a supplement and a complement to that of the family. . . . Estimates show that the monetary value of family care for older people residing in the community is substantial and greater than that provided by public agencies. These estimates do not include the psychological and emotional costs associated with the caregiving. . . .

> Family Caregiving and the Elderly:
> Policy Recommendations and Re-
> search Findings, issued by the New
> York State Office for the Aging,
> March 1983

The single greatest fear we have in this country is the fear of growing old, losing our mind, and being put away in a nursing home. It overshadows cancer as a national phobia. And its impact on the family is enormous.

> Dr. Robert N. Butler, chairman of
> the Department of Geriatrics and
> Adult Development, Mt. Sinai Medi-
> cal School[1]

There are classes for young mothers in the care of the newborn, but where can the daughter of a feeble mother find classes in parent care that would teach her how to bathe and dress an older person or how to cope with incontinence?

> A visiting nurse

1. As quoted in Didi Moore, "America's Neglected Elderly," New York *Times Magazine,* January 30, 1983.

❧ 1 ❧

LOOKING AHEAD
AND GETTING THINGS SAID

FAMILY CONFERENCES

It is generally agreed among geriatric social workers and other professionals who specialize in family relations that no matter how many adult children make up the family, responsibilities are not equally shared when parent care becomes necessary. It might be the oldest daughter with her own children, or the youngest who still lives "at home," or the daughter-in-law whose house is around the corner, or (much less commonly) a favorite son, but *one* member of the family almost invariably becomes the prime caregiver.[1] This doesn't mean that financial burdens aren't shared or that patterns of responsibility remain the same over the years. What *is* likely is that at any given moment, one family member will know exactly what's going on, will be called when there's a crisis, and will be the liaison with the others.

Since no two families are any more alike than two individuals, there is great diversity in caregiving arrangements. If yours is a family whose members are emotionally and geographically close to each other, you're in a good position to talk things out regularly and deal with changing circumstances, such as the death of one parent and the relocation of the other, or the need for a part-time housekeeper.

Even in families where adult children are separated by distance or by unfriendly feelings about each other, the essential thing to do is to set aside old resentments and sibling hostilities and even to welcome the return of the prodigal sister or brother for the sake

1. Sometime in the 1980s, the term *caregiver* began to replace *caretaker* among social workers. It does not yet appear in any dictionary, but its use is now so widespread that it is likely to receive official sanction any day.

of family cohesion. Some family conferences should be arranged without the parents so that feelings can be aired frankly, but the goal should be general agreement about how to proceed when a problem presents itself. Sometimes family meetings are called by one spouse without the knowledge of the other, when Father wants everyone's opinion about Mother's recent peculiar behavior, or when Mom finds her freedom limited now that Pop has retired and hangs around the house all day and what do the children think she should do about it.

When various options to improve your parents' situation are being considered, always consult them about their preferences *before* embarking on a plan of action. Unless or until parents become mentally incompetent or are diagnosed as clinically senile, their opinions should always be respected, and final decisions that affect their lives should remain with them. To be physically feeble is by no means to be feeble-minded, and family members should guard against their own or each other's tendency to treat their parents like incompetent children, or even worse, like intractable infants.

It may well be that you feel your parents continue to be more competent in many ways than you are, and seem to have an endless supply of physical stamina as they jog briskly into their seventies. In fact, many members of the generation that came through the Great Depression and weathered the crises of World War II seem to face their declining years with enviable self-reliance and dignity intact.

However, should the time come when you have to devote thought and effort to caring for your parents, face facts; deal with your feelings instead of denying them, and don't take on more responsibilities than you think you can handle without getting irritable and angry. *Don't make promises you won't be able to keep.* Better never to have said, "Mom, don't worry about ending up in a nursing home because we'll always be able to take care of you," than to have to admit at some future time that she'd be better off in an institution that provides full-time professional attention.

IF YOU'RE AN ONLY CHILD

Make a special effort to maintain contact with your aunts and uncles, especially those who are devoted to your parents. Including them in your life, and making it clear that you're pleased to be included in theirs, provides a firm foundation for calling on their help when it's needed. Your mother's sister may be happy to come around and do the marketing and cooking while your mother recovers from surgery; your father's brother may offer to drive him to his physical therapy sessions when the cast comes off his broken leg.

An unmarried woman with a demanding job or a single parent with a boring one may think she ought to invite her recently widowed mother to come and live with her. After all, she has no one else to turn to . . . it might be nice to enjoy occasional mothering and a good hot meal after a hard day . . . David wouldn't have to go to a special play group after school. . . .

But most family therapists agree that there aren't many aging parents who can live harmoniously with their children—and particularly when it's a mother and a daughter—unless they've been doing it without friction for decades. If both women want to be closer, and Mother doesn't mind moving out of her old neighborhood and away from her friends, you could help her find an apartment on the same street, or even in the same building. But to install her in a dwelling where her independence is threatened, and where seemingly buried mother-daughter conflicts about the "right" way to do things are acted out all over again— that's an arrangement likely to present more problems than it solves.

DEALING WITH BUREAUCRACIES: SURVIVAL TACTICS

BUREAUCRACY: a system of administration marked by officialism, red tape, and proliferation[2]

BUREAUCRAT: a government official who follows a narrow rigid formal routine or who is established with great authority in his own department[3]

The time is likely to come, if it hasn't already, when you'll need information from an official source—a city, county, state, or federal agency whose genuine reason for being is not to shuffle papers around but to be of service to you. Alas, many of these agencies are understaffed or poorly regulated or the rules are in the process of change or the computers have broken down. . . .

Here are some suggestions for keeping your sanity and your temper in the process of trying to find out what you want to know.

2. *Webster's Ninth New Collegiate Dictionary,* 1983.
3. Ibid.

Above all, be patient and persistent, and be prepared for a run-around, rudeness, busy signals, being put on hold, being disconnected while you're on hold, and wasting the better part of an hour with no results.

If you're consulting an agency on the phone, don't start out with the notion that it's a simple chore to be squeezed into a five-minute slot in your busy schedule. The more rushed you feel, the testier you'll get. Better, before you dial, to settle down with a notebook and pen and write down the date, the agency you're calling, the phone number, and the specific questions you want to have answered. When someone does pick up, ask for the person's name and write it down; then ask your questions and write down the answers. If the person you're talking to can't answer your questions, find out what agency to call and whom to ask for.

If you're consulting an agency in person, bring that notebook as well as something to read or do while you're waiting. Discuss the nature of your business with the receptionist to make sure you're in the right place. If you're told that you're in the wrong office, find out where to go and write down what you've been told. If you've waited around for an hour to see a particular employee and it turns out that the agency is right but the department isn't, find out where to go next and whom to see. Patience and organization are your greatest assets. During any interview with a lower-level government employee or an upper-echelon bureaucrat, always write down the person's name and take notes as the interview proceeds. The notebook you're carrying around should be the looseleaf variety, and you may eventually find it helpful to use pens that color-code the information you've been accumulating.

KEEP CALM AND KEEP YOUR PURPOSE IN MIND. What you want is information about options, services, entitlements, procedures, official forms, and how to speed up the process of getting the best solution (it will never be perfect) for your family's problem.

Don't be put off by high-handedness, but don't accept rudeness or incompetence either. When you think it necessary, ask to speak to a supervisor. In these endeavors, you're sure to meet helpful, sympathetic, and resourceful men and women, too, who understand what it means to serve the public, even though the term *public servant* has gone out of fashion. When you enter *their* names in your notebook, distinguish them in some way so that

when you have the time, you can send them a thank-you note—
and address a copy to their boss.

FINDING OUT ABOUT FINANCES

Some people can talk openly and honestly about money; others
can talk about everything but. The parent most difficult to deal
with when the need arises for making family decisions is the father
or mother who won't share *any* details about finances with anyone
but the accountant, and that's that. Then there are the parents
whose savings may have been depleted by the cost of coping with
a chronic illness and who say, "Never mind. We can struggle
along on what we've got." In such cases, it might be helpful—if
they don't want to impose on the children—to advise them to
investigate their eligibility for Supplementary Security Income
(SSI) in addition to their Social Security, and for food stamps.
Why should they "struggle" when they may be the very people for
whom these programs were created?

Fortunately, most parents share information about their resources with each other and with their offspring as they grow
older, especially if the sons and daughters are eventually going to
contribute to their support. In some instances, "eventually" can
mean overnight if a healthy sixty-year-old father dies of a heart
attack, leaving his financial affairs in a total mess and his widow
with nothing but large debts.

In families where an aging father might balk at talking about
his sources of income with his children, the children should encourage their mother to be present when Dad meets with the
accountant to prepare his tax returns. In families where mutual
consideration and trust are the general rule, the following matters
might be discussed:

- Are both parents receiving—or will they receive—their own
  Social Security benefits based on their individual work history?
- Does your father receive a pension and does it include benefits
  for his widow when he dies?
- Is your mother the prime beneficiary of his life insurance?
- Do your parents have a joint checking account and a joint sav-
  ings account?
- Considering the number of older women who have a difficult
  time establishing credit when they are widowed, does your

mother have any accounts in her own name against which *she* can apply for a loan during your father's lifetime? Does she have any credit cards in her own name?

- Is someone in the family in a position to provide—on short notice—a list of *parental assets,* including bank accounts; resale value of the house and car; rental income from real estate; assessed value of such valuables as jewelry, silver, art objects, or a coin or stamp collection; and *parental debts* including outstanding loans, mortgage payments, and unpaid bills on credit cards and charge accounts?
- Are all important documents relating to parental finances kept in the same place, and does at least one member of the family other than the parents have access to that place if necessary?

Changing Circumstances

In families where it is accepted that one member of the younger generation—whether a son, a daughter, or an in-law—will take the continuing responsibility for dealing with financial problems as they arise, the nature of the responsibility should be spelled out in detail.[4]

- Is this person to be the investment counselor for your parents without consulting other family members when giving his or her advice?
- Does the responsibility consist *only* in being the family member who is always informed of changing circumstances and making these changes known to other family members?
- Is this the family member responsible for arranging to set up a fund of contributions from other members when the parents' resources run low?

One of the major changes in the family's involvement with parental money problems is likely to occur when the father dies. If there's a will that leaves the widow well provided for, or she has her own money, she may still want to turn to a favorite family member for advice. If, on the other hand, she chooses to turn to an old friend, or her brother, or the family attorney, it may be that sons and daughters will feel resentful about not being consulted, or not being trusted. Consider, though, that not "depending" on the children for advice may be the widow's way of maintaining

4. The formalized power of attorney is discussed on page 8.

her autonomy or refusing to assign her favorite son the role of surrogate spouse in money matters.

If your mother comes through her bereavement determined to handle her own affairs in whatever way *she* sees fit, such determination should be respected and encouraged. The many widows in their sixties and seventies who are joining younger women in courses called "Managing Your Money" and "How to Be Your Own Investment Counselor" have been discovering that they needn't be entirely at the mercy of a banker or stockbroker in making their decisions.

Widows whose major concern about money is how to invest it wisely are, however, in the minority. More typical is the elderly widow trying to make ends meet while maintaining her own household—as most prefer to do. With a few exceptions, more than 80 percent of older women *don't* receive a pension, and for those who do, the median amount is about $3000 a year.

If your widowed mother is among the women who make up 71 percent of the elderly poor, with Social Security the major source of her income, family members may want to figure out ways of making her life a little easier. Many older women in straitened circumstances refuse to take money outright, even from a son or daughter who can afford to send a small monthly check. In such situations, generous impulses can take the form of such practical presents as a new winter coat, a round-trip ticket for a visit with an ailing sister who lives a thousand miles away, or the prepaid one-day-a-week services of a cleaning person.

Where There's a Will, There's Less Confusion Later

If your parents haven't written a will with the help of an attorney and deposited it with him or her, they should be urged to do so. If you're broaching the subject because you think it hasn't been attended to, you may have to convince your parents that you don't expect them to discuss the nature and extent of their assets, or to reveal the terms of the will to you, which, in fact, you'd prefer that they didn't.

With many elderly parents, the amount of material wealth involved has very little to do with the intensity of their feelings about how and to whom they wish to bequeath their legacy. And in many large families, who inherits the house and the cash is less significant than who inherits particular contents of the house or particular items of personal property. Many lawyers urge the maker of a will to list individual bequests in detail, including items whose value is merely sentimental (that's a very large *merely)* as well as family furniture and decorative objects formerly viewed with disdain and now fetching fancy prices.

Even when adult children are financially better off than their parents, the fact that no advance decisions were made about who is to get a favorite piece of jewelry or the family photo albums, or Father's chess set can eventually cause no end of bickering. (Which is not to say that the will in which everything is meticulously spelled out is a guarantee against hard feelings. Far from it —especially when the hard feelings are part of the pattern of how the offspring relate to each other.)

In families where more or less amicable feelings and rational behavior prevail, it can be suggested that parents take their children's and grandchildren's preferences—as well as those of other family members and dear friends—into account. If your mother or father would feel better knowing how much particular possessions are worth before they decide on their disposition, you can suggest that a qualified appraiser be called in to make an assessment.

In seeking an appraiser, your parents will find qualified professionals listed in the local classified telephone directory. The appraising industry is self-regulated, and appraisers are not licensed, but reliable credentials include membership in the Appraisers Association of America or the American Society of Appraisers.

POWER OF ATTORNEY AND PROBLEMS OF COMPETENCE

Have your parents considered giving the power of attorney to a responsible family member or trusted friend in the event of a serious accident or illness? (In confronting this eventuality, it should comfort you to know that most people retain their legal competence to the end of their lives.) Where husband and wife are both legally competent, each may wish to confer this power on the other. It is also common practice to choose a well-informed son or daughter or the family lawyer who is also a good friend.

While laws vary from state to state, power of attorney usually enables the recipient to manage all funds, sign some contracts, and transact most business in the other person's name. The extent of the power can be limited by the way in which the document is drawn up,[5] and it can be terminated at any time by revoking it in writing. It is also terminated in the event that your parent becomes incompetent *unless* the notarized document is a *durable power of attorney,*[6] that is, it states that at the time it was signed, it was the wish of the competent signer that the document should remain in force in the event of incompetence.

Some states, including New York, have passed a law that provides for a *conservatorship,* a designation conferred on the person or legal entity empowered to handle the estate of a disabled or incompetent person. If your parents live in one of the states that has passed a similar law, you might ask them to consider the advisability of naming a conservator in advance of any compelling necessity to have a court do so. A well-informed and trusted attorney should be able to answer all their questions and dispel suspicions about being rendered powerless by conniving family members.

HAVE YOUR PARENTS SIGNED A LIVING WILL?

Many older people often say—and they say it with conviction—that they don't want to be kept alive by tubes, transfusions, respirators, and other "heroic measures" at a time when they are terminally ill, or when irreversible brain damage has caused them to be comatose. But even though all individuals have the constitutional right to refuse such treatments when they are capable of making their wishes known, this right doesn't automatically extend to their families if they should attempt to carry out such previously stated wishes. When the time comes for close relatives in consultation with the doctor to make the crucial decision on behalf of the patient who can no longer communicate, such wishes may have no validity unless they can be backed up by the documentary evidence of a properly executed Living Will or similar declaration.

5. See the form on page 10 and 11.
6. See the bottom half of the Living Will form on page 21.

This power of attorney shall not be affected by the subsequent disability or incompetence of the principal.

To induce any third party to act hereunder, I hereby agree that any third party receiving a duly executed copy or facsimile of this instrument may act hereunder, and that revocation or termination hereof shall be ineffective as to such third party unless and until actual notice or knowledge of such revocation shall have been received by such third party, and I for myself and for my heirs, executors, legal representatives and assigns, hereby agree to indemnify and hold harmless any such third party from and against any and all claims that may arise against such third party by reason of such third party having relied on the provisions of this instrument.

In Witness Whereof, I have hereunto signed my name and affixed my seal this....................

day of.., 19........

....(Seal)

(Signature of Principal)

STATE OF   COUNTY OF   ss.:

On the   day of   19   before me personally came

to me known, and known to me to be the individual described in, and who executed the foregoing instrument, and he acknowledged to me that he executed the same.

TO

Power of Attorney

Statutory Short Form

Dated,............................., 19........

T 44—Statutory Short Form of General Power of Attorney:
   Disability Clause, if not desired cross out: 1-81
   Complies with Chap. 140, Laws of 1980

JULIUS BLUMBERG, INC.,
PUBLISHER, NYC 10013

Notice: The powers granted by this document are broad and sweeping. They are defined in New York General Obligations Law, Article 5, Title 15, sections 5-1502A through 5-1503, which expressly permits the use of any other or different form of power of attorney desired by the parties concerned.

𝕶𝖓𝖔𝖜 𝕬𝖑𝖑 𝕸𝖊𝖓 𝖇𝖞 𝕿𝖍𝖊𝖘𝖊 𝕻𝖗𝖊𝖘𝖊𝖓𝖙𝖘, *which are intended to constitute a GENERAL POWER OF ATTORNEY pursuant to Article 5. Title 15 of the New York General Obligations Law:*

That I

   (insert name and address of the principal)

do hereby appoint

   (insert name and address of the agent, or each agent, if more than one is designated)

my attorney(s)-in-fact TO ACT

   (a) If more than one agent is designated and the principal wishes each agent alone to be able to exercise the power conferred, insert in this blank the word "severally". Failure to make any insertion or the insertion of the word "jointly" will require the agents to act jointly.

In my name, place and stead in any way which I myself could do, if I were personally present, with respect to the following matters as each of them is defined in Title 15 of Article 5 of the New York General Obligations Law to the extent that I am permitted by law to act through an agent:

   [Strike out and initial in the opposite box any one or more of the subdivisions as to which the principal does NOT desire to give the agent authority. Such elimination of any one or more of subdivisions (A) to (L), inclusive, shall automatically constitute an elimination also of subdivision (M).]

To strike out any subdivision the principal must draw a line through the text of that subdivision AND write his initials in the box opposite.

(A) *real estate transactions;*   [   ]
(B) *chattel and goods transactions;*   [   ]
(C) *bond, share and commodity transactions;*   [   ]
(D) *banking transactions;*   [   ]
(E) *business operating transactions;*   [   ]
(F) *insurance transactions;*   [   ]
(G) *estate transactions;*   [   ]
(H) *claims and litigation;*   [   ]
(I)   *personal relationships and affairs;*   [   ]
(J) *benefits from military service;*   [   ]
(K) *records, reports and statements;*   [   ]
(L) *full and unqualified authority to my attorney(s)-in-fact to delegate any or all of the foregoing powers to any person or persons whom my attorney(s)-in-fact shall select;*   [   ]
(M) *all other matters; .*   [   ]

[Special provisions and limitations may be included in the statutory short form power if they conform to the requirements of section 5-1503 of the New York General Obligations Law.]

The problem of achieving a dignified death has become increasingly complicated in recent years by the progress in medical technology, which on the one hand can save lives, but on the other can prolong existence beyond any reasonable benefit in doing so.

In the meantime, the fine distinctions in the different life-sustaining procedures continue to be argued about in the courtroom. In January 1985, for example, the Supreme Court of New Jersey, one of the twelve states that have not yet enacted comprehensive Living Will legislation,[7] affirmed the constitutional right of competent patients to refuse medical treatment even if the refusal meant certain death, and it extended that right to nursing home patients who were comatose or in other ways incapable of expression *as long as there was evidence that such a refusal would have been their choice.* One consequence of this decision was the empowering of the state's Long Term Care Ombudsman to sanction requests by family members or legal guardians to authorize withdrawal of life-prolonging measures, including feeding tubes as well as respirators, from nursing home patients in that category. This distinction between feeding tubes and respirators has become critical in states with no comprehensive Living Will legislation where courts have indicated that the removal of an artificial feeding tube can be viewed as murder.

In New York, New Jersey, and other states where judges have been handing down case-by-case decisions stating that doctors and health care institutions must honor the directives of a Living Will, there are many legal authorities who feel that, in the absence of state legislation, such decisions may have little effect on the apprehensions of doctors and institutions about their vulnerability to costly malpractice litigation initiated by surviving family members.

In the midst of conflicting attitudes and confusion in the courts, the anguish of families and the dilemmas of doctors have not been forgotten. A step in the right direction was taken in 1985, when the National Conference of Commissioners of Uniform State Laws adopted a Uniform Rights of the Terminally Ill Act, which is being recommended to state legislatures. In formulating the provisions of this act, attempts have been made to incorporate the best aspects of the laws already passed and to do away with those aspects that lead to complications rather than clarification. The

7. As of June 1986, these states are Hawaii, Kentucky, Massachusetts, Michigan, Minnesota, Nebraska, New Jersey, New York, North Dakota, Ohio, Pennsylvania, and Rhode Island. All the other states have passed Living Will or Terminal Patients Rights legislation in one form or another.

adoption of a uniform act by all state legislatures would protect the rights of dying patients, relieve physicians of the threat of lawsuits, and impose a desirable consistency on hospital and nursing home procedures.

In the absence of such uniformity, many hospitals nationwide have established ethics committees and engaged professional philosophers to create official policies that will guide doctors on when *not* to resuscitate terminally ill patients through life-sustaining technological means. (It is well known that such means can ward off death not only for days and months, but in some cases, for years.) In California, which in 1976 was the first state to enact Living Will legislation, many hospitals, Stanford University Hospital among them, include a Living Will form in the packet of information presented to every patient at the time of admission. In New York State, where no such legislation has yet been enacted and the state hospital association provides no official guidelines or recommendations to its members on this matter, individual hospitals such as Mt. Sinai Medical Center in New York City will attach a copy of the patient's Living Will to the medical chart if asked to do so. At the same time, it will probably be pointed out to the patient and family members that the instructions in this document will be carried out only to the extent allowed by law.

In states with Living Will laws, a State Declaration form is the acceptable Living Will form for that state. You can write up your own declaration if you need to, but follow these guidelines offered by Colorado. These apply specifically in that state, but provide a good framework. (If your state has not passed Living Will legislation, see page 14.)

- A declaration may, but need not be, in the form set forth in law and must be witnessed by two persons who are neither beneficiaries of, or claimants against, your parent's estate, nor a physician or employee of a physician or health care facility in which your parent is a patient. If your parent is unable to sign the document, someone who fits the witness criteria may do so at your parent's request.
- You or your parent is responsible for notifying her physician of the existence of the declaration and/or its revocation.
- Before the declaration will be legally binding, the patient's terminal condition must be diagnosed and certified in writing by two physicians, one of whom is their attending physician. Once certified, there is a forty-eight hour waiting period before life-

sustaining procedures may be withdrawn. These procedures do not include nourishment, comfort or the alleviation of pain. [Colorado *does* distinguish between feeding tubes and respirators.] *If you wish artificial nutrition and hydration withheld or withdrawn, you should specify this in your document.*

- A declaration is invalid during pregnancy if it is believed that the fetus could develop to viable birth with continued application of life-sustaining procedures.
- The law does not permit active steps to terminate life. However, the withholding or withdrawal of life-sustaining procedures from a terminally ill patient does not, for any purpose, constitute suicide or homicide.
- The existence of a declaration can have no effect on the issuance or continuation of the patient's life insurance.
- It is advisable to initial the declaration periodically as further proof of the patient's sustained conviction.

A Typical Declaration Form Available in States with Living Will Laws

Here, for example, is the form distributed in Colorado:

STATE OF COLORADO

DECLARATION AS TO MEDICAL OR SURGICAL TREATMENT

I, _____, being of sound mind and at least eighteen years of age, direct that my life shall not be artificially prolonged under the circumstances set forth below and hereby declare that:

1. If at any time my attending physician and one other physician certify in writing that:

   a. I have an injury, disease, or illness which is not *curable or reversible* and which, in their judgment, is a terminal condition; and

   b. For a period of forty-eight consecutive hours or more, I have been unconscious, comatose, or otherwise *incompetent* so as to be unable to make or communicate responsible decisions concerning my person; then

I direct that life-sustaining procedures shall be withdrawn and withheld; it being understood that life-sustaining procedures shall not include any medical procedure or intervention for nourishment or considered necessary by the attending physician to provide comfort or alleviate pain.

2. I execute this declaration, as my free and voluntary act this

_____ day of _____, 19 _____.

By _____
Declarant

The foregoing instrument was signed and declared by _____ to be his declaration, in the presence of us, who, in his presence, in the presence of each other, and at his request, have signed our names below as witnesses, and we declare that, at the time of the execution of this instrument, the declarant, according to our best knowledge and belief, was of sound mind and under no constraint or undue influence.

Dated at _____, Colorado, this _____ day of _____, 19_____.

_____

Name and Address

_____

Name and Address

STATE OF COLORADO   )
)
County of _____)   ss.

SUBSCRIBED and sworn to before me by _____, the

declarant, and _____, and _____,

witnesses, as the voluntary act and deed of the declarant, this

day of _____, 19_____.

My commission expires:

NOTARY PUBLIC

Copies available from:

Concern for Dying
250 West 57th Street
New York, N.Y. 10107
(212) 246-6962

Statutory citation: COL. REV. STAT ACT 15-18-101-113; see also paragraphs 512-36-117 (1985)

The provisions of Colorado's law, summarized below, are more or less the same as laws passed by other states. Until the enactment of this legislation, no doctor was required to carry out the directives of a patient's Living Will. Now, however, the law spells out in detail the responsibilities of medical care personnel, the procedures that are to be followed, the rules governing compliance and immunity, and the relationship between the Living Will and insurance.

ON IMMUNITY FROM SUITS: Whereas before passage of the legislation, hospital personnel were always vulnerable to suits claiming malpractice, the new law provides that no physician, hospital, or staff person shall be subject to legal or licensing penalty for complying with the provisions of a Living Will.

ON PENALTIES: Any person who willfully conceals, defaces, damages, or destroys a Living Will without the consent of the signer, or who falsifies or forges a Living Will, or who willfully withholds information about the revocation of a Living Will, shall be punished by law.

ON REVOCATION: A Living Will can be revoked by its signer according to the law, "either orally or in writing, or by burning, tearing, obliterating, or destroying" the original document. The person's personal physician must be told, and other interested parties who have been given copies should also be informed of the revocation.

ON THE LIVING WILL AND INSURANCE: The law states that (1) withholding or withdrawing of life-sustaining procedures in compliance with a Living Will is neither suicide nor homicide; (2) the existence of a Living Will shall not affect life insurance in any way; (3) no insurer or provider of health care shall require a person to sign a Living Will in order to be insured or to receive health care services; (4) failure to sign a Living Will shall not affect any insurance rates.

If your parents live in one of the states that hasn't passed a similar law and they wish to sign a Living Will, they can request the form duplicated below from Concern for Dying, whose address appears at the bottom of the form. Organized in 1968 as the Euthanasia Educational Council, it was the first organization to produce and distribute Living Wills, and since that time, it has responded to over 7 million requests nationwide. It also supplies Living Wills in Braille and in Spanish. In 1983, the organization established a Living Will Registry, a computerized filing system that assigns a registry number to the participant. A copy of that person's Living Will is maintained in the files and kept up to date when changes are to be made in home address, instructions, and provisions.

THE LIVING WILL REGISTRY

In 1983, Concern for Dying instituted the Living Will Registry, a computerized file system where you may keep an up-to-date copy of your Living Will in our New York office.

What are the benefits of joining the Living Will Registry?

- CONCERN's staff will ensure that your form is filled out correctly, assign you a Registry Number and maintain a copy of your Living Will.
- CONCERN's staff will be able to refer to *your* personal document, explain procedures and options, and provide you with the latest case law or state legislation should you, your proxy or anyone else acting on your behalf need counselling or legal guidance in implementing your Living Will.
- You will receive a permanent, credit card size plastic mini-will with your Registry number imprinted on it. The mini-will, which contains your address, CONCERN's address and a short version of the Living Will, indicates that you have already filled out a full-sized, witnessed Living Will document.

How Do You Join the Living Will Registry?

- Review your Living Will, making sure it is up-to-date and contains any specific provisions that you want added.
- Mail a copy of your original, signed and witnessed document along with a check for $25.00 to:

> The Living Will Registry
> Concern for Dying
> 250 West 57th Street, Room 831
> New York, New York 10107

Revised January, 1984

The one-time Registry enrollment fee will cover the costs of processing and maintaining your Living Will and of issuing your new plastic mini-will.

■ If you have any address changes or wish to add or delete special provisions that you have included in your Living Will, please write to the Registry so that we can keep your file up to date.

TO MAKE BEST USE OF YOUR LIVING WILL

You may wish to add specific statements to the Living Will *in the space provided for that purpose above your signature.* Possible additional provisions are:

1. "Measures of artificial life-support in the face of impending death that I specifically refuse are:
   a) Electrical or mechanical resuscitation of my heart when it has stopped beating.
   b) Nasogastric tube feeding when I am paralyzed or unable to take nourishment by mouth.
   c) Mechanical respiration when I am no longer able to sustain my own breathing.
   d) _____ "

2. "I would like to live out my last days at home rather than in a hospital if it does not jeopardize the chance of my recovery to a meaningful and sentient life or does not impose an undue burden on my family."

3. "If any of my tissues are sound and would be of value as transplants to other people, I freely give my permission for such donation."

The optional Durable Power of Attorney feature allows you to name someone else to serve as your proxy in case you are unable to communicate your wishes. Should you choose to fill in this portion of the document, you must have your signature notarized.

If you choose more than one proxy for decision-making on your behalf, please give order of priority (1, 2, 3, etc.).

Space is provided at the bottom of the Living Will for notarization should you choose to have your Living Will witnessed by a Notary Public.

Remember . . .

- Sign and date your Living Will. Your two witnesses, who should not be blood relatives or beneficiaries of your property will, should also sign in the spaces provided.
- Discuss your Living Will with your doctors; if they agree with you, give them copies of your signed Living Will document for them to add to your medical file.
- Give copies of your signed Living Will to anyone who may be making decisions for you if you are unable to make them yourself.
- Look over your Living Will once a year, redate it and initial the new date to make it clear that your wishes have not changed.

The Concern for Dying newsletter is a quarterly publication reporting the most recent developments in the field of death and dying. It contains announcements of upcoming educational conferences, workshops and symposia, as well as reviews of current literature. The Newsletter is sent to anyone who contributes $5.00 or more annually to CONCERN FOR DYING.

☐ I would like to receive the Newsletter.
☐ I would like to enroll in the Living Will Registry

Additional materials available to contributors:

☐ Questions and Answers About the Living Will
☐ Selected articles and case histories
☐ A bibliography
☐ Information on films

A mini-will, a condensed version of the Living Will which can be carried in a wallet in case of accident or emergency, will be sent upon receipt of a contribution.

For information, call: (212) 246-6962

The space in the middle of the form enables the signer to include specific instructions about the particular artificial life support systems which are *not to be used,* in particular, a mechanical respirator when natural breathing has stopped; nasogastric feeding when nourishment by mouth becomes impossible; electrical or mechanical resuscitation of the heart when it has stopped beating. Instructions may also include a request to live out the last weeks of a terminal illness at home, and permission to donate healthy tissues or organs to be used as transplants for those who need them. (If one or both of your parents wears a MedicAlert bracelet or insignia, it can be similarly inscribed.)

The Durable Power of Attorney on the Living Will form is optional.

Doubts Should Be Discussed

If your parents haven't thought about signing a Living Will until now, they should be encouraged to discuss the decision with their doctor as well as with family members. It is especially important to have such a discussion with whoever is going to be the spokesperson, or is to be given the power of attorney, or named the legal guardian in the event of incompetence. However, parents should not be pressured into signing such a document if they resist doing so.

Procedures to Follow after Signing a Living Will

1. Two original printed forms should be filled out and signed in the presence of witnesses. Witnesses should not be heirs, the personal doctor, or employees of the doctor, hospital, or nursing home. The signatures need not be notarized except in cases where the signer also signs the Durable Power of Attorney option.
2. As many copies of the original should be made as are necessary for distribution to concerned parties.
3. One of the signed original declarations should be given to the prime care doctor and discussed with him or her to be sure that it will be attached to the signer's medical records, and that full compliance can be counted on.
4. If full compliance with the Living Will is not forthcoming, it

My Living Will
To My Family, My Physician, My Lawyer
and All Others Whom It May Concern

Death is as much a reality as birth, growth, maturity and old age—it is the one certainty of life. If the time comes when I can no longer take part in decisions for my own future, let this statement stand as an expression of my wishes and directions, while I am still of sound mind.

If at such a time the situation should arise in which there is no reasonable expectation of my recovery from extreme physical or mental disability, I direct that I be allowed to die and not be kept alive by medications, artificial means or "heroic measures". I do, however, ask that medication be mercifully administered to me to alleviate suffering even though this may shorten my remaining life.

This statement is made after careful consideration and is in accordance with my strong convictions and beliefs. I want the wishes and directions here expressed carried out to the extent permitted by law. Insofar as they are not legally enforceable, I hope that those to whom this Will is addressed will regard themselves as morally bound by these provisions.

(Optional specific provisions to be made in this space — see other side)

DURABLE POWER OF ATTORNEY (optional)

I hereby designate _____ to serve as my attorney-in-fact for the purpose of making medical treatment decisions. This power of attorney shall remain effective in the event that I become incompetent or otherwise unable to make such decisions for myself.

Optional Notarization:

"Sworn and subscribed to

before me this _____ day

of _____, 19_____."

_____
Notary Public
(seal)

Signed_____

Date _____

Witness _____

_____
Address

Witness _____

_____
Address

Copies of this request have been given to _____

_____   _____

(Optional)   My Living Will is registered with Concern for Dying (No. _____)

Distributed by Concern for Dying, 250 West 57th Street, New York, NY 10107 (212) 246-6962 may then be necessary for your parent to consider changing doctors.

5. The other signed original should be kept where it is easily accessible, preferably in a desk drawer, and *not* in a safety deposit box. It's a good idea to review the document and sign it anew each year. The copy in the doctor's possession can be signed again too.

6. A copy should be turned over to the spouse, all adult children, the closest friend, the family lawyer, and the pastor or rabbi.

7. A reduced copy, or a card provided for the purpose, should be carried in the wallet together with the Medicare card.

Additional information about Living Wills and the legislation affecting their execution is available from:

Concern for Dying
250 West 57th Street, New York, New York 10107
(212) 246-6962

DEATH AND THE DECEASED

In many religious denominations, especially those that are essentially congregational rather than orthodox and doctrinal, disposition of the deceased may be ruled by personal choice rather than by adherence to immutable ritual. Also, in families where religious observances no longer have any place in celebrating a birth or ritualizing a death, it is important to find out about the parents' preferences and see that they are written into the will. In this way there can be no eventual arguments among survivors about how to proceed.

It's possible that you may find discussions about death morbid and distasteful, but it's also possible that your parents may be ready and willing to talk about such matters, especially if they're still enjoying good health. After all, death is compellingly real to them: they've probably had to deal with the death of their own parents and of some of their friends or other family members. If you have any uncertainty about what their wishes might be, find out whether they want a religious funeral service and whether they prefer to be buried or cremated. If the choice is cremation, the family should arrive at an agreement about the disposition of the ashes.

Is there a family burial plot? Does your father belong to a fraternal organization whose benefits include a cemetery plot and partial payments for burial costs for himself and his spouse?

The Social Security Administration currently pays a death benefit of $255 only to the surviving spouse who had been living with the decedent, or to a dependent child under eighteen, or to a disabled adult child entitled to disability benefits. (Since 1981, a funeral director can no longer collect the Social Security death benefit under any circumstances, even on the authorization of the family.)

The Veteran's Administration also pays a death benefit to the surviving spouse. The amount is based on whether the cause of death is or is not attributable to a service-related disease or injury.

As you probably know either from experience or from glancing at discreet newspaper advertisements, you can depend on the help of the funeral home director or the staff of the mortuary to work out the details of the funeral and subsequent burial or cremation. What you may *not* know is that you need no longer be at the mercy of morticians at a time when you're too distraught to be thinking about saving money. In 1984, the Federal Trade Commission established the Funeral Rule, which now regulates funeral industry practices nationwide. This regulation enables you and your family to get detailed information about goods and services so that you can choose only those that you want and pay for only those that you've chosen. Funeral directors are required to provide price information on the phone, and if you make your inquiries in person, the establishment is required to give you an itemized price list which you can keep for purposes of selecting the provider who offers the arrangements and prices that meet your needs.

———————————

Additional useful information is contained in *The Consumer Guide to the FTC Funeral Rule,* available free of charge from the Consumer Inquiry Division of the FTC office that services your area, or by sending your request to:

Federal Trade Commission
Bureau of Consumer Protection
6th Street and Pennsylvania Avenue, N.W.
Washington, D.C. 20580

SEEK OUT A LOCAL SUPPORT GROUP—OR START ONE YOURSELF

One of the most encouraging and productive developments in recent years is the network of self-help groups for the adult sons and daughters of aging parents. In addition to providing information about community resources and down-to-earth solutions for daily problems, members share their feelings of helplessness, anger, inadequacy, and fatigue in ways that can make meetings a haven and give participants a healthy sense of solidarity.

An organization that helps establish regional groups, conducts workshops, maintains a referral service, and publishes a self-help manual and newsletter is:

Children of Aging Parents
2761 Trenton Road, Levittown, Pennsylvania 19056
(215) 946-4012

Another group that helps in the formation of local groups and provides speakers, cassettes, and other aids for conducting intergenerational workshops and community seminars is:

The National Support Center for Children of the Aging
Box 245, Swarthmore, Pennsylvania 19081
(215) 544-3605

PRIVATE GERIATRIC CARE MANAGERS

In October 1985, an assemblage of specialists—social workers, nurses, psychologists, and gerontologists, many of whom have left nonprofit agencies to set themselves up as private practitioners— met in New York City at their first national conference, "A Call to a New Profession." In Chapter 9, pages 237–39, you'll find detailed information about the professionals who call themselves private geriatric care managers: their services, fees, and the various ways in which client-consultant relationships are worked out.

In facing our parents' future, it's a consolation to know that many people never suffer from prolonged illness, mental deterioration, or the humiliation of poverty during their later years. While it's true that they have to adjust to changes in their activities—golf rather than tennis, swimming rather than skiing—severe limitations are widespread only among those who are over eighty-five. But even under the happiest circumstances, you may be called on for help as your parents grow older, or you'll be consulted for advice in an unanticipated emergency.

The purpose of the material in the preceding pages is to facilitate clear thinking when a crisis calls for prompt action. It's one of the facts of life that family members have their disagreements— parents with each other and with their close relatives, sons and daughters with their parents, and brothers and sisters among themselves. When such disagreements are resolved *before* a situation arises in which an immediate decision is essential, a calm consensus rather than bickering and confusion will rule the day.

As for the usual problems that may arise, a broader range of solutions is now available for helping you to help your parents in ways that are effective as well as mutually satisfying. In the material that follows, you'll be alerted to health problems that can be handled before they become disabling; you'll be able to offer practical and unexpected suggestions for leisure activities, alternative housing, and self-help. And thanks to recent developments in home care and day care for the elderly (as well as respite arrangements for you), neither you nor your parents need be haunted by the likelihood of a nursing home as the only possible destiny for their old age.

❧ 2 ❧

BEING ALERT
TO HEALTH AND SAFETY PROBLEMS

*People here can fall through the cracks. We wait until an older person
activates the medical system rather than assessing his or her condition
all along. The problem is that many elderly do not report their illnesses. They feel that if they are old, then being sick is normal. An
older person here has to almost literally fall on his knees before the
system intervenes. The later the intervention in the elderly, the more
difficult the recuperation. . . .*

Dr. Richard W. Besdine, of the geriatrics fellowship program at Harvard
University Medical School[1]

SOME COMMON HEALTH PROBLEMS OF AGING

Alcohol Abuse

Many people who were never "problem" drinkers in their
younger years gradually begin to abuse alcohol when they have to
deal with the stresses of aging. Occasional solitary drinking may
begin as a way of blunting the pain of loneliness following the
death of a beloved spouse, as an escape from the daily grind of
taking care of a chronically ill wife, as a cure for depression following a divorce after forty years of marriage. But what begins as
a means of coping with a problem may eventually become a problem in itself.

Alcohol abuse is especially damaging and dangerous to older
people not only because it harms the liver, kidneys, stomach,
heart, and brain, but also because it increases the likelihood of

1. As quoted in Christopher Hallowell, "New Focus on the Old," New York *Times
Magazine,* December 15, 1985.

serious falls at home, pedestrian accidents on the street, and disasters resulting from diminished alertness to danger. In older people, the confusion and forgetfulness produced by excessive drinking can easily be mistaken for mental illness requiring institutionalization. And a particular hazard for the elderly is the potentially deadly effect resulting from the mixture of alcohol with any of a number of their medications. According to a study conducted in 1982 by the National Institute on Aging, 10 to 15 percent of older patients seeking medical help had a drinking problem related to their ailment.

The first step in dealing with a parent who has a drinking problem is *your* willingness to recognize it *as a problem.* (It's not unusual for sons and daughters to refuse to make this one of their concerns; some actually encourage a certain amount of drinking, because, after all, it makes their parents "feel better." More insidious still is a family situation in which a younger member is denying the problem of alcoholism in his or her own life, and therefore can't face the parental problem either.)

What are the danger signals? In the flier "Aging and Alcohol Abuse," the National Institute on Aging suggests that the following symptoms indicate the need for help:

- Drinking to calm nerves, forget worries, or reduce depression
- Loss of interest in food
- Gulping drinks and drinking too fast
- Lying about drinking habits
- Drinking alone with increasing frequency
- Injuring oneself or someone else while intoxicated
- Getting drunk more than three or four times within the past year
- Needing to drink increasing amounts in order to get the desired effect
- Frequently acting irritable, resentful, or unreasonable during nondrinking periods
- Experiencing medical, social, or financial problems caused by drinking

And it is particularly important to be alert to increasing memory loss and blackouts attributable to alcohol consumption.

Once you've become aware of some of these danger signals, what's the most effective approach? It's generally agreed that you're more likely to be listened to if you present the problem in terms of concern about your parent's health rather than in terms of morality or "Aren't you ashamed of yourself?" (A typical response to that question is self-abasement, tears, apologies, promises to reform, and so on.) The late-onset alcohol abuser is trying to cope with real-life crises, frustrations, and diminished self-esteem, and you're not going to make his or her life easier by scolding or by worrying about what the neighbors think.

Defining alcohol abuse as an illness that requires treatment is the best approach. If you think you'll get some cooperation, suggest that together, the two of you can find the right kind of help. The local department for the aging, the family doctor, or a social service agency can refer you to a suitable program. (Don't neglect to find out from your parent's prime care doctor whether the drinking has been taken into account as a contributing factor in other disorders.)

Remember that older people feel more comfortable with their contemporaries, so it's a good idea to investigate the availability of a special treatment group for senior citizens. You can always start by calling the Alcoholics Anonymous (AA) headquarters in your parent's area. And whether you can count on parental cooperation or not, it's a good idea for you to check on an Al-Anon chapter in *your* area so that you can count on the supportive fellowship of others dealing with alcoholism as a family problem.

Additional information is available from:
Al-Anon National Information Center
1 Park Avenue, New York, New York 10016
(212) 683-1771

National Council on Alcoholism, with local offices in
    approximately 200 cities and towns across the United
    States, or write to the national headquarters at:
12 West 21st Street, New York, New York 10001

National Clearinghouse for Alcohol Information, a federal agency that supplies printed material and referrals
P.O. Box 2345, Rockville, Maryland 20852

Alzheimer's Disease

It used to be that when older people began to have serious memory lapses or showed signs of physical disorientation, they were categorized as "senile." Now, however, even though the last word has by no means been said on the subject, we know that Alzheimer's disease (officially called *senile dementia of the Alzheimer type*) is responsible for the severe and irreversible mental damage that affects about 2 million Americans: one in twenty over age sixty-five, and one in five over age eighty.

People with Alzheimer's disease are literally "losing" their mind because of the selective destruction of a small area of the brain (the hippocampus) that is responsible for creating and processing memories. The cause of the destruction that occurs in this organic brain disease has not yet been defined with absolute certainty. Some researchers are inclined to believe that the disease is caused by a virus, others that it may be the result of an immunological disorder. While no two cases are precisely the same, deterioration rarely occurs all at once. The stages from mild disability to total incapacity may occur within a brief three years, or they may go on for as long as fifteen or twenty.

By no means should you or anyone else make the snap judgment that your parent is suffering from "Alzheimer's" because of erratic behavior or memory loss. In 1985, at a conference for family members of Alzheimer victims held at the National Institutes of Health, Margaret M. Heckler, Secretary of Health and Human Services, informed her audience that as many as 15 to 30 percent of all Alzheimer diagnoses may be wrong. It was also pointed out by various experts that the disease had become a "garbage pail" diagnosis for mental diseases and disorders that might be curable if correctly diagnosed. Refined neuropsychological tests are needed to establish this diagnosis after eliminating other possible psychological, physical, and chemical causes for the symptoms. Such causes for memory lapses and personality changes as ministrokes, overmedication, malnutrition, alcoholism, and depression can be ruled out by a thorough examination as well as by a detailed history of the patient supplied by family members. And mental functions are assessed by sophisticated memory tests, drawing tests, and other laboratory procedures.

Living with a parent suffering from Alzheimer's disease requires enormous patience and caregiving skills, even in the early stages of the disease. Since safety precautions are essential, physical changes in the environment are necessary. It's especially difficult to deal with the fact that a loving and beloved parent has been transformed into a demanding, irrational, and often a frightening stranger. How to balance feelings of guilt and of angry desperation is the problem faced by family members, not to mention that practically no official recognition has been given to financial burdens and glaringly inadequate facilities for long-term care.

Some cities and states are establishing day-care center programs that provide respite for families and suitable activities for patients. Dr. Burton V. Reifler, founding director of the Alzheimer's Research Program at the University of Washington, has pointed out that "incurable does not mean untreatable."[2] However, although some treatment facilities are making progress in helping Alzheimer's victims achieve optimal function, such facilities are not easy to find. Recent years have seen the creation of a network of supportive resources.

The Alzheimer's Disease and Related Disorders Association has 125 chapters in 44 states and the District of Columbia. If you can't find a telephone listing for a local chapter, contact the organization's national office at:

    360 North Michigan Avenue, Suite 601
    Chicago, Illinois 60601
    (312) 853-3060

The association supplies informational brochures for caregivers as well as an up-to-date reading list.

In 1984, the New York City Alzheimer's Resource Center was established to provide families with information about where to go for advice and help for legal and financial problems, long-term care, how to apply for federal assistance, and where to go for private counseling. Sponsored by the city's Department on Aging, it is the first such clearinghouse in the United States. It is open from nine to five Monday through Friday and is located at:

2. New York *Times,* May 7, 1985.

260 Broadway (near Chambers Street)
New York, New York 10007
(212) 577-0815—and don't lose patience!

Arteriosclerosis

Also called *peripheral arteriosclerosis,* this is a condition in which the hardening and narrowing of the arteries of the leg result in circulatory impairment. The loss of blood supply to the muscles causes stiffness and shooting pains, often in the form of night cramps that disturb sleep. The reduction of blood supply to the skin, especially of the feet and toes, causes abnormal and uncomfortable sensitivity to cold.

More life-threatening than peripheral arteriosclerosis is *atherosclerosis,* the condition in which fatty substances and other foreign materials are deposited in the inner lining of the arteries, especially of the coronary arteries. When these deposits, known as "plaques," cause the channels through which the blood must flow to become increasingly clogged, the likelihood of heart disease increases.

As your parents get older, be alert to signs of shortness of breath, and pay attention to any mention of chest pains, dizziness, cold hands and feet, leg cramps, and other problems attributable to circulatory impairment. Don't take the responsibility of advising this or that treatment in the form of a low-cholesterol or a crash diet, or a fitness routine. See that an appointment is made with the doctor for an electrocardiogram and other diagnostic tests that can measure the extent of the problem. Treatment may be medical and/or surgical, with additional recommendations about diet and exercise. If coronary bypass surgery is recommended, be sure that your parent gets a second opinion from a reputable cardiologist.

Arthritis

When your parent begins to complain about feeling creaky in the morning or of not being able to sleep because of aching joints, don't assume that such discomforts are an inevitable consequence of aging and needn't be taken seriously. While it may be true that arthritis is incurable, it *can* be treated, and its crippling effects could be avoided by many more people if the right steps were taken promptly to preserve as much normal joint function as possible. (Also see Osteoarthritis, page 40.)

Be especially vigilant in guarding your parent against the quack treatments on which unwary and gullible victims spend an estimated $1 billion a year. Such treatments range from copper bracelets, to "herbal" medicines, to elixirs of dubious composition, to fad diets of unproved value. Dr. Harry Spiera, chief of the Division of Rheumatology at the Mt. Sinai Medical Center, and a member of the Board of Governors of the Arthritis Foundation, is one of many distinguished authorities who believes that there is no hard evidence on the relation between diet and arthritis. He has also pointed out that repeated injections of steroids may have a deteriorative effect on cartilage.

Reliable information on the nature of various forms of arthritis and the most effective ways to treat them, as well as referrals to rheumatologists and special community services, can be obtained from one of the seventy local chapters of the Arthritis Foundation. If you can't find a local listing, write to the national office:

> The Arthritis Foundation
> 1314 Spring Street, N.W.
> Atlanta, Georgia 30309

Emphysema

This insidious lung disease comes on slowly and is usually found among older men and women who have been—and continue to be—heavy smokers. It is characterized by the eventual destruction of the tiny air sacs in the lungs that supply the blood with oxygen. While air pollutants in the form of urban smog and occupational dusts and fumes are partially responsible for tissue damage, they in no way compare with the damage done by the self-pollution of smoking.

The development of chronic bronchitis is signaled by an intermittent "smoker's cough," but emphysema proceeds silently. As the alveolar tissue (air sacs) becomes increasingly stretched and eventually ruptured, the extra effort required to breathe puts a cumulatively damaging strain on the heart.

Although the damage is irreversible, the earlier the condition is discovered, the more effective the treatment. If you can't get your parent to stop smoking, or if you think the abandoned habit may already have been damaging, be on the alert for increasing breathlessness following any slight exertion. Because a conventional chest X ray may not pick up the signs of tissue impairment, suggest that your parent ask the doctor to perform a test of lung capacity with a spirometer. This test is an accurate indicator of the extent of air flow obstruction.

Helpful information about emphysema, chronic bronchitis, and the various forms of respiratory malfunction known as chronic obstructive lung disease (COLD) can be obtained from the national headquarters of the American Lung Association, 1740 Broadway, New York, New York 10019, or by contacting the regional chapter listed in the local telephone directory.

Hearing Loss

In the hearing process, a complicated relay system is set in motion by the impact of sound waves on the eardrum. The vibrations of the eardrum (tympanum) are transmitted to the three tiny bones that lie behind it in the chamber called the middle ear. The movements of these tiny bones (ossicles) send ripples into the fluid contained in the inner ear (cochlea). The movements of the fluid are transformed into impulses carried by the auditory nerve to the brain, where the impulses are interpreted as the messages of speech, music, unpleasant noise, and all the other sounds of daily life. When this complicated relay system is interrupted at any point along the way, the result is hearing impairment.

There are two main types of hearing loss: *conduction deafness* (also called bone deafness), caused by damage to some part of the middle ear, and *nerve deafness,* resulting from damage to the inner ear or the auditory nerve. While serious hearing loss is by no means inevitable in older people, three out of ten over the age of sixty-five have some degree of impairment; over the age of seventy, the percentage increases dramatically.

The most common cause of the conduction hearing loss that accompanies aging is *otosclerosis* (see page 43).

Nerve Deafness

This condition may result from disease, accidents involving skull fractures, and the effects of certain medications. The great advances that have been made in the design of hearing aids and in microsurgical techniques can help most people suffering from conduction deafness. And recently, there is new hope for people whose nerve deafness was presumed to be beyond treatment. The latest development is an electronic device surgically implanted in the cochlea. This implant stimulates the auditory nerve electronically so that it can send messages to the brain.

You can play a critical role in helping your parent find the right way to compensate for hearing loss. First of all, you can be sensitive to the fact that not everything you're saying is heard, especially if you aren't speaking face to face. (As deafness sets in, many people unconsciously become quite skilled in compensatory lipreading.) Even though your parent may deny that the impairment exists, suggest an appointment with an otologist (a physician who is an ear specialist) to find out the extent of the problem. It may be something as simple as a heavy accumulation of earwax that needs flushing out; on the other hand, it may be a tumor or infection that needs prompt treatment. If the doctor thinks the next step is evaluation by an audiologist for the best type of hearing aid, your parent must be given a signed statement to the person who fits and sells these devices in order to be able to buy one. (The U.S. Food and Drug Administration established rules governing such sales after many complaints about fraudulent claims and the exploitation of the unsuspecting elderly.)

If increasing deafness has resulted in the personality changes that accompany loss of communication with others, it's a good idea to steer your parent in the direction of a good ear specialist and also an accredited lipreading instructor. (The doctor can be consulted for a referral.) As a matter of fact, considering the incidence of deafness among the elderly, you might join your parent in a lipreading course even though you don't suffer from the impairment. It's a special skill that may be useful some time in the future.

Information about research developments and local resources as well as general literature are available from the following organizations:

The Deafness Research Foundation
55 East 34th Street, New York, NY 10016
(212) 684-6556
Toll-free calls from outside New York State:
(800) 535-3233

The American Deafness and Rehabilitation Association
814 Thayer Avenue, Silver Springs, Maryland 20910
(301) 589-0880

Self-Help for Hard-of-Hearing People (90 state groups)
4848 Battery Lane, Suite 100,
Bethesda, Maryland 20814
(301) 657-2248

If your hearing-impaired parent is a dog lover, you might look into a new program that trains "hearing dogs" to respond at once to noises and to lead the owner to their source. Certified dogs are being placed with suitable applicants, and most states recognize their right to enter public places with the handicapped person. Information about the training program in your parent's area is available from:

The American Humane Association
9725 East Hamden Avenue, Denver, Colorado 80231

Heart Failure

While the term may sound sinister, it doesn't mean that the heart has stopped beating but that its efficiency has been impaired so that it is no longer strong enough to maintain normal circulation throughout the body. When the impairment occurs in an older person—that is, someone who hasn't gone through life with a "weak" heart because of a congenital defect or a childhood bout with rheumatic fever—it is usually the result of a long period of uncontrolled high blood pressure, a heart attack, or coronary artery disease. The condition may also be called *congestive* heart failure, a term that refers to the condition in which a deterioration of the heart's pumping action causes a backup of the blood returning to the heart through the veins. As a result, some of the fluid in the blood is expelled through the thin walls of the smaller blood vessels into the surrounding tissue. As the fluid piles up, it leads to swelling, or edema, typically causing swollen ankles. Congestion in the lungs ("water" or "fluid" in the lungs) is manifested by wheezing and shortness of breath.

Keep an eye on your parent's ankles; watch out for puffy fingers too, and when you hear signs of breathing difficulties, it's time to suggest a checkup. Don't panic, and don't convey unnecessary anxiety. Go along to the doctor if you can. Following a thorough examination and an electrocardiogram, treatment will probably include digitalis in one or another form to strengthen the heart muscle's action, a salt-restricted diet, and a diuretic—with supplementary potassium if necessary.

When the heart beats irregularly or too slowly, the cause may be a disruption of the electrical transmission system between the upper and lower chambers. When this *natural* pacemaker fails to function in a normal way, an *artificial* pacemaker is implanted in the body and connected to the heart by wires through which electrical impulses are sent for the purpose of maintaining a reliable heartbeat. The artificial pacemaker automatically turns on when the rate is too slow and turns off when the heart can maintain a satisfactory beat on its own.

A brief hospital stay is required for installing the device, followed by regular visits to the cardiologist for checkups of the power pack that supplies the electric current. Office visits are interspersed with checkups by telemetry from your parent's home phone to the phone in the doctor's office. Depending on the nature of the power pack, it may last for more than ten years. Replacement is accomplished under local anesthesia.

When the question of a pacemaker comes up, you can reassure your parent that it isn't going to interfere with *any* normal activities, including swimming.

If your parent's prime care physician thinks a pacemaker is indicated, get a second opinion from a cardiologist, who may offer other solutions. When the decision is made to have the pacemaker installed, find out where the operation will be performed and ask to meet the surgeon who will do the operation.

If you'd like general information on research, diet recommendations, exercise programs, and the like, write to:

The American Heart Association
7320 Greenvale Avenue, Dallas, Texas 75231
(214) 750-5300 and
Heartlife (formerly the Association of Heart Patients)
P.O. Box 54305, Atlanta, Georgia 30308
(404) 523-0826

High Blood Pressure (Hypertension)

One of the mysterious aspects of high blood pressure is that in most cases, it produces no symptoms and cannot be traced to a specific treatable underlying cause. In about 90 percent of the people with abnormally high readings, the disorder comes under the heading of "benign" or "essential" high blood pressure. However, since even "mild" or "moderate" cases place additional strain on the aging heart, arteries, and kidneys, you can help your parents avoid hypertension-induced strokes, heart attacks, or kidney failure by seeing that their blood pressure is properly monitored and correctly treated if necessary.

WHAT DO THE MEASUREMENTS MEAN? As the blood circulates through the body, the pumping action of the heart causes the blood to push or press against the walls of the arteries through which it flows. Every complete heartbeat creates two different pressures: the systolic pressure, when the heart contracts and forces the blood through the arteries; and the diastolic pressure, when the heart relaxes between beats. The systolic pressure is the higher number, the diastolic the lower, and since the heart is at rest more often than it beats, the diastolic pressure is closer to the average pressure and therefore the more important measurement. Even though there's no agreement about what reading is *normal* for people who are over sixty and in decent health, treatment and supervision are indicated when the bottom number is consistently over 95; that is, for your parents, readings might range from 120/ 80 to 135/85 to 140/90 without causing undue alarm unless there are complicating factors requiring close evaluation. In any case, treatment for high blood pressure shouldn't be initiated until your parent has had at least three measurements at consecutive times but always under the most relaxing circumstances.

Suppose the bottom reading is somewhere between 90 and 95, and it's generally agreed that it would be better to bring it down than to see it rise to a dangerous level. The first recommendation might be a combination of weight loss through diet and exercise, cutting down on salt, and cutting out coffee and cigarettes. If this regimen brings the pressure down to safe levels, there's no need to add any medication to the treatment. (In point of fact, it's possible that part of the problem may be caused by an over-the-counter medication that your parent takes routinely without realizing its harmful effect on blood pressure. Two especially dangerous categories are decongestants and so-called appetite depressants.)

If your parent can't handle the doctor's suggestions and the condition poses a threat to well-being, it may be essential to prescribe medication. If this is to be the treatment, find out from the doctor whether any side effects of the medicine should be anticipated.

———————

An excellent source of information about hypertension is the federally funded

> National High Blood Pressure Education Program
> National Institutes of Health
> Bethesda, Maryland 20014

———————

Malnutrition

Malnutrition doesn't necessarily mean not eating enough of the right foods; it can also mean eating too much of the wrong ones. Older people are especially likely to have poor eating habits for a variety of reasons: they may have to pinch pennies to make ends meet; they may go through periods of depression or disability during which marketing and cooking seem insurmountably difficult. They may have trouble chewing because of ill-fitting dentures or missing teeth, and so live on soft foods lacking essential nutrients. Or they may survive precariously on fast food or processed food likely to be dangerously high in salt and sugar as well as cholesterol. In addition, many older people cling to old-fashioned ways of preparing food: too much frying, and too much boiling away of important nutrients. Over and above everything else, remember that as your parents grow older, they are likely to be susceptible to nutritional deficiencies because their bodies become less able to absorb the necessary nutrients from the food they do eat.

If you feed one or both of your parents in your own house, you can (subtly) supervise not only what they eat but how much. Since people over sixty are advised to keep their weight down, and since they aren't likely to get enough exercise, they need fewer calories. But that means that less food must contain all the essential nourishment. Grandpa's portion of lean meat, vegetables, and brown bread should be smaller than a teenager's, and everyone will benefit if the salt shaker is banished from the table.

If you're keeping an eye on parents who live nearby, you might do some unobtrusive snooping to see whether there are too many processed foods on hand that are likely to contain too much salt: soups, crackers, tomato juice, potato chips, and the like; or too much animal fat: bacon, sausages, rich cheeses, butter. If you were raised on overcooked vegetables, bring a steamer and an assortment of spinach, cauliflower, yams, mushrooms, cabbage, and squash, so that you can demonstrate how quick and easy—not to mention how nourishing—the steaming method of food preparation can be. Find out if perishable food is being stored beyond its time, and make sure that whoever does the marketing takes note of the last date of sale on dairy products. Get the message across that leftovers should be eaten promptly, and that instead of sniffing to find out if something is "spoiled," the rule to follow is "When in doubt, throw it out."

The aging parent who lives alone is the person most likely to be improperly nourished. Your widowed or divorced mother may be depressed and demoralized. ("I have no one to cook for.") If it's your father who's living on his own, you may hear, "But I've never cooked for myself." In such cases, it's important to find out whether what appears to be increasing physical decrepitude is attributable to a faulty diet. You can ask your parent to do you a favor and keep a list of the food eaten over the period of a week ("and no cheating please"). Make it sound like a game rather than a chore.

There are indications that one third of all elderly Americans aren't getting enough of the nutrients necessary for maintaining good health, and the federally funded Congregate Meals Program is an attempt to provide a partial corrective. This program is *not* a form of welfare, nor was it meant to be. Under the Older Americans Act, it was designed to enable senior citizens to come together for a wholesome and nutritious repast and enjoy one another's companionship as well as the food. Some participants may want to make a contribution, but no one should feel forced to do so. (It wouldn't be amiss if you found out how the program is carried out in your parent's area, and if you feel that some aspects need improving, you can make your suggestions to the proper administrator.)

Many communities offer other solutions that combine practical sense with some imagination: senior citizen cooking classes for men only ("I finally learned how to roast a chicken and it's so easy!"); regularly scheduled get-togethers of older women for shared meals and recipe exchanges; other morale-building activities, discussed in the next chapter, that result in a renewed interest in self-care.

Of course, many parents will take suggestions from their doctor or their friends, but not from their children. If this is the case in your family and you're concerned about your parents' diet, see if you can get their physician to have a heart-to-heart talk with them and to prepare a list of do's and don'ts that should be followed. If circumstances make it necessary to do so, you (or the doctor) might point out the potential dangers of self-medication with megadoses of this or that vitamin or mineral, or involvement with this or that food fad that can do more harm than good.

The general rule that parents have always been urged to follow for the well-being of their children—SET A GOOD EXAMPLE!—is the same rule that you're now in a position to follow vis-à-vis your parents when it comes to good nutrition.

If your mother or father is scheduled to return home after hospitalization, find out from the social service department whether a consultation with a nutritionist is advisable.

Osteoarthritis

Osteoarthritis is the joint inflammation most likely to affect your aging parent, more likely your mother. In this "wear and tear" condition, the cartilage, which is the normally smooth and elastic connective tissue that "hinges" the joints, becomes rough, swollen, and inflamed. Pain and impaired function are the result.

As soon as your parent shows signs of osteoarthritis, it's a good idea to encourage a visit to the doctor for a treatment plan. Nowadays, a better understanding of degenerative joint disease has resulted in comprehensive treatment that goes beyond the use of over-the-counter painkillers. (Of these, aspirin remains the cheapest and most effective medicine because of its anti-inflammatory *and* analgesic properties.) One aspect of therapy is the use of particular exercises, combined with essential warm-up techniques, that are designed to stretch and strengthen arthritic joints and maintain maximum mobility of other susceptible joints. Even in cases of eventual impairment of function, surgical replacements of hip, shoulder, and knee joints have arrived at such a level of success that countless older people are active and pain-free instead of being more or less immobilized or disabled.

Osteoporosis

Have you suddenly noticed that your parents seem to be shrinking, or that your mother's spine isn't as straight as it used to be? The cause is osteoporosis, a condition of aging in which the bones become increasingly porous, brittle, and weak. Changes in height and posture occur because the spinal vertebrae begin to collapse as their weight-bearing capacity diminishes. In many instances, this condition leads to chronic back pain. A more serious consequence is that a hip fracture or a broken arm may follow what seemed to be a not very serious fall.

There appears to be no single cause for the loss of bone compactness and strength. It is known that up to the middle years, bone tissue is replaced at approximately the same rate at which it is lost. However, in many older people, and especially in postmenopausal women, the breakdown of bone tissue outpaces the body's ability to compensate for the loss. Among the risk factors that seem to contribute to the problem are heredity, heavy smoking, excessive use of alcohol, low calcium–high protein diet, chronic illness, and lack of exercise. Over the years, when these circumstances cause the calcium blood level to plummet, the body restores the essential balance by withdrawing the calcium from the bones. Women appear to be especially vulnerable to this silent depletion of bone tissue not only because of hormonal changes, but through the demands of pregnancy and nursing, and in many cases, because of habitual crash dieting.

According to Dr. Marjorie Luckey, codirector of the Osteo-porosis and Metabolic Bone Disease Program at the Mt. Sinai Medical Center, one out of every three women over sixty has osteoporosis; after seventy-five, one out of every two, and after eighty, the condition is responsible for 50 percent of all hip frac-tures.

There's no way you can be sure that your parents—especially your mother—ought to have special attention because of bone fragility. (In many cases, the condition isn't detectable even in an X-ray examination.) Nor is there any reason to assume that osteo-porosis is inevitable. The people in their sixties and seventies whose bones are likely to be in good condition are those who don't smoke, drink in moderation if at all, stay away from caffeine, and incorporate some exercise into their daily routine. Above all, their diet is high in calcium, which means a daily intake of about 1200 milligrams. (For women over sixty-five, Dr. Luckey recommends 1500 milligrams.)

Here's a rundown on how you can advise your parents to eat in order to achieve that amount:

An excellent source of calcium is milk. An eight-ounce glass of milk contains about 290 milligrams of calcium. The listed amounts of the following foods contain about as much calcium as a glass of milk.

	Calories
8-ounce glass of whole milk	159
8-ounce glass of skim milk	88
1 ounce Swiss cheese	105
1/2 cup creamed cottage cheese (low-fat)	335
15 ounces cream cheese	1590
1 cup turnip greens	29
2 cups broccoli	80
3 cups raisins	1257
2 cups canned shrimp	296
1/2 cup canned salmon (with bones)	188
3 ounces sardines (with bones)	264
1/2 pound tofu	164

Dr. Luckey has also made the following recommendations, which you can pass along to your mother: Decrease the intake of dietary protein; avoid taking megadoses of vitamins A and D, both of which cause bone loss; cut out smoking, drink very little alcohol, and make exercise part of the daily routine.[3] While some authorities consider calcium pills less effective than calcium in the diet, their use as a supplement is advisable especially if your parents don't like milk or don't digest it easily. Your mother might ask her doctor whether she should take supplementary pills regularly. (Dr. Luckey recommends calcium carbonate and warns against pills containing dolomite or bone meal.) If your mother is on a low-cholesterol diet, she can increase the high-calcium vegetables and cut down on whole milk and cheese.

Since a negative calcium balance can be created by some medications, especially those containing cortisone, neither parent should be taking such prescription drugs without careful monitoring. If your mother has been placed on long-term estrogen maintenance therapy, find out why—either from her or from her doctor. A significant number of doctors believe that the postmenopausal decrease in the female steroid hormone estrogen is the primary cause of osteoporosis in older women, although there is no definitive scientific evidence that this is so. On the other hand, most gynecologists support the contention that long-term estrogen replacement therapy increases the risk of cancer of the lining of the uterus (endometrial cancer) and is associated with increased incidence of hypertension and strokes.

Otosclerosis

In this condition, which is twice as common among older women as among older men, overgrowth of the bony tissue slowly immobilizes one of the three bones of hearing (the stapes) so that it can no longer vibrate normally, thereby failing to play its role in the relaying of sound waves. It is the most common cause of the conduction hearing loss that accompanies aging. (See also Nerve Deafness.)

Parkinson's Disease

This degenerative brain disease, also called *parkinsonism,* and sometimes *shaking palsy,* affects movement, but it does not impair

3. These recommendations were presented at a conference cosponsored by the Older Women's League and the Mt. Sinai Medical Center Community Health Program in 1985 in New York City.

intellectual capabilities. It is characterized by increasing muscular rigidity and the development of a tremor, usually of the hand, and often of the head. About half a million older people in this country (approximately 1 person in 100 over age fifty) suffer from this disorder in a form severe enough to send them to seek help. It is a disorder for which there is no cure, but its symptoms can be alleviated to a considerable degree by various drugs developed in recent decades.

Parkinsonism is not hereditary, and the underlying cause is unknown. It has been established that the involuntary shaking and the progressive rigidity of the muscles result from a deficiency of the chemical dopamine, which transmits messages between nerve cells in the portion of the brain called the *basal ganglia.* The deficiency occurs when the cells that normally produce the chemical have worn out. The major advance in treating parkinsonism occurred when the compensatory drug L-dopa was developed in the 1960s. In most cases, the progressive effects of the disease can be minimized by a variety of medications whose effectiveness is evaluated on a trial-and-error basis, enabling the patient to choose the one that provides the greatest benefits with the fewest adverse side effects.

If you notice that your parent has developed a tremor, the first thing to check out is whether the shaking is produced as a side effect of a particular psychotropic drug such as Thorazine. If this is in fact the case, the tremor stops when the medication is discontinued. But then a decision has to be made about which is more disabling: the drug-induced tremor or the return of the psychotic syndrome when the drug is withdrawn.

If along with the tremor, you notice that movement is slower and stiffer and that speech is somewhat slurred, a neurologist should be consulted. You may have to insist on this consultation (if the prime care physician hasn't already made a point of it), since even a consideration of the likelihood of parkinsonism has been known to precipitate a depression.

When the diagnosis is established on the basis of symptoms, medical history, and responses to a group of neuropsychological tests, treatment usually begins with drugs that are milder than L-dopa. An exercise plan is often part of the treatment. It appears that stressful situations such as a family upheaval or an illness will aggravate the condition, so try to arrange for as much peace and loving care as possible. Don't make your parent feel stupid and incompetent just because of slow speech and halting movements.

Encourage the continuation of social relationships and participation in family gatherings. (Young grandchildren should be briefed so that their behavior is considerate. If they have the example of *their* parents' thoughtfulness, they won't need much coaching.)

When physical therapy is combined with medication, you might ask for a demonstration of the recommended exercises so that you can applaud the efforts. And be sure that the instructions about medication are followed to the letter. In most cases, this means that the drug is not to be combined with alcohol, antihistamines, or antidepressants.

An invaluable source of support for patients and their families can be found in the self-help groups that concern themselves with the most effective ways to deal with the physical and emotional problems presented by parkinsonism. For information about the group closest to you and your parents, contact:

> The Parkinson Support Groups of America
> 11376 Cherry Hill Road, Apt. 204
> Beltsville, Maryland 20705
> (301) 937-1545

Free pamphlets and general information are available from:

> The American Parkinson Disease Association
> 116 John Street, New York, New York 10038
> (212) 732-9550; outside New York State, call
> (800) 223-2732

> The National Parkinson Foundation Inc.
> 1501 Northwest Ninth Avenue, Miami, Florida 33136
> (305) 547-6666

> The United Parkinson Foundation
> 360 West Superior Street, Chicago, Illinois 60610
> (312) 664-2344

Vision Impairment

After the age of sixty, nine out of ten people have eyesight problems. Fortunately, many of these problems can be satisfactorily solved by prescription eyeglasses or contact lenses. However, visual impairment may be caused by conditions that require prompt attention—either medical or surgical.

Glaucoma. This is potentially one of the most damaging disorders of the aging eye. If you yourself are over forty, you should have been alerted to the importance of having an annual check for the onset of this condition since, if it isn't treated as soon as it is detected, it can do irreversible harm to the optic nerve. This is what happens: In the normal eye, the fluid (aqueous humor) that fills the areas between the cornea, the iris, and the lens is constantly renewed and drained away into the bloodstream through channels near the cornea. When the drainage system no longer functions efficiently, the fluid backs up, and the resulting accumulation starts to press against the retina, damaging the nerves that control side vision. If the pressure is unrelieved and continues to increase, it eventually impinges on the optic nerve at the back of the eye, destroying frontal vision as well.

In its early stages, glaucoma produces no symptoms, but an ophthalmologist can detect its onset with the help of a device that measures pressure within the eyeball. This diagnostic test is quick and painless and enables the doctor to initiate treatment that will halt the progress of the disease in its earliest phase. Treatment with eyedrops can either decrease the amount of fluid produced or increase the amount removed. In more advanced cases, surgery may be recommended to open up new channels for fluid drainage.

If your parent's glaucoma is being treated with eyedrops, they must be used with meticulous attention. An older person who lives alone may have some trouble either remembering to use the drops every morning and evening, or differentiating between the two types that have been prescribed, or getting the drop *into* the eye. In such cases, you might make a practical arrangement with a dependable neighbor or a responsible teenager for administering the drops, but if you do so, be sure to get your parent's approval in advance.

Older people with glaucoma may or may not have been alerted about the importance of avoiding certain medications with potentially dangerous effects on their eye condition. When a new medicine is prescribed by some other specialist or by the prime care physician, find out whether the doctor knows about the glaucoma. You and/or your parent can also check with the pharmacist about whether the new medication is contraindicated for glaucoma patients, and if it is, the matter should be discussed with the doctor for further instructions.

Cataracts. Like glaucoma, this eye disorder can be detected at its inception by an ophthalmologist long before it produces any vision impairment. Cataract formation occurs almost imperceptibly, causing the normally crystalline lens to become cloudy. As the process continues, or as the cataract "ripens," it blocks the passage of light to the retina and results in progressive loss of vision. When your parents have their annual eye checkup, they will be told if cataract formation is detected, and the condition will be monitored. You may be aware of the problem before they are if there are complaints about the dimness of the lighting, or about occasional double vision.

Cataracts that develop late in life are a leading cause of blindness in people over sixty because so many older people are afraid of eye surgery and don't know that the removal of cataracts is one of the safest operations performed today. You can give them that assurance, and tell them that *when* to have the operation done is a matter of individual choice after taking several options into account. You can help in the decision making when you find out what the options are. Some older people whose chief pleasure is reading or fine handwork want the cloudiness eliminated as soon as it interferes with sharp vision. If there's a cataract in one eye only, there may be no need to make the quick decision about surgery. If cataracts have developed in both eyes but at a somewhat different rate, they may both be removed during the same hospital stay but with an interval of about a week between the two operations. In deciding on how to advise your parent, consider the fact that some specialists believe that cataract removal should not be scheduled until the vision in one eye is seriously impaired and the healthier eye has begun to deteriorate too.

In many instances, no surgery is necessary at all. The obstructive effect of "immature" cataracts can be offset by eyeglasses, contact lenses, or a trial-and-error combination of stronger indoor lighting and stronger lenses.

Older people with diabetes are particularly vulnerable to the specific threat to vision known as *diabetic retinopathy.* In this condition, the diabetes may lead to a bulging and eventual hemorrhaging of the tiny blood vessels on the retina. Early diagnosis makes a critical difference in successful treatment, which may involve the use of lasers.

The condition called *macular degeneration* has been known to impair the vision of a significant number of people over sixty-five, but it hasn't received much general attention until comparatively recently. Don't panic if you're told that this disorder is responsible for the deterioration in your parent's eyesight. Macular degeneration, which affects the part of the eye that receives and analyzes light from the center of the visual field, doesn't progress to blindness. If your parent can't be helped by laser treatment, you can provide large-type books and newspapers, good strong lighting, and a high-powered magnifying glass. You might also investigate some of the optical devices designed to maximize the visual capabilities of the impaired eyes.

You and your parents can benefit from a Home Eye Test Kit for Adults, which contains distance and near vision tests and the Amsler Grid Test for macular degeneration. The kit also lists the problems that should be checked by an eye doctor. Send your request plus one dollar to:

The National Society to Prevent Blindness
79 Madison Avenue, New York, New York 10016

Another source of useful information is the free catalog "Products for People with Vision Problems" available from:

The American Foundation for the Blind
15 West 16th Street, New York, New York 10011

Of all the pleasure-giving provisions you can initiate for a parent who is legally blind, none is likely to be more satisfying than participation in the Talking Books Program. Without any charge, this program delivers long-playing records and cassettes of a variety of books and magazines for every taste, selected by the participant from catalogs that are kept up to date. It also provides a slow-speed record player as well as a cassette deck. With documentation of your parent's visual impairment from an ophthalmologist, arrangements for participation in the Talking Books Program can be made through the local library, or by writing to:

The Library for the Blind and Handicapped
Library of Congress, Washington, D.C. 20542

MEDIC ALERT

Millions of people with potentially life-threatening health problems wear a bracelet or necklace with a waterproof ID that spells out the nature of the disability—heart failure, diabetes, allergy to certain medications, and the like. The Medic Alert emblem, which is worn at all times, also contains the individual's membership number and a twenty-four-hour emergency telephone number which can be called collect from anywhere in the world for up-to-date information about the wearer. Medic Alert is supported by membership fees and donations. If your parent has a health problem that might produce an emergency in a public place or while traveling alone, the Medic Alert emblem can be a lifesaver.

For additional information, write to the national headquarters:

Medic Alert, P.O. Box 1009, Turlock, California 95081
or call the toll-free number: 1-800-344-3226
In New York City, the organization can be reached at:
777 United Nations Plaza, New York, New York 10017
(212) 697-7470

COPING WITH NUISANCE COMPLAINTS

Although they aren't in the same category with major diseases, there are many conditions that can make daily life uncomfortable for your parents—and unnecessarily so. These are problems that can usually be resolved by understanding their cause or by a change in habits. You can also contribute a great deal to your parents' well-being by promoting the idea that they should be more alert to the messages from their own bodies than to the messages from TV commercials for over-the-counter remedies.

Chilblains

When people grow older and circulation becomes more sluggish, their sensitivity to cold increases, especially in the extremities. This sensitivity is the underlying cause of chilblains, a local inflammation most commonly affecting the face, ears, hands, and feet, and sometimes the tip of the nose. Symptoms are swelling, reddish-blue discoloration, itching, and burning. Since the inflammation is most likely to occur when the air is damp as well as cold, the most effective treatment is to bring your parent indoors at once into a warm, dry environment. Remove all clothing and pat—don't rub or chafe—the inflamed areas with a soft, dry towel. *Don't* permit the affected areas to be soaked in hot water. Fleece-lined slippers and gloves can be worn indoors until the condition improves.

Since chilblains are easier to prevent than to treat, you might (once again) remind your parent to wear the proper clothing when going out in nasty weather: wool or part-wool socks and gloves, earmuffs, and a hat. To be especially avoided by the elderly with poor circulation are footwear and gloves made entirely of synthetics. And no smoking!

Constipation

Judging from TV commercials, it isn't only the older generation that's concerned with constipation. And unfortunately, copywriters never tire of equating "irregularity" with moodiness and fatigue, or of implying that a "sluggish" bowel means that the body is retaining "poisons" likely to do incalculable harm. It's true that many people in their sixties and seventies become constipated, but if a medical checkup has found no organic basis for the problem, it's probably due to faulty eating habits, lack of exercise, or years of ill-advised overmedication with strong laxatives. And if constipation is a recent manifestation, find out whether the complaint is a side effect of a particular medication, especially one of the psychotropic drugs prescribed for depression or other mental illness.

Unless a doctor has given other advice, you can suggest the following: more whole grain breads and cereals, more fresh and cooked vegetables, and fresh or stewed fruit for dessert instead of pastry. Lots of liquid is a big help too—not in the form of alcoholic beverages or those containing large amounts of caffeine or sugar, but just plain water, eight glasses a day, or several glasses of skim milk. Use *no* stimulant laxatives; bulk laxatives made from fiber extracts, such as Metamucil, can be helpful when taken with a glass of water or fruit juice. Use only those stool softeners, such as Colace, that don't contain a laxative. Give *no* enemas unless prescribed by a physician.

Dental Problems

Poor dental hygiene, avoidance of dental checkups, missing teeth, dentures that don't fit properly—any of these circumstances can cause trouble during the later years. If your parents have had a long association with a competent dentist and have managed to preserve most of their teeth, they are among the fortunate few of their generation. (Consider the fact that half the people in the United States are toothless by the time they reach sixty-five.)

Two problems your parents may be dealing with because of partial toothlessness are an inability to chew properly, thus restricting their diet to soft foods which may not provide essential nutrients; and gaping spaces which make speech unintelligible, have a negative effect on appearance, and cause many older people to withdraw from social contact.

If your parent is about to join the ranks of more than 50 million Americans who wear partial or complete dentures, you can help investigate various options. In a few states, there are now legalized clinics operated by "denturists," technicians who specialize in the fitting and preparation of dentures. In most parts of the United States, however, dentists are still considered the only professionals properly trained to do this work because they can diagnose conditions that may jeopardize the total health of the mouth and gums if not correctly treated before the dentures are made.

Good dental work can be expensive (bad dental work can be just as expensive), and some older people are lucky enough to be covered by a health insurance plan that pays part of the cost. With such coverage, the patient may be free to choose an individual dentist who is expected to submit a pretreatment plan for approval. If your parent has no such coverage and money is in short supply, but there's no urgency about time, find out whether there's an accessible clinic connected with a school of dentistry.

While the work may proceed slowly in such clinics, it may be of a better quality than that of a private clinic whose profits are based on quick patient turnover. Parents on Medicaid are entitled to dental services. Medicare recipients are not.

If your parent has an especially complicated problem, you might seek out a specialist in geriatric dentistry. Such specialists are sometimes available for consultation at clinics connected with university hospitals.

If you can't make a satisfactory contact with such a specialist and the family dentist can't provide a referral, request the information from:

> Dr. Marie Jacobs, Secretary
> The American Society for Geriatric Dentistry
> Loyola University
> 2160 South First Avenue, Maywood, Illinois 60153

Dry Eyes

A marked decrease in the production of tears after the age of sixty results in the "dry eye syndrome," which is about nine times more prevalent among women than among men. In a few cases, it may be connected with rheumatoid arthritis, but if your mother isn't suffering from that disorder, and complains that her eyes feel "sandy" and irritated, or that she often has the "foreign body in my eye" sensation, she probably should be using *replacement tears.* There are two main types, both nonprescription, and unless her ophthalmologist thinks one is better than the other, you might advise her to experiment until she finds which brand gives her the best results. Since these drops come in a plastic squeeze bottle and needn't be refrigerated, they can be kept within easy reach in the drawer of a bedside night table.

Dry Mouth

Salivary insufficiency, a common condition among older people, can cause difficulty not only in chewing and swallowing, but also in speaking clearly. A constantly dry mouth also leads to an increase in cavities because food is more likely to stick to the teeth, and this in turn results in the problem of bad breath. If the decrease in saliva is directly attributable to aging, practical measures can include the frequent use of mouthwashes and the occasional use of hard sour candies. However, if your parent is taking one of the psychotropic drugs prescribed for anxiety, depression, or severe mental illness, dry mouth may well be a side effect of the medication. You might discuss the problem with the doctor who prescribed the medication and get some suggestions for relief of the discomfort.

Fatigue

When an older person who used to be enterprising and energetic begins to say, "I feel tired all the time," something other than "getting older" is likely to be the cause of generalized fatigue. Since the condition may be remediable without a medical checkup, you can be helpful by exploring a few obvious causes: poor health habits that include an inadequate diet, smoking, too little fresh air and exercise. Maybe the cumulative results of wearing the wrong shoes have caught up with your mother, in which case see if you can get her to give up the heels that are too high for everyday use in favor of more sensible footwear.

Of course the sudden onset of fatigue may be a warning of an undiagnosed illness, signaling the need for a thorough checkup. Among the conditions associated with chronic tiredness are anemia, tuberculosis, heart disease, diabetes, and cancer. When you become aware that complaints about fatigue are accompanied by signs of boredom verging on depression, the problem is likely to be more psychological than physical. And if you think your parent is suffering not from a deficiency of energy but from a lack of motivation, you may find some useful suggestions in Chapter 3, "Helping Your Parents Maintain a Cheerful Outlook." Insomnia, which partially accounts for fatigue in many older people (younger ones too), is discussed below.

Insomnia

When aging parents speak about sleeping "poorly," it's a good idea to find out whether they mean that their sleep is constantly interrupted, or that they find it difficult to fall asleep, or that they wake up much too early. It *is* true that as we age, we seem to need less sleep, but it's equally true that older people have to contend with "broken" sleep: having to get up in the middle of the night to urinate; being roused by acutely painful leg cramps or by the sound of the spouse's snoring. Troublesome as these interruptions may be, most people manage to get back to sleep unless there are other problems that keep them awake. Of these, the most common are chronic depression or anxiety about failing health, dependency, money, one's own death, and even more, the death of the spouse who is the main caregiver. If you can get your parents to talk to you about these feelings (and they probably will if they don't think you'll pooh-pooh them), you may be able to provide much-needed emotional support. Such conversations, undertaken with your ears and your heart open, offering sympathetic reassurance and sensible suggestions, can be more beneficial than tranquilizers and sleeping pills.

Insomnia may also be connected with circumstances that can be changed or eliminated: the very medications that are supposed to "cure" it—barbiturates and other sleeping pills—can actually lead to addiction and the disruption of normal sleep patterns. (If this appears to be the case with your parent, *don't* take the responsibility of urging abrupt discontinuation of the drugs. Withdrawal from such medication should always be gradual and supervised by a physician.)

If you've been investigating various relaxation techniques on your own behalf, your parents might be helped by them too, especially as an aid to "unwinding" at bedtime instead of "trying" to fall asleep. *Never* suggest "a good stiff drink" as a sleeping potion. In some cases, alcohol is the reason for the sleep problems, and it can be dangerous when combined with a long list of medications.

It may be that difficulty in falling asleep at night is the result of taking too many little naps during the day and/or having too little exercise. Also, sensitivity to caffeine may be so acute that it should be ruled out altogether, not only before bedtime. Older people who have the habit of staying in bed for the better part of the morning when there is no compelling reason for doing so should be encouraged to establish more or less regular hours for rising and retiring. And as a bedtime routine, a glass of warm milk with a bit of honey is likely to be a more effective and safer soporific than a shot of whiskey.

Ringing in the Ears

Older people are sometimes unwilling to mention this persistent nuisance because they're afraid they'll be told that they're "hearing things." But complaints about hissing, buzzing noises (the phenomenon is known as *tinnitus)* are easy enough to differentiate from auditory hallucinations by a few simple questions. In some cases, ringing in the ears unaccompanied by any other symptoms can be a temporary side effect of certain antibiotics. It may also be associated with the use of diuretics or aspirin and such medicines as indomethacin (prescribed for arthritis) or quinidine (prescribed for certain heart ailments).

Where the cause is no more complicated than obstruction of the eustachian tube by earwax, the ringing sounds go when the ear is flushed out by a doctor. An ear specialist may find that the noises are attributable to otosclerosis, or to a tumor. If a physician can't find a treatable cause and the sounds continue to distress your parent, you might inquire about the effectiveness of ultrasound irradiation of parts of the inner ear. A less drastic treatment is a transmitting device that masks the sounds when it is inserted in the ear.

KNOWING WHO'S WHO IN HEALTH CARE

Your parents may be fortunate in having maintained a relationship with a prime care physician who knows their history and who answers all their questions and yours. It's also possible that over the years, they've been referred to one specialist or another without involving you in the experience. However, as they get older and their circumstances change, they may want your advice more often, or you may feel that you should participate in decision making with them.

Since the many specialties and subspecialties can be somewhat bewildering, it's helpful to know about the ones most often consulted. Unfortunately, doctors may designate themselves "specialists" without having spent the necessary additional years as resident physicians in a hospital accredited in their chosen field. This extra training is a requirement for certification, which is conferred after passing an examination conducted by a board of specialists in the selected field of practice. You *know* that the doctor to whom

your parents have been referred is a certified specialist when the
initials M.D. are followed by (among others): F.A.C.C., which
stands for Fellow of the American College of Cardiology, or
F.A.C.G., for Fellow of the American College of Gastroenterol-
ogy, and so on.

There's nothing to prevent an M.D. from being a self-styled
surgeon, and it is therefore important to check on credentials
when your parent is to have an operation. Whatever barriers are
put in your way, find out whether the person who is to do the
surgery is a Fellow of the American College of Surgeons
(F.A.C.S.). If you can't get a look at a framed diploma in a consultation room, you can get the information in the comprehensive
American Medical Association Directory, which should be available at your local library. If your parents are members of a health
maintenance organization or a similar group plan, you can check
on the credentials of the participating physicians in the same
source if they haven't been made available any other way.

Doctors of Medicine (M.D.s)

Sometimes called G.P.s (general practitioners), M.D.s are physicians who treat diseases and injuries, do checkups, prescribe
medications, and do some minor surgery. They make referrals to
specialists when they think it necessary. All M.D.s have completed medical school course requirements as well as additional
graduate education. They must be licensed in the state in which
they practice.

Family Practitioners

These M.D.s come closest to what used to be called the family
doctor, although their training is far more extensive and demanding. The practice of family medicine, which provides comprehensive care on a continuing basis for the young and old, male and
female members of the same family, was certified as a medical
specialty in 1969. It was the first specialty to require continuous
recertification by examination every six years.

Internists

Internists are M.D.s who specialize in the diagnosis of diseases
in adults and their treatment by medical means. An internist

doesn't deliver babies or perform surgery. Some limit their practice to particular specialties.

Doctors of Osteopathic Medicine (D.O.s)

D.O.s receive the same training as M.D.s and are their professional equivalent. In addition to medication and surgery, manipulation of bones and muscles is also used by D.O.s as a method of treatment.

Medical Specialists

Any of the above doctors may refer your parents to one of the following specialists, all of whom are M.D.s:

Cardiologists—heart and coronary artery specialist.

Dermatologists—skin specialist.

Endocrinologists—a specialist in the glands and hormones and in such diseases as diabetes.

Gastroenterologists—a specialist in diseases of the digestive tract, including ulcers, and of the intestines, such as irritable bowel syndrome.

Gynecologists—specialist in the female reproductive system, often consulted during menopause.

Neurologists—specialist in disorders of the brain and nervous system, such as parkinsonism and Alzheimer's disease.

Oncologists—tumor and cancer specialist.

Ophthalmologists—eye specialist who also performs eye surgery.

Orthopedists—surgical specialist who operates and treats injuries and disorders of the bones, joints, muscles, and connective tissue.

Otolaryngologists—also called an ENT specialist (for ear, nose, and throat).

Physical Medicine and Rehabilitation Specialists—an M.D. who specializes in restoring normal function to patients who have had a stroke, and in correcting disabilities resulting from an accident or injury.

Proctologists—specialist in the medical and surgical treatment of disorders and diseases of the anus and rectum.

Radiologists—specialist in the diagnostic and therapeutic use of X rays, sonography, radioactive substance, and CAT scanners.

Nuclear medicine is the branch of radiology that uses radioactive isotopes in detecting and treating disease.

Rheumatologists—specialist in arthritis and rheumatism.

Surgeons—a general surgeon is qualified to perform any type of surgery. However, many surgeons specialize in particular kinds of operations: brain, chest, heart, stomach, etc.

Urologists—specialist in the urinary system of both sexes and the male reproductive system.

The U.S. Department of Health and Human Services provides a second opinion hot line that gives the names of local agencies throughout the United States offering lists of medical specialists. The toll-free number is 1-800-638-6833. [Maryland has its own number: 1-800-492-6603.] Second opinions are covered by Medicare and most other insurance plans.

Mental Health Specialists

Psychiatrists are M.D.s trained in the diagnosis and treatment of mental and emotional disorders. They may prescribe medicines known as *psychotropic* or *mood-altering* drugs, administer electroshock treatment, and conduct counseling sessions. Older people may be referred to psychiatrists who specialize in geriatric problems. Medicare helps to pay for psychiatric costs on both an inpatient and an outpatient basis.

Psychoanalysts may or may not be M.D.s. Their treatment of mental illness is based on Freudian theory.

Clinical Psychologists are not M.D.s. They may be called "Doctor" because they have an academic Ph.D. If they have a master's degree, they are not called "Doctor." Clinical psychologists may specialize in family therapy or they may counsel patients on a one-to-one basis. When this category of counselor works directly with an M.D. (customarily with a psychiatrist), services are partly paid for by Medicare.

NOTE: *Psychotherapy* is the general category for the treatment of mental and emotional disorders. A *psychotherapist* may be a psychiatrist, a psychoanalyst, a psychologist, or a "lay" (that is, nonprofessional) analyst. For a more detailed list of mental health counsellors, see page 105.

Eye Specialists

Ophthalmologists are M.D.s who specialize in the diagnosis and treatment, medically and surgically, of eye disorders. They also do refractions and prescribe eyeglasses and contact lenses. Your parents should have a continuing relationship with an ophthalmologist.

Optometrists are not medical doctors. After graduation from college, they attend a school of optometry for three years. Their training enables them to prescribe and adjust eyeglasses and contact lenses. Although they are permitted in some states to *use* certain drugs, they may not *prescribe* any medication. When an eye disorder requires sophisticated diagnosis and medical or surgical treatment, the patient is referred to an ophthalmologist. A limited number of optometric services may be covered by Medicare.

Opticians fill the corrective prescriptions ordered by the ophthalmologist or optometrist. They are essentially lens grinders who rarely connect with the public. Opticians are licensed in over twenty states.

Dental Specialists

Dentists (D.D.S. stands for Doctor of Dental Surgery) treat tooth decay and gum disease, fill cavities, extract teeth, provide dentures, and routinely check for cancer inside the mouth. They recommend regular checkups for preventive care of teeth and gums, and they can prescribe medication when necessary. Some dentists specialize in complicated tooth extraction and jaw surgery. A specialist in root canal work is an *endodontist,* a specialist in gum diseases is a *periodontist,* and one who straightens teeth is an *orthodontist.*

Dental Hygienists clean and polish teeth, teach people about effective tooth hygiene, and take X rays. They work under the supervision of a dentist and must be licensed by the state in which they practice. Their services are not paid for by Medicare.

Foot Care

Podiatrists (D.P.M. stands for Doctor of Podiatric Medicine) are licensed by the state in which they practice after completing four years of professional school. They diagnose and treat diseases and injuries of the feet. They perform operations to remove bunions and to repair injuries, design corrective devices for orthopedic comfort, and prescribe drugs relating to local conditions only. Where a foot condition occurs because of systemic involvement, the patient is referred to an M.D.

Other Members of the Health Care Family

In recent years, several new categories of health professionals have been established to facilitate the work of M.D.s and to provide as much personalized patient care as possible. If your parents are participants in a health maintenance organization or a similar group plan, they may be examined by a physician's assistant or a nurse practitioner rather than by an M.D.

Audiologists are specialists who test patients for hearing loss. They recommend hearing aids, and in some cases, sell them. They usually have a master's degree in their specialty, and most states require that they be licensed.

Nurse Practitioners (N.P.s) are registered nurses who have been additionally trained to conduct physical examinations and diagnostic tests for the purpose of counseling and treating patients. Just as there are nurse practitioners who specialize in midwifery or in the care and treatment of newborns, there are now many nurse practitioners whose specialty is geriatrics. N.P.s may make house calls when the doctor is too busy to do so; they may be in charge of a rural health facility; or they may be on the staff of a hospital, day-care facility, or nursing home. The regulations governing their activities differ from state to state. When their services are performed under a doctor's supervision, they are partially paid by Medicare.

Occupational Therapists (O.T.s) provide individualized programs of mental and/or physical activity to promote recovery from injury or illness. Correctly conceived, occupational therapy isn't mere busy work or distraction from pain. It is concerned with building the patient's confidence by providing new capabilities that go beyond rehabilitation for participation in normal activities. Properly staffed hospitals, nursing homes, and adult day-care centers employ occupational therapists who may call on the services of performing artists and crafts people as well as experts in exercise programs. Occupational therapists play a practical role in teaching stroke victims how to accommodate themselves to new ways of getting dressed, preparing a meal, and getting around in their own dwelling when they leave the treatment facility. Medicare pays for some of the costs for outpatient referrals by a doctor and for all costs when the patient is in a hospital, skilled nursing facility, or rehabilitation center.

Physical Therapists (P.T.s) are trained to establish or restore mobility, strength, and/or function to parts of the body impaired by accident, injury, illness, or prolonged disuse. Among the means used are exercise, manipulation, heat application, hydrotherapy (hot or cold water), and mobilization. Acupressure (also known as *shiatsu)* is a form of massage that may be used for muscle rehabilitation. (Since *acupuncture* is an invasive technique that punctures the patient's skin, only an M.D. may perform it except in those states where acupuncturists are officially licensed.) Medicare pays for a portion of the costs for outpatient treatment initiated at a doctor's request. When physical therapy is an aspect of team treatment in a hospital, rehabilitation center, or at home following a stroke, Medicare pays for specified treatment.

Physician's Assistants (P.A.s) are trained to take over many of the tasks that used to be performed only by doctors. They take medical histories, conduct physical examinations, perform routine diagnostic procedures, and present the patient with a treatment plan. In some states, they are permitted to prescribe drugs and to consult with the supervising doctor on the phone rather than in person. The services of a P.A. are partially paid for by Medicare when they are performed under the supervision of a doctor in a professional setting.

Registered Dietitians (R.D.s) are specialists in dietary counseling. They are accredited by an examination following an approved undergraduate program augmented by an internship. R.D.s are in charge of menu planning in hospitals, day-care facilities, and nursing homes.

Registered Nurses (R.N.s) Depending on state licensing requirements, R.N.s may have from two to four years of special training in an accredited nursing school usually attached to a hospital. Some R.N.s prefer to work with patients as staff members of a health care facility; others may be employed only as a private nurse responsible for only one patient. Many R.N.s are engaged in administration, teaching, and public health. In recent years, more and more R.N.s are participating in graduate programs offering advanced training in pediatrics, intensive care, and geriatrics. When your parent is in a hospital, private duty nurses are not paid for by Medicare. Many hospitals maintain a nurses' registry office where you can order and pay for private nurses in advance for specific eight-hour shifts during your parent's hospital stay. While this may be a great luxury, it can be comforting to know that a nurse will be at the bedside at the moment of arrival from the recovery room following a major operation.

Speech/Language Therapists are specialists who not only correct such impediments as a lisp or a stammer. They especially evaluate and treat patients who have suffered impairment or loss of speech/language function. The disability is commonly associated with a stroke, or it may result from the surgical removal of the vocal chords or a disease of the nervous system. If your parent is undergoing therapy for restoration of normal speech function, you can encourage every effort, cooperate with the speech therapist in continuing the exercises, and try not to lose patience with the uphill struggle to reestablish communication.

Within specified limits, the services of both an audiologist and a speech therapist are covered by Medicare.

In addition to the resources mentioned in connection with specific disorders, the following health organizations can be consulted. Many of these service organizations have individual chapters listed in local telephone directories. If you can't find an affiliate near you or your parents, write to the address given below.

Allergy   The American Allergy Association
P.O. Box 7273
Menlo Park, California 94026

Asthma & Allergy Foundation of America
1302 18th Street, N.W., Washington, D.C. 20036

Cancer   The American Cancer Society
777 Third Avenue, New York, New York 10017

Diabetes   American Diabetes Association
2 Park Avenue, New York, New York 10016

Kidney   National Kidney Foundation
Disease   2 Park Avenue, New York, New York 10016

Self-Help Groups

For a list of the relevant groups that meet in your and your parents' area to discuss the physical and emotional concerns affecting your family, send your request for information, plus a stamped self-addressed envelope to:

The National Self-Help Clearing House
CUNY Graduate Center
33 West 42d Street, Room 1222
New York, New York 10036

Don't overlook the resources of your local library, and don't hesitate to consult the reference librarian about books that don't circulate.

INCREASING YOUR PARENTS' SAFETY AT HOME

Whether your parents maintain their own household or are part of yours, you can help them avert accidents by looking at their living quarters as well as their habits around the house with a critical eye. Keep in mind that there's no place like home for accidents. An estimated 3 million are suffered by the elderly in their own dwelling, and in the seventy-five and older age group, falls are the major cause of accidental death. Other preventable tragedies include serious burns and poisoning. At high risk is an old person who lives alone or who is left home alone all day by busy family members and who has impaired vision and/or unsteady mobility because of a chronic ailment or alcoholism. Smokers present special problems at all times.

Here are some practical ways to make your parents' living quarters safer as well as some suggestions to give them in the interest of reducing their exposure to danger.

In the Bathroom:
- Install grab bars at a 45-degree angle next to the toilet, on the bathtub wall, and in the shower stall.
- Be sure that there's a nonskid rubber mat in the bathtub and shower at all times as well as a rug with a nonskid undersurface on the floor.
- If possible, have the temperature of the water coming from the shower thermostatically controlled. If not, the water temperature should be stabilized *before* getting into the shower.

In the Kitchen:
- If your mother does her own housekeeping, see that staples and dishes are stored in shelves that are easily accessible. Whether in your house or her own, she should *never* be permitted to stand on a chair in order to reach anything. Every kitchen should be provided with a sturdy step stool.
- Check all the pots and pans she uses and get rid of all those with wobbly handles. You can replace them together by taking a trip to a local thrift shop, to a church rummage sale, or if bargain hunting fails, to the local variety store.
- Discourage the use of cooking utensils too heavy to be moved or carried by frail or arthritic hands.

- Suggest that pot handles be turned inward at all times.
- Mark the "off" indicator for the oven and range with high-visibility fluorescent paint. ("I forgot to turn off the oven" is a common cause of household disasters.)
- If your mother is using a microwave oven, be sure that she understands all the precautions.

In the Living Room:
- Remove all scatter rugs.
- Make sure there are no electric wires running across the floor.
- Do not place furniture in a way that obstructs passage from one room to another.
- Make *sure* there is good lighting.

In the Bedroom:
- Arrange the furniture so that there is unobstructed access from the bed to a window, to the door, and to the bathroom.
- Install a night light to illuminate the path from the bedroom to the bathroom.
- Avoid electric blankets. Because an older person with poor circulation in the extremities might be insensitive to the cumulative damage done by an electric blanket, it's probably safer for a parent who complains of cold feet to wear loose-fitting woolen bed socks at night.

Protection Against Accidental Falls:
- Replace all one-step elevations by ramps.
- Make sure that all steps indoors and out are free of clutter at all times.
- Repair all holes and tears in stairway carpeting.
- Provide good light in passageways and at the top and bottom of stairways.

Protection Against Accidental Fires:
- Install smoke detectors in all levels of the dwelling.
- Have an unbreakable rule against smoking in bed, and if your parent has a habit of drowsing on the couch or in an easy chair, smoking shouldn't be permitted except in the kitchen.
- Replace frayed electric cords and broken plugs promptly.
- Keep space heaters far away from curtains and drapes,

and

If your mother spends much time around the house wearing a lounging robe or housecoat, it should be midcalf or above ankle-length. Floor-length garments are responsible for many falls. Nor should she be permitted near a stove surface when she's wearing a garment with long, loose sleeves.

"Safety for Older Consumers: A Home Safety Checklist" is a brochure that can be obtained without charge by writing to:

The Consumer Product Safety Commission
Washington, D.C. 20207
or by calling this toll-free number: 1-800-638-2772

If your parent would have any difficulty using the phone in an emergency, find out about the services provided by the telephone company in your area for people with impaired vision, hearing, speech, or movement.

The New York Telephone Company's Communication Center for Disabled Customers, 1095 Avenue of the Americas, New York, New York 10036, supplies a booklet entitled "Services for Special Needs" to interested customers.

"First Aid in the Home" is a wall chart containing information on emergency procedures and suggestions for the safe storage of medicines. It is available free of charge from:

The Council on Family Health
420 Lexington Avenue, New York, New York 10017

SAFETY AND VEHICLES

Pedestrian Problems

The over-sixty-five age group has the highest number of pedestrian fatalities. If you think your parents aren't alert enough to dangers from moving vehicles, take the time to impress them with the importance of *paying attention* when they're on foot. Even a brief walk from the parking area to the shopping mall can be dangerous for someone who moves slowly, has faulty vision, and is too busy talking to be aware of what's going on.

Make sure they understand that their safety depends on obeying the rules, and it should never be assumed that the driver will see them or be able to stop in time if they're crossing against the light or in the middle of the street. It's especially dangerous to cross between parked cars or from any place other than the designated crosswalk.

Behind the Wheel

When you're a passenger in your parents' car, you can set a good example by buckling into your seat belt and seeing that they do the same.

If you notice that your mother's or father's driving is increasingly erratic and represents a danger to all concerned, try to find out whether slowed-down reflexes and wavering attentiveness are attributable to a natural deterioration of responsiveness or to the effects of a particular medication. If any drug regularly taken is accompanied by the warning that it produces drowsiness, that warning should be heeded absolutely and some other person should do the driving.

PROTECTION AGAINST CRIME

Older people, especially older women who live alone, feel especially vulnerable to burglars, muggers, and purse snatchers. Whether your mother is more or less alone in your house all day, or whether your parents have their own household, here are some precautionary measures you can spell out for them:

- Valuables should be kept in a rented safety deposit box, not at home. For emergency access to the box by family members, two signature cards should be on file with the bank vault attendant.
- The front door should never be opened to a stranger even when it is equipped with a chain lock. Your mother or father can be civil but at the same time should insist that the purpose of the call be stated from the outside. If the caller appears to have a reason for being admitted, he or she should be asked to place an official ID under the door. (A common ploy used by criminals

to get into people's houses is to announce that they are utility inspectors.)

- When no one is going to be home for several days, arrange to have a neighbor pick up the mail and other delivered items.
- If, on returning home, even after an absence of only an hour or so, there are signs that the door or windows have been tampered with, tell your parents *not* to go inside to investigate. Call the police and enter the house together.

Neighborhood Safety

If your parents have relocated recently, or if they continue to live in an area that has "deteriorated," don't undermine their confidence by criticizing their neighbors. Older people have found that the best protection against crime is a self-help neighborhood group that meets regularly and knows the local crime prevention officer. Members of such groups watch out for each other, accompany each other on shopping expeditions, and are generally helpful and supportive as the need arises.

If your parents are living in a neighborhood where street crime has increased and no such self-help group exists, you might encourage them to take the initiative in starting one.

Tell your mother when you have the occasion to do so and even though you may have told her before, *not* to put her purse on the floor in a restaurant or at the theater, but to keep it in her lap, and *not* to carry her keys, money, credit cards, and practically all her worldly possessions in her purse. Some sensible older women never buy any street clothes that don't have pockets, and many, when they're out and around, keep their keys someplace on their person, separate from any cards or other IDs that contain their house address.

CON ARTISTS AND SCAMS

You may occasionally have been annoyed by what you consider to be your parents'—and particularly your mother's—excessive distrust of all strangers, but there are circumstances where such suspicions should be reinforced by you, or instilled where they don't exist.

Many older people are victimized by fast-talking swindlers and con artists, especially when easy money-making schemes or bargains are offered as bait. Tell your parents to be especially wary of:

- Friendly strangers who offer goods or services at cut-rate prices.
- Financial advisers or "consultants" or fortune-tellers who ask that money be turned over to them for profitable investment.
- People wearing fancy uniforms or presenting impressive business cards with high-sounding titles next to their names.
- Any stranger who encourages discussion about details of personal finances.
- Any and all projects or involvements that require being sworn to secrecy.

You might also suggest that if your parents have been approached by any fraudulent operator and have been smart enough to resist the bait, it would be a service to others if the incident were described in detail to the police. But even more important, if they have been gullible enough to be taken in, and the perpetrator has vanished with their money, they should be encouraged to give you the necessary information for reporting the occurrence to the right legal authority. (Try not to make them feel guilty. The victims of scams feel stupid and ashamed enough without your adding insult to injury.)

———————

The booklet "Senior Citizens Against Crime" is available on request from:

The Office of Justice, Assistance, Research, & Statistics
United States Department of Justice
Washington, D.C. 20531

———————

3

HELPING YOUR PARENTS
MAINTAIN A CHEERFUL OUTLOOK

Many younger people have parents who are wonderful role models. They rarely complain or feel sorry for themselves, and not only can they cope with their own problems, they're still offering help of one kind or another to their adult "children." They don't live in the past; they take a genuine interest in others, or they care passionately about gardening, or about traveling, or they're determined to improve their English or learn how to use a word processor. Well into their old age, in spite of arthritis or failing eyesight, off they go when they can—to rally support for a better housing program, to volunteer at the children's hospital, or to augment their modest means at the part-time job they enjoy.

What's their secret? They seem to know that excessive self-concern is the enemy of well-being. One seventy-year-old sums it up by saying, "The world out there is much more interesting than *I* am."

But even the most independent and self-reliant parents (not to mention those who always need a boost in self-confidence) go through times of transition when they need your help and encouragement, when they have to face dramatic changes in circumstance: loss of their spouse, anxieties about money, the unexpected move to another state by an only son and the only grandchild.

During such times—and at all times—there are many ways in which you can help your parents without being patronizing. You can encourage them to call on resources of their own that they may never have known they had, and you can call their attention to resources in the community and in the world beyond their usual horizons that they may not have been aware of.

MEMBERSHIP IN ADVOCACY ORGANIZATIONS

Have you been paying close attention to the social programs for the aging that are constantly being cut nowadays for the benefit of military spending? Do you keep track of moves to tamper with Social Security benefits and Medicare? It wasn't all that long ago (unless fifty years seem like forever to you) when the sons and daughters and other family members were expected to take total responsibility for the older folks who had no financial means of their own. And if they couldn't count on family support in those good old days, they had no alternative but to shuffle off to the county poorhouse or the state-supported old folks home.

There may be lots of badmouthing of social programs and entitlement, but it should be kept in mind that the *first* legislation providing the elderly with well-earned benefits for their later years was the Social Security Program, enacted in 1935. The Medicare program was enacted in 1965, and Medicaid in 1966. It should be obvious to aging parents *and* to their adult children that any cuts in these programs represent a threat to both generations.

The American Association of Retired Persons (AARP)

Among the groups lobbying to protect these programs as well as speaking out for older Americans is the AARP, a nonprofit, nonpartisan organization open to anyone fifty years or older, whether retired or not. Established in 1958, it now has more than 19 million members, many of whom are active participants in community, state, and national affairs.

If your mother and/or father isn't an AARP member, one of the most helpful gifts you can give them is a membership. It's a great bargain: the "dues" are five dollars a year (spouse included), and the amount covers a six-issue subscription to *Modern Maturity*, an informative and entertaining magazine, plus eleven issues of the *AARP News Bulletin*.

Dedicated to helping older Americans achieve retirement lives of independence, dignity, and purpose, the AARP knows that the most effective way to reach this goal is by playing an active role in practical politics. In addition to offering your parents the opportunity for participation in the organization's volunteer state legislative committees maintained in all fifty states and the District of

Columbia, the AARP provides many other special programs and resources in the fields of consumer affairs, energy conservation, driver retraining, lifetime learning, interreligious liaison, senior employment, tax counseling, and widowed persons resources. Other low-cost benefits to members include group health insurance; nonprofit pharmacy services; and hotel, motel, and car rental discounts.

For a membership application, write to:

> AARP Membership Division
> 215 Long Beach Boulevard,
> Long Beach, California 90801

The Gray Panthers

This is a more militant group, and one that you can join *with* your parents, since the approach is intergenerational: people of all ages working together for the benefit of each. The organization was started about fifteen years ago by Maggie Kuhn, a church worker in Philadelphia, when she was forced to resign her job at sixty-five. Since that time, the Gray Panthers have established a network of over a hundred chapters in twenty-seven states, whose activities focus on fighting agism in all its forms, whether the prejudice takes the form of mandatory retirement, or discrimination against the young or the old in social programs, or stereotyping the old as "weak and ineffectual" and the young as "mindless and oversexed."

The Gray Panthers have been pioneers in the movement for intergenerational housing so that older and younger people who can't afford a home on their own can make a true home together, and as they put it, "care for each other and share the full scope of human experience."

Joining the Gray Panthers with your parents is an excellent way to participate in the same experiences and discuss them from different points of view. For your parents, getting out and fighting for programs that benefit young and old alike can be energizing as well as enlightening and productive. And there are plenty of activities to get involved in: petition drives, media monitoring, protest marches against Social Security cuts.

If there's no listing in your telephone directory for the Gray Panthers, you can write for information about the organization and how to join it. Address your request to:

The Gray Panthers
3635 Chestnut Street, Philadelphia, Pennsylvania 19104

OWL—For Women Only

The acronym OWL stands for Older Women's League, which has established itself within only about seven years as a national network of activists concerned with the problems of midlife and older women: pay equity, retirement benefits, insurance for dependent spouses, job training programs for displaced homemakers, adequate housing, and physical and mental well-being in the later years.

If your mother is bored with playing bridge and going to benefit lunches, or if she feels isolated in a rural area and wants a "we" to identify with, she would probably enjoy an OWL membership. There are approximately a hundred groups from coast to coast, and should your mother decide to become a member, it can be a source of comfort to you to know that she will have found new friends with similar interests as well as a "sisterhood" that she can count on in an emergency. Whether there's a crisis involving transportation or a substitute home aide, OWLs pride themselves on the speed with which they fly to help each other. A member of the San Diego group recently pointed out that in addition to working hard to change legislation that will improve the quality of life for older women, "We have to be aware of the need within our own membership. Older women know how to make do with what they have, but when their health fails, or their car decides to stop running, or their circumstances change into crisis, someone who cares needs to know."

Even if your mother doesn't want to go to meetings, she may want to receive the OWL *Observer,* the national newspaper which is mailed out ten times yearly. Subscriptions are included in the five-dollar membership fee.

————————————◆————————————

If you'd like to investigate further, and there's no local listing for the Older Women's League, write to:

OWL National Office, Lower Level B
1325 G Street, N.W., Washington, D.C. 20005

————————————◆————————————

And if your mother looks back with nostalgia on her earlier years as an activist in union or in radical politics, her experience as a speaker and organizer would be welcomed by the National Organization for Women.

SELF-HELP GROUPS

The self-help movement is one of the most rapidly growing support systems in the United States today. Modeled on Alcoholics Anonymous, which had its modest beginnings fifty years ago and now has about thirty thousand chapters in the United States and twice that number worldwide, self-help groups have been proliferating at an astonishing rate within the last ten years. One of their attractions to older people is that members aren't treated as the *beneficiaries* of the group's altruism. They aren't perceived as recipients only, but as active participants able to share a lifetime of experience, to offer a mature perspective, or to provide an unexpected solution to a problem that has brought young and old alike into the same room.

It is estimated that there are now about five hundred thousand actively functioning self-help groups in the United States and Canada, and they deal with practically every problem you can think of. The groups usually come under one of these categories: self-care groups for people suffering from a particular physical or mental disability and related groups for their friends and family; behavior modification groups such as those for alcoholics, overeaters, gamblers, debtors, drug users (there are individual groups for those who want to kick the smoking habit, cocaine addiction, Valium dependency, etc.); advocacy groups for minorities such as homosexuals, the elderly, and the homeless; self-improvement, self-fulfillment groups; and those that focus on a particularly stressful circumstance.

Almost all of them function in the same way. Their effectiveness is based on the concept that members help each other without the intrusion of professionals unless their guidance is specifically requested or they are invited as guest speakers. There are no fees; necessary funds may be raised by donations or benefit parties. Meetings are usually held in no-rent facilities such as community centers, church or synagogue facilities, or a member's home. Programs are self-determined, and a "buddy system" is often encouraged for crisis support.

There are currently thirty regional self-help clearinghouses that collect and disseminate information about local groups and offer guidance in the establishing of new ones.

If you and/or your parents have any difficulty locating the nearest information center, a list of local clearinghouses throughout the United States is available from:

> The National Self-Help Clearing House
> CUNY Graduate Center
> 33 West 42d Street, Room 1222
> New York, New York 10036

Enclose a stamped, self-addressed envelope with your request.

READING MATTER THAT MATTERS FOR OLDER PEOPLE

In addition to organizational involvement and peer group support, reading remains an important source of self-reliance for the aging, not just anything in print, but intelligently prepared material from reliable sources. If your parents don't know about the Consumer Information Catalog, your local library should have copies on hand for free distribution. The Consumer Information Center was set up in 1970 to help federal agencies disseminate information useful to the public at large. The catalog is published four times a year and offers pamphlets on a wide range of subjects. Most of the publications are free; the rest are available at a nominal cost. A handy guide called "Age Pages," compiled by the National Institute on Aging, deals with matters of concern to you and your parents. It costs two dollars. Other pamphlets cover a broad range of subjects, including nutrition, financial planning, house repairs, travel, and how to buy a used car.

If you have difficulty locating a catalog, request one from:

The Consumer Information Center
P.O. Box 100, Pueblo, Colorado 81002

A variety of well-written informative publications is offered in the catalog of the Public Affairs Committee, established fifty years ago "to educate the American public on vital economic and social problems." Included in the current list of 175 titles are "The Rights of Patients," "Sex after Sixty-five," "A Dying Person and the Family," "Getting Ready to Retire," "Health Foods: Facts and Fakes," and "You and Your Alcoholic Parent." The pamphlets are $1 each.

Request a free catalog from:

The Public Affairs Committee Inc.
381 Park Avenue South, New York, New York 10016
(212) 683-4331

MAINTAINING FAMILY TIES

In some families in which the generations have separate households, parents, especially Mother, and maybe even Mother-in-law, expect to be phoned every day even though they live only a few minutes away from each other. If the ritual is a source of comfort and pleasure for both generations, it's a fine way to maintain contact. In many instances, however, sons and daughters of aging parents (as well as the aging parents themselves!) are too busy or too distant for daily phoning. Also there are those with sufficient self-knowledge to anticipate that what begins as an agreeable ritual can develop into a tyranny. Should there be a mutual agreement about the best way to stay in touch if you're separated by a considerable distance? Should there be an established arrangement for back-and-forth visiting if you live nearby? Are spontaneous spur-of-the-moment invitations better than oh-my-god-it's-Friday-night-again dinner dates?

In most cases, *some* plan for visiting and phoning is preferable to none at all, but a plan that's too rigid may end up by causing resentment. Think about what suits you and your parents best, talk about what's possible, and then make an arrangement that includes the phone, letters, and visits. If your parents are the only "family" you've got, it doesn't hurt to let them know that they're an important part of your life even though you don't see them very often.

Of course, if you have children of your own, your relations with your parents take on an added dimension. Many women who are no longer living with the father of their children and who have gone back to work or back to school are only too happy to be able to make a mutually agreeable arrangement with Grandma whereby she moves in and takes on matriarchal responsibilities. Or maybe the grandparents live near enough for their dwelling to provide home base for your kids when they come home from school.

If your parents live too far away for the children to be able to visit them often, it's a good idea to encourage letter writing as soon as elementary printing skills are acquired. (Telephone conversations aren't likely to need encouragement—on the contrary.) Aging parents are usually thrilled by the sight of such communications, and the children may make their first attempts to write down some words. (Don't correct spelling unless you're asked to do so. Many grandparents think childish misspellings are "cute.")

Try to share special events in the lives of the children by sending your parents color photos whenever you can: birthday parties, school performances, the first Halloween costume, the older child with the new baby. Photocopies of report cards that everyone in the family can be proud of are likely to be carried in Grandma's wallet for the whole world to see, but be careful about promoting favoritism for the child who is a good student at the expense of the sibling whose school achievements are on a different level, or in a different area altogether.

One of the most effective ways to breathe life into intergenerational communication over distance is the use of tape recordings. If your parents don't own a cassette deck as part of their audio equipment, consider giving them one with a supply of tapes the next time there's an occasion for a special present. And if you don't have one, maybe it's time to get one so that the children can make tapes and receive them from your parents. Tapes can be more gratifying (and less expensive in the long run) than long-distance phone calls because the tapes can be played over and over to the endless satisfaction of young and old alike.

Many children are encouraged at home and at school to explore their ethnicity or to find out how things used to be when the grandparents were growing up in this country or in some other part of the world. Whether your parents had an early life of hardship or of ease, it can be a great source of pleasure to them to be asked to share their memories with the very young: what games they played, what school was like, what foods they loved, how holidays were celebrated, how *their* parents treated them, what *you* were like as a child, what folk and fairy tales they remember. (Such explorations might well be a learning experience for you as well as for your children.)

Many parents have found that as their children move into their teens, grandparents often assume a more important role. According to Professor Bert Cohler, member of the Committee of Human Development at the University of Chicago, "Teenagers are turning to their grandparents for advice because they have the time, money, and experience to help teenagers resolve important issues such as career choices."[1] They also rely on their grandparents for guidance rather than on their parents because they find the oldest generation more objective.

Colleen Johnson, associate professor of medical anthropology at the University of California Medical Center in San Francisco has pointed out that grandparents and teenagers often become closer after the parents are divorced.[2] Her studies indicate that under those circumstances, teenage girls tend to become especially close to their maternal grandmother.

There are, on the other hand, many grandparents who wish they could be closer to their grandchildren but don't know how to

1. New York *Times,* April 15, 1985.
2. Ibid.

fulfill the desire without seeming too pushy. In families where the parents of growing children have maintained affectionate and open relationships with *their* parents, the grandchildren are likely to do the same. But even in the best of circumstances, youngsters approaching their teens often reject *all* authority figures in the flight toward independence. The loss of contact is especially painful to the grandparents because they are at a stage of their own lives when they often feel thwarted in their efforts to share their skills, accumulated experiences, and knowledge (maybe even their wisdom) with the generation that's just coming up.

Your parents may be among those many grandparents who are finding a satisfactory solution to the problem of alienation by talking to each other in an already existing self-help group, or they may decide to start such a group of their own among their friends and be surprised at how many members eventually turn up. If you feel family ties would be improved for the benefit of all three generations, you might suggest participation in such a group.

If your parents live in the New York City area, another option is available for a fee. An organization has recently been established "to promote a mutually nurturing and caring intergenerational society by eliminating ageism and generational separation." For additional information, write to:

The Foundation for Grandparenting
10 West Hyatt Avenue, Mt. Kisco, New York 10549
(914) 241-0682

SPLINTERED FAMILIES AND VISITING RIGHTS

If you're a parent who has remarried, or if remarriage has made you a stepparent, you may be one of the many men and women facing the practical and emotionally charged problem that exists when children from a former relationship and their grandparents want to connect with each other. This situation can be especially troublesome following a rancorous divorce or separation. Until recently, grandparental visitation rights in cases of a dissolved union have been dealt with in a haphazard collection of state laws.

In 1985, however, a resolution was introduced in the U.S. House of Representatives by Rep. Mario Biaggi, Democrat, of New York, expressing congressional support for the development and enactment in each state of a uniform law giving grandparents adequate rights to visit grandchildren after the dissolution of a marriage.

SOLVING PROBLEMS OF BOREDOM AND LONELINESS

Whatever our family situation, there's scarcely an age at which we don't occasionally feel bored, lonely, disconnected, and at a loss about how to get through the next few hours. With older people especially, objective circumstances are often the chief cause of such feelings. Moving in with a son or a daughter after the death of a spouse often means leaving a familiar neighborhood and a group of accessible friends and community connections. It also may mean staying home alone all day while other members of the family are at work and school. Or perhaps your widowed parent has decided to remain in the same dwelling at a considerable distance from you, and has discovered that with the death of a spouse, social arrangements with other couples eventually diminish and disappear. And if your widowed mother doesn't drive, getting around alone or depending on the thoughtfulness of friends may lead to increasing isolation.

If, however, you honestly think that your parent's attitudes and behavior are the essential cause of the isolation, you might try having a heart-to-heart chat the next time you hear complaints about being lonely. It would be more productive to have such a conversation not on the phone, but face to face, so that your physical presence, facial expressions, opportunities for hand holding can contribute to the positive aspects of the message you're trying to communicate. Above all, be supportive and understanding rather than negative and impatient. Don't put your parent on the defensive, and don't provide openings for being accused of lack of sympathy and consideration. Here goes:

"Mom, maybe your standards are too high and you're too critical of your new neighbors. I'll bet you have more in common with those women than you think. Never mind illnesses and operations and money worries. Talk about your last vacation. Show pictures. Ask to see pictures of their grandchildren. Instead of disapproving of the young single parents who go to work, maybe you could compliment them on how well they're doing. Maybe you could even let them know they can call on you in an emergency and so can the children. . . ."

"Pop, you *know* I have to go to my in-laws every other Thanksgiving. I know it's hard since mother's gone, but you've still got a lot to be thankful for—your health is pretty good, you've got a good pension, your apartment is comfortable. You don't have to feel sorry for yourself on holidays. Instead of waiting for Aunt Cathy to invite you to a turkey dinner, why don't you invite her and Uncle Ben to a restaurant for a change? Or maybe you could suggest to a couple of the widows at the Center that you'll all get together and make dinner for your crony who's home alone with a broken leg. . . ."

Alternatives to Living Alone

While most parents prefer to make it on their own if they can, there are those who don't like living alone but don't want to move in with their adult children even if invited to. Fortunately for all parties, and thanks to enterprising individuals and newly organized community resources, there's no need for an elderly person to live alone in a utility flat or in the dwelling that holds too many memories of the departed spouse.

Among the living arrangements you can help your solitary parent investigate are: becoming a boarder in a well-run boardinghouse, renting the spare room to a student or a congenial roommate-companion, participating in a shared housing plan, or moving in with a congenial family in the neighborhood.

During the nineteenth century, according to Clark University's Professor Tamara Hareven, founder of the *Journal of Family History,* one fourth to one third of Americans either lived in someone else's house or took in boarders. She points out that it wasn't "the mythical three-generational family living in the same house" that helped the young people who left the farm to work in factories, but moving in with city households. Dr. Hareven proposes a reversal of this pattern as a solution to the increasing isolation of older men and women "willing to trade privacy for companionship." When they move in with dissatisfied young mothers "whose families have too much privacy and whose children are growing up without seeing older people and learning from them," all the generations can benefit.[3]

Perhaps your father would enjoy having a housemate now that your mother's gone. According to Housing Alternatives for Seniors, a nonprofit organization in Los Angeles, "Many find that moving in with a roommate is easier than moving in with their own children. Others like the arrangement because they don't have to give up their possessions or abandon their hobbies and activities the way they often do when they move into an institution."[4]

Grass roots organizations similar to the one in California have been springing up all over the country. Whether they function under the supervision of city or state services for the aged or are community funded and supported, the more reliable and professional ones use the services of a trained social worker and counselors who evaluate the specified requirements of the applicants so that congenial pairing can be worked out.

If your father would like to try such an arrangement, either to help with the rent or the upkeep of the house, or to find a congenial companion, you might have to initiate the procedure. When he finds the person who seems right to *him* and whose references have been carefully checked by the social agency and by him (your father, too, will be checked out), give them both your best wishes, withdraw from the situation, and keep your misgivings to yourself unless there's some flagrant irregularity that requires your attention. If the arrangement has been made through a social service agency, the caseworker will probably be aware of the legal aspects of sharing an apartment. If the arrangement has been made more informally, the parties involved should know that state legislatures have been revising the housing law so that elderly renters can share their apartment with other elderly people and add the roommate's name to the lease. Before such revisions, this formal acknowledgment wasn't possible, and the roommate could therefore be evicted if the leaseholder of record vacated the premises.

A 1980s version of communal living is another alternative to a retirement home or a small apartment. Organized by social service agencies, this plan enables five residents to live in a single-family house and share chores, meals, and "common" rooms and at the same time have their private sleeping quarters. Most resi-

3. New York *Times,* April 17, 1980.
4. New York *Times,* July 31, 1980.

dents don't want too many services provided for them since if they're physically able to be in charge of their own lives, they prefer to do the housekeeping on their own.

Of particular interest to those sons and daughters who have assumed some or most of the financial responsibility for an aging parent is the fact that in 1983, the United States Department of Housing and Urban Development (HUD) was directed by Congress to authorize the use of federal rent subsidies for shared residences for the elderly. Thus, this type of housing is not only more civilized and congenial than institutionalized living for older people who are ambulatory and capable of self-care; it is also more cost-effective. Savings have been spelled out in these terms: An apartment in a housing complex for the elderly averages $450 a month, or $5400 a year; participation in a shared home averages $200 a month, or $2400 a year. Nursing homes range in annual cost from $15,000 to $30,000 per person; the annual cost for an individual participant in a shared residence is $9000 to $14,000 if all meals and housekeeping services are included, or $6000 to $7200 if only some meals and services are included.[5]

Many cities and states are sponsoring variations of shared housing. Several years ago, the New York State Division of Housing and Community Renewal established the Shared Housing Option Program (SHOP), which facilitates one-to-one matching as well as "accessory apartments," which are essentially independent private living quarters in the unused space of a private home. For further information, write to:

SHOP, New York State Division of Housing and Community Renewal
2 World Trade Center, New York, New York 10047
(212) 488-3228

The National Shared Housing Resource Center
6344 Greene Street, Philadelphia, Pennsylvania 19144
(215) 848-1220

5. New York *Times*, January 31, 1985.

is a national nonprofit organization that promotes shared housing programs and intergenerational housing options for older people on a local and regional level. In addition to functioning as a national clearinghouse and building coalitions to support these housing options, it publishes the *Shared Housing Quarterly,* available by subscription for $15 annually.

For the ambulatory elderly who can take care of themselves, there are 115,000 apartments sponsored by the United States Department of Housing and Urban Development. The units are designed for easy access, and the rents are based on income. Further information is available from the local Area Agency on Aging.

Another source of information is the 42-page booklet *Housing Options for Older Americans.* For a free copy, send your request to:

The AARP Housing Program
1909 K Street, N.W., Washington, D.C. 20049

"I Don't Feel Lonely, I Feel *Useless*"

An older woman who managed to juggle homemaking, child-rearing, a job, and community activism isn't likely to face an identity crisis when the children leave, and her husband dies. Of course she'll take time adjusting to the empty nest, and of course she'll grieve the loss of her spouse. But eventually, she'll continue to find fulfillment in some of the activities that were part of her self-definition. But for the many elderly women whose sense of self has always been determined in relation to the *other*—as somebody's daughter, somebody's wife, somebody's mother—an attempt to achieve an independent identity can be a painful experience, especially when the attempt is postponed until the age of sixty or later. This is almost entirely a female problem, since men have usually created an independent identity early in life.

If your mother now feels useless because she's no longer "needed" by anyone, you can help her explore new ways of continuing to serve others outside the immediate range of home and family, and at the same time develop confidence in herself as an autonomous human being.

If she enjoys being with children, you might help her investigate volunteer programs in hospitals and day-care centers where there is a need for surrogate grandmothers to tell stories, read books, help at mealtimes. If she would like to get out and around and enjoys driving, clinics and health organizations are always looking for volunteer chauffeurs who can transport handicapped patients. Does she find spiritual comfort in being helpful to the homebound? You can encourage her to arrange a schedule of visiting, doing errands, and cooking an occasional meal for a friend or neighbor less fortunate than she. Was your mother once a competent secretary? She might want to volunteer as an office worker in a not-for-profit organization—her favorite charity perhaps, or a health hotline, or the local public radio station. If she's a good cook and complains about not having anyone to cook for anymore, point out that widowers who live alone and who hang out at the senior center might profit from her cooking lessons. Many men never light the oven after their wife dies, and if there are cooking facilities at the center, a resourceful woman can show the men how to roast a chicken or prepare a nourishing soup or make a beef stew or simmer prunes and apricots or steam vegetables. And who knows what social events might result from inspiring improperly fed men to try their skills in their own kitchens?

Many of these activities and a long list of others have been formalized under the federal government's ACTION program, which has created three individual Older Americans Volunteer Programs: the Retired Senior Volunteer Program (RSVP), the Foster Grandparent Program (FGP), and the Senior Companion Program (SCP). All programs are open to both sexes of any race, color, national origin, political beliefs, or religion. Each individual program has its own requirements:

RSVP volunteers must be age sixty or older and retired. There are no income or education requirements. Participants may choose from assignments compiled by the local RSVP office, and they are provided with transportation to and from volunteer sites. They are given preservice orientation and in-service instruction, and they are involved in projects that use their talents and knowledge.

The Foster Grandparent Program is open to low-income men and women who volunteer to work with children who have special needs. They receive forty hours of preservice orientation and monthly in-service training sessions. In return for twenty hours of sustained personal attention to handicapped youngsters, they receive a small tax-free stipend, transportation allowance, hot meals while in service, accident insurance, and an annual physical examination.

The Senior Companion Program is open to low-income men and women sixty years old or over who are part of a comprehensive care plan to help homebound elderly people to continue to live as independently as possible. These volunteers serve not only as companions, but also as advocates for the aged by helping them find the community resources appropriate to their needs. Participants in this program are given the same advantages as those in the Foster Grandparent Program.

There are ten ACTION regional offices throughout the United States. If you can't find a telephone listing for the office that covers your parents' area, call 1-800-424-8580 toll-free for further information.

THE ADVANTAGES OF SWAPPING SKILLS AND SERVICES

Have your parents caught up with the recently revived practice of bartering skills and services on a one-to-one basis? Most older men and women are capable of performing some essential task or providing a necessary service in exchange for similar services rendered in another area of expertise. Money need never change hands, and both parties to such agreements can have the satisfaction of being useful to others at the same time that they find the solution to a particular need of their own.

If the idea is greeted with enthusiasm, here are some of the possibilities you can explore with your mother and/or father: What chores or tasks can they perform for other people? What would they appreciate having someone else do for them? You might have to explain that there really is a need out there in the community for someone who knows how to rewire a lamp or repair a rickety table or who can improve someone's bridge-playing skill.

Maybe your mother would be happy to do some house-sitting, plant-watering, pet-feeding, and mail-collecting for vacationers in exchange for leaf-raking and a few necessary plumbing repairs. Baby-sitting and afternoon child care can be offered in exchange for chauffering services. The possibilities are unlimited. And how should they go about promoting what they have to offer and what they're looking for as a swap? By advertising in the community newspaper and the senior citizen publication, by posting attractively hand-lettered notices (photocopied from a single master) on bulletin boards in local laundromats and markets, or by putting them in people's mailboxes around town.

Here are some services to offer and/or to ask for: carpentry, minor plumbing and electrical repairs, typing, light housework, reading aloud, mending and alterations, auto repair, baby-sitting, tutoring, chauffeuring, breadbaking, house-sitting, dog-walking, gardening, practice in speaking English or a foreign language, gamesmanship in bridge or chess or Scrabble, photography lessons, cooking lessons. Your mother might even locate someone who'd be happy to tune her piano or repair her TV in exchange for a mutually agreed upon supply of her banana bread and pumpkin muffins.

There's no doubt that many of these skills and services are marketable at a price. If you've watched your mother collect what appeared to be a lot of junk and organize her own profitable tag sale, you might suggest that she advertise her availability for such projects on a percentage basis of the cash return. Families who are moving or who have finally decided that the time has come for a basement-to-attic cleanup and who are too concerned with other commitments might be delighted to turn the whole project over to a capable organizer.

Some women have developed an elegant handwriting especially suitable for invitations to large parties and receptions. Payment could be arranged by the piece or by the job. Baking scrumptious birthday cakes, whipping up impressive desserts, supplying soups and salads for dinner parties or take-out food shops can become a profitable enterprise now that so many younger married women are working full time.

Encourage your mother to explore the part-time job market not only if the money would come in handy but also because a job would give a necessary structure to her days, and it might be great for her self-esteem too. Getting out and spending several hours a day or several days a week as a cashier, salesperson, office worker, or library clerk can be a more effective remedy for depression than Valium, especially for women who live alone. And if your mother's taking a job means she has to leave your father to his own resources, he may decide to investigate similar possibilities. If he's a whiz at household repairs, he can advertise his services for a nominal fee. Single mothers and widows might form the nucleus of an appreciative clientele. Also, in spite of computers, there's still a need for competent tutoring in math and science.

Some older women get a new lease on life in communities where the time-honored role of baby-sitter has been elevated to that of "nanny" by professional working women desperate for someone capable, responsible, and intelligent to care for the baby when they go back to their job.

Selling Handicrafts

Special opportunities exist for parents who can handcraft one-of-a-kind objects of genuine merit. Creative crochet or knitting, carved wooden chess men or decoys or soldiers, personalized petit point, quilted coverlets, handpainted trays, dollhouse furniture in "period" styles, patiently crafted fish lures, witty and sturdily made stuffed animals, hand-embroidered pillows, appliquéd ter-rycloth beach bags—there's no end to the objects for which there's a demand. A parent may have all the necessary skills, but you may have to supply a push in the right direction and perhaps some suggestions about color, design, and current taste, keeping all comments as positive as possible, and resisting the temptation to take over.

Elder Craftsman Inc. is a not-for-profit organization that "educates, encourages, and advises older people in the making of fine handicrafts, thereby improving the quality of their lives and adding to their dignity, their creative satisfaction, and their income." It operates its own retail shops, which sell the work of more than nine hundred older handcrafters from around the country, and among its publications is a partial listing of the craft shops and co-ops to be found nationwide.

For a copy of *Opportunities in Crafts for Older Adults,* send a check or money order for $1 to:

Elder Craftsman Inc.
135 East 65th Street, New York, New York 10021

KEEPING TRACK OF EARNINGS

If your mother is gainfully employed outside the home after years of having been a "dependent," or if she's suddenly making money in a cottage industry of her own devising, you may have to help her set up a system of keeping track of her earnings and her deductions. Certainly she may be perfectly competent to do this on her own, or she may prefer the services of an accountant. It appears that some older people are confused about how much money they can earn without jeopardizing their Social Security benefits. As of June 1985, no adjustment is made in the recipient's checks if maximum *net* earnings don't exceed the following amounts: $5400 for people who are sixty to sixty-five; $7320 for those who are sixty-five through sixty-nine, and there is no limit placed on the earnings of recipients over 70. (President Reagan has informed us that he returns his Social Security check.)

There's no question that most older people prefer to manage their own affairs without depending on financial assistance from their offspring, and most of them do. And with all the talk about government handouts, it should be kept in mind that Social Security checks are their *due,* not their dole. However, many parents want to continue to work into their later years not only for the sake of their mental well-being, but because they need the money. Aside from the more obvious resources for job opportunities such as want ads, employment agencies, and community programs designed with senior workers in mind, the local library should be consulted for guidance to be found in pamphlets and brochures. Many city and state departments on the aging also sponsor special vocational retraining workshops for seniors.

Related information is available from:

Office of National Programs for Older Workers
U.S. Department of Labor
Employment and Training Administration
601 D Street, N.W., Room 6122
Washington, D.C. 20213

A YEARNING FOR LEARNING

Continuing Education

There are the mothers and fathers who say, "If only I could have continued my education!" or "I always wanted to go to college, but I had to help support the family," or "I stood on my feet all day for eighty cents an hour and came home to run the household after my mother died. Who had time or strength for night school?"

It's the generation that came to adulthood in the 1930s, the survivors of the Great Depression, talking sometimes bitterly, sometimes proudly of what they had to do without.

And there are the parents who turned twenty-one in time to face the disruptions of World War II. "College? I learned the facts of life in the infantry overseas." "The GI Bill? I had to take over the family business when my father got sick." "Education? You forget I was a war bride and your older brother was born in 1943."

But what about now? Are you still hearing sighs of regret about your educational advantages and their missed opportunities? Is "If only . . ." a constant theme? Call their bluff. Find out how serious your mother and/or your father is about the hunger for knowledge. It's a hunger that's easy to satisfy nowadays. Maybe all they need is a little encouragement from you and reassurances about their ability to participate even though their memory isn't all that wonderful anymore.

But you can point out that if they take courses involving discussion, attitudes, and personal experience, they needn't cope with a decreasing ability to remember facts or to memorize the conjugations of irregular verbs. They can contribute a refreshing point of

view and a perspective different from that of their younger class-
mates when discussing local politics or novels or poetry or femi-
nism or the history of the union movement.

Courses for older Americans are everywhere. Practically all institutions of higher learning offer extension courses—"continuing
education" and "lifelong learning" programs. Religious centers
and libraries offer lecture series on current events; the local "Y"
engages specialists to teach everything from "Relaxing with
Yoga" to "Elementary Spanish." Museums clear up some of the
mysteries of modern art. Community newspapers and library bulletin boards are a good source of information about courses, and
they usually feature those that are offered free or at reduced prices
for senior citizens.

Sometimes the profusion of possibilities can be bewildering. If
your parent finds it hard to decide how to be a student all over
again, you can help by having a few exploratory conversations.
Does your dad want to learn more about a subject he already
knows something about, or does he want to start from scratch?
Would he like to become a better photographer so that he can
bring home really good pictures the next time he goes on a trip or
be able to photograph the grandchildren properly during their
early years? Does your mom want to take a course in the history
of the great religions so that she can understand her Jewish/Cath-
olic/Baptist/Moslem friend better? Or take a class in elementary
drawing so that she can "make a cat" or "do a picture of Daddy"
at the behest of a grandchild?

Sometimes idle curiosity can be transformed into intense interest through exposure to a gifted teacher or a lively group. "Oh, if
only I could write! What a story my life has been!" "So take a
course in creative writing, Mom." "I've always wanted to know
how the stockmarket works." "Here's a series called 'What Happens on Wall Street,' Dad."

The National Council on the Aging has been helping local
communities organize discussion group programs known as
"Self-discovery Through the Humanities." Since 1976 over
twelve hundred such groups have participated, with the essential materials provided free of charge by the council. Program units concentrate on themes from literature, history,
folklore, drama, philosophy, and the visual arts. Program

packages include anthologies, guides for discussion leaders, tapes, posters, and press releases. With support from the National Endowment for the Humanities, the council offers the program to any senior center or organization that serves older people.

If your parents' community hasn't yet begun to take advantage of the "Self-discovery Through the Humanities" program, details about participation are available from:

The Senior Center Humanities Program
National Council on the Aging, Inc.
600 Maryland Avenue, S.W., West Wing 100
Washington, D.C. 20024
(202) 479-1200

Hobbies

A hobby is another good starting point for getting an older person out of the house with a continuing purpose. Maybe you'll have to supply your mother with some literature about creating an indoor greenhouse to get her to expand her houseplant activities. If your father has collected old postcards with early scenes of his native city, call his attention to a course on the subject being given by the local historical society, and it's possible he'll be off and running to the library for books on his specialty, to flea markets for undiscovered treasures, and to postcard collectors' conventions to catch up on current market values.

In some families the collecting instinct seems to be a strong genetic trait: the youngest male brags about his growing batch of baseball cards with the same acquisitive enthusiasm that Grandpa shows when he adds to his stamp albums. Whenever possible, get the generations together for sessions of "show and tell."

The competitive spirit seems to run in families too. Even though it may have lain dormant since your father retired as the company's outstanding salesman, try evoking his sense of competition by calling his attention to the numerous tournaments and contests "for seniors only." Never mind the weekly Bingo games. Remind him that he used to be a terrific bowler—"and look, here's a bowling battle restricted to players who are seventy and older."

If he used to enjoy board games but hasn't played recently, tell him to look into the chess or checkers contest for seniors. And your mother might get a glint in her eye if you locate an ongoing Scrabble tournament for "oldsters only."

TAKING ADVANTAGE OF TRAVEL BARGAINS

Your parents probably know about special rates offered by planes, trains, and buses as well as by cruise ships. However, they may not know about year-round reductions and excursion bargains. It's all very well to join a senior citizen outing to a nearby vacation spot, but see if you can get your mother to join a tour group that's going somewhat farther afield. If a congenial family member or a friend can go with her, so much the better. She might even discover that she can manage on her own in a group of all ages unified by a singular interest and be proud of herself for coping so well. Many timorous widows used to depending on their spouse to make all travel arrangements find out that they're pretty competent when they have to deal with the big world by themselves. And what's more, many learn to like the freedom of not having to defer constantly to someone else's wishes about what to see and where to go and when to eat.

Consider collecting a batch of colorful travel folders featuring special tours at a discount, and if you can afford the time and money, one such tour of your mother's choice would make a memorable sixty-fifth or seventieth birthday present, especially if she's coming out of a depression after an illness or a bereavement.

If one or both parents can still enjoy camping and sightseeing in natural settings rather than in cities, be sure they know about the lifetime Golden Age Passport entitling people over sixty-two to visit this country's national parks at no charge.

For information about the procedure for making personal application for the passport, write to:

National Park Service
U.S. Department of the Interior
18th and C Streets, N.W., Room 1003
Washington, D.C. 20240

Elderhosteling

Do your parents and their friends know about Elderhostel? This program offers older people a unique combination: the excitement of exploring new places and the satisfaction of broadening intellectual horizons. From its modest beginnings less than ten years ago, Elderhostel has become a network consisting of over seven hundred participating institutions located in all fifty states as well as in foreign countries. The program enables older people to register for brief summer courses conducted in small groups while they live in campus dormitories or residential facilities close to classes and dining areas.

Anyone is eligible who is sixty or over or whose participating spouse or companion qualifies. The courses, which aren't for credit, are open to all participants regardless of whether they never completed elementary school or have a postgraduate degree. The offerings in a recent 125-page summer catalog range from "Antique Furniture Styles and the Decorative Arts" at Pennsylvania State University to "Jazz in the 1940s" at the University of North Carolina to "Scandinavian Culture" at the University of Wisconsin to "Scotland, Story of a Nation" at the University of Dundee in Scotland.

Most of the programs given in the United States begin on Sunday evening and end on Saturday morning. The maximum charge for all programs in this country is $195 (slightly higher in Alaska and Hawaii) and includes registration costs, living accommodations for six nights, all meals—from Sunday dinner to Saturday breakfast—five days of classes, and extracurricular activities. Travel arrangements must be paid for independently.

If your parents can explore these opportunities together, so much the better. If your widowed or divorced parent isn't venturesome enough to go alone, encourage him or her to discuss Elderhosteling with a friend or relative, or maybe you'd like to be the Elderhostel companion so that you can travel and take a few courses together.

In studying the catalog for possibilities, you'll find that not only is the course content described in detail, but extracurricular activities and the environs as well. Here's a typical example: "Hampshire is a small innovative liberal arts college in the Connecticut River Valley, near the historic village of Amherst and the lively town of Northampton. Green and lush in the summer, the campus offers ready access to nearby scenic and cultural attractions, and provides fine recreational activities, including a glass-enclosed indoor/outdoor swimming pool, hiking exercise trails, and outdoor tennis courts."

And here's another: "University of Wyoming, Wyoming's only four-year educational institution, is located in Laramie, the 'Gem City of the Plains,' (elevation 7200 feet). The spectacular Snowy Range and Medicine Bow National Forest to the west, provide picnicking/camping area and opportunities for field trips. During its popular summer school sessions, the University's diversified cultural activities are highlighted by the Western Arts Music Festival. Clean air and blue skies combine with Western hospitality to welcome the Elderhosteler to southeastern Wyoming."

As a first exposure to travel adventure and learning, just sitting around and *reading* the catalog can be an inspiration and energizer to parents and their friends who may be stuck in the same rut when it comes to summer plans.

The easiest way to find out more about the Elderhostel program is at the local public library. The organization has placed a special version of all the catalogs at all libraries—main and branch facilities—throughout the United States and Canada. Over seventeen thousand libraries have cooperated with Elderhostel in this endeavor, and to facilitate quick action, the catalogs contain tear-out registration forms that can be used by potential hostelers.

For those families that find the cost of getting there and the cost of registration beyond their means—in most cases, it's a one-week-only deal—some financial assistance is available. For information and application forms, write to:

Hostelships
Elderhostel
80 Boylston Street, Suite 400
Boston, Massachusetts 02116

Seasonal catalogs containing national and international course offerings are available from the same address. If your mother or father wants a quick answer to a particular question, call (617) 426-8056.

EXERCISE FOR ENJOYMENT

Some older people are involved in special exercise programs as part of rehabilitation therapy after a stroke or a fall, or as treatment for arthritis. But what about exercise for the pure pleasure of it?

Many parents need no prodding. Separately or together, or with friends, they play tennis and golf, go bicycling, swim in the summer, and go to a gym in cold weather. But what about a mother or a father in reasonably good health who spends too much time moping around the house or watching television or driving short distances instead of setting out there on foot? With the right clothes, comfortable shoes, and yes, a cane if necessary, and a congenial companion—a dog will certainly do—walking is a wonderful form of exercise that can lighten the spirits and keep the body limber. Lots of people remember with affectionate approval the sight of ex-President Harry Truman taking his thirty-minute morning "constitutional" when he was well into his eighties.

If you live near your mother, you might consider inviting her for a weekly walk instead of an outing in the car. If there's a grandchild old enough and responsible enough to join Grandpa on a hike through the park every Saturday morning—weather permitting—both generations would benefit from the experience.

Many special interests can be combined with walking: there are local birdwatching groups and groups that specialize in nature hikes; urban historical societies and other groups concerned with architectural preservation organize walking tours to explore neighborhoods that elderly people might be too apprehensive about investigating on their own. If you live at a distance from a widowed parent, you might look into some of these options the next time you visit and maybe even plan to participate in a group outing together.

There are men who never lose the desire to "keep score" as a way of improving their record. Maybe giving your father a pedometer for Father's Day instead of the usual tie or toiletries will inspire him to do more walking. If he's still a bit of a gambler, he might even challenge one of his poker-playing pals to a daily walkathon to find out who's the better man on his feet.

If there's a decent-sized lawn in front of your parents' house, a gift that might get them off the porch regularly is a croquet set. You can play the game with them from time to time, and if there are no grandchildren to compete with them, they can invite the neighbor's children to join them and keep a running score.

Shall We Dance?

Many younger people are astonished—and sometimes more than a little embarrassed—when their supposedly creaky ancient parents participate in an energetic folk dance at a wedding or a festival. Pleasure is apparent in their knowledge of the steps and their ability to teach "the children" some of the complicated figures. But folk dancing and square dancing needn't be restricted to special occasions. In many cities, parks departments sponsor regular groups led by knowledgeable callers; the "Y" as well as many religious and ethnic organizations offer instruction to all ages. If your mother is too shy to check out the possibilities by herself, suggest that she go with a friend or neighbor. Or if you can arrange to go with her, who knows—you may be tempted to relive some of the more "folkloric" aspects of the 1960s.

Ballroom dancing on a regular basis is another way to exercise and socialize at the same time. Few of us are so tough that we don't get a little teary when we see couples in their seventies glide into a graceful waltz or two-step. If you think your mother or father looks "silly" whirling around with each other or with a friendly partner, try to remember what you looked like when you did the twist, or what your children look like when they gyrate to their favorite rock group. If your father feels great when he's on a dance floor, suggest that he do it more often.

Workshops for older people interested in modern dance and in unconventional approaches to movement can be found at local colleges and in extension courses. Find out if visiting is possible before enrollment. If your mother is enthusiastic but worried about the enrollment costs, you might offer her a check for the tuition as a Christmas or birthday gift.

Not a Rowing Machine—The Real Thing

A program pioneered several years ago in Tennessee by then seventy-eight-year-old Chris Kelm was known as Rowing for the Handicapped. In 1981, the U.S. Rowing Association started a similar venture in Philadelphia, and more recently new programs have been springing up under the same auspices in various parts of the country. The programs emphasize participation by seniors who may be somewhat incapacitated by arthritis or other handicaps of aging but who can still have a wonderful time handling those oars together.

If your father feels most alive when he's out in a boat and wants to enjoy the companionship of his contemporaries while getting a workout under expert supervision and supersafe conditions, you can help him find out whether there's a program in his vicinity.

For information, write to:

> The U.S. Rowing Association
> #4 Boathouse Row
> Philadelphia, Pennsylvania 19130

BROADER HORIZONS FOR THE HOMEBOUND AND HANDICAPPED

Resourcefulness, imagination, and the encouragement of others —those are assets of inestimable value to older people whose activities are restricted by infirmities. A parent in a wheelchair, or one who must spend long hours in bed, or whose sight is almost gone, can still draw on a variety of inner strengths if the motivation is there. Dependence on tranquilizers or alcohol, a lack of interaction with interesting people, and constant exposure to television have their dehumanizing effects, but you'd be surprised at how many people of your parents' age can bounce back when offered the right incentives.

A man or a woman whose brain/mind functions are more or less intact (or can be restored to comparatively good health by the removal of all but the most essential drugs) can be helped to transcend many limitations. Creativity can be encouraged by providing the right materials: art supplies for drawing and painting, clay for modeling, or tapes and a tape recorder for reliving the past or "telling" stories that can be transcribed and edited. It's not necessary to have much mobility—and it's never too late to learn to play the recorder. If there's a piano in your mother's home and she can still see well enough to sight-read, call the local conservatory or the high school music department and try to find someone who'd enjoy the opportunity to play music for four hands with her. Find a teenager on the high school chess team who would benefit from playing the game with your father several hours weekly if that used to be his passion. Language skills can be the basis for regularly scheduled visits by people of various ages who'd like to improve their conversational facility in Italian or Spanish or Yiddish—or English.

For a parent who depends on the radio for intellectual stimulation and good music, it's convenient to have two radios—one with the dial set at the Public Radio's FM frequency, and the other for the AM frequency if each outlet offers different programming.

You're old enough to know how vividly your own earlier years are recaptured by the sound of the popular music you listened to over and over again—whether it was the Beatles or Elvis or early Bob Dylan. Well, the evocative sound for your parents is something different, but the effect is the same. Someone who is housebound, or whose sight is failing but whose ears are as sharp as ever, will review happy memories through a record or cassette collection of old favorites, insufferably saccharine though they may sound to you. And if there are grandchildren in the family, they'd probably cherish (if not now, then as they grow older), hearing a "memory" tape that begins, "I remember dancing the Lindy to that Benny Goodman number," or "I remember hearing Ethel Merman sing 'Anything Goes' on Broadway in that musical."

A parent who is homebound because of seriously impaired vision or who as a consequence of a stroke or neuromuscular disease is unable to hold a book is eligible to participate in the Talking Books program of the Library of Congress. (See page 49 for details.)

Taking care of plants and watching them flourish can be a source of pleasure to older people who can't move around much. If the windowsill is too shallow to accommodate an interesting assortment, you can provide your mother with a table on casters that can hold lots of pots and be moved around the room to follow the sunlight. Some plant lovers prefer a wide variety of cactuses and succulents because they're easy to care for; others have a talent and passion for African violets, and there are those who proudly share their chives, mint, and basil grown from seeds. Home aides or visitors are usually happy to help with the chores of repotting and transplanting.

PETS AS A SOURCE OF PLEASURE AND WELL-BEING

Never mind about all the cartoons that make fun of the little old ladies and their canaries and cats and pampered poodles. It turns out that pet owners have the last laugh.

In a flyer promoting the Cornell Companion Animals Program, the new role of pets as "therapeutic facilitators" is spelled out in the following observations by Dr. Leo K. Bustad, dean of the Veterinary College at Washington State University:

> Many elderly people have discovered that animal companions satisfy some of their greatest needs. Pets restore order to their lives; provide a more secure grasp of reality; and link their owners to a community of caring, concern, sacrifice, and intense emotional relationships. When older people withdraw from active participation in daily human affairs, the nonhuman environment in general, and animals in particular can become increasingly important. Animals have boundless capacity for acceptance, adoration, attention, forgiveness, and unconditional love. Although the potential for significant benefits to a great variety of people exists through association with companion animals, the potential seems greatest in the elderly, for whom the bond with animal companions is perhaps stronger and more profound than at any other age.[6]

Here are some conclusions established by another authority on the interaction between pets and people, Dr. Erika Friedmann, professor of health science at Brooklyn College. Dr. Friedmann is also affiliated with the School of Veterinary Medicine at the University of Pennsylvania:

> Caring for a pet provides a sense of being needed and self-worth similar to that obtained from caring for other people. Taking re-

6. Leo K. Bustad and Linda Hines, "Placement of Animals with the Elderly—Benefits and Strategies," *California Veterinarian,* August 1982.

sponsibility for a pet can be especially important to patients whose activities are limited due to chronic diseases, handicaps, or social isolation. Caring for a pet often facilitates caring for oneself. The requirements of keeping a pet healthy have been used as an inducement for maintaining healthy living conditions for pet owners.

On the basis of continuing research, Dr. Friedmann and her colleagues have concluded that "because pets can decrease owners' depression, anxiety, and sympathetic nervous system arousal," they can therefore decrease the incidence or slow the progression of "a broad spectrum of chronic diseases, including coronary heart disease, hypertension, and diabetes."

There is mounting evidence that older people temporarily hospitalized for surgery or acute illness are motivated to "get better quicker" so that they can go home to their pet; that those temporarily immobilized by an accident manage to recover more quickly than anticipated because they are "needed" and they prefer not to entrust their pet to another person's care.

The Cornell University program that connects pets with people is only one of many similar projects initiated as a result of these findings. A University of Minnesota study of 774 health care facilities disclosed that "about half were using pets to help their residents [because] dramatic improvements in outlook and ability have been noted among nursing home residents as a result of pet programs."[7] In practical terms, one of the most heartening results of these studies for those of our parents who may eventually be in a nursing home is the fact that state laws are being enacted that give nursing home residents the right to have a "collective pet."

If you're a creature lover yourself, you don't need all this scientific evidence to justify your or anyone else's feelings about the comforts and joys of pet ownership. But if you find it ridiculous that so much care and concern should be lavished on a nonhuman, or if you resent the fact that your parent's pet is the recipient of more attention and the source of more pride than you are, it might be a good idea to distance yourself from the situation so that you can arrive at a better understanding of what's going on.

Those of us who haven't yet reached our later years and survived the loss of a spouse, siblings, old friends, and perhaps even a son or a daughter may not realize how tragic the death of an adored pet can be. Such a death may represent not only the loss of a beloved creature but all other losses as well, and therefore bear a

7. Jane Brody, "Owning a Pet Can Have Therapeutic Value," New York *Times*, August 11, 1982.

burden of grief out of all proportion to the particular circumstance.

A wise son or daughter won't ridicule or minimize this mourning. It should be respected and permitted to run its course, and when the worst is over, perhaps a replacement might be considered. However, in this situation as in all others involving a pet, never present one as a surprise unless you're absolutely sure the surprise will be a welcome one.

If you're considering giving your parent a dog or a cat or a bird, or even an aquarium to care for, make sure you've taken into account such matters as allergies, "no pet" clauses in a lease, or similar prohibitions. (Thanks to unremitting efforts by senior citizen advocates, such prohibitions are significantly on the wane in housing for the elderly.)

If the preference is for a dog, and no particular breed is specified, find out whether it wouldn't be sensible to choose one small enough to be paper-trained so that it needn't be walked in very bad weather. When a companion-housekeeper, housemate, or family member is part of the household, this person's attitudes toward a new member of the menage should be taken into account, especially if responsibilities are to be shared.

BEING ALERT TO SIGNS OF DEPRESSION

Many older people who have survived wars, cultural dislocation, and economic hardship take a more philosophical view of what life is about than their sons and daughters do. They don't think it's "sick" to be sad, or "morbid" to be melancholy as a reaction to the inevitable tragedies that befall most of us. In fact, it would be unnatural *not* to feel grief when confronting the death of someone dear, or a change of circumstance that appears to deprive the future of any interest or promise.

But what if there's no such clear-cut cause for signs of depression? You notice that your usually spiffy father has begun to neglect his appearance and complains about not being able to sleep. Or your mother sits around and cries a lot and cancels her usual social commitments. When you spend time with her, she keeps asking you why she should go on living.

It's not a good idea to ignore such signals and assume that in time, things will change for the better. Nor is it helpful to pooh-

pooh the feelings of someone who is visibly depressed, or to mini-mize the misery that depression can cause.

One practical measure to take is a survey of all your parent's medications and find out from the prescribing doctor or from a reference book (try *Physicians' Desk Reference* or *Physicians' Drug Manual)* at the library whether mood changes might be attribut-able to any of them. Separately or in combination, drugs such as barbiturates, estrogens, cortisone, digitalis, amphetamines, and beta-blockers are known to cause depression in some people. And on the subject of drugs, try as tactfully as possible to find out whether an increase in alcoholic intake might be a significant fac-tor.

If it's been more than six months since your parent had a checkup, it might turn out that a thorough physical examination will reveal a previously undiagnosed but treatable condition. Or it may be that there has been a deterioration in hearing or eyesight that can be corrected.

Another factor known to contribute to depression, especially in the elderly who spend little time out of doors during the winter, is a lack of exposure to sunlight or full-spectrum light. At a 1985 conference sponsored by the New York Academy of Sciences on the biological and medical effects of light, sunlight was said to be indispensable not only for promoting the health of the bones, but also for increasing alertness and counteracting depression. The condition known as SAD (*seasonal affective disorder*) is one that causes many people to become withdrawn and depressed during the winter months. Dr. Alfred Levy, a research psychiatrist at the National Institute of Mental Health, thinks that for this type of depression, the most effective treatment is a good dose of sunlight in the morning and late afternoon.

If you can manage to do so, or if you can find a suitable com-panion for your parents, plan to have them do various errands on foot instead of by car, and suggest activities that will require time out of doors. Proper clothing, preferably in layers, should make it possible to brave the cold on a sunny day when there's no strong wind, and everyone will benefit from getting out of the house during the winter doldrums. One word of warning: There are medications that cause what's called a *photosensitivity reaction* in some people when they're exposed to sunlight. Some of these medications are the sulfonamides and tetracyclines, the fungicide griseofulving, thiazide diuretics, as well as some of the common tranquilizers.

Some Other Practical Suggestions

Many people—both young and old—experience a self-limiting depression that runs its course in a few weeks or months without requiring professional intervention. If your parent has good and bad days, there are various ways in which you and other family members can be helpful. You can enhance the older person's feeling of usefulness by subtly assigning small tasks that need to be done (not mere busywork); you might suggest some form of group exercise—aerobics or relaxation techniques.

If you're in a position to know that some of your mother's friends and relatives (maybe even one of your siblings) are contributing to her depression by wearing her out with long telephone conversations or interminable visits during which the talk always turns to disease, divorce, disaster, and death, tactful but firm interference on your part is in order. If it's your mother's best friend or her sister who turns up regularly with wearisome tales of woe (boredom is extremely exhausting), suggest they go to a movie together rather than sit around the house. Or try to see that when they have lunch together, a younger, more cheerful third person is present.

Signs of Deepening Depression

When you become aware over a period of months that your parent's depression has been intensifying rather than diminishing, that withdrawal from normal communication is increasing, sleep loss and loss of appetite are becoming more of a threat to well-being, the time has come to find help. There are other signals to take note of and to report to the therapist when the time comes for an interview: an inability to concentrate, picking quarrels, compulsive rituals, hysterical fear of animals, refusal to be in any enclosed space such as an elevator (claustrophobia), or unwillingness to leave the house (agoraphobia). Bizarre behavior and the expression of paranoid feelings are also typical of clinical depression and shouldn't at first glance be confused with indications of senility—of the Alzheimer type or any other type.

Many younger people, when they have their first prolonged encounter with someone suffering from severe depression—and especially if that "someone" is a parent—tend to think that certain aspects of the illness are a "performance" or "a bid for attention" and that talk about suicide is "another way to make me feel guilty." Maybe, maybe not. Whatever anger and resentment a son or a daughter might feel in the presence of a seriously depressed parent, the bottom line *intention* of the parental message is "Help me!"

Types of Therapists

Therapists fall into these major groups:

1. *Psychiatrists* are medical doctors who have special training and experience in treating mental and emotional disorders. They are qualified to administer electroshock therapy and to prescribe drugs.
2. *Clinical psychologists* are trained in clinical diagnosis and therapy, and may or may not have a doctor's degree (Ph.D.) in psychology.
3. *Clinical social workers* have a master's degree and sometimes a doctor's degree in social work, with additional training in psychotherapy.
4. *Qualified family counselors* usually have a master's degree in psychology and additional training in therapy.

Since only psychiatrists and other M.D.s can prescribe medication, the other categories of therapists frequently are associated with them for this purpose.

Types of Therapy

There's much less talk nowadays than there used to be about "schools" of therapy—Freudian, Jungian, Horney devotees—and much more talk about psychotropic drugs, cognitive therapy, and self-help. Before discussing professional approaches to depression, it should be mentioned that there are self-help groups whose purpose it is to provide guidance and relief for the depressed patient as well as other groups which offer support for the family members dealing with the problem (as discussed on p. 74).

Group therapy conducted under the supervision of a psychiatrist or a psychologist, with or without individual therapy, can be especially effective for older people whose self-image has been undermined or who feel unique in their misery. It isn't recommended for people who are inarticulate, who feel there's something "shameful about discussing personal problems in 'public,' " or who are extremely defensive, even when criticism is constructive.

When a patient is too depressed to be responsive to one-to-one "talking" therapy, two main alternatives are available: drug therapy with antidepressants and tranquilizers, and electroshock (electroconvulsive) therapy consisting of a series of electric shocks delivered to the brain. (In California, there is a movement to outlaw this treatment.)

Finding the right therapy for a seriously depressed parent is no simple matter in view of the disagreement among the specialists themselves. Seek out someone whose judgment you trust in these matters: the family doctor, minister, priest, or rabbi; a relative or good friend who has coped effectively with a similar problem; a psychiatric social worker connected with a social service agency specializing in the disorders of the aged.

If there's a conveniently located medical school in the area, try to connect with the faculty members who teach the courses in geriatric medicine or the psychiatrist who specializes in geriatric patients and find out about arranging for a consultation.

Whatever course you decide to pursue on your parent's behalf, remember the following: a psychiatrist does *not* give the patient a physical examination; only a physician, that is, an M.D., can prescribe drugs; and antidepressant drugs and tranquilizers are not a cure for depression but rather a temporary expedient to help the patient achieve the psychological equilibrium necessary for the progress of other forms of therapy or counseling.

Other referral sources for local therapists include:

The American Psychological Association
1200 17th Street, N.W., Washington, D.C. 20036

The National Association of Social Workers
7981 Eastern Avenue, Silver Springs, Maryland 20910

as well as local telephone listings for the Mental Health Association, the Department of Mental Health, and for psychiatric nurses, the state or county nurses' association.

There is an increasing awareness on the part of the medical profession that sensitivity to drugs increases with age. Many doctors are therefore adjusting the doses of the psychotropic drugs for people over sixty-five in order to minimize the undesirable side effects of dizziness, fainting, and decrease in blood pressure.

If your parent's depression is being treated with drugs, the person who is in touch with day-to-day events should promptly notify the prescribing physician about such reactions, or other untoward manifestations that seem to be attributable to the drugs.

Some Facts About Finances

Payment for therapists and counselors depends in many instances on the duration of the therapy, the type of therapist, the nature of your parent's medical insurance, and in which of the fifty states the treatment is taking place. During the first consultation with the therapist, costs, insurance coverage, and number of sessions covered should be spelled out so that there is no eventual misunderstanding about money. Clinical psychologists are licensed in all fifty states, and (as of June 1985) forty states and the District of Columbia have "freedom of choice" laws requiring insurance companies to reimburse psychologists for therapy if patients prefer them to psychiatrists. Social workers are licensed in thirty-five states, but only fifteen states (California, Florida, Kansas, Louisiana, Maine, Maryland, Massachusetts, Montana, New Hampshire, New York, Oklahoma, Oregon, Tennessee, Utah, and Virginia) require that insurance companies reimburse them for psychotherapy or counseling. Family counselors are licensed in only nine states, but California is the only state in which reimbursement for therapy by insurance companies is legally required.

As of 1985, Medicare pays up to 50 percent of the charge for outpatient mental health services up to a maximum of $500 a year.

The following figures give some indication of the range of fees nationwide for therapy by the various mental health professionals: For psychiatrists in private practice, the median fee per session is $90; for clinical psychologists, $65; and for social workers, $50. Some social workers and family counselors may charge no more than $25 or $30 a session.[8]

8. New York *Times*, April 30, 1985.

It is generally agreed that higher fees don't necessarily mean more effective therapy or therapy of a higher quality. In the therapeutic relationship, as in all complex relationships, there are many variables, and of these, a critical consideration is that the "chemistry" should be right between patient and therapist. If after several sessions, your parent feels that the relationship isn't productive, you should seriously consider seeking help elsewhere.

BEREAVEMENT

According to recent estimates, there are approximately 11 million widows and 2 million widowers in the United States. But while the death of a spouse is the most common bereavement experienced by an aging parent, and while it may be the most disorienting, it isn't necessarily the most poignant. With more people living into their seventies and eighties, there's an increasing number of older people who outlive an adult son who died of a heart attack or a daughter who died of cancer. Not only is this reversal universally recognized as tragic, but in addition, the survivors are often deeply concerned about who will take care of them, who will call them, who is left to understand them, and who will bury them. And it comes as a surprise to many younger people that an aging parent will be devastated by the death of a very old mother or father, or of a brother or a life-long friend.

It used to be assumed that observance of the rituals of mourning provided a transition between the need to withdraw from the everyday world, and the need to return to it. Spiritual comfort about the meaning of life and death could be achieved in conversations with the family's minister, priest, or rabbi. While many mourners still have these sources of solace, there are widows, widowers, and older people in general who may be in need of special counseling.

It has been observed that many widows will turn first to their doctor. But a brisk and competent (in most instances) male doctor isn't necessarily the best source for supportive counseling unless he also happens to be an especially understanding human being, one who makes it possible for the woman to discuss her deepest anxieties and her feelings of guilt or of anger. It is only within the last decade that most medical schools have recognized the need to give doctors-to-be lecture and discussion courses in dying and death. Such courses are designed to explore the young students' attitudes to dying and death and thereby to facilitate understanding and communication not only between the doctor and the terminal patient, but also between the doctor and the surviving family members. The book most frequently cited in these courses is *Questions and Answers on Death and Dying* by Elisabeth Kübler-Ross.

An insightful family doctor will be alert to any signs that the widow has been turning to alcohol for comfort, and also will be especially careful about monitoring a prescription for sleeping pills. Nor should tranquilizers or antidepressants be handed out without a careful evaluation, since it is the considered opinion of many researchers that the mourner should *not* be anesthetized against grief; that the process of an individual's mourning should be allowed to run its course unless it assumes pathological proportions.

What about widowers? It would appear that the best thing your father can do if he survives your mother is to remarry or take up residence with a woman who will share a life with him. A twelve-year study by Johns Hopkins researchers of four thousand men and women found that while a husband's death had practically no effect on the mortality rate of women, men were much more likely to die within several years of the death of their wife than men of the same age who were married.[9] Among the reasons given for the disparity is the fact that men have been socialized to hide their feelings and therefore don't permit themselves to go through the grieving process essential for the eventual recovery of equilibrium. Another authority, Robert Fulton, who directs the Center for Death Education and Research at the University of Minnesota, points out that "men who belonged to a generation that relied heavily on a wife to provide emotional support and physical comfort" are generally reluctant to seek professional help to tide them over troubled times. Statistics for remarrying, however, are on the side of the widowers, because after sixty-five, they are significantly outnumbered by available women. A widower who embarks on a courtship with what appears to be unseemly haste may provoke the disapproval of his sons and daughters, but in terms of his own well-being, it would appear that Father knows best.

9. New York *Times,* September 12, 1983.

Peer Support and Professional Counseling for the Bereaved

In 1973, the AARP became the first organization to develop programs on a national scale to serve the newly widowed. These programs were the result of studies indicating that grieving men and women receive the most effective help from those who have gone through similar experiences and have rebuilt their lives. AARP Widowed Persons Service Programs now function in more than 170 communities with the cooperation and cosponsorship of a network of local organizations including religious groups, mental health and social service agencies, and educational institutions.

Recently widowed parents should be encouraged to participate unless other resources are being explored. The organization has also prepared a comprehensive directory of services in the United States and Canada, as well as a guide for widowed persons. The guide, *On Being Alone,* deals in a realistic and sympathetic way with such subjects as family adjustment, personal and social adjustment, financial and legal affairs, employment, and housing. It also includes a selected bibliography and referral suggestions.

———

Inquiries about local Widowed Persons Service Programs should be addressed to:

Widowed Persons Service
American Association of Retired Persons
1909 K Street, N.W., Washington, D.C. 20049

For a single copy of *On Being Alone,* write to:

AARP Widowed Persons Service
Box 199, Long Beach, California 90801

———

Bereavement counseling by a professional specialist may be necessary if your parent appears to be suffering from what can be considered pathological grief. Most bereaved people are distressed and depressed on and off for many months following the death, but when acute grief continues to be immobilizing for a year or more, the family should consider the advisability of special therapy.

In some areas, there are organizations that specialize in bereavement counseling. For example, in Washington, D.C., a nondenominational "safe house" for the bereaved was established at St. Francis Center, where private therapy sessions are part of a broad program. In the San Francisco area, there are more than fifty groups offering bereavement counseling. A pioneering group in New York City known as the Bereavement and Loss Center is a nonsectarian center that offers therapy following a death or anticipating one. Treatment may be long-term or brief, conducted on a group basis or individually by psychiatrists, psychiatric social workers, and an advisory staff of medical doctors, attorneys, and financial experts. Sessions are by appointment.

Even though professionals are available to help the bereaved find the way back to the satisfactions of daily life, in the final analysis it is the person's built-in strengths and the support of family and friends that will make the critical difference.

How You Can Help

- If you live at a considerable distance from the widowed parent and you don't have a family of your own, make an effort to take time off so that you can spend some time together. If that isn't practical, invite your bereaved parent to spend some time with you. And if that won't work out, keep the lines of communication open and call up as often as you can.
- When you hear remarks such as, "I shouldn't have let him die in a hospital among strangers," or "I should have let the business run itself so that we finally could have taken that trip to Europe," or "Maybe if I had insisted on a different doctor . . ." the most supportive thing you can do is to be reassuring and positive. If in fact you think that mistakes were made, ask yourself what can possibly be accomplished at this date by being critical rather than comforting. In most situations, observations that begin "You *should* have . . ." can only be hurtful.
- Try to talk to the surviving parent about the one who died. Recall pleasant times together. Tell anecdotes about your childhood memories. If you have children of your own and the death is their first experience of this kind, talk to them too. "I remember when . . ." "Do you remember when . . ." These recollections may cause tears, but tears are an effective way to re-

duce stress. Most people concede that they feel better after crying. Sometimes widowed fathers need to be encouraged to cry rather than to put on a brave and stoic front.

- Find out whether you can be helpful in reviewing clothes and personal possessions so that they can be given to relatives, friends, neighbors, or personal charities.

- Discourage premature decisions about making major changes. Regaining some stability is a good idea before a widow or a widower sells a house, shuffles money and other assets around, or completely rewrites a will. Try not to push for decisions about the immediate future. Wait until the newly single parent is less distraught before asking about preferences in new living arrangements.

- Encourage as much continuity as possible in maintaining social connections. If a widowed parent turns to an old friend of the opposite sex for solace and understanding, it serves no purpose for the children to pronounce judgments about "disloyalty to the dead," etc., etc.

- If your widowed parent finds comfort in a self-help group of other widowed persons and begins to make new friends whose social, educational, or economic background are at considerable variance from what you're accustomed to, be content that companionship is available rather than critical about the "suitability" of the people, unless of course you have reason to believe that your parent's safety or well-being might be at risk.

- If you can get any messages through during the months of mourning, point out that being self-reliant after years of dependency can be very difficult at first, but it has the compensations of discovering new ways of being. Many widows who always relied on their husband for decisions about vacation plans, money matters, and social life eventually find out that they enjoy being independent in their old age.

❧ 4 ❧

MAKING SENSE
OF YOUR PARENTS' MEDICINES

According to figures recently released by the General Accounting Office, senior citizens consume more than 25 percent of the prescription and over-the-counter drugs used in this country even though they make up only 11 percent of the population. An FDA report, "Drug Utilization in the U.S.," found that people seventy years old and older fill an average of thirteen prescriptions a year.[1] Some of these are refills for maintenance drugs, but other studies indicate that some older patients may get as many as fourteen to eighteen *different* drugs during one year.[2] And as for patients in nursing homes, these studies say that some of the institutionalized old are likely to be taking as many as thirty different medications.

Do our parents know what they're doing with all those drugs? Do *you* know what they're doing? Do all those medications make sense, and are your parents using them sensibly?

Among the results of a nationwide survey commissioned by the AARP are the following: More than one third of the 1001 respondents experienced side effects from their prescribed medicines, and of these side effects, about one third were reported as "very serious"; 45 percent said that doctors don't always ask them what other prescription medications they're taking; and nearly two thirds were not always asked about nonprescription drug use. A significant difference in the attitude toward older patients is revealed in the following finding: "Older people are *less likely* to receive information about prescription drugs from their doctor or pharmacist. For example, 41% of the elderly surveyed said that they were never told about side effects by their physician as compared with 29% of the middle-aged."[3]

1. New York *Times,* March 16, 1985.
2. *FDA Consumer,* September 1983.
3. *AARP News Bulletin,* December 1984.

Who should take responsibility for the inadequate dissemination of essential information to our aging parents? And even more basic questions are: How necessary are all those drugs to their well-being? Are they being prescribed in the right doses? What is their cumulative effect after ten years? After twenty years?

More and more advocates of our elderly insist that they are "overmedicated" compared to their peers in other countries. In addition, it is being pointed out that as people grow older, they respond differently to drugs they are expected to take for "maintenance" for the rest of their lives. As their metabolism changes with age, they may excrete less of a powerful chemical than a younger person would. They therefore may be retaining damaging amounts of a substance that can interact negatively with some other prescribed drug.

For reasons not yet thoroughly understood, people in their sixties and seventies—not to mention their eighties—are likely to be more sensitive to such drugs as tranquilizers, antihistamines, antidepressants, and those prescribed for parkinsonism. This extra sensitivity produces dramatic negative side effects not associated with what are considered to be "normal" doses. Such negative side effects may also occur following self-medication with nonprescription drugs, especially in combinations not monitored by a physician. One such dangerous (and common) mixture occurs when a prescription tranquilizer or antihistamine is casually combined with an over-the-counter cough medicine containing alcohol.

Responding to pressures from many quarters, the FDA has begun to investigate the need for developing guidelines for the geriatric testing of drugs. Such guidelines may be difficult to arrive at since pharmaceutical manufacturers don't usually risk testing their products on older people. However, aging *women* have a special stake in promoting these tests *before* maintenance drugs reach the market. As matters now stand, because on the average, women outlive men by ten years, and because there are twice as many women as men in the seventy-five and older age group, old women are now the drug industry's guinea pigs for the effects of long-term use of medications for chronic conditions.

This aspect of informal "experimentation" was emphasized by a delegate from the Older Women's League at an FDA Consumer Exchange meeting held in Washington in 1984. Addressing herself to the main topic, "Drug Use and the Elderly," Alice Quinlan maintained that attention was not being directed to the older part of the population either in the clinical testing of drugs or in the adverse reaction to drugs already on the market, nor have manufacturers and physicians given enough consideration to the altered response of the elderly to drugs.

Among the suggestions she made were the following: that elderly patients participate in the testing of drugs in proportion to their likely use of them; that drug studies be redesigned to include more women—now underrepresented—so that significant sex differences in older patients can be studied in premarketing trials; and especially, that experiments should run long enough to provide information about how older women will be affected by the long-term use of drugs prescribed for hypertension, diabetes, heart conditions, and similar chronic disorders. If this isn't done, she pointed out that "women become the unwitting participants in uncontrolled mass testing of drugs."

As the concerned family member of aging parents, you can help keep their medication to an effective minimum by maintaining regular communication with them and their prime care physician as well as their pharmacist if possible. The information that follows is designed to alert you to some of the more typical problems and the practical ways of dealing with them.

To provide essential material to the FDA that will assist drug manufacturers and health professionals in the surveillance of drugs, family members of the elderly are urged to report an adverse reaction to a drug not only to the prescribing doctor, but to the FDA as well. Write to:

The Division of Drug Experience HFN 730
FDA
5600 Fishers Lane, Rockville, Maryland 20857

and request a Drug Experience Report Form on which to supply the facts.

JUST WHAT DID THE DOCTOR ORDER?

Many older people wince when you refer to the contents of all those bottles as "drugs," which they usually prefer to call "my

medications." Is there in fact any difference between a *medicine*
and a *drug?* The problem of defining terms precisely is no small
matter if you're trying to keep track of your parents' prescription
drugs and over-the-counter medications and self-prescribed vitamins and herbal nostrums from health food stores, and maybe
even a quack remedy or two.

Does a good dictionary clarify matters? *Webster's Ninth* defines
medicine thus: "(a) a substance or preparation used in treating
disease; (b) something that affects well-being." And what about
drug? The first definition given by the same source is "any substance used as a medicine or an ingredient in a medicine."

Does the official definition of *drug* used by the Food and Drug
Administration clear up the question? Here it is: (1) a substance
recognized in an official pharmacopoeia or formulary;   (2) a substance intended for use in the diagnosis, cure mitigation, treatment, or prevention of disease;   (3) a substance other than food
intended to affect the structure or function of the body;   (4) a
substance intended for use as a component of a medicine, but not
a device, component, part, or accessory of the device.

Well, that's what those substances are in all those containers.
However, ambiguities abound. At what point, for instance, does a
vitamin, which in required daily amounts is a nutrient or food,
become a drug as in definition 3? If your mother is a devoted
purchaser of such "health food" scams as kelp, or if she's just
discovered a new miracle vitamin and is taking megadoses of it, it
wouldn't be amiss to check such self-treatments with her doctor.

Is Every Drug Available in Generic Form?

Why was it only recently that people began to talk about generic drugs and the savings they represent? What was going on
before they became available? According to William F. Haddad,
president of the Generic Pharmaceutical Industry Association,
this is the story:

> In the fifties, every state in the Union quietly enacted laws prohibit-
> ing the substitution of generic drugs. They also banned comparative
> price advertising, a ban which the Supreme Court later ruled was
> illegal. Beginning in the midseventies, every state in the Union ex-
> cept Indiana, passed legislation that not only permitted the substitu-
> tion of generic drugs, but was specifically designed to encourage
> their use.

Even though every drug has a generic name that usually describes its chemical components, the generic form may not yet be available to consumers because the patent that protects the manufacturer's exclusivity for seventeen years has not yet run out. In this connection, Mr. Haddad observed:

Now that laws in 49 states encourage generic prescribing, and the Federal Trade Commission promotes generic use, the major pharmaceutical companies are attempting to restrict consumer access to lower-priced drugs by asking Congress to *extend patent protection for prescription drugs for up to seven more years!* [Haddad's italics.] That could cost consumers $1,000,000,000 a year.

When a patent does expire, any company that plans to market a generic equivalent must receive FDA approval. Of particular interest in this connection is the fact that while Inderal, the heart and hypertension medicine prescribed for millions of older Americans, lost its patent protection in 1984, more than a year elapsed before its generic equivalent, propanolol, reached the market at less than half the price.

Thanks to pressure from senior citizen lobbyists, consumer groups, and drugstore chains, prescriptions filled with generic drugs increased 13 percent in a recent year (1983), while the prescription drug market grew less than 3 percent in the same year. There are some circumstances, however, where the substitution is discouraged by the physician, supposedly because of the absence or presence of a particular variable that might affect some patients adversely. And when the patent for Valium ran out in 1985, a spokesman for Hoffman–La Roche contended that the company still had "concern about the bioequivalency of the generic versions." In response to this concern, Margaret Heckler, then secretary of Health and Human Services, said, "Generic drugs are subject to the same stringent FDA standards as brand-names." A few other facts are relevant: In 1984, about 9 million Americans spent $350 million for Valium. Now, three pharmaceutical companies, including Parke-Davis, are marketing the generic equivalent, diazepam, at a saving of approximately 40 percent to consumers.

———

You can check all your parents' prescriptions for their generic equivalents by sending for a copy of the *List of Interchangeable Drugs,* free upon request from:

The Generic Pharmaceutical Industry Association
200 Madison Avenue, Suite 2404
New York, New York 10016

Getting Clear Instructions and Following Them

If you're taking some of the responsibility for a parent's well-being, here are some sobering facts: 33 to 50 percent of all prescription drugs are used incorrectly, and as many as 2.7 million hospital admissions can be traced to drug-induced problems.[4] The Boston Collaborative Drug Surveillance Program at Boston University, a clearinghouse for information on the side effects of drugs, estimates that $4.5 billion is spent on hospital bills and over a hundred deaths result each year from drug interactions.[5]

Many of these disasters are the result of carelessness, but as older patients increasingly go to specialists without telling each one about the medications prescribed by every other one, they are likely to end up with dangerous drug combinations. It's easy enough to blame the physician for not taking the time to ask you or your parent about all routinely used medications, but the most effective way to find out what you need to know for your parent's sake—who may be too timid or too deferential in the doctor's presence—is for *you* to ask.

When accompanying your mother or father to the prime care doctor, or to a rheumatologist, a cardiologist, an allergist, a neurologist, a psychiatrist, here's a sensible way to proceed:

On the first visit to any physician (and that includes an ophthalmologist too), all your parent's current medications, both prescription and nonprescription, should be taken along in a plastic bag. If the doctor doesn't ask what medicines are now being taken, a special point should be made of handing over the collection for inspection. The doctor should also be informed of any sensitivity to particular substances or antibiotics. If your parent is a recovered alcoholic, that should be mentioned too.

If at the conclusion of the consultation a prescription is forthcoming, it should be accompanied by verbal instructions. If you think the instructions are incomplete or unclear, feel free to ask the relevant questions and write down the answers. (The fastest

4. *AARP News Bulletin,* April 1985.
5. New York *Times,* July 21, 1984.

way to do this is to write or type the questions in advance of the visit, leaving spaces for the answers, and make a batch of photocopies so that you or your parent can always have the questionnaire handy.) If you think all this is too much trouble, or your parent thinks it's an imposition on the doctor, be assured that in the long run, the procedure saves needless phone calls and avoids potentially dangerous consequences. Any physician or physician's assistant who gets huffy about answering such questions or gives the questioner the brush-off should be viewed with suspicion.

Here are some basic questions to ask about a prescription:

- If the name of the medication isn't written clearly enough to read, what is it?
- Is the prescription signed to indicate that a generic equivalent may be substituted? If not, why not?
- What is the medicine supposed to do? If it's an antibiotic, what bacterial infection is it supposed to fight?
- What side effects should be expected?
- How often and in what amounts should it be taken?
- Does "three times a day" mean morning, noon, and night? Before meals, with meals, after meals?
- What does "take on an empty stomach" mean? (Usually it means one hour before, or two hours after a meal.)
- If the instructions say "Every six hours," does that mean getting up in the middle of the night to take the medicine?
- For how many days should it be taken? How soon should it be expected to work? Should it be discontinued when the symptoms are gone?
- Should it be refilled without another appointment?
- What are the foods, beverages, and/or other drugs (including nonprescription drugs) that should be avoided while taking this medicine?
- Does it have to be refrigerated?
- What is the best time to call the doctor if there are any untoward reactions?
- Is there some way of treating the condition that doesn't involve medication—for example, weight loss, changes in diet, exercise, bed rest, hot baths?

If your parent is fortunate enough to be the patient of a physician who provides most of this information *without* being asked, you'll find that having the questionnaire makes it easier to write down what you're told. No matter how good your memory is, some vitally important detail is likely to be forgotten, and even though the pharmacist is supposed to put basic instructions on the label when the prescription is filled, they will never—or rarely—be as complete as you want them to be.

Demystifying Prescriptions

Pharmacists are taught enough Latin to be able to read a physician's prescription. But why shouldn't you and your parents be able to read the prescription too? Since more and more patients are asking that question, more and more doctors are writing their prescriptions in English. (Not that that's a satisfactory solution to the problem of intelligibility. If you're friendly with the family's pharmacist, ask him or her how often the doctor has to be called to decipher the instructions.)

Here's a more or less typical prescription:

ROBERT J. ROE M.D.

3 Ivy Pl. Gorham, Maine 04038 Tel. 838-2466 Reg. No. 77254

NAME Mrs. Evelyn Crossland   AGE 67

ADDRESS RR 4 Box 37   DATE 9/21/85

R

Dolobid
500 mg tabs
#xii
ii stat, then 1 q 8-12 h
Refill 3X   PRN pain

Dr. _____   Dr. _____
Dispense as Written   Substitution Permissible

This prescription will be filled generically unless physician signs on line stating "Dispense as Written."

And here's what it means:

Dolobid is the name of the medication; *500 mg tabs* means that each tablet contains 500 milligrams of the medication; *#xii* means the prescription is written for 12 pills; *ii STAT, then 1 q 8– 12h* means 2 tablets are to be taken immediately, then one every 8 to 12 hours; *PRN* means as necessary (to deal with *pain*). And the placement of the signature means that a generic substitute is permissible.

You can learn a lot about your parents' medications from the FDA publication *Here Are Some Things You Should Know About Prescription Drugs,* available on request from:

Rx Drugs, Department 62
Pueblo, Colorado 81009

PRESCRIPTION DRUGS AND THEIR GENERIC EQUIVALENTS

The following is a list of some of the many drugs now available in generic form. However, state regulations can supercede FDA approval of generic equivalents. Generic forms of drugs preceded by an * are expected to be available before the end of 1985. (Source: Generic Pharmaceutical Industry Association's *List of Interchangeable Drugs*; **Source for purpose and possible side effects, *Physician's Drug Manual*)

BRAND NAME	GENERIC	PURPOSE**	SOME POSSIBLE ADVERSE SIDE EFFECTS**
ACHROMYCIN V TETRACYN	Tetracycline HCL	to fight bacterial infection	gastrointestinal disturbance
ALDOMET	Methyldopa	to reduce high blood pressure	headache, dizziness, gastrointestinal disturbance, liver disorder
ALDORIL	Methyldopa and Hydrochlorothiazide	combination drug to reduce high blood pressure and act as a diuretic	liver disorder, decreased libido, headache, dizziness, psychic and gastrointestinal disturbances, tremor, sedation
ANTIVERT	Meclizine HCL	to control nausea and vomiting	drowsiness, dry mouth, blurred vision
ATIVAN	Lorazepam	to reduce anxiety and insomnia	sedation, dizziness, disorientation, gastrointestinal disturbances, visual disturbance
BENADRYL	Diphenhydramine HCL	antihistamine to reduce allergic reactions; also for motion sickness and parkinsonism	sleepiness, dizziness, confusion, blurred vision, gastrointestinal disturbances

(Continued on next page)

BRAND NAME	GENERIC	PURPOSE**	SOME POSSIBLE ADVERSE SIDE EFFECTS**
BUTAZOLIDIN	Phenylbutazone	to treat rheumatoid arthritis, acute gouty arthritis	because this is a powerful drug causing a long list of adverse reactions, use is recommended only for patients unresponsive to other therapies
COMPAZINE	Prochlorperazine	to control severe nausea and vomiting and to reduce anxiety	muscle spasms, pseudoparkinsonism, drowsiness, dizziness, agitation, dry mouth, constipation, blurred vision
DALMANE	Flurazepam HCL	to treat insomnia	rash, nausea, blurred vision, hangover, psychic and/or physical dependence may develop in addiction-prone individuals
ELAVIL	Amitriptyline HCL	antidepressant	palpitations, confusion, insomnia, dry mouth, numbness
E.E.S.	Erythromycin Ethylsuccinate	to fight bacterial infection (staph, strep) and prophylaxis against bacterial endocarditis	gastrointestinal disturbances, rash
EQUANIL (MILTOWN)	Meprobamate	to lessen anxiety and tension by producing sedation	drowsiness, dizziness, slurred speech, headache, gastrointestinal disturbances
HYDRODIURIL	Hydrochlorothiazide	to reduce blood pressure and fluid accumulation	gastrointestinal disturbances, dizziness, headache, jaundice, constipation
INDERAL	Propranolol	beta blocker for heart ailments, high blood pressure, migraine	disturbed heartbeat, dizziness, fatigue, visual and gastrointestinal disturbances

(Continued on next page)

BRAND NAME	GENERIC	PURPOSE**	SOME POSSIBLE ADVERSE SIDE EFFECTS
INDOCIN	Indomethacin	to treat rheumatoid, osteo- and gouty arthritis	headache, dizziness, depression, muscle weakness, psychic disturbances, ringing in the ears, palpitation, liver disorder
LANOXIN	Digoxin	to treat congestive heart failure	loss of appetite, gastrointestinal disturbances, blurred vision, arrhythmias, headache, apathy
LASIX	Furosemide	diuretic used to treat high blood pressure	loss of appetite, gastrointestinal disturbances, dizziness, headache, ringing in the ears, blurred vision
LIBRIUM	Chlordiazepoxide HCL	tranquilizer	drowsiness, confusion, nausea, constipation
LOMOTIL	Diphenoxylate HCL with Atropine Sulfate	to control diarrhea	nausea, vomiting, cramps, dizziness, drowsiness, restlessness, depression
MOTRIN (Advil)	Ibuprofen	to reduce arthritis pain	nausea, cramps, heartburn, constipation, dizziness, headache, ringing in the ears
NEMBUTAL	Pentobarbital sodium	sedation to treat insomnia	severe depression, drowsiness, hangover, allergic reactions, circulatory collapse, psychic and/or physical dependence in addiction-prone individuals
ORINASE	Tolbutamide	to treat diabetes	nausea, heartburn, headache, rash, liver disorder
PEN-VEE K V-CILLIN K	Penicillin V Potassium	antibiotic treatment for strep and staph infections; short-term prophylaxis against bacterial endocarditis	nausea, diarrhea, rash; if allergic to penicillin very serious and dangerous side effects can occur

(Continued on next page)

BRAND NAME	GENERIC	PURPOSE**	SOME POSSIBLE ADVERSE SIDE EFFECTS
PERCODAN	Aspirin: Oxycodone HCL	a strong analgesic for moderately severe pain	lightheadedness, dizziness, sedation, constipation, vomiting, nausea
QUINORA	Quindine Sulfate	to regulate heart arrhythmias	dizziness, tremor, blurred vision, ringing in the ears, gastrointestinal disturbances
*SERAX	Oxazepam	to treat anxiety and agitation	mild drowsiness, dizziness, headache, slurred speech, tremor, nausea
STELAZINE	Trifluoperazine HCL	major tranquilizer to treat psychotic disorders	drowsiness, dizziness, tremors, dry mouth, blurred vision, gastrointestinal disturbances
THORAZINE	Chlorpromazine HCL	major tranquilizer to treat psychotic disorders and acutely agitated, manic, or disturbed hospitalized patients	dizziness, tremor, psychotic symptoms, epileptic seizures, cardiovascular disturbances, dry mouth, constipation, vision impairment
TRIAVIL	Perphenazine/ Amitriptyline	to treat depressive symptoms of schizophrenia; also depression and anxiety associated with chronic physical disease	cardiovascular disturbances, confusion, disorientation, hallucinations, dry mouth, blurred vision, altered liver function, gastrointestinal disturbances, constipation
TYLENOL with CODEINE	Acetaminophen with Codeine phosphate	to reduce pain and fever	dizziness, sedation, nausea, vomiting, constipation
VALIUM	Diazepam	minor tranquilizer	drowsiness, fatigue, sleep disturbance, cardiac disturbances, constipation, psychic and/or physical dependence may develop in addiction-prone individuals

PROBLEMS OF DRUG DEPENDENCY

Consider the fact that most doctors are men and most patients over sixty-five are women. Consider also that most older women have been culturally conditioned to be trusting and respectful toward their doctors. And if the doctor is more or less typical of *his* cultural conditioning, he's likely to think that older women are emotional hypochondriacs. A female patient may be twice his age, but between them, they may set up a Big-Daddy-Knows-What's-Good-For-You situation that requires tactful vigilance on the part of a younger family member.

For example, twice as many women as men take psychoactive drugs, and the elderly receive 39 percent of all sleeping pills, according to Dr. Leslie Hartley Gise, professor in the Division of Liaison Psychiatry at the Mt. Sinai Medical Center. She points out that 80 percent of women alcoholics are also addicted to tranquilizers, and that iatrogenic alcoholism is initiated by doctors who recommend drinking as a tranquilizer, especially to older women who go into a depression when their children leave the nest. *(Iatrogenic* means "caused or induced by medical treatment." The mother's morphine addiction in *Long Day's Journey into Night* is a classic example.)

Another dangerous assumption on the part of many physicians is that when an older woman describes the acute discomfort of such physical conditions as arthritis or colitis, the "real" underlying problem, or the exacerbating circumstance, is psychological. And on the basis of this questionable assumption, they write prescriptions for *combination* drugs without alerting the patient or the family to the possible consequences. Among these drugs are Librax, which combines the generic tranquilizing agent in Librium (chlordiazepoxide HCL) with drugs that treat gastrointestinal problems; and Donnatol, which contains the barbiturate phenobarbital plus drugs that treat colitis or parkinsonism. Not only can the sedative and/or "feel good" ingredients result in physical and psychological addiction; they can lead to disaster when combined with other drugs, and especially when combined with alcohol.

It has been mentioned earlier that the FDA and the medical and pharmaceutical establishments have begun to investigate the need for correcting drug dosages for patients as they go into their sixties, seventies, and eighties. It doesn't take much in the way of a tranquilizer or a sedative, especially when combined with an antihistamine and an "innocent" drink, to produce confusion, slurred speech, or memory impairment in an elderly person. More sinister still, as critical faculties and alertness are increasingly jeopardized by dependence on drugs that "keep the patient calm" or "help her to get a good night's sleep," the family may begin to assume that "Mom's got signs of Alzheimer's" or "We have to think of full-time care because she's too confused to take care of herself."

There's no reason to assume that it's "only natural and normal" for your mother to be unable to concentrate or to be disoriented just because she's getting older. Take a critical look at the prescription pills she's been taking regularly. If you think it would be productive to do so, arrange to see her physician so that you can find out about the contents of all her medications and the effect they're likely to have over a long period.

Should the session with the doctor be less than satisfactory, you might try discussing the problem with the pharmacist who's been filling the prescriptions, and as a last resort, you can check out the drugs at your local library. Ask for the *Physicians' Drug Manual* or the *Physicians' Desk Reference*.

Family members who see nothing wrong with encouraging their mother to use tranquilizers, antidepressants, sleeping pills, or "a relaxing drink" as the easiest way to cope with the sorrows of bereavement should give serious thought to other recommendations. An elderly woman who is grieving because of her husband's death, or is depressed because of the terminal illness of a beloved brother or sister, or is trying to cope with the inevitability of her fading looks and failing powers, may find inner resources for dealing with such circumstances if she gets other kinds of support: the family's acceptance of grief as a natural and necessary expression; the seeking out of suitable self-help groups; the encouragement of rituals of mourning that are still part of the older generation's reality even though the young people have abandoned them. And above all, using the phone, letters, visits, and remembrances to strengthen the emotional support that makes mothers continue to feel essential to their adult offsprings' well-being.

THE IMPORTANCE OF THE PHARMACIST

Maybe you don't remember "the corner drugstore," but people of your parents' generation usually have happy recollections of the local pharmacist who owned his establishment, greeted his customers by name, spoke to their doctors regularly, and took the time to answer questions. If your parents have been able to maintain a relationship with such a treasure (or have found a reasonable facsimile in a conveniently located shopping center), you should get to know him or her if you don't already.

Nowadays many people have to deal with a chain store pharmacist who is confined to a cubicle in a huge establishment with the inventory of a mini–department store. But even in such cases, it should be possible to create a personal relationship. A pharmacist who is competent and approachable and who takes a genuine interest in the customers can play a vital role in preventing drug disasters.

Many pharmacists have begun to keep records that include the customers' allergies, special sensitivities, and the like, as well as their physician's name and whether they prefer their medications packed in containers with childproof caps or simple screw-on tops. And if your parent is homebound, or lives alone and needs prompt emergency service from time to time, try to make sure that the pharmacist will be cooperative about phoning the physician for an essential prescription and arranging to have it delivered, accepting payment by check if necessary.

Computerized Information

If your parents live in an area where there's a choice of pharmacies, they might be able to connect with one where patient information is being computerized. In 1984, Bruce H. Colligen, director of special studies for the National Association of Chain Drug Stores, reported that while only about 20 percent were computerized, he anticipated that by 1990, the number would be up to 90–95 percent.[6] In stores where the computer system is being tested or has already been installed, your parents would be asked to fill out a "patient profile" form that provides the pharmacist with

6. Ibid.

essential information: name, address, phone number, physician's name, food and drug allergies, chronic conditions, and all medications usually taken.

When your mother or father comes in with a new prescription, the computer enables the pharmacist to see whether there might be any dangerous interactions between the new medication and those that are already part of the daily regimen. If this should be the case, the pharmacist then calls the doctor to have the problem resolved.

Computers are also a quick way of telling the pharmacist whether patients are refilling prescriptions too often or not often enough—another problem to be discussed with the doctor.

In keeping track of your parents' medications, the question of adverse interaction is of prime importance. Many health care authorities feel that the responsibility should remain with the physician, but in view of the new products approved by the FDA each year—in 1984 alone, seventy-five new drugs came on the market —it would seem that only a computer can supply dependable data on demand.

You have reason to be concerned about the potential dangers of drug interaction if your parents are taking as many as four or five prescription medications on a regular basis plus one or two that they prescribe for themselves. Recently, it was reported that a chain of over a hundred drugstores based in St. Louis has developed computerized data indicating seventeen thousand possible adverse interactions.[7] According to the president, Harlan Steinbaum, these range from headaches and nausea to depression, internal bleeding, and death. In one year during which member stores used the data, 15 to 17 percent of the prescriptions that were presented involved a potential hazard to the patient.

Unfortunately, once your parents become part of the computer input of a particular drug store chain or independent pharmacy, any bargain hopping will make it difficult for the "patient profile" to be complete in any one place. They could ask that medications bought elsewhere be added to their data base, but the pharmacist probably won't be too pleased. On the other hand, if your parents have been faithful to one pharmacist who is using computer data, they can ask for their printout if and when they move out of his area.

7. Ibid.

Special Payment Plans

In practically all neighborhoods, there are pharmacists who offer a discount of 10 to 15 percent to senior citizens on Medicare, and who also accept Medicaid payment. Some states have established special payment plans for prescription medicines which might benefit your parents if they live on a fixed income that falls below the official minimum.

A typical program is New Jersey's PAAD (Pharmaceutical Assistance to the Aged and Disabled), under which those who qualify pay only $2 of the total cost of each prescribed drug, and PAAD pays the rest.

The local office for the aging in your parents' area can supply information about similar plans for which they might be eligible.

OVERHAULING THOSE OVER-THE-COUNTER DRUGS

Do your parents suffer from arthritis? Insomnia? Hemorrhoids? Acid indigestion? Constipation? Tired blood? Nutritional deficiencies? Help is at hand, right there on the television screen and within easy reach on supermarket shelves.

The old and the very old who can get around and buy their own remedies represent a gold mine for the nonprescription drug industry. Not only are they likely to get a heavier dose of advertising than other age groups because they watch more television than their busy sons and daughters; they also hope to minimize or "cure" their ailments with inexpensive remedies that don't involve yet another trip to the doctor, who will give them yet another prescription for a costly drug. And many older people have the notion that even if the over-the-counter medications won't help them much, they can't do them much harm either.

This raises the basic issue that has been occupying the attention of the FDA since 1962, when Congress passed legislation requiring that the ingredients in an approved over-the-counter drug not only had to be *safe* (that requirement was contained in a law passed in 1938), but also had to be *effective.* Four years later, in 1966, the FDA asked the National Academy of Science of the National Research Council to evaluate a broad sampling of nonprescription drugs then on the market. The results: Only 25 percent of those evaluated were found to be effective for even one use.

Not until 1972 did the FDA launch what has come to be known as the OTC (Over-The-Counter) Drug Review, whose purpose has been to study 500,000 brands of drugs so that the ineffective ones can be removed from the market as required by the 1962 legislation. Seventeen panels of qualified experts were appointed, and eleven years later, in 1983, it was announced by the FDA that the fifty-eight reports submitted came to the conclusion that of the more than seven hundred ingredients in over-the-counter medications, only about one third could be considered effective.[8] The rest were either ineffective or unsafe, and in a large number of cases, the experts couldn't come to any conclusions because of an insufficiency of data.

And have all these ineffective and/or unsafe products been taken off the market? Not as of 1985, and the way things are going at the FDA, probably not until 1990 if then.

In the meantime, another group has devoted itself to reviewing nonprescription drugs. The Health Research Group, founded by Ralph Nader and consisting largely of physicians and laboratory scientists, has published a book called *Over-the-Counter Pills That Don't Work,* in which the authors discuss common health problems, when to consult a doctor, and when to try alternative treatment. The book is available in local bookstores, or by mail from The Health Research Group, Dept. 22, 2000 P Street, N.W., Washington, D.C. 20036. The price is $6.95. The group also recommends a long list of over-the-counter drugs and their generic equivalents already found to be both safe and effective by the FDA advisory panels. It also names those drugs on which there is joint agreement as to ineffective and/or unsafe ingredients.

In trying to make some sense of the contents of your parents' medicine cabinet, you might be helped by knowing that among the products that both the FDA advisers and the Ralph Nader Health Research Group say *yes* to are: all painkillers that contain nothing but aspirin or acetaminophen; all laxatives whose main ingredient is psyllium (a natural seed that becomes gelatinous when ingested); and the antacids Gelusil, Maalox, Rolaids, Tums, and milk of magnesia. Among the products that both groups found to be either unsafe or ineffective or both are Anacin Maximum Strength, Excedrin Extra Strength, Dristan 12 hr. Nasal Decongestant, Sinutabs Extra Strength, Vicks Cough Syrup, Triaminicin, and Preparation H Ointment and Suppositories.

8. New York *Times,* October 10, 1983.

Some of these remain on store shelves; some have already been removed.

And while you're helping your parent edit the medicines, check the expiration date on each container and dispose of the drugs too old to be effective.

Checking on Alcohol Content

There's an insidious problem connected with nonprescription drugs that requires your attention especially if you have a parent who regularly takes a sleeping pill containing phenobarbital, a tranquilizer, or an antihistamine that produces drowsiness. The problem is this: There are many over-the-counter medicines that contain a considerable amount of alcohol. Here, for example, is a selection from the open shelves of a chain pharmacy (May 1985): Comtrex Multi-Symptom Cold Reliever is 20 percent alcohol by volume; Nyquil Night Time Colds Medicine is 25 percent alcohol; Robitussin Night Relief Colds Formula is 25 percent alcohol; Geritol (iron supplement) is 12 percent alcohol.

Obviously the physician who prescribed the medication that must not be combined with alcohol is in no position to check up on the patient who has been conned into buying a "strong effective" over-the-counter remedy for coughs and colds. Nor do pharmacists, even the most attentive ones, have any control over what their customers are buying from the open shelves. Who then is to take the responsibility for alerting people in their sixties and seventies and eighties (for some of whom even the "usual" amount of the prescription drugs in question may produce dizziness and disorientation) of the potential dangers of self-medication with over-the-counter preparations that may contain as much as one-fifth to one-quarter alcohol? No one but the patients themselves or concerned family members.

Overdoses of Over-the-Counter Vitamins

Older people may be told by their physician to include a multivitamin capsule in their daily regimen to compensate for possible deficiencies in their diet. Many more, however, regularly take vitamins in self-prescribed combinations, and more dangerous still, in megadoses. If your parents are doing this, you must try to convey the message that vitamins in large doses are *drugs* and not nutrients, and that when the bundle of medicines in the plastic bag is taken to the doctor for review, the containers of vitamins and mineral supplements *must* be included.

There are several reasons for alerting the prime care physician to this type of self-medication, which is sometimes the recommendation of a self-styled "nutritionist." Claims that megadoses of vitamins can "cure" cancer or heart conditions have led some older people to take as much as ten times the recommended vitamin allowance without telling their doctor what they're doing. And there are instances where what they're doing is interfering with a medical treatment that has been proved effective for a chronic condition, or jeopardizing the validity of particular medical tests that are indispensable for the correct diagnosis of symptoms.

A particularly dangerous aspect of self-medication with megadoses of vitamins is that often, when faced with negative results, the victim decides to stop the vitamin intake altogether, which leads to a withdrawal crisis in the body's artificially hyped-up chemistry.

If you become aware of bottles of vitamins in the parental drug arsenal, see if you can find out what they're doing there, and the next time a doctor's visit is scheduled, have them checked out, together with the over-the-counter laxative, pain reliever, cough medicine, and antihistamine.

A Helpful Development

Because there have been unpleasant and sometimes life-threatening incidents resulting from even tiny amounts of heretofore unspecified inactive ingredients in nonprescription drugs, the principal manufacturers of these drugs have voluntarily been listing colorings, preservatives, and similar components on package labels. This listing makes it possible to prevent those infrequent but serious occurrences in which an individual may be allergic to a particular substance in what normally might seem to be insignificant amounts.

Overdose Toxicity of Over-the-Counter Painkillers

According to the American Association of Poison Control Centers, pharmaceuticals are responsible for the majority of reported human poisonings that occur in the home. Of these, the single drug most involved is the nonprescription drug acetaminophen, sold under the name of Tylenol, Panadol, Datril, and Anacin 3. This conclusion is the result of studies undertaken by Whitehall Laboratories. These painkillers are completely safe when used according to package instructions, but your parents should be warned that a significant overdose can cause serious trouble. A significant overdose is 2½ times the amount recommended. In the case of acetaminophen, such overdoses may lead to acute liver damage. Similar overdoses of aspirin may lead to respiratory failure. Of the various over-the-counter analgesics, it would appear that ibuprofen (sold as Advil) involves the least damaging consequences when taken in overdoses.

GUARDING AGAINST MISHAPS

Failing memory, impaired alertness caused by overmedication, poor eyesight, inadequate communication between doctor and patient—these are among the many causes of mishaps with drugs. According to a survey conducted in Minnesota by a professor of nursing among the elderly who lived independently and were responsible for their own health care, "Fewer than 5% of those taking prescription drugs knew enough to ensure safe use." In the interests of economy, some older people might reduce the dosage of an expensive drug to the point where it becomes ineffective; others think that as long as they paid for a particular medication, they should use up the entire contents even though it might be a risky thing to do.

If you want your parents to get the greatest benefit from their medicines at the same time that they are safeguarded against unnecessary risks and accidents, here are some suggestions:

- If they are on several maintenance drugs, find out whether the prescribed dose should be adjusted as they grow older.
- Give them a magnifying glass so that they can read the tiny print on package labels and drug company literature accompanying most medication.
- Since the late 1970s, drug manufacturers have been required to put an expiration date on labels or containers. However, a pharmacist's label may carry only the date of the prescription. Ask the doctor whether the prescription container should have an expiration date as well.
- If your parent thinks there's any reason for discontinuing a

medication or changing the dosage, the physician must be consulted before doing so.

- Even if your mother and father are taking some of the same prescription medicines, they should each have their own containers and prescription numbers. Under no circumstances should prescription drugs be shared with any family member or friend who seems to be suffering from the same condition.

- Sometimes an older person forgets to take a particular medicine or has had to skip a few doses while the prescription was being refilled. The wrong thing to do is to take a double dose to make up for those missed. The right thing to do is to ask the physician how to proceed.

- A medication that has been discontinued on the advice of the physician when the symptoms have subsided shouldn't be used again when the symptoms recur six months later. The physician should be consulted before resuming the medication. There are many reasons for doing this: The physician should always know what medication the patient is taking at any given time; other medicines for some other condition may have been prescribed in the intervening six months that may interact negatively with the former medicine; in the time elapsed, a better and more effective drug may have come on the market that should be substituted for the old one.

- The containers of medicines that are taken daily can be grouped in a shallow container and kept on the dining table except for those which, like eyedrops, may have to be refrigerated. The dining table is a practical place to keep drugs because they often have to be taken before, with, or after meals.

- Pills that have to be taken at bedtime should *not* be kept at the bedside table, but rather on another surface such as a chest of drawers a few steps distant from the bed. Distancing the drugs reduces the possibility of taking the wrong dose or the wrong combination when half asleep. *At bedtime* is most safely interpreted as *before getting into bed.*

- If your parents have their own dwelling and their medications are capped with screw-on tops rather than with those that are childproof, remind them to put all bottles and containers where your children—or any children—can't get their hands on them.

- Discourage your mother from taking pills out of their prescription containers and carrying them around in a pillbox. If medication is to accompany her on a visit or weekend trip, the pharmacist's containers should go along with her. A scramble of pills in a pillbox can lead to unnecessary confusion.

■ Prescription drugs discontinued on the doctor's advice, or those whose expiration date has arrived, shouldn't be given to anyone else. They should be discarded promptly by flushing them down the toilet and throwing the containers out with the garbage unless the label carries the pharmacist's refillable instructions.

DRUGS AND DRIVING, DRIVING AND DRINKING, DRINKING AND DRUGS: IN ANY COMBINATION, THEY SPELL DANGER

Even when they're functioning at top capability, many older people are a menace to themselves and to others on the road. Their physical reflexes aren't as quick as they used to be; their vision may be somewhat impaired; they can no longer make the split-second decisions demanded by present-day driving circumstances.

Consider then how much more perilous the situation becomes because of the effect of medications such as tranquilizers and antihistamines. Not until recently has there been serious research on the relationship between legal drugs and auto accidents. A study conducted in Dallas found Valium (diazepam) in the blood of 10 percent of drivers killed in car crashes.[9] Other studies indicate that drivers who take antihistamines have significantly more accidents than those who have no allergies.

We know how much more sensitive people become to drugs as they grow older, and even though they've been warned by medical authorities and drug manufacturers not to do so, countless lawabiding senior citizens insist on getting behind the wheel when they're too drowsy and slowed down to drive safely.

If your parents are a cause for concern in this regard, you might call their attention to the printed warnings that accompany the medication. If the reaction is stubborn resistance, you may have to involve the family doctor: either the drug should be withdrawn (it may not be as essential to parental well-being as driving is), or the car keys should be turned over to someone else.

"Drunk driving" has been getting lots of attention recently, but what about older people who aren't alcoholics or "problem drink-

9. New York *Times*, December 22, 1984.

ers" but who don't think twice about getting behind the wheel after they've had three beers at a picnic or half a bottle of wine with dinner? If you're anxious about your parent's drinking and driving pattern, take the time to discuss it in a friendly way. Make it clear that you don't object to drinking as such, but there are times when a soft drink or a fruit juice makes more sense than an alcoholic beverage.

Unfortunately, there are many families in which eighteen-year-olds and forty-year-olds have their own problems with drinking and driving. If you're in such a situation vis-à-vis your spouse and your children and the family car, as well as with a recalcitrant parent, you may want to seek help from a family counselor.

Even a moderate amount of alcohol can produce undesirable results when combined with particular prescription and nonprescription drugs regularly taken by older people. The National Institute on Aging has pointed out that alcohol can intensify the brain-depressing effects of the "minor" tranquilizers—Valium (diazepam), Librium (chlordiazepoxide), Miltown (meprobamate); barbiturates compounded of phenobarbital; painkillers such as Demerol (meperidine); and antihistamines—both those prescribed for allergies and those that are found in nonprescription cold remedies.[10] The same federal source points out that "the use of alcohol can cause other drugs to be metabolized more rapidly, producing exaggerated responses. Such drugs include anticonvulsants (Dilantin), anticoagulants (coumadin), and antidiabetic drugs (Orinase). In some people, aspirin can cause bleeding in the stomach and intestines. Alcohol also irritates the stomach and can aggravate the bleeding. The combination of alcohol and diuretics can reduce blood pressure in some individuals, producing dizziness."

Other warnings about alcohol and medication: It can interfere with the effectiveness of antidiabetic medicine by raising blood sugar levels. It can cause nausea and vomiting when combined with certain antibiotics. It can result in a risky rise in blood pressure when combined with MAO-inhibiting drugs such as the antidepressants Nardin (phenelzine) and Marplan (isocarboxazid). It can lead to overdose by destroying the coating of time-release capsules so that the drugs are absorbed with undesirable speed.

10. *Age Page,* November 1983.

A QUICK LOOK AT QUACKERY

A 1984 congressional report covering the results of a four-year investigation into health frauds contained the information that elderly Americans were spending upwards of $10 billion each year on quack remedies. The largest amount—5 billion—was being spent on cancer remedies of no proven effectiveness; three billion for worthless cures for arthritis; and most of the rest on products guaranteed to counteract the effects of aging. The investigation, which was supervised by Congressman Claude Pepper, noted that while people who were sixty-five and older made up less than 12 percent of the population, they were the victims of 60 percent of all health frauds.

The consequences go beyond the economic exploitation of gullible older people desperate to diminish their suffering. At the time the report was issued, Congressman Pepper was quoted as saying, "Over 75% of the products reviewed by the committee were found to be potentially harmful or dangerous. In addition to the loss of money paid for nonexistent cures, individuals who purchased them are exposing themselves to hazards ranging from blindness to the acceleration of cancer, aggravation of arthritis, convulsions, heart palpitations, insulin shock, and death."

False cure promoters who prey on older women's fear of aging are making millions of dollars even though the claims for various herbs, "secret formulas," and vitamin megadoses have never been scientifically substantiated. Is your mother still smoking, drinking too much, and eating too little at the same time that she's gobbling up "youth" remedies and covering her face with expensive goo? If she isn't beyond the reach of reason, suggest that good health habits cost very little and will keep her looking better longer than overpriced fakery.

You can protect your parents not only from spending their money foolishly but also from the possibility of jeopardizing their health. Try to alert them to the fact that medical quackery is a big business conducted by shrewd operators who manage to stay within the law by clever and misleading wording of their advertising. Tell them to watch out for mail-order promotions or door-to-door pitches about a "miracle cure" or an "important breakthrough" and that show "before and after" photographs or signed testimonials from "overjoyed" users.

If your parent defends such frauds with the argument that "the government wouldn't allow the product to be sold if it was illegal or harmful," you might quote Congressman Pepper, who blames the FDA for spending only 1 percent of its budget on the control of quackery, and who says that law enforcement in this area takes lots of time and money because it has to be done on a case-by-case basis.

However, if your parent tells you in no uncertain terms that the "miracle" cure produced wonderful results, and that it's working better than anything the doctor prescribed, you'll have to decide whether you want to go into an explanation of the placebo effect, or whether to let well enough alone and be grateful for the powers of suggestibility.

You can present your parents with a summary of the House of Representatives report *Quackery: A $10 Billion Scandal* by requesting a free copy from:

> The Honorable Claude Pepper
> Health and Long-Term Care Subcommittee
> Room 715, House Annex
> U.S. House of Representatives
> Washington, D.C. 20515

Since the U.S. Postal Service is empowered to investigate mail fraud, send a sample of any mail-order quackery to the local post office, with a photocopy of the advertisement and your letter of complaint to the Chief Postal Inspector, Washington, D.C. 20260.

❧ 5 ❧

HELPING YOUR PARENTS
MAKE THEIR WAY THROUGH
THE HEALTH INSURANCE MAZE

Medicare . . . Medicaid . . . medigap . . . HMOs . . . supplements . . . DRGs . . . spending down . . . HCFA . . . Part A . . . Part B . . . prepayment . . . PROs . . . private hospitals . . . and MONEY MONEY MONEY.

Does it take an M.B.A. or a Ph.D. to figure out the most effective ways to help your parents deal with the confusion surrounding health care insurance? Whatever is required in the way of expertise to sort out the facts, one thing is clear to practically everybody: the problem of rising health care costs isn't a personal family matter; it's a national crisis.

Putting the situation in historical perspective provides a few interesting ironies and some surprises. When a federally operated health insurance program was first proposed in the 1940s, it was militantly opposed by the American Medical Association and by Republicans who saw the program as an un-American form of "socialized" medicine. In 1965, the Medicare bill was finally passed in spite of the continued opposition of the AMA and conservative politicians, who offered alternatives that were hopelessly inadequate for the needs of the elderly. At the time of the enactment of the legislation, only half of those over sixty-five had any health insurance at all. For the half who did have private coverage, the usual policy paid no more than $10 a day for hospitalization at a time when the average hospital cost was $40 a day. It was obvious to President Johnson and to anyone else who knew how much money most retired people had at their disposal—and to anyone who could do simple arithmetic—that adequate coverage was *not* provided by private insurance, and that therefore average older Americans couldn't afford to pay hospital bills without pauperizing themselves and their families. Of course, as an alternative, they could always become public charges at tax-supported institutions.

In 1985, twenty years after the adoption of Medicare for the elderly and Medicaid for the poor, 50 million Americans participated in these programs at a combined cost of $93 billion. "Medicaid and Medicare grew faster than we expected," said Wilber J. Cohen, a former Secretary of Health, Education, and Welfare, who was one of the architects of the program, "because the true extent of the unmet need was not appreciated by the American Medical Association or me or anyone else in the Government."[1]

Other developments were also not "appreciated" or anticipated: In the fifteen years from 1967 to 1985, beneficiaries of Medicare services soared from 19.5 million to 30 million; in the five years from 1967 to 1972, the Bureau of Labor Statistics estimated that while the Consumer Price Index for all items rose 25 percent, the cost of physicians' services rose 34 percent and hospital room rates went up 74 percent. And when Dr. James H. Sammons, executive vice-president of the AMA was asked whether his organization now supports Medicare, the response was, "You bet we do. We also support Medicaid. We have spent the last twenty years trying very hard to make these programs work, and I think they have worked. We oppose President Reagan's proposed reductions in both programs."[2]

There is no doubt that the increase in the life expectancy of our parents in the last two decades is partially attributable to easier access to health care. (It is also attributable to physical fitness programs, better diet, and a decrease in smoking.) However, when we assess President Johnson's prediction in 1965 that the passage of the Medicare bill would mean that "older citizens would no longer have to fear that illness will wipe out their savings, eat up their income, and destroy lifelong hope of dignity and independence," we can only say that the prediction was a well-intentioned wish rather than an accurate projection into the 1980s.

One major reason for all the confusion and competition in the health insurance field is that older people are trying to figure out a way of closing the gap between total medical costs and what Medicare pays for. According to the House Select Committee on Aging, the elderly aren't any better off now than they were before

1. New York *Times*, April 20, 1985.
2. Ibid.

Medicare. They spent about 15 percent of their income on health care twenty years ago, and they're spending the same amount now. Although Medicare pays approximately 40 percent of their health care costs, these costs have risen nearly 900 percent during that period, and the Medicare deductibles keep going up too.

With the government curtailing rather than increasing Medicare benefits, and the income of most of our parents fixed at a level inadequate to bridge the gap between what Medicare pays for and what they have to pay for themselves, we now have another type of insurance for the elderly—sometimes called Medicare supplements, and familiarly known as "medigap."

But there remains the specter that haunts many families—the devastating effects of a chronic illness on family members in terms of the psychological burdens and financial expenses involved in long-term care for a physically and/or mentally disabled parent. Many families have already been faced with the harsh reality of how best to combine their personal assets and various government entitlements in order to provide the most humane and individualized care at home for a father in the early stages of Alzheimer's disease or a mother crippled by rheumatoid arthritis. When there is general agreement among sons and daughters—and the spouse who can still function more or less independently—that a good nursing home is the best solution for the seriously disabled and increasingly incompetent parent, the question of money always arises. As of now, there is practically no private long-term insurance to cover this circumstance, a circumstance that affects an ever-increasing number of people as more and more Americans live to be very old. Whereas the norm used to be the three-generation family, it's no longer unusual to be part of a four-generation family. Statistics indicate that 60 percent of the people between the ages of fifty and sixty-five are responsible for the care of a family member who is eighty years old or older, and that percentage is expected to continue to grow with each decade. By the year 2000, according to current predictions, the seventy-five-to-eighty-five age group will grow from 7.7 million to 12.2 million, but more significantly, the eighty-five and over population will more than double—from 2.2 million to 5.1 million. The effect of these figures is causing more and more Americans to find themselves trapped in stressful situations because while science is keeping more and more people alive longer and longer, society hasn't figured out how to provide for their well-being as they become less capable of caring for themselves.

In the wings are private companies calculating the feasibility and profitability of long-term health care insurance. The federal government has been making calculations of its own indicating that such insurance, if available, would redirect Medicaid expenditures in ways that would benefit the truly needy as well as all taxpayers. Suggestions have been made by various advocacy organizations that long-term health insurance could be sold to younger family members for the benefit of coverage for their elders, and that the purchasers should be able to deduct the premiums for tax credit.

Legislation has already been proposed in the Senate that would encourage the development of consumer standards for this type of coverage. The designation for the proposed bill is S1378. It may have an embattled history, but it should be interesting to keep an eye on how the voting goes as "The Longer Term Care Insurance Promotion and Protection Act of 1985" makes its way through Congress. In the meantime, the material that follows is intended to provide you with a better understanding of the options now available to your parents.

MEDICARE

Medicare is the federal health insurance program for some disabled people and for practically all people sixty-five or older no matter what their income and no matter where they live in the United States or its commonwealth islands. As the program now functions, it pays for approximately 40 percent of the health costs of the average elderly American. It is currently under severe attack by advocates for the elderly and their families because it excludes from its benefits approximately 6.5 million chronically ill people who need some form of long-term nonskilled nursing care. Alzheimer victims are the ones most frequently in the news nowadays, but they are the newcomers on a long list that includes survivors of strokes, people disabled by parkinsonism, and those enfeebled by the cumulative effects of old age.

This exclusion may well be attributable to the powerful forces that had to be placated in order to get the program enacted at all. These forces—hospitals, skilled nursing facilities, and the American Medical Association—essentially wrote themselves into the Medicare program to the exclusion of the providers of custodial care. Because of this unrealistic assessment of the long-term needs

of the old and the very old, their sons and daughters—and their
spouses—often have no alternative but to turn to Medicaid for the
help that Medicare denies them.

In point of fact, although some of the language and the provisions require close reading and careful interpretation, one paragraph is clear and unambiguous. It appears on page 7 of *Your
Medicare Handbook* (April 1985 edition) following the warning
that "Under the law, Medicare does not cover custodial care.
. . ." and it says:

> Care is considered custodial when it is primarily for the purpose of
> meeting personal needs and could be provided by persons without
> professional skills or training. For example, custodial care includes
> help in walking, getting in and out of bed, bathing, dressing, eating,
> and taking medicine. Even if you are in a participating hospital or
> skilled nursing facility or you are receiving care from a participating
> home health agency, Medicare does not cover your care if it is
> mainly custodial. . . .

At the same time that the program is being criticized in many
quarters because of its inadequacies, the recent administration in
Washington has made every effort to reduce the Medicare budget
by revising payment procedures and inaugurating new standards
for hospital disbursements. Before trying to figure out the meaning of headlines such as "Discharging Elderly Patients Quicker
and Sicker," "Elderly See Share of Hospital Costs Soar," or
"Study Says Medicare Rule Blurs Cost of Treatment," it is necessary to take a close look at what the Medicare program *does* cover
and how it works.

Two Separate Health Care Programs

Medicare consists of two distinctly separate programs which
can be summarized as follows:

Hospital Insurance, also called Part A, provides partial coverage for your parents on the basis of their own or each other's
Social Security benefits. That is, if your father is a recipient of
these benefits and your mother isn't because she never worked,
she is entitled *as his spouse* to receive Medicare benefits when she
reaches age sixty-five. The same would be true for a couple in
which the wife was the wage earner receiving Social Security payments on her retirement and the husband was not going to receive

Social Security benefits on retirement because he had lived off an inheritance. As the spouse of the female recipient, he would be entitled to receive Medicare benefits when *he* reached age sixty-five.

Hospital insurance, or Part A of the Medicare program, helps to pay for the following services for a strictly defined period: inpatient services in an accredited hospital, a post-hospital skilled nursing facility, as well as for home *health* care and hospice care. There is no premium payment for this insurance. In 1985, Part A Medicare recipients were responsible for paying the first $400 of their hospital bills. This amount is known as the *hospital insurance deductible.*

Medical Insurance, also called Part B, pays for part of the cost of physicians' services, outpatient hospital services, outpatient physical, speech, and/or occupational therapy, home health care (not to be confused with homemaker or custodial services), and other outpatient health services. Part B is not free. The basic medical insurance premium has been rising by small amounts each year. (Through December 1985, the monthly premium was $15.50.) Most Social Security recipients elect to have this amount deducted from their monthly benefit checks. These payments are tax deductible at the end of the year. The medical insurance deductible is $75 in approved charges for the year, and after your parents have paid out that amount, Medicare medical insurance pays 80 percent of the approved charges for the rest of the year. The beneficiary is responsible for paying the remaining 20 percent.

A Closer Look at Medicare Part A: Hospital Insurance

When you examine the *Medicare Handbook,* which spells out most (but by no means all) of the details of how hospital coverage works, you discover that the insurance can "help" the recipient pay more often than it pays the whole bill outright. When your parent is admitted to a Medicare-participating hospital for inpatient treatment as prescribed by a physician, Medicare pays for all specified services for the first sixty days (less the $400 deductible). If your parent's stay must continue beyond sixty days, Medicare pays for all specified services minus $100 for each day after the sixtieth day. From the sixty-first day through the ninetieth day, the hospital may charge the patient for the $100 a day. Any continuous hospital stay up to ninety days followed by sixty continu-

MEDICARE (PART A): HOSPITAL INSURANCE—COVERED SERVICES PER BENEFIT PERIOD(1)			
Service	Benefit	Medicare Pays**	You Pay**
HOSPITALIZATION	First 60 days	All but $400	$400
Semiprivate room and board, general nursing and miscellaneous hospital services and supplies.	61st to 90th day	All but $100 a day	$100 a day
	91st to 150th day	All but $200 a day	$200 a day
	Beyond 150 days	Nothing	All costs
POSTHOSPITAL SKILLED NURSING FACILITY CARE . . . In a facility approved by Medicare. You must have been in a hospital for at least 3 days and enter the facility within 30 days after hospital discharge. (2)	First 20 days	100% of approved amount	Nothing
	Additional 80 days	All but $50 a day	$50 a day
	Beyond 100 days	Nothing	All costs
HOME HEALTH CARE	Unlimited visits as medically necessary	Full cost	Nothing
HOSPICE CARE	Two 90-day periods and one 30-day period	All but limited costs for outpatient drugs and inpatient respite care.	Limited cost sharing for outpatient drugs and inpatient respite care.
BLOOD	Blood	All but first 3 pints	For first 3 pints

*60 Reserve Days may be used only once, days used are not renewable
**These figures are for 1985 and are subject to change each year.
(1) A Benefit Period begins on the first day you receive service as an inpatient in a hospital and ends after you have been out of the hospital or skilled nursing facility for 60 days in a row.
(2) Medicare and private insurance will not pay for most nursing home care. You pay for custodial care and most care in a nursing home.

Source: *Guide to Health Insurance for People with Medicare,* U.S. Department of Health and Human Services, Jan. 1985.

ous days out of the hospital (or out of a skilled nursing care or rehabilitation facility) is considered a *benefit* period. If your parent's doctor orders readmission for inpatient treatment *before* this benefit period ends, your parent doesn't have to pay the $400 deductible all over again. Your parent is entitled to an unlimited number of benefit periods in a Medicare-approved facility with the following exception: 190 days of care in a participating *psychiatric* hospital is the absolute for which Medicare can help to pay during a person's lifetime.

Hospice Care Benefits consist of two ninety-day periods and one thirty-day period during which Medicare pays for all covered services required by the terminal illness as well as for treatment of an unrelated condition. (See Chapter 7, pages 205–8, for a detailed discussion of hospice care.) The only deductibles for which the patient is partially responsible are the cost of drugs and inpatient respite care. As defined in the April 1985 *Medicare Handbook,* "Respite care is a short-term inpatient stay which may be necessary for the patient in order to give temporary relief to the person who regularly assists with home care. Inpatient respite care is limited each time to stays of no more than five days in a row."

To return to an examination of general hospital coverage: Suppose your parent requires a continuation of treatment in a hospital or skilled nursing facility beyond the insurable ninety-day period? For this circumstance, an additional special sixty days known as *reserve* days are provided to be used during the patient's lifetime. These sixty days are special indeed. They can be used a few at a time or all at once, but no matter when they're used, the patient must pay (in 1985) $200 for each day of services. Medicare pays the rest.

During any period of hospitalization, Part A does *not* pay for the services of your parent's physician even though the services are provided in a hospital. The doctor's bills are paid under the provisions described in Medicare Medical Insurance Part B. That is, if your parent has already paid the (1985) $75 deductible in doctors' fees, Medicare will pay 80 percent of the bills for the rest of the year. Your parent pays the remaining 20 percent.

The Services Paid For by Medicare When Your Parent Is Hospitalized. The following are the services that the hospital is being paid for, and to which your parent is therefore fully entitled. If you think they are being withheld even though they are necessary, don't hesitate to speak to your parent's physician first, and if that doesn't bring satisfactory results, write out a list of particulars and make an appointment to speak to the hospital administrator or the administrator's surrogate. Your parent is entitled to:

- A bed in a semiprivate room containing no more than four beds.
- All meals. If a special diet has been ordered, make sure that the instructions have been followed. Find out from the doctor or the floor nurse whether the food is to be salt-free, sugar-free, fat-free, or high in a particular nutrient, and then check out the meals being served when you come to visit.
- Regular nursing services. This means the service of registered nurses, nurses' aides, and other personnel *on the hospital staff* who carry out the doctor's orders for the well-being of the patient. Not only does the quality and quantity of the service vary from hospital to hospital, but it may vary from section to section of the same hospital depending on the floor nurse in charge, and from room to room and bed to bed depending on the clout of the particular physician or the importance of the particular patient. If you think your father or mother is being

too demanding, take that into account when you try to assess the nursing services. On the other hand, older people are often unwilling to complain about incompetent or inadequate nursing service, not to mention downright rudeness, because they're fearful of the consequences. (Hospital staff members, on the other hand, feel that TV programs have given the public some highly dubious expectations about what hospital life is like.) If your parent is genuinely pleased and appreciative of the nurses' efforts, the family should convey this information. If, on the other hand, you feel that there are legitimate complaints about the attitude or competence of nurses and their aides to the extent that your parent's progress is being affected, speak to the doctor about what should be done to improve the situation.

When your parent is a hospital inpatient, Medicare also pays for the cost of special care units (intensive care, coronary care, etc.), drugs, laboratory tests, X rays, and CAT scans; in cases of surgery, the use of the operating room, anesthesia services, and the recovery room, and rehabilitation therapy as needed. If your parent is the recipient of blood transfusions, Medicare pays these costs unless the particular hospital has the policy of charging a nonreplacement fee for the first three pints of blood. In the very rare instances where this policy prevails, your parent has the option of paying the fee or arranging to have this amount of blood replaced either by a family member or by another acceptable source.

What Medicare Does **Not** *Pay For During Hospitalization.* As a Medicare recipient, your parent is *not* entitled to payment for:

- The installation of a telephone, a radio, or a television.
- The additional cost of a private room except under special circumstances.
- Private duty nurses.

Whether or not to pay for private duty nurses when a parent is to be hospitalized is a matter that should be given some consideration. (In cases where a supplementary policy covers private duty nursing, be sure that the terms of the coverage apply to the particular circumstance.) Find out from the physician in charge of your parent whether staff nursing is attentive enough to obviate the need for the expense of private duty nurses even for the first day following major surgery. Also, you can find out about the experiences that other family members or your parents' friends have had in the same hospital. Of course if your parent insists on private duty nurses and is in a position to pay for them, or if you'd like to provide nurses for one or two shifts as a special present, you can arrange to order them at the nurses' registry in the hospital. On a national basis, these services range from $14 to $22 *per hour* for an eight-hour shift. (Rates are higher for intensive care private duty.)

Prospective Payment System and DRGs.   Before examining Medicare coverage for a patient who is transferred from a hospital to a skilled nursing facility, some clarification is in order about how your parents are being affected by the new way in which hospitals are being paid by Medicare. From the time of the program's inception, hospitals were paid for the cost of all essential services to the patient during the length of time the attending physician decided that hospitalization was necessary. In 1983, following concerted pressure from the Reagan administration to cut health care costs, Congress passed a law specifying that hospitals be paid the same amount, *set in advance,* for each Medicare patient with a particular illness, *regardless of the length of the hospital stay.* This prospective payment system is based on classifications known as Diagnosis Related Groups, referred to as DRGs, of which there are now 470. These groups were arrived at by computerizing the various circumstances that cause Medicare beneficiaries to be hospitalized. Thus, no matter how long the doctor decides your parent should remain in the hospital after gallbladder surgery complicated by postoperative infection, or a hysterectomy followed by pneumonia, the hospital is paid by Medicare only for the time allotted to those particular DRGs. This new payment system has already produced significant differences in the length of time that patients are hospitalized. For example, the average hospital stay for Medicare recipients dropped from 9.5 days in 1983 before the new system was initiated, to 7.5 days in 1984—a decrease of 20 percent because of the revised payment arrangement.

There has been plenty of criticism on several grounds directed at this "cost containment" reform of Medicare hospital insurance. With a fixed price for specific illnesses, there is now a strong incentive to send patients home even earlier than the allowable stay so that hospitals can keep the extra money. In a survey conducted by the American Medical Association and reported in the New York *Times,* more than 60 percent of the 7800 physicians who responded said that they fear a decline in the quality of care because of "government interference in doctors' decisions."[3] The July 1984 issue of the *New England Journal of Medicine* contained the results of a study conducted by Johns Hopkins University's Medical School which indicated that while two patients may be admitted to their respective hospitals for the "same" DRG and for which each hospital will receive the same payment, one patient may be in much worse shape than the other and may therefore require a much longer hospital stay. It turns out therefore that some hospitals are being paid too much and some too little. These variations in the need for longer hospitalization are discernible not by computer, but by the physician in charge of the patient. In this connection, the National Public Radio reported on June 20, 1985, that 43 percent of the AMA membership said that some hospitals were exerting pressure to have patients discharged promptly no matter what their condition by putting the relevant DRG data on the patient's chart as a reminder to the doctor. Thus doctors feel that they are being forced into an adversarial position with the hospital. When Senator John Heinz, Republican from Pennsylvania and chairman of the Committee on Aging, was confronted with a report on the new payment system, his response to the savings that were indicated was that they "showed that patients are moved out of hospitals "sicker and quicker."

Some Safeguards Against High-handedness. You've already been notified by the April 1985 *Your Medicare Handbook* that "Medicare does not cover custodial care. . . ." That particular sentence goes on to explain that Medicare also doesn't cover care that is not "reasonable and necessary" for the diagnosis or treatment of an illness or injury. The warning is spelled out as follows for your parents:

> If a doctor places you in a hospital or skilled nursing facility when the kind of care you need could be provided elsewhere, your stay would not be considered reasonable and necessary. So Medicare could not cover your stay. If you stay in a hospital or skilled nursing facility longer than you need to be there, Medicare payments would end when further inpatient care is no longer reasonable and necessary.

And the next paragraph goes on to say:

3. July 30, 1985.

To help Medicare decide whether inpatient hospital care is reasonable and necessary, there are Peer Review Organizations (PROs) in each State. Each PRO is made up of local doctors who review the care prescribed by their fellow doctors. Medicare hospital insurance cannot pay for any inpatient hospital care that the Peer Review Organization finds is not necessary.

Fifty-four Peer Review Organizations were set up nationwide between July and November 1984. They were established not only to help the government cut health care costs by promoting outpatient treatment, but also to guarantee the quality of Medicare services. As a result of mounting concern and criticism by members of Congress and by advocates for the elderly, rules have been established under which PROs are required to disclose the following information to consumers about individual hospitals: the mortality rate for different types of surgery, the number of patients who develop postoperative infections, the average length of hospital stays, how often the hospital performs various procedures, and how much it charges for them. The disclosures give the names of hospitals and individual departments, but not the names of doctors and their patients, and in issuing this information, the PROs may also include their assessment of the quality of care at the hospital in question.

You can find out the name of the Peer Review Organization associated with the hospital of concern to your parents, as well as the types of information the particular group makes available by writing to:

> Director, Office of Medical Review
> Health Standards Quality Bureau
> Health Care Financing Administration
> Meadows East Building, 6300 Security Boulevard
> Baltimore, Maryland 21207

Additional Patient Protection. In January 1986, Ronald J. Wylie, acting director of the Office of Beneficiary Services in the Health Care Financing Administration, announced that hospitals would have to inform Medicare patients at the time of admission that they have a right to challenge a premature discharge by appealing to the local Peer Review Organization, and that this appeal can be initiated while the patient is still in the hospital, as soon as he or she is informed that discharge has been scheduled for a particular date. The review organization is given three days in which to hand down a decision. With this new ruling, there's no need to wait until your parent is sent home in order to register a formal objection to the hospital's judgment.

This recent ruling is the result of a consensus by the Senate Special Committee on Aging, the inspector general of the Department of Health and Human Services, and the General Accounting Office that patients were, in fact, being discharged "quicker and sicker" under the new DRG payment system. With this new right of appeal the following arrangements prevail: If in reviewing the appeal, the PRO deems the discharge appropriate, your parent is *not* liable for hospital charges until three days *after* that specified date. If, on the other hand, the PRO finds the discharge date premature, your parent can remain in the hospital, and no matter what the DRG indicates in terms of payment, the hospital must bear the additional cost of the stay. It is therefore important that when a parent on Medicare is admitted to a hospital, he or she, as well as a family member, has been officially informed of the patient's right to challenge the hospital's decision to send the patient home too soon.

Medicare Part A and Skilled Nursing Facilities. Medicare beneficiaries, their families, and advocacy organizations for the elderly have been increasingly concerned about the insufficiency of Medicare coverage for chronic illness that requires a long-term combination of occasional skilled nursing care and daily "custodial" care. The *Medicare Handbook* clearly spells out the circumstances under which Part A hospital insurance can *help* pay for nursing home care. Among the limitations that you and your parents must take into consideration are the following:

- Most nursing homes in the United States are *not* skilled nursing facilities.
- Many skilled nursing facilities are *not* certified by Medicare.
- In certain facilities, only *some* portions participate in Medicare.
- Medicare will not pay for the care of anyone who needs skilled nursing care or rehabilitation services only once or twice a week and who needs custodial care the remainder of the time.

(See Chapter 8, "When a Nursing Home Is the Right Answer," pp. 209–34.)

A Closer Look at Medicare Part B: Medical Insurance

MEDICARE (PART B): MEDICAL INSURANCE—COVERED SERVICES PER CALENDAR YEAR			
Service	Benefit	Medicare Pays	You Pay
MEDICAL EXPENSE Physician's services, inpatient and out-patient medical services and supplies, physical and speech therapy, ambulance, etc.	Medicare pays for medical services in or out of the hospital. Some insurance policies pay less (or nothing) for hospital outpatient medical services or services in a doctor's office.	80% approved amount (after $75 deductible)	$75 deductible* plus 20% of balance of approved amount (plus any charge above approved amount)**
HOME HEALTH CARE	Unlimited visits as medically necessary	Full cost	Nothing
OUTPATIENT HOSPITAL TREATMENT	Unlimited as medically necessary	80% of approved amount (after $75 deductible)	Subject to deductible plus 20% of balance of approved amount
BLOOD	Blood	80% of approved amount (after first 3 pints)	For first 3 pints plus 20% of balance of approved amount

*Once you have had $75 of expense for covered services in 1985, the Part B deductible does not apply to any further covered services you receive the rest of the year.

**YOU PAY FOR charges higher than the amount approved by Medicare unless the doctor or supplier agrees to accept Medicare's approved amount as the total charge for services rendered. (See page 16.)

Source: *Guide to Health Insurance for People with Medicare,* U.S. Department of Health and Human Services, Jan. 1985.

Unlike the hospital coverage which is available to practically everyone who is sixty-five or older, the medical coverage is *optional*. To receive these benefits, participants pay a tax-deductible monthly premium of $15.50 (1985), which is subtracted from the recipient's monthly Social Security check. The medical insurance pays *part* of the cost of doctors' bills, certain specified ambulance transportation, outpatient care, outpatient therapy services, home health care (skilled nursing), and certain other health services and supplies not covered by Part A.

Before any payments are made in a given year, your parent must have paid a total of $75 of approved charges. After this deductible amount has been met, medical insurance pays for 80 percent of approved charges for the rest of the year, and your parent is responsible for the additional 20 percent. *Approved* or *allowable* charges are based *not* on the doctor's or supplier's current fees, but on amounts approved and regulated under a procedure prescribed in Medicare law. In recent years, there has been an ongoing battle between the medical profession and Medicare on the question of physicians' fees, their willingness to "freeze" their fees for Medicare participation, and their willingness to participate in the program altogether.

Under Part B, there are two ways in which doctors and suppliers are paid. In the *assignment* procedure, which can save the patient time and money, doctors receive the medical insurance payment directly from Medicare. Medicare pays 80 percent of the approved charge after subtracting (1) any part of the $75 deductible not yet met by the patient, and (2) the remaining 20 percent of the approved charge which is the coinsurance.

When doctors *don't* accept assignment, they bill the patient directly for their fees, even when these fees are larger than those approved by Medicare. Your parent then submits a claim for payment to the local Medicare carrier, which in turn pays the patient 80 percent of the *approved* charge (not 80 percent of the doctor's fee paid by the patient) after the $75 deductible has been met.

The form is extremely straightforward and simple to fill out.

How to Fill Out a Medicare Form

Indispensable to a complete understanding of how Medicare coverage works in all its details is the most recent edition of *Your Medicare Handbook.* This publication (the April 1985 edition is seventy-two pages long) is available on request in person, in writing, or by phone at all Social Security offices. Even if your parents are not yet sixty-five, it's a good idea to begin to become familiar with how the system works, especially if they are considering the purchase of other types of health insurance. Also available is a free booklet called "How to Fill Out a Medicare Claim Form."

The names and addresses of Medicare-participating doctors and suppliers are listed in the Med Pard *(Med*icare *Par*ticipating *D*octors) Directory, available for your inspection at any Social Security office and at the local Area Agency on Aging. Based on the provisions of the Freedom of Information Act, you or your parents are entitled to photocopy up to forty-nine pages of this government document free of charge. If this procedure turns out to be too much of a hassle, you can buy your own copy of the directory for $2 from the local Medicare carrier, whose name and address you will find at the back of *Your Medicare Handbook.*

PATIENT'S REQUEST FOR MEDICARE PAYMENT

IMPORTANT— SEE OTHER SIDE FOR INSTRUCTIONS

PLEASE TYPE OR PRINT INFORMATION   MEDICAL INSURANCE BENEFITS SOCIAL SECURITY ACT

NOTICE: Anyone who misrepresents or falsifies essential information requested by this form may upon conviction be subject to fine and imprisonment under Federal Law. No Part B Medicare benefits may be paid unless this form is received as required by existing law and regulations (20 CFR 422.510).

1   Name of Beneficiary From Health Insurance Card

(First)   (Middle)   (Last)

SEND COMPLETED FORM TO:

Blue Cross & Blue Shield
of Greater New York
P.O. Box 535
Murray Hill Station
New York, New York 10016

2   Claim Number From Health Insurance Card

☐ Male

☐ Female

3   Patient's Mailing Address (City, State, Zip Code)
Check here if this is a new address   → ☐

(Street or P.O. Box—Include Apartment number)

(City)   (State)   (Zip)

3b   Telephone Number
(Include Area Code)

4   Describe The Illness or Injury for Which Patient Received Treatment

4b   Was illness or injury connected with employment?

☐ Yes

☐ No

5   If any medical expenses will be or could be paid by your private insurance organization, State Agency, (Medicaid), or the VA complete block 5 below.

Name and Address of other insurance, State Agency (Medicaid), or VA office

Policy or Medical
Assistance Number

NOTE: If you DO NOT want payment information on this claim released put an (x) here   → ☐

I authorize Any Holder of Medical or Other Information About Me to Release to the Social Security Administration and Health Care Financing Administration or Its Intermediaries or Carriers any Information Needed for This or a Related Medicare Claim. I Permit a copy of this Authorization to be Used in Place of the Original, and Request Payment of Medical Insurance Benefits to Me.

6   Signature of Patient (If patient is unable to sign, see Block 6 on other side.)

6b   Date Signed

IMPORTANT!

ATTACH ITEMIZED BILLS FROM YOUR DOCTOR(S)
OR SUPPLIER(S) TO THE BACK OF THIS FORM.

HOW TO FILL OUT THIS MEDICARE FORM

Medicare will pay you directly when you complete this form and attach an itemized bill from your doctor or supplier. Your bill does not have to be paid before you submit this claim for payment, but you MUST attach an itemized bill in order for Medicare to process this claim.

FOLLOW THESE INSTRUCTIONS CAREFULLY:

A. Completion of this form.

Block 1. Print your name exactly as it is shown on your Medicare Card.

Block 2. Print your Health Insurance Claim Number including the letter at the end exactly as it is shown on your Medicare card.

Blocks 3 through 5. Complete the information in these Blocks as Requested.

Block 6. Be sure to sign your name. If you cannot write your name, make an (X) mark. Then have a witness sign his or her name and address in Block 6 too.

If you are completing this form for another Medicare patient you should write (By) and sign your name and address in Block 6. You also should show your relationship to the patient and briefly explain why the patient cannot sign.

Block 6b. Print the date you completed this form.

B. Each itemized bill MUST show all of the following information:

● Date of each service.

● Place of each service   —Doctor's Office   —Independent Laboratory
                        —Outpatient Hospital   —Nursing Home
                        —Patient's Home   —Inpatient Hospital

● Description of each surgical or medical service or supply furnished.

● Charge for EACH service.

● Doctor's or supplier's name and address. Many times a bill will show the name of Several doctors or suppliers. IT IS VERY IMPORTANT THE ONE WHO TREATED YOU BE IDENTIFIED. Simply circle his/her name on the bill.

● It is helpful if the diagnosis is also shown. If not, be sure you have completed block 4 of this form.

● Mark out any services for which you have already filed a Medicare claim.

● If the patient is deceased please contact your Social Security office for instructions on how to file a claim.

COLLECTION AND USE OF MEDICARE INFORMATION

We are authorized by the Health Care Financing Administration to ask you for information needed in the administration of the Medicare program. Authority to collect information is in section 205(a), 1872 and 1875 of the Social Security Act, as amended.

The information we obtain to complete your Medicare claim is used to identify you and to determine your eligibility. It is also used to decide if the services and supplies you received are covered by Medicare and to insure that proper payment is made.

The information may also be given to other providers of services, carriers, intermediaries, medical review boards, and other organizations as necessary to administer the Medicare program. For example, it may be necessary to disclose information about the Medicare benefits you have used to a hospital or doctor.

With one exception, which is discussed below, there are no penalties under social security law for refusing to supply information. However, failure to furnish information regarding the medical services rendered or the amount charged would prevent payment of the claim. Failure to furnish any other information, such as name or claim number, would delay payment of the claim.

It is mandatory that you tell us if you are being treated for a work related injury so we can determine whether worker's compensation will pay for the treatment. Section 1877 (a) (3) of the Social Security Act provides Criminal penalties for withholding this information.

*U.S. GPO: 1984-795-029

Medicaid

In order to understand what Medicaid is and how it works, it is important to differentiate it from Medicare.

Medicare is an *insurance* program that pays hospital and medical bills with funds held in trust by the federal government for eligible recipients. Medicaid is an *assistance* program that pays such bills with money from federal, state, and local taxes for eligible people.

Medicare is a federal program that operates in the same way all over the United States for almost everyone sixty-five years old or older and without regard for income differences. Because Medicaid is a partnership between federal and state governments, states design their own programs within federal guidelines. Thus Medicaid differs from state to state in its eligibility requirements and its entitlements.

Both Medicare and Medicaid are part of the Social Security Act. Government employees, health professionals, and social workers often call Medicare Title 18 and Medicaid Title 19. Both Medicare and Medicaid (in its federal aspect) are under the jurisdiction of the Health Care Financing Administration of the U.S. Department of Health and Human Services. And both programs must be operated in compliance with Title VI of the Civil Rights Act of 1964, which states:

> No person in the United States shall, on the ground of race, color, or national origin, be excluded from participation in, be denied the benefit of, or be subject to discrimination under any program or activity receiving Federal financial assistance.

Medicaid Eligibility. Among the people eligible for Medicaid are those who are sixty-five and over who receive public assistance or Supplemental Security Income (SSI), or whose income and assets are judged by the local department of social services to be insufficient for their medical expenses. States vary considerably in the strictness of the income and resources standards they apply to determine eligibility.

If you have any reason to think that a parent will be in need of Medicaid assistance within the next few years, you would be well advised to take a good look at the Application for Medical Assistance. A Medicaid "kit" can be requested by phone, by letter, or in person at the local Welfare or Medicaid office of your state's department of social services. The blue pages for State Government Offices and City Government Offices in your telephone directory will have a listing for Medicaid as such under the "Social Services" heading.

When you examine the application form—which may be ten pages long—don't be daunted by the prospect of complicated procedures and detailed documentation required for establishing the proof of the statements made by your parent on the form. This documentation must be presented (photocopies may be accepted) during the personal interview by the applicant (that is, your parent), or, in cases of blindness or other disability, by you or some other representative. Among the items usually requested for inspection are all documents showing income from Social Security payments, pensions, insurance, SSI; all bankbooks; receipts for expenditures for rent and utilities; proof of age; and proof of health insurance coverage.

Any other insurance your parent has must be listed on the application form. In addition to Medicare, coverage might include Blue Cross/Blue Shield, Worker's Compensation, and third-party insurance benefits resulting from an automobile accident or other injuries. Applicants for Medicaid who are enrolled in a health maintenance organization or similar group plan should consult their Medicaid office for details on the use of Medicaid in such circumstances. Payment of health insurance premiums is one of the few legitimate deductions from gross income taken into account in establishing Medicaid eligibility.

Limits to Reserve Assets and Income. In considering Medicaid eligibility, most states limit the amount of money and property in reserve assets to under $3000 for a household of one person, and under $4500 for a household of two. Assets are defined as cash on hand, cash in savings accounts, stocks and bonds, and the cash value of a life insurance policy. The following items are *not* part of the eligibility calculation: the house (privately owned and lived in), group or other insurance with no loan value, an automobile, personal effects, and household effects.

The transfer of nonexempt property (property that is considered in establishing the allowable reserve level) for the purpose of qualifying for Medicaid may cause the applicant to be deemed ineligible. This "spending down" gambit has been considered by administrative rulings and by court decisions. If it is a relevant factor in your parents' situation, you and they should receive legal advice *before* a Medicaid application is made.

If your parent lives alone, the permissible annual income in most states is under $5000. If your parents live together, the permissible annual income for a family of two is under $7000. (These figures are on the high side of the Medicaid allowance in those states where Medicaid applicants must meet the public assistance (welfare) eligibility criteria before they can apply for medical assistance. They may be on the low side for New York and California.)

The *income* criterion is applied to items such as interest on savings, dividends from stocks, Social Security benefits, union pension payments, and in those circumstances where they are claimed as tax deductions by the donors, contributions from legally responsible family members.

Medicaid and Surplus Income. In some states—New York State is one—a person may be accepted into the Medicaid program if in any one month, his or her medical expenses are equal to or greater than the surplus income. Details about how the Surplus Income Program works are available from your parents' local Medicaid office.

Services Covered by Medicaid. People who are receiving Medicare benefits can also receive Medicaid as supplemental assistance if their eligibility is established. Medicaid will pay for certain services and items *not* covered by Medicare, and also provides necessary coverage when Medicare benefits are exhausted. In all participating states, Medicaid pays for all the following:

- Inpatient and outpatient hospital care
- Laboratory and X-ray procedures
- Skilled nursing facility services[4]
- Physicians' services
- Screening, diagnosis, and treatment of children under twenty-one
- Home health care services

4. It is under this entitlement that accredited nursing homes are reimbursed when the patient's Medicare benefits are exhausted and savings and income from other sources are inadequate. See Chapter 8.

- Family planning services[5]
- Rural health clinic services

In many states, Medicaid also pays for the following, although some restrictions may be applied:

- Care in a health-related facility
- Treatment by dentists and podiatrists
- Eye care and eyeglasses
- Hearing aids
- Treatment in a psychiatric hospital (for patients under twenty-one and over sixty-four) or in a mental health facility
- Drugs included on an official List of Medicaid Reimbursable Prescription Drugs. Those not included may be considered after a special application form is submitted.
- Physical, occupational, and speech therapy
- Transportation to Medicaid-covered services

How Medicaid Works. Applicants who are accepted into the program receive a Medicaid Identification Card. In some cases, the card is issued monthly, in others, quarterly, and for those who are expected to be permanent recipients, an ID card may be issued annually. A code letter on the card indicates the nature of the holder's entitlements.

This card must be shown to the physician, dentist, druggist, or other health care provider at the time of each visit. The recipient always asks in advance whether the provider accepts Medicaid payment. Once the provider accepts a Medicaid patient, the provider must accept payment from Medicaid as *payment in full.* The patient is asked to sign a billing form stating that the service was received. If your parents become Medicaid recipients, they should be advised *never* to sign a blank form. Eventually Medicaid may send the recipient a form to be completed in order to verify that the service for which Medicaid was billed was actually received.

Responsibilities of Medicaid Recipients. If your parents receive Medicaid benefits, they must report changes in income or assets or a change of residence to a different county or a different state. Giving false information or withholding relevant information to local social service authorities in order to qualify for Medicaid is

5. In some states, campaigns have been mounted to end Medicaid payment for abortions.

against the law. Lending or selling a Medicaid ID card is subject to severe penalties.

Legally responsible relatives are required, if able, to contribute to the support of their dependents who receive Medicaid. In the case of one's parents, this means that a spouse is responsible for a spouse. *Adult children are not legally responsible for their parents.* And as for spousal responsibilities, these are increasingly being defined by the courts, case by case. The following decision received nationwide attention:

Medicaid and Spouse Support: The Rose "Septuagenarian" Case. In January 1985, a seventy-two-year-old New York woman went into Queens County Family Court with a suit against her husband of fifty years for support payment. To preserve her anonymity, the woman is known as Rose "Septuagenarian," and by that name, the case which was decided in her favor has achieved landmark status.

This wasn't a typical case involving wrangles, rancor, and evasion of marital responsibility. At issue was the question of priorities.

The couple had been able to manage on a combined annual income of under $20,000 made up of the husband David's pension and Social Security payments, which added up to $13,750, and Rose's Social Security payments of $4800. But when David had to go into a nursing home, nearly all of *his* annual assets were used to reimburse Medicaid for the cost of his care. Presuming that the nursing home in this instance charged about $25,000 a year, Medicaid took the position that it was entitled to most of David's income. For Rose, the noninstitutionalized spouse, the Medicaid program set aside an allowance equal to the public assistance level.

Rose, however, was requesting support payments of $1225 a month, which, when combined with her own Social Security allotment, would enable her to maintain a modest standard of living instead of dooming her to a life of impoverishment for her remaining years because of her husband's illness.

The legal basis for Rose's claims was a provision in New York State's Social Service Law that exempts court-ordered support payments from consideration when Medicaid eligibility is being computed. But the New York City Department of Social Services, in contesting that position, insisted that the provision which had been cited in Rose's behalf was limited to support orders which had been issued before Medicaid funds had been extended to a patient.

Family Court Judge Jeffry H. Gallet who heard the case, ruled in favor of Rose, concluding that even though there was no prior case law or legislative history on which to base a resolution of the problem, it was appropriate in this instance to issue a support order that would shield all of David's income from the demands of Medicaid repayment. Judge Gallet also cited Section 411 of the Family Law Act, which requires that a spouse pay "fair and reasonable support" based on the parties' circumstances. He pointed out that if that law were to be subordinated to the Medicaid rule cited by the city department, many women would be effectively sentenced to "complete disruption of their lives at a time when they are extremely vulnerable," adding that a denial of Rose's support petition would be particularly unfair to the women of her generation, who "because they were denied an equal opportunity to fulfill their economic potential in the employment market, are more likely to be economically dependent on their husbands."

The judge ordered that David's entire income minus $50 a month be turned over to Rose as "spouse support." Since David was already a Medicaid patient in the nursing home, his situation remained unaltered as a result of this judgment. And since he and Rose had never been in an adversarial position, she continued to visit him regularly as before.

Anticipating that the New York City Department of Social Service and other allied agencies would appeal his judgment, Judge Gallet pointed out in his written decision that "Appellate Courts have held that spouses have a proprietary interest in their spouse's pension in matrimonial actions" and that when these courts considered the question of whether basic Social Security benefits were public assistance or insurance, they found them to be "akin to an annuity" and "not a form of public assistance." If Social Security benefits were a form of public assistance, "the petitioner would not be able to consider them a potential source for her support."

Judge Gallet has earned the gratitude not only of Rose "Septuagenarian" but also of countless women who hope that his decision will point the way for new legislation that will address itself to the problem he described so humanely and accurately. "We must note that an overwhelming majority of women are younger than their husbands. In addition, actuarial tables tell us that a woman of 70 will outlive her seventy-five-year-old husband by more than 11 years. From these facts, together with the common knowledge that medical costs for many illnesses of old age are beyond the financial means of most American families, we can reasonably draw the conclusion that husbands are more likely to require care which will deplete the marital assets than their wives, who are likely to be the economically weaker spouse."

It has been pointed out with considerable justification that, if there were a reversal of the statistics that resulted in widespread impoverishment of elderly men rather than women, state legislatures would long since have modified the Medicaid rules.

SOME LEGAL ALTERNATIVES TO "DIVORCE OR DIVEST." Farsighted lawmakers who have been doing their arithmetic homework have figured out that given the ever-growing numbers of women who will live into their eighties, it would benefit the entire community if fewer of them were forced into pauperism and public support because of Medicaid divestiture pressure. In the long run, taxpayers would have to spend fewer dollars if there were a more equitable and rational solution to the problem of the impoverishment of the noninstitutionalized spouse. As matters now stand in most states, she eventually becomes an impoverished widow on welfare for the rest of her days.

This problem is one that not only concerns the abstract "taxpayer" but is especially poignant for many of the sons and daughters of the elderly. They watch their parents "spend down" to accommodate the "minimum assets" requirements of Medicaid at the same time that they confront the tragedy of a father's impending institutionalization because of Alzheimer's disease, or they play a collusive role in the divorce of parents who have amicably agreed that their savings of a lifetime should be turned over to the spouse who is well in order to circumvent a decade or more of total penury or dependence on "the children." Surely there must be better solutions than these.

And in fact, California has already passed a law enabling a couple to sign an agreement that divides joint assets in half when one member enters a nursing home, thus protecting the funds of the uninstitutionalized spouse from the requirements of Medicaid. Advocates for the elderly are pressing for a uniform law that would make a "separation of assets" agreement an automatic legal procedure when one member is institutionalized. In this way, problems such as hiring a lawyer or getting the signature of a spouse who may be legally incompetent can be avoided.

ARE YOUR PARENTS LIKELY TO CONFRONT THIS PROBLEM? If there is any possibility that one of your parents will have to be partially or totally subsidized by Medicaid when entering a nursing facility at the same time that the other parent is well enough to remain at home, be sure to find out well in advance what steps can be taken to protect the equity of the well parent in the couple's joint assets. Such information should be available through a social service agency that has its own legal department or that can refer you to lawyers who specialize in advocacy for the aged and their families. The Bar Association in your own or your parents' area may also be called on for a suitable referral.

Supplementary Insurance: "Medigap" Policies

When older people began to realize that Medicare coverage was by no means adequate for their health care needs, they panicked about the extent of out-of-pocket costs involved in deductibles and copayments. It didn't take long for unscrupulous insurance agents to exploit these fears, with the result that their elderly victims were sometimes high pressured into buying five, six, and sometimes as many as ten policies. In the late 1970s, Congressman Claude Pepper's House Committee on Aging inaugurated hearings into what the committee staff described as a "colossal racket." Among the results of one of the committee's surveys was the revelation that the beneficiaries of more than half of the Medicare supplement policies then on the market were receiving less than fifty cents in benefits for every dollar they were paying in premiums.

Thanks to these congressional investigations and to others initiated by several states, the National Association of Insurance Commissioners developed standards for Medicare supplement policies that by 1980 became the model for laws in states where such laws did not already exist. (As of January 1986, Rhode Island and Nevada remain the only two states that have not yet passed such laws according to the NAIC.) Among the most important *minimum* legal requirements for Medicare supplement insurance policy coverage are the following:

1. Hospital copayment for days 61 to 90.
2. Hospital copayment for Medicare "lifetime reserve days."
3. Ninety percent of hospital expenses for 365 days after all Medicare benefits have been used up.

4. Twenty percent of Medicare-approved charges for Part B expenses. (A deductible of up to $200 can be required for these copayments.)
5. Claims occurring *six months or more* after the date when the policy was bought, regardless of whether the claim arises from a pre-existing condition.

Many Medicare supplement policies provide benefits that go beyond these minimum requirements. For example, in 1985, the American Association of Retired Persons (AARP) offered its members a Group Health Insurance Program Medicare Supplement Plus Plan with the Prudential Insurance Company of America, for a monthly premium of $19.50. The AARP plan covers the claims shown in the chart on page 166.

Medicare's deductibles and copayments effective January 1, 1985.
* In each calendar year, you must pay the first $200 of Medicare eligible expenses not paid by Medicare. These expenses must be incurred while you are covered by this plan.

DEFINITIONS

Skilled nursing facility and hospital means a Medicare-approved institution in which confinement is medically necessary. The skilled nursing care received must meet applicable standards of medical practice and be of the type eligible under Medicare Part A. Confinement in a skilled nursing facility must begin within thirty days of a hospital stay (of at least three days) or a prior skilled nursing facility stay and be for the same condition. *Custodial care does not qualify as an eligible expense.*

Benefit period means a period of time, determined under Medicare. It begins with the day you enter a hospital as an inpatient and ends when you have been out of a hospital or skilled nursing facility for sixty days in a row.

Other Possibilities for Medigap Coverage

If your parents haven't considered participation in this type of group coverage, or if they don't have the option of a continuation of group coverage when they retire from a job, they can investigate the Medicare Supplement policies offered to *individuals*. For example, for an annual premium of approximately $440 payable

	EACH BENEFIT PERIOD	MEDICARE PAYS	AARP's MEDICARE SUPPLEMENT PLUS PAYS YOU
MEDICARE PART A HOSPITALIZATION	Days 1-60	All but $400.00	$400.00
	Days 61-90	All but $100.00 a day	$100.00 a day
	Day 91+	All but $200.00 a day (only if using "Lifetime Reserve Days")	$200.00 a day (60 day maximum when not using "Lifetime Reserve Days")
	Day 91+	Nothing after "Lifetime Reserve Days" are exhausted	100% of eligible expenses up to lifetime maximum of 365 days
MEDICARE PART A SKILLED NURSING FACILITY	Days 1-20	All eligible expenses	Nothing. Benefits are paid by Medicare
	Days 21-100	All but $50.00 a day	$50.00 a day
	Days 101-365	Nothing	$100.00 a day
MEDICARE PART B DOCTORS' CARE	For any calendar year	80% of eligible expenses (after $75 deductible)	Remaining 20% of Medicare eligible expenses (after $200 deductible)*
IN-HOSPITAL PRIVATE DUTY NURSING	Day 1 through duration of hospital-ization	Nothing	Up to $30.00 per 8 hour shift for Registered Nurse . . . Up to $25.00 per 8 hour shift for Licensed Practical (Vocational) Nurse. Up to 3 shifts per day, 60 shifts per Benefit Period for RN and LPN combined.

quarterly, a Blue Cross/Blue Shield policy in this category provides the following when combined with Medicare: 455 days of full coverage for hospital confinement, and 100 days of full coverage in a skilled nursing facility; the supplemental surgical-medical benefits include 20 percent payment of Medicare's approved charge for services received while an inpatient in a hospital, for outpatient emergency care for accidental injury, and for ambulatory dialysis or surgery anywhere. This particular individual Medigap policy also covers extensive home health care benefits as an alternative to hospitalization or confinement in a skilled nursing facility.

If you're helping your parents evaluate various offerings of Medicare supplement coverage, remember to find out whether they are eligible for Medicaid *before* they invest in any other coverage. If they meet the requirements for Medicaid in their state, then Medicaid becomes their Medicare supplement.

Health Maintenance Organizations (HMOs). Until comparatively recently, membership in health maintenance organizations operating for the profit of the participating doctors and hospitals had been restricted for the most part to people who were still gainfully employed and their families. This restricted market was preferred because the health care costs of a younger and healthier part of the population are obviously lower than those of the over-sixty-five group. Older people are a riskier investment because they are likelier to have chronic illness and to require expensive diagnostic tests and more extensive hospitalization. Recently, however, Medicare and Medicaid have been encouraging their beneficiaries to use HMOs precisely because they reduce health care costs by cutting down on what have been called "unnecessary" medical procedures and hospitalization. (Since HMOs make *preventive* health care a top priority, periodic checkups can discover early onset of a condition that is treatable on an outpatient basis.)

Beginning in 1985, Medicare began to prepay for services provided by HMOs, paying 95 percent of the average cost per patient in the particular HMO service area. This figure translates into an average payment of about $2200 per person per year. According to the Department of Health and Human Services, the number of HMOs nationwide with which Medicare contracted for services has increased from 70 in 1985 to 164 by January 1986, and of the

18 million HMO members, more than 600,000 are Medicare beneficiaries.

HOW HMOS WORK. A health maintenance organization is a prepaid plan that combines the functions of an insurance company *and* a doctor/hospital. Instead of paying a regular premium to the insurance company, then, in case of illness, paying the doctor at the time of the visit, and then having to wait (sometimes for more than a month) for reimbursement, payment is made *only* to the HMO. Thus, in return for the prepaid premium, health care costs are covered and the health care itself is provided.

When Medicare signs a contract with a particular HMO, the prepayment plan must offer at least all the services offered by Medicare, and it may offer additional services as well. Some of these extra services may be offered free; others may require additional prepayments.

There are two basic types of health maintenance organizations: group practice and individual practice. Group practice HMOs must be affiliated with a hospital and provide services at one or more central locations. In other words, your parent would have to go to the center for all treatment. Therefore, in most parts of the country, a switch to an HMO means that your parent would give up the freedom to choose any doctor or hospital. However, the "individual practice" HMO that most companies and hospitals are offering in the New York area and in some large cities elsewhere permit patients to receive care in a doctor's office—even the doctor they go to now—as long as the doctor participates in the HMO. For doctors who join such organizations, the trade-off consists in giving up some of their private practice fees in exchange for a guaranteed monthly payment for each patient that the HMO assigns to them. In addition to this guaranteed income, participating doctors share in the profits of the organization.

In most cases, both the group and the individual type limit their membership to people living within the specified area of the affiliated doctors and facilities. This is called the HMO service area. Both types use affiliated hospitals and skilled nursing facilities (nursing homes) when inpatient care of this type is required. Some of the largest group practice HMOs own their own hospitals.

In the typical HMO, a member is assigned a primary care physician who usually has been trained as an internist or a family practitioner. Specialists are available in those areas specified in the member's coverage. These usually include eye care, hearing, arthritis, heart and circulatory disease, gynecology, urology, surgery, and pathology. In addition to a staff of physicians, HMOs often make use of qualified nurse-practitioners or physician assistants to handle routine patient visits. Laboratory and radiology services are likely to be available in the same center.

THE COMPETITION GROWS. Blue Cross/Blue Shield, which has been one of the most active not-for-profit providers of supplementary insurance to Medicare beneficiaries, has now become an aggressive competitor for HMO dollars. For example, *Total Health Care 65* is a federally qualified health maintenance organization sponsored by Blue Cross/Blue Shield of Kansas City, Missouri. In its promotional literature this HMO ("It's Medicare and much more!") offers a comprehensive health care plan that, in addition to Medicare benefits, pays for:

> Unlimited hospitalization
> Unlimited physician services
> Routine vision and hearing services
> Preventive services
> Private duty nursing ($2000 annual maximum)
> Prescription drugs ($5 per thirty-four-day supply)
> Expanded skilled nursing facility benefits

These and other services not covered or only partially covered by Medicare are provided for monthly premium payments ranging (in 1986) from $23.68 for males and $19.92 for females in the 65–69 age group, to $36.63 for males and $32.87 for females in the 80–84 age group.

In the promotional literature, the following answer is given to explain why the monthly premiums are lower than the average supplementary plan:

> Total Health Care . . . believes that access to preventive care ultimately reduces the need for more expensive acute care. By providing fully covered health checkups, tests, and other early detection medical services, experience shows that *Total Health Care 65* will spend less on hospitalizations, surgeries, and other treatment for advanced disease.

Unlike some HMOs whose roster of primary care physicians and hospital affiliations is limited to a particular area, this particular plan points out that while medical services for members must be "performed, prescribed, or authorized" by a primary care physician chosen from its register of more than a hundred private practice physicians located throughout the metropolitan Kansas City area, "It is entirely possible that your current physician is a *Total Health Care 65* physician." And when the need for a specialist or hospital care arises, "Virtually all specialists and hospitals in the Kansas City area are available. Over 850 specialists have contracted for the program."

There is, however, an "Important Notice" included in the brochure, which says, in part:

> If the doctor you currently see is not on the enclosed list of . . . physicians, then you must change doctors. After joining *Total Health Care 65*, any medical care you receive must be coordinated by your Primary Care Physician. If you see another physician, or if you are hospitalized without authorization from your Primary Care Physician, then neither *Total Health Care 65* nor Medicare will pay the bills. You and your Primary Care Physician will be partners in keeping you healthy and arranging for proper medical care when you need it.

It is this aspect of HMOs—the "coordination by your Primary Care Physician," who is referred to in some quarters as "the gatekeeper"—that has come under critical scrutiny by many advocates of quality health care for the elderly. If the primary care physician has to approve all referrals to a specialist, and if—as is the case in many HMO plans—the primary care physician is provided with a financial incentive *not* to make such referrals, then specialist referral and hospitalization may be deferred and withheld not on the basis of medical criteria but because of economic considerations. Also, if *efficient* "cost containment" leads to an increase in the profits shared by HMO doctors, who decides whether a particular medical procedure, test, or hospital inpatient assignment is "unnecessary"?

If your parents are considering membership in a health maintenance organization, here are some factors to be weighed:

ADVANTAGES

- Because HMOs work within a budget, *preventive* health care is a top priority.
- The fixed premium covers comprehensive services, thus making it possible to calculate annual health care expenses in advance.
- Your parents are spared the nuisance of filling out reimbursement forms and having to wait to be repaid for out-of-pocket payments to physicians.

- All health services—laboratories, X-ray services, pharmacies, as well as the prime care physician and specialists—are conveniently located in one area.
- Periodic checkups that are rarely performed as part of conventional insurance plans keep patients informed about the onset of conditions that need attention, sometimes even before any symptoms appear.
- Since all the patient's medical records are in one place, they are available on a twenty-four-hour-a-day, seven-day-a-week basis. This easy access can be a big help in an emergency.
- Because of the competitive situation that has developed in health insurance, HMOs may prove to be the best value for the money spent.

DISADVANTAGES

- In many HMOs, participants have practically no choice of physician or hospital.
- The only Medicare-contracted HMO in the area may be inconvenient to get to, especially in an emergency. If you're the family member who chauffeurs your parents to and from doctors' appointments, the distance involved should be taken into consideration.
- Since participation in only *one* HMO is permitted, membership isn't practical if your parents move from one part of their state to another—or to another state altogether—when the seasons change, unless arrangements can be made with a reciprocating HMO.
- Since groups vary in their benefits, a careful check must be made before joining.
- Because until the recent implementation of Medicare reimbursement, very few people over sixty-five were enrolled in HMOs (the AARP put this figure at 5 percent in 1985), not many HMO doctors have had extensive experience in dealing with geriatric problems.
- If your parents have maintained a more than satisfactory relationship with their prime care physician over a long period, no other doctor may compare favorably no matter how competent he or she is.

AND SOME CAUTIONARY QUESTIONS

- Have you asked family members and your parents' friends who are HMO participants and Medicare recipients whether they intend to renew their contracts?
- If your parents have some other health plan that supplements Medicare, have they checked the comparative benefits?
- Have they visited the HMO center and been cordially received when they—and you—ask questions such as:

How long does it take to get an appointment?
What kind of certification do the physicians have?
Are they board-certified in their specialties?
Does the HMO include a neurologist and a proctologist?
Do members have the right to a second opinion?
Does the HMO have more than one hospital connection?
How much time is the patient expected to spend with doctors' assistants and other paraprofessionals rather than with the doctors themselves?
If the area HMO is *not* contracted with Medicare, what are the rights of Medicare recipients?

If you can't keep all these questions in mind when you and your parents make your inspection visit, jot them down on a slip of paper and leave plenty of room for the answers.

———————

With funding from the Health Care Financing Administration of the U.S. Department of Health and Human Services, the AARP has been conducting a consumer education program to familiarize Medicare recipients with the advantages of HMO participation. Trained volunteers have been addressing senior citizen groups, religious organizations, and AARP chapter meetings in five targeted areas: Philadelphia, Detroit, Tampa, Bridgeport/New Haven, and San Francisco/Oakland. The organization has also prepared a free booklet, "More Health for Your Dollar—An Older Person's Guide to HMOs." Send your request to:

AARP, P.O. Box 2400, Long Beach, California 90801

The Health Care Financing Administration has also prepared a booklet called "Medicare and Prepayment Plans: Health Maintenance Organizations and Competitive Medical

Plans." The booklet can be obtained at local Social Security offices.

Private Hospitals Selling Health Insurance. The latest development in the health insurance field and one likely to have far-reaching consequences is the challenge to nonprofit organizations such as Blue Cross/Blue Shield by private, profit-seeking hospital chains. The chains entered the insurance business at about the same time that the federal government replaced its system of reimbursing hospitals for costs with the DRG system of predetermined payments which is now in effect.

Most hospital chain insurance plans have a ceiling on lifetime benefits, and by offering special discounts, they expect subscribers to use the private hospitals that are part of their corporate arrangement. Blue Cross/Blue Shield and similar health insurance companies do not impose limitations on benefits for "high-risk" participants, and these companies have been and continue to be committed to freedom of choice (except when the company also offers an HMO plan).

Hospital chains, which typically consist of hundreds of private hospitals in various parts of the country under one corporate management, have been buying large insurance companies in order to be able to sell health insurance in various states. This strategy would appear to guarantee full use of private hospital beds by the subscribers.

As of September 1986, it is not yet clear what the relationship will be between these incorporated private hospitals and the Medicare/Medicaid programs. What *is* an important factor is that some states (including New York State) have enacted legislation prohibiting hospital chains from *owning* hospitals, even though they may manage them.

In a recent interview Dr. Paul Elwood, the health specialist who conceived of and named health maintenance organizations, said that "conventional health insurance is dead," and with hospital chains moving into insurance, "we're witnessing the industrialization of medicine. We're going to end up with the majority of medical care in the U.S. delivered by 10 to 15 corporations. These will be 'supermeds' replacing individual physicians, staffs, clinics, hospitals, and insurance companies."[6]

6. New York *Times,* July 5, 1985.

The response of the American Medical Association to this vision of the future will have a great deal to do with whether the prophecy becomes fact. In the meantime, families with aging parents who are trying to figure out the most advantageous ways of extending their insurance coverage should keep an eye on this new development and how they will be affected by it.

Some of the corporate entities to watch are American Medical International, based in Beverly Hills, California, with a chain of 129 hospitals offering a health insurance plan known as *Amicare;* the Nashville-based Hospital Corporation of America, which owns and operates 360 hospitals and promotes the *PriMed* health insurance plan; and the Louisville-based Humana Corporation, with 84 private hospitals under its wing and an insurance plan called *Humana Care Plus.*

Some Final Suggestions

- If your parent is between ages sixty-five and sixty-nine and has on-the-job health insurance coverage in addition to Medicare, he or she should find out about continuing membership following retirement. All options offered by a former employer or by a union should be investigated.
- Some people buy more policies than they need. It's more effective to have a single comprehensive policy that *adds* to Medicare coverage rather than several small ones whose benefits duplicate each other.
- If you're helping your parent read promotional brochures, be sure to check for exclusions for preexisting conditions. If, for example, your father has a history of glaucoma treatment and he fractures his leg in a fall, the insurer may refuse to honor his claim because it is attributable to bad eyesight.
- Advise your parents to avoid any policy that insures against a specific disease. The more inclusive the policy, the better.
- When your parents consider policies that supplement their Medicare benefits, be sure they understand what "gaps" are covered.
- Since HMOs differ in their cost, convenience, and flexibility, all available plans should be closely compared.
- Some policies are automatically renewable for life. Your parents should avoid any policy that gives the company the right to refuse renewal on an individual basis.
- Every state has consumer protection laws that dictate the way insurance companies must function. An insurance agent must

be licensed by the state, and your parents have a right to ask to see that license.

- If any irregularities are suspected, or if you have any complaints on behalf of your parents, you can bring these to the attention of the Better Business Bureau in your area or to the Consumer Service Department of the state's Insurance Department.

A GUIDE TO HEALTH INSURANCE FOR PEOPLE WITH MEDICARE is a detailed brochure developed jointly by the National Association of Insurance Commissioners and the Health Care Financing Administration of the U.S. Department of Health and Human Services. It is updated regularly and is available free at all Social Security offices.

❧ 6 ❧

ADULT DAY CARE:
A RECENT DEVELOPMENT

The myth may be the sanctity of the family, but the reality is
inadequate day care for the very young and the old at a time when
more women than ever are working because they must. And it
should be painfully clear by now that when it comes to providing
creative solutions to social problems, "the private sector" isn't
going to be heard from if the solution doesn't involve taking
money to the bank.

The concept of day care for the elderly doesn't take much imagination. It has been a flourishing institution in several European
countries for quite a while. But it took a combination of circumstances to get the movement going in this country: more and more
of the primary caregivers—the daughters and daughters-in-law—
working full time; increasing criticism of the premature and unsuitable institutionalization of the elderly; the success of several
pilot programs; and finally, in 1979, the organization of the National Institute on Adult Daycare as a unit of the National Council on the Aging.

Since its beginnings, the institute has been the focal point for
adult day care activity. It has promoted the concept as a practical
community-based option for disabled older people. It has provided the technical assistance necessary for establishing new programs. It has formulated standards and urged their adoption so
that an adult day care center in Maine functions in the same
civilized, professional, and humane way as a center in Virginia. In
addition, the institute promotes the improvement of services
through an exchange of information at national and regional seminars, and stimulates research projects whose results can form the
basis of practical solutions to such problems as interim care for

Alzheimer patients and how best to combine day care and home care as an alternative to institutionalization.

Soon after the creation of the National Institute on Adult Daycare, in April 1980, the subcommittee on Health and Long Term Care of the House of Representatives Select Committee on Aging conducted hearings on adult day care programs. During these hearings, advocates stressed the effectiveness of the already existing programs in terms of cost to the federal government and benefits to the participants. To the aging and their families, it had become obvious that adult day care was a concept whose practical applications were long overdue. To legislators, it was becoming apparent that they were expected to get moving.

In 1982, the National Institute on Adult Daycare initiated the celebration of the first National Adult Day Care Center Week. By 1983, there were over nine hundred centers in cities, counties, and towns nationwide in every state except Wyoming and New Hampshire. When President Reagan proclaimed the celebratory week the following year, he was joined by proclamations from governors, mayors, and county officials from coast to coast. And by 1984, the institute announced that these programs "are indeed bridging the gap between independent living and long-term institutionalization, making a positive difference in the lives of disabled adults and their families."

EXACTLY WHAT IS ADULT DAY CARE?

Adult day care is the general term for a wide range of programs offering community-based services in a group setting to older, functionally impaired adults, to younger disabled adults, and to their families and caregivers. Such programs are also known as geriatric day care, day health care, and day hospital care. Their main focus is to maintain or improve the level of mentally or physically impaired adults who can't be left alone during the day, yet who don't need round-the-clock nursing care.

Well-run programs have many obvious advantages: They offer their participants the opportunity to spend their days in a stimulating environment of their peers at the same time that they receive supportive professional attention, *and* they offer concerned sons and daughters as well as caregiving spouses a positive and practical alternative to the premature and inappropriate institutionalization of a parent—or husband or wife.

What's the Difference Between a Senior Center and Adult Day Care?

Senior centers were originally established to provide social activities for older people who were essentially able to manage their own lives and who weren't in need of daily supportive services. Of the more than five thousand senior centers nationwide, many offer much more than coffee and conversation. Some act as a clearinghouse for information about legal and financial problems. Many participate in the federally funded hot meal program, and a large number count on the services of a social worker who plans outings, classes, and fund-raising parties. But senior centers do not offer an *individualized* plan of medical and social services for each participant.

An adult day care center, on the other hand, expects participants to attend on a scheduled basis so that they can benefit from a suitable combination of the following services in addition to supervision and daily hot meals and snacks: transportation, exercise, occupational therapy, counseling, ongoing medical and social evaluation, regularly scheduled health screening, reality orientation, physical and/or speech therapy. The participant's changing condition and the recommendations of the physician in charge are the most important considerations in determining the program. If, for example, your father enters a day care program after being hospitalized for a mild stroke that somewhat impaired his speech and the use of one hand, his doctor will recommend speech therapy and physical therapy. When maximum results have been achieved in these two areas, a new evaluation may find that he should be spending time with the reality orientation group. A woman recently widowed and immobilized by grief may have to spend many sessions with a bereavement counselor. As she regains her emotional equilibrium, her doctor may recommend that her program be changed to include participation in exercise classes as therapy for her arthritis.

An adult day care center may be directly connected with a local hospital or clinic, or it may be a separate facility that uses some of the professional services of a nursing home. In some communities where social services are planned with imagination and good sense, adult day care centers are being established back-to-back with child day care centers to encourage interaction between the generations. By creating a sense of family and mutual dependence, this arrangement can be a happy experience for young and old alike.

SOME PIONEERING PROGRAMS

Here are three adult day care programs that have served as models for many others that followed. All three originated in the 1970s, and though their participants varied as a group from each other, each program enabled the elderly for whom it was designed to maintain as much independence as possible in a familiar community setting.

The day care center in Omaha, Nebraska, is situated in an area where one quarter of the population is over sixty-five, and of these, many live in rural isolation. It is seven miles from the Archbishop Bergan Mercy Hospital, which coordinates the day care services with a home health care program. As described by Sister Stella M. Neill, its first director, the center's staff includes a social worker, a supervisor, a geriatric technician, and an activity coordinator.[1] The hospital provides the services of a registered nurse, and its dietary department prepares and delivers hot meals every day. Occupational, physical, and speech therapy are available as needed. Other services include housing assistance and counseling, health education, nutrition information, group discussions, and community excursions. Volunteers are brought into the center to organize Bible study, foreign language sessions, and arts and crafts activities. The daily fee of $15 (in 1981) also covers two-way transportation within a five-mile radius. When the participants' charts were reviewed several years ago, results indicated that more than half were living alone, and about one third used the facility only twice a week.

Since 1975, the Support Center in Wheaton, Maryland, has been serving about twenty-four participants—blacks, Hispanics, Caucasians, some on Medicaid, many paying privately—elderly men and women with Alzheimer's, arthritis, parkinsonism, and the aftereffects of a stroke.[2] Most live with their families, some live in foster homes, and a few live alone. Essential forms of therapy are provided when prescribed by a physician. The center transports its members to medical and dental appointments if caregiv-

---

1. Hospital Progress, March 1981.
2. Frances Goldstein and Stephanie Egly, "Adult Day Care: An Extension of the Family," *Aging,* No. 348, 1985.

ers aren't able to take time off from work to do so. The physical setting is attractively furnished and decorated. A small kitchen enables participants to prepare special treats, and the resident pet is a tame rabbit who likes to be cuddled. In addition to a well-run arts and crafts program, activities include "armchair travel," during which a particular country becomes the focus of attention. The resource librarian supplies books, films, and slide shows, and when Greece was the favored place, the proper ethnic foods were prepared. According to the authors' account, everyone enjoyed the egg lemon soup and the Greek salad.

The Wheaton Center is funded in a variety of ways: The Maryland Department of Health and Hygiene has provided a grant that subsidizes care for low- and moderate-income participants; Medicaid certification of the center enables it to receive reimbursement for the clients who receive Medicaid. Private participants are charged from $20 to $33 a day depending on their financial resources. Donations from community groups are sometimes spent on essentials, but often they are used for art materials, records, and the extras that enrich daily experience.

Part of the success of this center is attributable to an active and involved board of directors consisting of nine representatives from private and public life who function on a volunteer basis. The fact that several board members are the sons and daughters of parents who used to be participants of the center is a special acknowledgment of its important role in family life in the community.

The program known as Geriatric Day Care was established in the Bronx, in the early 1970s, at the Jewish Home and Hospital for the Aged, one of the oldest, largest, and most respected nonprofit geriatric centers in the United States. This program, the first of its kind in New York City, has pointed the way for similar services elsewhere, especially in those communities where supplementary health services are not easily available. To be eligible, the participant must live within a radius of about 3½ miles of city streets, be sixty years old or older, ambulatory and continent, and capable of eating a meal without help. The participant must also be the patient of a primary care physician in the community with whom the day care personnel can remain in close contact so that continuing readjustments can be made in daily health and medical services.

A complete physical examination is required at the time of admission and once a year thereafter. On the basis of the results, medical, emotional, social, and nursing needs are evaluated so that an individual treatment plan can be developed. Among the supplementary services are psychiatric consultation, hearing tests, dentistry, ophthalmology, and podiatry. Occupational, physical, and speech therapies are integrated into the daily schedule when the need is present. Social services are available to participants and members of their family. In addition to a hot meal and snacks every day, birthday parties, planned entertainment, and other recreations are part of the program. Shopping days are scheduled for wardrobe replenishment. An annual outing for lunch in a restaurant is a special event, and every effort is made to help these group members to maintain their strong community ties. And just as they go into the community as part of the program, the resources of the community come to them in dance performances, concerts, slide shows, and lectures on current events.

The participants are a pretty lively bunch. Of the current group of seventy-five, sixty-five live alone, eight live with a spouse, and only two live with another family member. There are about six times as many women as men. Some come to the center only two or three days a week; others are there for the five weekdays and the Sunday program. Most have sons and daughters who live in the metropolitan area—in Westchester or Long Island—and both generations feel that geriatric day care is a practical solution that provides peace of mind for the children while preserving autonomy for the parents. A goodly number also depend on the assistance of a visiting housekeeper (not provided by the center) who comes by several times a week to help with cleaning, laundry, marketing, and other tasks.

Like most programs of this kind, it is reimbursable by Medicaid. Patients in a position to pay are billed at $35.50 a day, and any cost of services exceeding this amount is absorbed by the program.

Additional information about this program can be obtained from:

The Jewish Home and Hospital for the Aged
Kingsbridge Center, Greenwall Pavilion
2545 University Avenue, Bronx, New York 10468
(212) 579-0220

GERIATRIC DAY CARE FOR THE BLIND AND THE VISUALLY IMPAIRED

According to the National Institute on Adult Daycare, there are currently only two programs in the United States offering comprehensive day care services for an elderly person with severe sight impairment. Both programs, one in the Bronx, the other in the city of Yonkers in New York, have been developed under the auspices of the Jewish Guild for the Blind, a nonsectarian, nonprofit agency that has been a pioneer since 1914 in responding to community needs.

Like the Geriatric Day Care program, the Guild Day Care program in the Bronx is affiliated with the Jewish Home and Hospital for the Aged, and it offers similar services, plus vision rehabilitation, adaptation training in regaining skills and personal confidence in cooking, dressing, and maintaining personal hygiene. Activities that foster independence and pride include adult education courses, discussion groups, a variety of crafts, and participation in exercise and dance.

The Guild Day Care program in Yonkers, which is associated with the Home for the Aged Blind, is run in much the same way. Both programs are reimbursable by Medicaid, or participants may pay on a private basis.

Additional information about the Guild program for Bronx residents is available by calling (212) 579-0502. If your parent is a suitable applicant and is a resident of southern Westchester, you can find out more about the Guild program in Yonkers by calling (212) 365-3700 or (914) 963-4661.

A SAMPLING OF DAY CARE PROGRAMS NATIONWIDE

Montana continues to be the only state that offers no adult day care services (as of 1986); and practically everywhere else, the availability of such services is woefully inadequate to the growing need for them. If there's a well-run program in your parents' area, do what you can to keep it going. And if a good day care center is needed to ease their situation and yours, do what you can to rally community support for establishing one.

Here's a sampling of current services:

ALASKA   While adult day care services are limited, of the four centers in the state, the one in Anchorage is also an Alzheimer's Disease Center that operates Monday through Friday from 7:30 A.M. to 5 P.M.

HAWAII   According to a recent report by the governor on long-term care resources, Hawaiians live longer than the elderly in any other state and are second only to the Swedish for longevity in the entire world. Taking this factor into account, the state sponsors many facilities for the aging, among which are a variety of day care centers. As officially defined, day care for the elderly means "an organized program of personal care, social service, therapy, group and leisure activities during part of the day in a licensed facility." (Hawaii is one of the states that has formulated standards for licensing. One requirement is that there must be one staff member for every six participants.) Centers vary in their admission requirements, special services, and fees. The Central Oahu Senior Day Care Center, which is open five days a week, is for disabled seniors fifty years old or older who can't be left alone for long periods. The fees are $310 per month, $17 per day, plus a nominal fee for a hot meal.

The only facility on the island of Hawaii is the Hilo Center, which offers transportation, hot lunches and snacks, physical therapy and massage, individual counseling, health screening, excursions, dance and exercise, health care, and remotivation therapy. It has also established a "reminiscence" program, in which the elderly participants whose memory may be failing, or whose sense of self is increasingly threatened by isolation, have the opportunity to talk about their accomplishments of the past, when they were competent parents, important wage earners, respected citizens. Shared reminiscence in a group directed by a trained counselor can restore self-esteem and thereby lighten the burden of depression in old age.

The Hilo Center accepts older adults who are ambulatory but with a physical or mental handicap that necessitates protective or supportive care during the day, those who are socially impaired or isolated, and stroke victims in need of speech and physical therapy. Referrals to this center are made by hospitals, by social workers, by health agencies, and by family application. Fees are $300 per month, with state reimbursement of $275 for those who are eligible. Financial assistance on various levels is based on individual assessment.

The Wilcox Adult Day Care Center in Lihue on the island of Kauai specializes in Alzheimer patients and offers reality orientation and reminiscing programs in addition to other basic services, including a staff member trained in first aid and in working with the disabled elderly.

ILLINOIS   Adult day care in this state is part of a well-organized Community Care Program. The 1986 plan presented by the Department on Aging defines the service in the following way: Direct care and supervision of adults over sixty outside the individual's home for any portion of the twenty-four-hour day in order to provide personal attention, promote social, physical, and emotional well-being, and offer alternatives to institutional care. Activities include development of a participant care plan based on the recommendations of the individual's personal physician; assistance with personal care and hygiene; leisure-time activities and recreation; preparing and administering medications, changing dressings, and the like; continuing physical assessment with suitable exercise and treatment programs; a daily congregate meal and snacks; two-way transportation; maintaining the participant's record; and providing information about and referral to other social services.

RHODE ISLAND   As described by the Department of Elderly Affairs, "Elderly day care is designed especially for convalescing seniors and for family situations in which home care for an elderly person strains family relations. This 5-day per week program can supplement home care and enable frail elderly persons to remain in their own home. Day care centers provide transportation, lunch, health services, group activities, social rehabilitation, and recreational activities. Payment for services is generally based on a sliding scale." As of 1986, the state maintains eleven centers.

VIRGINIA   In 1978, the Department for the Aging established the Virginia Institute on Adult Day Care, which was given the responsibility for "working in communities to support the impaired elderly and their families." The institute was one of the earliest agencies of this kind in the United States, and since that time has organized fifteen centers offering a broad range of services.

If your parents live in a state that does *not* license adult day care programs and you'd like to evaluate a particular program on your own, you can send for "Standards for Adult Day Care," prepared by the National Council on the Aging. Send your request with a check or money order for $7.50 to the Council at:

> 600 Maryland Avenue, S.W., West Wing 100
> Washington, D.C. 20024

If you would like some guidelines based on the standards set forth in this publication, here is a partial list of things to look for:

HOW TO EVALUATE AN ADULT DAY CARE FACILITY

1. Ask to see the written policy statement which spells out the target population served by the facility.
2. Find out whether there is a policy of excluding people with a history of violent or antisocial behavior or who are actively alcoholic or drug addicted.
3. Do records of individual participants include: Medical and assessment information regularly brought up-to-date? Signed authorization for medical emergency care if necessary? Reports on the participant's activities?
4. The ratio of staff to participants should be one to eight. If the program serves an especially high percentage of severely impaired men and women, the ratio should be one to five. (Volunteers included in these calculations should meet the same job qualifications as paid staff members.)
5. Staff members should include:
   - An experienced *director,* preferably one who has a professional degree in the field of health and human services.
   - A trained *social worker* or counselor who, in addition to other duties, meets regularly with family members and who can provide them with necessary information about community resources and entitlements.
   - A *registered nurse* or a licensed practical nurse supervised by an RN.

- An *activities director* with an academic degree in a field related to occupational therapy, therapeutic recreation through the arts, or physical education.
- Licensed therapists (as regular staff members or consultants) with state credentials in physical, speech, and occupational therapy.

6. Each participant's plan should include:
   - An assessment of needs, objectives of care, and specific activities for the achievement of these objectives.
   - Regular reassessment of this plan as necessary, or at least every six months.
7. One midday meal should be part of every participant's program, and this meal should provide one third of an adult's nutritional requirements (modifications recommended by the physician in the diet should be followed as necessary).
8. In addition to meeting the participant's physical requirements, programs should be planned around intellectual, cultural, social, and emotional needs.
9. A monthly calendar of activities and menus should be prepared and posted and copies made available to family members as requested.
10. Meetings of participants should be scheduled so that they can make recommendations to the staff.
11. In assessing the inside and outside of the facility, check the following:
    - Accommodations for the physically handicapped
    - Adequacy of lighting in all areas
    - Noise levels and soundproofing
    - Temperature control
    - Availability of comfortable furniture, cheerful furnishings, and generally attractive decor
    - Safety equipment
    - Procedures for fire safety and fire drills
    - Sanitary storing and preparation of food

RESPITE CARE

Respite care is an offshoot of adult day care. Neither of these services should be confused with informal, improvisational arrangements made for the temporary convenience of caregivers and their charges. If you're the prime caregiver of your ailing father, and you're going on a week's vacation (for *respite* from this responsibility), you might ask his sister to take care of him in your absence, or if his live-in home aide has a family crisis of her own to attend to, her informal respite arrangement might involve having your father stay with you while she's gone. Under the best circumstances, respite care, like adult day care, is administered by an official agency which sets guidelines for how a service is to be operated and funded.

On a nationwide basis, respite programs differ widely depending on their setting and the services they offer. Whether the dependent elderly person participates on an occasional and temporary basis or on a regular weekly or monthly schedule, *the basic purpose is to provide a period of relief for the family member or members responsible for primary care.* While respite care isn't meant to replace other specialized services, it is another community-based option designed to reduce family stress and help to prevent the premature institutionalizing of aging parents.

According to the National Institute on Daycare, the respite care programs administered by Wisconsin's Office on Aging have been models for the rest of the country. As described in that office's *Handbook of Caregiver Support Resources,* state funding has been made available "for the purpose of determining what constitutes an effective system of community based respite care that meets the needs of the families of the several dependent populations." Pilot projects have been established throughout the state in a variety of community-based settings: the home of the caregiver, a foster family or group home very near the family, or an adult day care facility.

Among the factors that have been deemed basic to the success of a respite care program are the establishment of an advisory committee, accessible and ongoing public information, an experienced community coordinator, an adequate supply of capable respite workers, a worker training program, and continuing coordination and cooperation with other service agencies.

In many states, respite care can be provided on a temporary basis by a local geriatric center which offers round-the-clock services that include professional nursing care as well as supervised social activities. In New York State, for example, the cost of respite stay in an institution ranges from about $25 to $75 a day, and stays may be as brief as a weekend or as long as a month.

The New York State Association of Homes for the Aging has been testing the concept of temporary institutional care in a project that involves eight facilities. Additional information about the facilities offering short-term respite care is available by writing to the association at 194 Washington Avenue, Albany, New York 12210, or by phoning (518) 449-2702.

HOW IS ADULT DAY CARE PAID FOR?

If your parent is a Medicaid recipient, full payment for participation in a day care program is provided in many states, including New York State. If your parent doesn't qualify for Medicaid and is sixty-five years old or older, Medicare will pay for only those aspects of day care that are part of a rehabilitation program authorized by a physician—specifically for physical and/or speech therapy. In some states, coverage for day care is provided by private health insurance.

Unfortunately, funding by the government and by private groups for day care and respite services is based on the arbitrary distinction between "social needs," for which no money is available, and "skilled nursing care," which is covered as a "medical" benefit. However, thanks to the combined efforts of the National Institute on Adult Day Care, enlightened policymakers, and such advocacy groups as the Children of Aging Parents, the AARP, the Gray Panthers, and others, there is an ever-increasing awareness of the need for a more realistic and humane solution to the problems associated with the continuum of long-term care.

Information about adult day care centers can be provided by your parents' physician, the social service department of the local hospital, community service organizations, and the area office of the state's Department on Aging.

❧ 7 ❧

HOME CARE:
HOW EVERYONE BENEFITS

Home care is becoming increasingly accepted as the wave of the future in long-term care—more appropriate for the majority of older people than a nursing home and generally less costly as well. And we have made a great deal of progress in the last few years in expanding the availability of home care under Medicare. . . .

Congressman Claude Pepper[1]

Clearly society has to respond to its older people in new ways, when the older segment of the population is increasing three times faster than its younger population. The real need is for an integrated array of services delivered in the elderly person's own community. If there were an adequate social support system for the elderly, many of the 12 to 18 percent of them who are now in institutions could be cared for at home. Inadequacies in our present long-term care system will multiply until we can offer a complete and integrated package of health and human services to the elderly.

Janet S. Sainer, Commissioner of
the New York City Department for
the Aging[2]

$4 Million Project Seeks to Keep the Aged Home
Headline, New York *Times*[3]

Until comparatively recently, there has been a widespread prejudice on the part of the health care system against paying for *any* in-home services for the aging. Nowadays, thanks to mounting pressures from advocates for the aging and their families as well

1. *Ask Claude Pepper* (Doubleday, Garden City, N.Y.).
2. Roberta S. Brill, "New York City Home Care Project: A Coordinated Health and Social Service Approach," *Aging,* March-April 1982.
3. September 15, 1985.

as increasing evidence of the cost-effectiveness of home care, more and more temporarily disabled and chronically enfeebled older people are being rehabilitated and maintained at home. And without a doubt, that's where they prefer to be, rather than in a hospital or a nursing home.

The United States spends about $30 million annually on nursing home care, about half of which is contributed by state-administered Medicaid programs. But according to the National Council on Aging, in-home/community care averages about $5000 a year per recipient, whereas the annual cost of a nursing home ranges from $20,000 to $50,000 depending on the quality of the services.

At the same time that many Washington policymakers insist that the family should bear all the burdens of caring for the elderly, state legislators have been taking a more enlightened and realistic view of the problem. The result over the past few years has been a significant increase in state and community-sponsored home care programs that provide the kind of long-term care not covered by most insurance and beyond the means of most families.

Sons, daughters, and spouses continue to be the most active participants in the care of the ailing elderly (at least 5 million Americans are caring for a parent on any given day),[4] but even when family members are willing and able to accept these responsibilities, there are simply no longer as many sons and daughters and nieces and nephews as there used to be. And family members tend to scatter rather than to remain in or near the old homestead or the deteriorating neighborhood of their elders. Even when the generations live close to each other or in the same house, the younger women are likely to be working all day, and friends and neighbors can't be counted on day in and day out. Thus, home care, once the province of kith and kin with occasional help from a visiting nurse, has become a major industry.

The National Homecaring Council estimates that there are now approximately eight thousand agencies providing some aspect of home care at an annual cost of $3 million. About five thousand of these have received Medicare certification. Services are provided by physicians, social workers, registered nurses, several types of therapists, and nutritionists, as well as by homemakers, health aides, and people who handle miscellaneous chores.

4. "Who's Taking Care of Our Parents?" *Newsweek,* May 6, 1985.

The professionalization of home care as an alternative to institutionalization goes back no farther than the mid-1940s when the director of New York's Montefiore Hospital, Dr. E. M. Bluestone, developed several hospital-based coordinated home-care programs. These treatment programs were carried out by a team in which the social worker played an indispensable role along with the physician and the nurse.[5]

From that time to this, the hospital social worker, in consultation with the physician, continues to play a significant role in establishing and individualizing home care programs and in acting as the source of information about "providers" of essential services. More and more hospitals are establishing geriatric assessment units that offer guidance for the family about home care. Also, as mandated by the Older Americans Act, practically every state has established Area Agencies for the Aging responsible for disseminating information not only about home health care providers, but also about community outreach programs, meals-on-wheels, and volunteer resources within the scope of their jurisdiction.[6]

ADVANTAGES

If you've taken on the responsibility of doing so, it's by no means a simple matter to set up a short-term (not to mention a long-term) home care arrangement that will be satisfactory in every detail to all concerned. But even though it may be far from perfect and may require lots of time and effort in terms of changing personnel, sudden crises, and parental complaints, properly organized home care has great advantages when compared with prolonged hospitalization or unsuitable institutionalization.

- An older person, especially one who is partially disabled or increasingly frail, derives all the benefits of feeling safe and secure in familiar surroundings.
- Rather than suffering from feelings of helplessness and disorientation that can lead to emotional regression, the patient at home has a sense of independence and greater control over treatment.

5. Celia Hailperin, "Twenty-five Years of Home Care Service," *Home Care: Living with Dying* (Columbia University Press, New York, 1979).
6. See the state-by-state listing in the Appendix for details on these agencies, including their address and phone number and the area served.

- Instead of yielding all authority to the professional staff of an institution, the homebound parent can discuss options and prognosis with the physician, visiting nurse, and therapists in a relaxed and unpressured way.
- Recovery is hastened by the informal presence of family and friends.
- Home-cooked meals, even when conforming to the instructions of a nutritionist, mean a great deal to older people who are set in their ways.
- Family members can consult with the social worker and other members of the treatment team about realistic long-term goals.
- During home care, family members can make useful and practical contributions to the patient's well-being rather than feeling helpless and useless as hospital visitors.
- The physician and therapists as well as the social worker can rely on family members to report the details of the patient's condition and progress.

HOW IS MY PARENT'S ELIGIBILITY
FOR HOME CARE ESTABLISHED?

Evaluation by a physician and a screening process are the basis on which a person's eligibility for a skilled nursing facility is established. Life-threatening conditions such as advanced diabetes, serious respiratory or circulatory impairment, and debilitating hypertension are taken into account; the screening process may deal with such matters as incontinence, dependence on a wheelchair for mobility, and signs of senility onset.

This evaluation can be made before your parent is discharged from the hospital; it may also be made when the patient or a family member requests removal from a nursing home so that the care can be administered at home. Eligibility for home care may be established while the person is still living in the community but has become so enfeebled that home care is the alternative to institutionalization.

If your parent is about to be discharged from the hospital or from a rehabilitation facility, you can find out from the patient service department how much home care he or she is entitled to under the insurance that covered the hospitalization.

What happens when insurance coverage for short-term care runs out and your parent is in need of continuing nonprofessional care? Or what about a parent who has a chronic disability that doesn't call for hospitalization but does need long-term home-maker/health aide services? Unless savings and family resources can cover these costs, the first practical step is to find out about your parent's entitlements or eligibility for experimental state-sup-ported programs, or for pilot projects paid for by private funds, by philanthropically supported geriatric centers (often attached to hospitals), or by a particular Area Agency for the Aging.

In cases where ambiguity or differing opinions becloud the issue of your parent's rights to financial assistance and home care, or you are being given the runaround by bureaucrats whose com-puters contradict each other, you can take the problem to a social worker at a nonprofit agency that specializes in family services and has a fee schedule based on ability to pay. (See Chapter 9, pages 245–46, for information about nonprofit, nonsectarian agen-cies sponsored by religious philanthropies.) Geriatric social work-ers in these agencies are well acquainted with available resources and solutions and can counsel both parents and offspring on how to achieve maximum benefits that are within family means.

Yet another option in arranging for care at home as an alterna-tive to institutionalization is to consult a geriatric "case manage-ment" specialist who has a private clientele. This option is dis-cussed in Chapter 9.

HOW IS HOME CARE PAID FOR?

Depending on the state in which your parents live, the state of their finances, and the nature of their needs, in-home services may be paid for partially or entirely by Medicare, Medicaid, supple-mentary insurance, a group insurance plan, a health maintenance organization, and/or by community programs subsidized by phil-anthropic organizations or local efforts. Some federal funds—the amounts depend on budget cuts—are also, under the jurisdiction of the Older Americans Act, distributed to local, county, or com-munity Offices for the Aging for home services for individuals over sixty, regardless of income. Where the need is great, services are limited to families with marginal resources. Some funds also originate in "Block Grants to the States for Social Services" as specified under Title 20 of the Social Security Act.

Veterans and their spouses and their children may benefit from the Veterans Administration's "improved pension program" when there is a need for "aid and attendance" for a non-service-associated disability. The extent of the benefits is determined by the individual's economic circumstances and may be applied to any type of home care.

Under group coverage, retirees and their spouses usually receive certain home care services through corporate and union pension plans.

In many states, private health insurance plans are required by law to include coverage for home care under the same conditions that apply to Medicare. In some cases, the policy itself may not spell out this coverage, and you may have to call the company or speak to the agent to find out the details. Blue Cross/Blue Shield, for example, has prepared an informative pamphlet called "Home Health Care" but the pamphlet may not have been received by all policyholders over sixty-five.

For most families of modest or middle income, the problems of payment begin when insurance coverage for maintenance care runs out. Parents who talked about "putting something aside" because "we don't want to come to the children for help" didn't realize how quickly a lifetime of savings could be exhausted by living long beyond their expectations. Even though home health care purchased for a dependent parent is a deductible allowance under the federal tax law, it's still quite costly, and if the care has to go on and on, there's no reason to expect even the most devoted sons and daughters to impoverish themselves and their own families in the process.

The alternative for many middle class older people is to use up their own savings to the point where they become eligible for Medicaid, or to embark on a "spending down" ploy that will eventually help them achieve Medicaid eligibility. This calculated reduction of assets usually consists of transferring savings accounts, securities, and the like to ownership by an adult son or daughter.

When the Senate's Special Committee on Aging conducted hearings (in September 1984) on the role of private insurance coverage for the care of the chronically ill, Senator John Heinz (R., Pa.), committee chairman, had this to say: "Our nation's middle class can insure their cars against theft and damage, their houses against flood, fire, and earthquakes, their children against the cost of college and braces, and their families against the risk of an early death. But when it comes to insuring against the single greatest threat to their life savings and their emotional reserves—the costs of longterm care—Americans face a major market void."[7]

WHAT SERVICES ARE PROVIDED BY HOME CARE?

The home treatment plan is drawn up by the physician in charge often in consultation with the social worker who remains in charge of coordinating the services and evaluating the ongoing needs of the patient and the family. Professional personnel are always licensed, certified, or registered by the state, and their services are paid for by the patient's insurance as covered by the terms of the policy. Nonprofessional aides and homemakers must come from agencies accredited to receive Medicare/Medicaid, or other insurance payments.

Here are some of the professional and nonprofessional personnel whose services may be specified as part of your parent's home treatment:

- A physical therapist for the rehabilitation of mobility following a stroke, an injury, or an accident, also for maintaining a level of muscular movement in the face of severe arthritis or surgery involving a joint.
- A speech therapist for the restoration of communication skills disabled by a stroke or by cancer surgery.
- A respiration therapist for a patient with lung function impaired by surgery.
- An occupational therapist for a patient whose disablement or impairment requires learning new ways of getting dressed, bathing, and doing household chores.
- A registered nurse to check on the patient's blood pressure, heart, and temperature two or three times a week, and to provide part-time skilled nursing care for as many hours a week as the doctor in charge deems necessary.
- A home health aide for bathing and dressing the patient and tending to matters of grooming, safety, and other aspects of personal care. (A home health aide may also be called a "nurses' assistant.")
- A homemaker or housekeeper to market, cook, and do light housekeeping. In some cases, these duties might be combined with those of a health aide.

7. As reported in the National Institute on Adult Daycare *News*, November 1984.

Volunteer support services depend on the resources of the community and should be explored in detail. The local Area Agency on Aging is a reliable clearinghouse for such information. You can also check the bulletin board at the nearest senior citizen center, call the office of the United Way, and contact such organizations as the PTA, Boy Scouts, Junior League, and philanthropic groups, both denominational and nondenominational. They can either provide the services themselves or refer you to volunteers who help the homebound by running errands, accompanying the patient to the doctor or dentist, reading the newspaper aloud, or arranging intergenerational visiting. Local chapters of voluntary health organizations usually can be counted on to provide some essential services to victims of the diseases that concern them as well as to offer family counseling.

If there is a self-help group in your neighborhood for Children of Aging Parents, you're likely to find some well-informed participants ready to share the results of their own experiences and to make helpful suggestions. See Chapter 1, page 24, for the address of the central office, which can supply you with information about the most conveniently located group.

THE TRANSITION TO SELF-RELIANCE: HOW THE FAMILY CAN HELP

If your parent has spent some time in a hospital or an extended care facility, the supervising physician and attending nurses generally promote and applaud all efforts to achieve self-reliance. When you and other family members visit during the last few days of transition from hospital to home, try to do the same instead of rushing to be helpful.

Very few older people need to be *totally* dependent on others for all the activities of daily life. The majority, even when they're frail or partially disabled, will take pride in fending for themselves when the tasks are within the range of their capabilities. "I can do it by myself" is the slogan that signifies good morale and recovery. Waiting to be waited on rather than accepting the challenge of regaining or maintaining whatever level of competence is possible is a capitulation to helplessness.

When the home care program includes an aide, you may not be in a position to keep an eye on how matters are handled during her hours of attendance. But if, when you visit, you think your mother is ready to brush her own hair or cut up her own food or spend more time walking about, get this message across to the aide as tactfully as possible. If your father is the patient, and he's ready to shave himself again or can dial his own phone calls, encourage him to do so.

PARTICIPATING IN HOME CARE

If possible, try to arrange to be on the premises when the visiting nurse or the therapists are scheduled to appear so that you can write down their special instructions and discuss these with the health aide. If particular exercises are to be done on a regular schedule, you can ask the aide to be sure the schedule is followed. In addition, your physical presence, your encouragement, and your interest in your parent's progress can contribute immeasurably to his or her morale.

There is an aspect of home care in which you may have to play the role of mediator. Of course all rational beings know that no one is perfect. But there's knowing and knowing. When it comes to having realistic expectations about the woman who is going to function as part-time homemaker and personal care provider, you may have to deal with a series of complaints.

Obviously, if the person's performance is conspicuously unsatisfactory, the complaints should be presented to the agency that assigned her, or to the social worker who is supervising your mother's care. But it should also be taken into account that your mother might feel depressed about her diminishing competence and independence, and that having another woman (even if it were to be her own daughter or sister) take over her domain (even temporarily) is calculated to make her resentful and irritable. This reaction is more likely to occur if she's unaccustomed to having other people "do" for her.

Whatever the reasons, it's not unusual to have the homemaker subjected to close and critical scrutiny. Even though she may be competent and agreeable, you may hear complaints about her talking too much, or that she isn't warm and understanding, or that she's sloppy in the kitchen, or that she doesn't know how to follow a recipe, or she dawdles when she goes shopping. And if, on one occasion, a grocery receipt is misplaced, you may hear muttered suspicions about being "robbed blind."

If it's your widowed father who's the recipient of the services, he may appreciate having a woman around to look after him again, but "She certainly doesn't cook the way your mother did . . . she has a funny accent . . . she forgets to turn off the lights. . . ."

Before you scold your parents for being supercritical, or before you get huffy with the aide, hang around in an inconspicuous way for a few hours when you can, or arrange to be on hand for lunch from time to time so that you can make your own estimate of what's going on.

Given the nature of your parent's needs and temperament, try to figure out which attributes are important and which are secondary. What do the trade-offs have to be? If it's a choice, maybe your mother would prefer someone who is meticulously neat and clean rather than someone who is sympathetic and chatty. Or on her scale of values, she may feel it's much more important to have someone around who adores the cats as much as she does and never mind that the glasses don't sparkle.

When your father is the one who's homebound, he may not give you a full bill of particulars if you casually ask, "How's it going, Pop?" Maybe what's needed is a leisurely heart-to-heart talk during which you might find out that he's very uncomfortable having "such a young woman" help him with his shower, or "lots of times I don't know what she's saying because she talks so fast."

Unless there's a major mismatching of parent and service providers, you can act as an intermediary and tactfully iron out most difficulties and misunderstandings.

MAKING YOUR EXPECTATIONS KNOWN

If the homemaker/health aide has been provided by an agency certified to receive payment by Medicare or Medicaid, it's likely that she has received instruction in how to do her job. However, the family member who is more or less supervising home care should know that requirements for certification can vary widely from state to state. For a rigorous set of performance expectations, consider the following as spelled out in a booklet entitled "In-home Personal Care and Homemaker Chore Service Standards" published by the Missouri Department of Social Services of the Division of Aging:

- Meal planning, preparation, and cleanup.
- Making beds and changing sheets with the recipient in or out of bed as required.
- Brushing, combing, and shampooing hair.
- Giving bed baths and assisting with tub baths.
- Brushing teeth when the recipient is unable to do so.
- Cleaning and cutting fingernails and toenails (except for diabetic service recipient).
- Shaving with an electric razor.
- Giving assistance in transferring to and from the bed to a wheelchair, walker, or chair.
- Assisting with ordinarily self-administered medications (opening bottles, getting water).
- Performing such household services (if related to medical need) as are essential to the service recipient's health and comfort at home. (Changing and laundering bedlinens, rearranging furniture so that the recipient can move about more safely and easily.)

The "Standards" brochure also points out that the agency providing the in-home services is expected to prepare in written form and distribute to all employees and volunteers a code of ethics that shall include, at a minimum, the following:

- No use of the service recipient's car.
- No consumption of the service recipient's food or drink.
- No use of the service recipient's telephone for personal calls.
- No discussion of own or other's personal problems, or religious or political beliefs with service recipient.
- No acceptance of gifts or tips.
- No bringing of friends or relatives to service recipient's house.
- No consumption of alcoholic beverages, or use of medicine or drugs for any purpose other than medical, in the service recipient's home, or prior to service delivery.
- No smoking in service recipient's home.
- No solicitation of money or goods for personal gain from the service recipient.
- No breach of the service recipient's privacy/confidentiality of records.
- The personal care workers may eat personal lunch in the service recipient's home with the consent of the service recipient.
- The personal care worker may use the service recipient's bathroom facilities.

Many of these performance expectations are based on an arrangement in which the agency is reimbursed for no more than four hours a day, sixty hours in any month.

There's no doubt that many of these expectations sound more rigid than necessary, but as anyone who's ever been in a position of authority knows, better results can be achieved by starting out with clear-cut rules and eventually deviating from them than by starting out with an "anything goes" attitude and then trying to establish order. Even if the aide's services are required on a full-time live-in basis either temporarily or into the unforeseeable future and begins to seem like a member of the family, there should be mutually understood ground rules. And if a weekend relief aide is part of the home care arrangement, the same rules should apply.

It should go without saying that a live-in aide has rights and privileges: a comfortable bed, a certain amount of privacy, reasonable access to the phone for incoming and outgoing calls. She should not be expected to do any heavy housecleaning, and if meals are provided, an adjustment can be made in the hourly or daily rate of pay.

Keeping the Patient's Environment Clean and Functioning Properly

When the home care program is being carried out in *your* home where your parent has a room of his or her own and the aide provides only part-time services, you're in a practical position to see that the environment is cheerful and well-maintained. But if your parents are in their own dwelling, and one of them is more or less in charge of the situation while the other is the recipient of care, you might make an occasional check to see that certain aspects of the house or apartment aren't gradually falling into disrepair. Such routine checks are especially important if your ailing parent lives alone and the necessary chores are beyond the province of the home health aide.

Is a faucet dripping? Is it time for the exterminator? Should summer screens be installed? If your parent lives in an apartment complex where maintenance workers are available by appointment, the aide should be asked to make the necessary arrangements as the needs arise. If repairs and chores have to be handled independently, find out from the social worker whether the community program for the aged has a referral group that provides handyman services.

A SAMPLING OF HOME CARE PROGRAMS

The following descriptions are intended to give you a general idea of the types of programs that have recently been developed by several states:

CONNECTICUT   The home care program, known as the Promotion of Independent Living, is administered through Connecticut Community Care Inc. (CCCI). This agency has established a case management service that assesses, coordinates, and monitors the needs of a frail elderly person so that home care is maintained as an appropriate alternative to institutionalization. Members of the family are invited to participate in the development of the program. *Eligibility* is based on age (60+), Connecticut residency, and economic need. *Priority* is given to minority elderly and to those who have already been inappropriately institutionalized. Fees are based on income. The client's contribution is determined when the care plan is established, and when services begin, the client is billed by the agency supplying the services. CCCI also arranges home care programs for clients who pay privately.

FLORIDA   A Home Care for the Elderly program is supervised by the Department of Health and Rehabilitative Services. The legislative intent of the program is to use the family and friends of the frail, elderly person as the informal service support network that functions as an alternative to institutionalization. This program encourages "the provision of such care in a full-time family-type arrangement in a private home by a person or group of persons, whether relative or non-relative, on a nonprofit basis." The department's subsidy payments to the "home care service provider" cover the following three areas:

1. The costs of clothing, food, housing, and incidentals
2. Payments for medical, pharmaceutical, and dental services essential to maintain the health of the elderly person, and not covered by Medicare, Medicaid, or any other form of insurance
3. When necessary, special supplements to provide for any services and specialized care required to maintain the health and well-being of the elderly person

The program's goal—the provision of care and services comparable to those of a skilled care facility or a nursing home—is achieved by coordinating the support network of professional therapists, home aides, and psychiatric care, which is supervised by an Adult Services counselor and supported by the necessary subsidy payments. The recipient's level of functional impairment and dependence on others is reassessed every few months to determine whether requirements for services have changed. As indicated in the summary of the program, "When necessary, additional in-home health services and care may be provided and reimbursed . . . to include home nursing, personal care, home health aides, medical, therapeutic, and respite care services. Rental, lease, or purchase of essential health-related equipment and mechanical devices is also authorized."

KENTUCKY The Division of Aging Services has developed a program of community-based in-home services for elderly residents who are at risk of long-term care institutionalization. The program is viewed as an indispensable component of the continuum of care directed toward optimizing the individual's ability to maintain function and postpone increasing enfeeblement. It therefore allows older people to remain close to their families in their own familiar surroundings, "thereby enhancing their sense of worth and wellbeing while attending to their physical needs."

In contrast to the *Home Health Program,* the *Homecare Program* doesn't require a physician's order because it uses a social model with a *health* component rather than with a *medical* component. (In accordance with state legislation, home health aide services must be purchased from licensed agencies and are relatively expensive. They are therefore not used when the less expensive homemaker/personal care services are appropriate and safe.) Homecare services as developed in the state's program include case management and assessment as well as homemaker, respite, chore, home repair, home-delivered meals, escort and/or home health aide, as these needs are identified.

In 1984, the Homecare Program provided in-home services to over seven thousand older Kentuckians who were at risk of long-term institutionalization. The Division of Aging Services, in collaboration with the University of Kentucky's Multidisciplinary Center of Gerontology, has also developed several training programs for homecare providers. Summer courses that have been offered include "Principles and Practices of Gerontology," "Alzheimer's Disease and other Dementias," "Case Management," in addition to workshops in various aspects of health care and networking. The Kentucky Cabinet for Human Resources has also prepared an attractive informative booklet on home care that describes what home care is, what it isn't, examples of services, eligibility, payment, and procedures for becoming a recipient. (See the state-by-state listing in the Appendix for the address of the Kentucky Cabinet for Human Resources if you wish to order this booklet.)

NEW YORK STATE In Suffolk County (Long Island) the Department of Health Services has received funding through the state's "Nursing Home without Walls" legislation to establish a typical community-based program that aims to provide health care for patients in their own home. The state pays 75 percent of the costs for patients who meet the criteria for such care and whose home environment is judged to be suitable for it. Medical treatment is supervised by the patient's private physician, and available services include nursing; speech, physical, and respiratory therapy; twenty-four-hour emergency response systems; social day care; congregate meals; and transportation. The program is supervised by a public health nurse.

Another program sponsored by the same state law is based at the Jewish Home and Hospital for the Aged in New York City. Each patient's needs are evaluated and the care plan is coordinated in consultation with the patient's private physician, who need not be affiliated with the hospital. Services include professional nursing care, social work assistance, therapy services, nutritional counseling, personal care workers, housekeepers, home health aides, medical equipment and supplies, laboratory services, and round-the-clock emergency coverage. Depending on need and eligibility, respite care, social transportation, and Meals-on-Wheels are also provided. Included in the home care plan are professional supervision of the patient's care plan on a continuing basis, ongoing contact with the patient's physician, training the patient and the patient's family members to assume appropriate care responsibilities, and providing consultation in times of stress. A special aspect of this program is the prompt availability of hospital or nursing home inpatient care when needed.

PENNSYLVANIA The Department of Aging has broadened the scope of its Long Term Care and Assessment Program (known as LAMP) so that in addition to providing comprehensive health and social assessments for persons applying for public subsidy for nursing home care, it also now provides service management and a broad range of community services for people remaining in their own homes. In 1983–84, the state legislature earmarked $5 million for LAMP and its accompanying in-home program which includes health and chore services and home-delivered meals. Another $5 million was allocated to attendant care where it was deemed necessary. Various sources supplied an additional $12 million to expand all in-home services provided by the state's Area Agencies on Aging for the frail and homebound.

Some Promising New Developments

A recent report by the AARP on state lawmakers and home care points out that because of cuts in federal spending, many states are taking more responsibility for exploring the cost effectiveness of in-home services as an alternative to institutionalization for Medicaid recipients.[8] Among the 1985–86 state budgets for such programs are: Florida—$9 million; Illinois—$60 million; Georgia—$2 million. Wisconsin, which already has a model day care program, plans to allocate $20 million for a pilot home care program called "Community Options."

In September 1985, it was announced that $4.2 million was being provided by seven private philanthropies for the development of new alternatives to institutionalization.[9] Known as the Living at Home Project, the funds will be distributed among a dozen cities for the creation of programs that can serve as models for the rest of the country. The grants will be given to local agencies so that home services to the elderly can be coordinated in a single program with one information center, thus simplifying the efforts of all members of the family to set up suitable arrangements.

The director of the Living at Home Project, Dr. Morton D. Bogdonoff, professor of medicine at Cornell Medical School, hopes that programs will be created that will not only provide basic in-home services for the elderly but will also find ways of bringing genuine enjoyment into their lives. One way of doing this, he suggested, would be to devise means whereby older people who are more or less homebound can continue to do some kind of useful work on a structured part-time basis.

8. *AARP News Bulletin,* July-August 1985.
9. New York *Times,* September 15, 1985.

If you're planning to involve yourself in a parent's home care arrangements, or if you want to know more about how to promote your parent's rights in dealing with various service agencies, the following publications provide useful information:

Home Care is available free from:

The National Association for Home Care
519 C Street, N.E., Stanton Park,
Washington D.C. 20002
(202) 547-7424

Information on Home Health Services is available free from:

AARP Fulfillment
Box 2400, Long Beach, California 90801

and in collaboration with the Council of Better Business Bureaus, the National HomeCaring Council publishes a comprehensive brochure

All About Home Care: A Consumer's Guide. Send your request together with $2 and a self-addressed stamped business envelope to:

The National HomeCaring Council
235 Park Avenue South, New York, N.Y. 10003

HOSPICE CARE AT HOME

It used to be that terminally ill patients and their families didn't have much choice about the kind of care that would be available to dignify the last few months of life, and where that care would be administered. Now, thanks to the development of the hospice movement following the establishment of the first program in New Haven by the Yale medical faculty a little more than a decade ago, there are over 1300 hospice organizations coast to coast. Of these, according to the National Hospice Organization, 185 are accredited for Medicare payment. For a patient to qualify for insurance benefits, a physician must certify that the patient's life expectancy doesn't exceed six months. Ninety percent of those who qualify have cancer.

Wherever possible, hospice care is administered in the patient's home rather than in a hospital. The continuum of services, in some cases on a twenty-four-hour basis, includes training family members and friends to care for the patient. The underlying philosophy of all hospice programs is that for a person with only a limited time to live, symptoms should be relieved and pain alleviated. Until comparatively recently, this philosophy has been—and in some quarters continues to be—resisted by the conventional medical establishment, dedicated as it has always been to prolonging the patient's life wherever possible by any available means.

Another aspect of the movement is that it essentially transfers control of patient care to the patient and the family. Louise Bracknell, former director of the National Hospice Organization, has pointed out that the movement "sees the person not just as a physical being, but as a social, spiritual, and psychological being, with needs in all those areas. We treat the patient and the family as a unit. At the most vulnerable time in the patient's life, we bring the health system to them."

Whether the program is based in the home or in a special hospice setting, unlimited visiting hours are possible, extra beds are provided for live-in guests, and the presence of grandchildren, even very young ones, is encouraged. A favorite pet is permitted too—all the elements that support the dying person's sense of self.

Under the best of circumstances, hospice staff is available to the family on a daily, round-the-clock basis. Consultations with family members and friends occur regularly so that they are trained in as many aspects of caregiving as they can handle. Mary Cooke, the hospice director at Cabrini Medical Center in Manhattan, has said that because a major focus of the program is the relief of pain, a majority of patients receive morphine. She remembers that, as a nurse before the hospice philosophy, "We didn't use it; it was not even discussed."[10]

Most hospice programs also do what they can to ease the pain of loss for the family. Bereavement counseling may continue for months after the patient's death, and efforts are made to help the widowed spouse and/or the bereft sons and daughters deal with

10. New York *Times,* December 24, 1983.

the stress of changing relationships and new problems within the family.

How does a program work when no family member lives nearby, or it isn't possible for a son or daughter to move in with a parent who has only a few months of living left? What happens when the parent insists on remaining in solitary but familiar surroundings rather than transferring to an unfamiliar hospice setting? Some programs are flexible enough to accede to the wishes of the terminal patient by providing all the necessary professional in-home services, such as a visiting nurse and social worker, as well as setting up schedules that rely on community volunteers to visit, act as companions, read aloud, play Scrabble, and be on hand to handle emergencies.

There's no doubt that hospice care may impose a considerable emotional burden on family members, but there are many families who feel that such care imparts a personal dignity and meaning to the end of life unachievable in a conventional hospital environment.

If you want to locate a hospice program in your own or your parents' area, information can be provided by local hospitals, state hospice organizations, and visiting nurses associations. Medicare and private insurance companies can also be consulted.

A list of local hospice organizations is available from:

The National Hospice Organization
1901 North Fort Myer Drive, Suite 401
Arlington, Virginia 22209
(703) 243-5900

An informative brochure, *The Basics of Hospice,* is also sent on request.

To find out about the formal accreditation of a particular hospice program, consult:

The Joint Commission on Accreditation of Hospitals
875 North Michigan Avenue, Chicago, Illinois 60611
(312) 642-6061

Local units of the various cancer care organizations, such as the National Cancer Foundation and the United Cancer Council, provide information and social services for patients and their families that augment a hospice program.

8

WHEN A NURSING HOME IS THE RIGHT ANSWER

Despite ongoing significant problems, there is no doubt that continual improvements are being made in America's nursing homes. In fact, we believe these improvements are made primarily a) because a state/ federal government regulatory structure does exist which has the respect and understanding of many concerned providers striving to uphold the publicly developed standards and to become a model for others, and b) because of the growing knowledge, concern, and involvement of the public, particularly represented by citizenry advocacy groups, long-term care ombudsman programs, resident and family organizations.

National Citizen's Coalition for
Nursing Home Reform[1]

Some of the anti-nursing home people just haven't seen a lot of good nursing homes, but I can assure you that there are many of them . . . and research shows that nursing home residents do much better when family members and community are involved.

Dr. Rose Dobrof, director of the
Brookdale Center on Aging at
Hunter College[2]

Even if you've planned ahead, you'll probably feel scared to death, confused, and vulnerable about the process of finding a nursing home.

Iris Freeman, Director of the
18,000-member Nursing Home
Residents Advocates in
Minneapolis[3]

1. Preamble to the Consumer Statement of Principles for the Nursing Home Regulatory System, September 1983.
2. New York *Times,* November 15, 1984.
3. Ibid.

While only 5 percent of people over sixty-five live out their last years in a nursing home, four times that many, that is, 20 percent or one old person in five, are likely to spend some time in an institutionalized setting in the span of a lifetime. In many cases, a brief stay occurs as a transition between hospitalization and return to normal life; in others, it occurs when the family caregiver is temporarily indisposed or unavailable.

With guidance by the physician in charge and the social services of the hospital and/or the community, these transitory episodes can be accomplished without traumatizing the patient or the family, especially if both have been psychologically prepared for the change in routine. And since the cost for a *temporary* stay in a skilled nursing facility is partially (or in some instances entirely) paid for by Medicare combined with supplementary insurance, the event doesn't represent a financial crisis either. (Health care insurance is discussed in Chapter 5.)

But who are the 5 percent who constitute the regular nursing home population? Their median age is eighty-one; almost half are childless, and more than two thirds are women. Typical patients are those with a combination of increasingly disabling medical conditions, or those whose mental impairment has become too difficult to cope with in a family setting. The fact that there are twice as many institutionalized women as men is accounted for by their greater longevity. A corollary of this circumstance is that in those cases where the prime caregiver of a chronically ill woman is her husband, his death is likely to result in her eventual institutionalization.

Most adult sons and daughters make enormous efforts to find ways of caring for ailing and disabled parents. But when it becomes inceasingly obvious that the capabilities of family members, even when combined with community resources of day care and home care, are an inadequate or inappropriate solution for the parent's increasing disability and dependence, a nursing home is the inevitable answer.

The most effective way in which loving concern can be expressed in anticipation of this decision is to take the time and make the effort to find a nursing home that answers your parent's needs and meets the family's standards.

The material that follows is intended to provide the basis for making an informed choice.

Families should be prepared to face these facts about finances:

- Medicare does *not* pay for an extended stay in a nursing home.
- The cost of most good nursing homes averages about $2500 a month, and this amount may not cover "extras."
- The average nursing home resident must usually convert to Medicaid payments in less than two years.
- In some states, the noninstitutionalized mate must go on public welfare before Medicaid payments are made available for nursing home coverage.
- The federal government continues to give serious consideration to enacting laws that would require adult children to provide some support for aging parents.
- The most expensive facilities do not necessarily provide the best care.

LEVELS OF CARE

There are three distinct categories of institutionalized living for the elderly, and they are defined by the different levels of care and supervision they provide. A *home for the aged* or a *congregate living arrangement* offers the minimum level of care; an *intermediate care facility (ICF)*, also known as a *health-related facility* or a *home with nursing supervision*, provides skilled nursing supervision and personal care on a daily basis; a chronic and convalescent nursing home, known as a *skilled nursing facility (SNF)*, provides continuous skilled nursing care for those with an unstable or chronic condition requiring round-the-clock supervision and personal attention. It has become increasingly common to house all three facilities in different sections or on different floors of one large complex, known as a *geriatric center*. Such a center may be affiliated with a nearby hospital. Depending on the person's needs at any particular time, one or another level of care may provide the greatest benefits at the least expense. Admission to and/or change from one level of care to another is always based on professional assessment.

The home for the aged, similar to the traditional "old folks' home," is not, strictly speaking, a nursing home. It usually offers basic services for old people who can still function more or less independently—that is, they are physically and mentally able to handle their daily needs, and are capable of assuming responsibility for taking their own medication. Room and board are provided as well as recreation, and residents may come and go as they wish, knowing that their meals will be served in a social setting. They are relieved of the anxiety of being isolated or alone in an emergency, and their families can enjoy a similar peace of mind. Such an arrangement may be the considered preference of someone who enjoys group living with peers rather than living alone with intermittent help from a family member, or living with a family member who has come to resent the responsibility. If the time arrives when the resident of such a facility begins to find it difficult to cope with the activities of daily living, or requires help in handling a medical routine, or has begun to show signs of mental deterioration requiring closer supervision, professional assessment will indicate the need for transfer to an intermediate care facility.

An intermediate care facility or health-related facility provides regular nursing services, but not on a twenty-four-hour basis. The assessment for admission is a stable or controlled condition requiring minimal skilled nursing services, the need for some professional supervision, and/or a limited program of therapy following a stroke or an injury. Some patients in this facility may be in transition between a hospital stay and a return home. Many, however, are likely to be in transition from this level of care to a skilled nursing facility because of a deterioration in their condition and an increase in their needs.

A skilled nursing facility is a nursing home most akin to a hospital with a twenty-four-hour nursing staff. It offers continuing medical supervision, rehabilitation therapy as needed, and ongoing assessment of unstable or chronic conditions. While many residents will remain permanently, some will leave when they are sufficiently rehabilitated after a major stroke or heart attack.

HOW ARE NURSING HOMES OWNED, MANAGED, AND REGULATED?

According to recent statistics, there are over 23,000 nursing homes in this country and they contain over 1½ million beds. About 80 percent of the facilities are proprietary—that is, they are privately owned, and operated to earn the highest rate of profit for the owner, usually a corporation. About 15 percent are run by nonprofit charitable organizations and sponsored by religious, fraternal, union, and community groups, many with private foundation endowments. The remaining 5 percent are run by various government agencies.

As a private industry, nursing homes are a big business, estimated at $27.3 billion in 1984. A growing development in the industry is ownership by large interstate chains. In 1983, some thirty-two companies operated 17 percent of all nursing homes; figures projected by a corporate official indicate that by 1990, 50 percent of all beds will be found in facilities operated by between five to ten companies.

Another marked trend is the increase in the size of the individual facilities. Whereas in 1961 the average nursing home contained 25 beds, the number had risen to 66 beds in 1980. In that year, 40 percent of all nursing home beds were in facilities that contained from 100 to 199 beds. Whatever the defects and virtues of this increase in the number of patients in any given facility—on the one hand, greater depersonalization in relationships between staff and residents, on the other, a broader spectrum of services—there can be little doubt that cost accounting in terms of profit returns per bed has played a significant role in this growth.

The "private sector" claims that under free enterprise and the competitive battle for the consumer's dollar, the public eventually receives the best value for its money. Perhaps this mechanism prevails when owners can maximize their profits by catering only to a rich clientele. But the great majority of nursing homes can function only if the staggering costs of the care they provide is paid for by government dollars (in the long run, it's we the people).

Licensing Requirements

For residents in facilities that accept *only* people who pay out of private funds, the primary regulatory protection is provided by state licensing procedures. All state governments require that nursing homes be licensed, and it is through the standards established by the licensing agency for acceptable business practices and level of services that consumers are protected. Regulations vary from state to state. A facility must be licensed by the *state* before it is eligible to receive *federal* certification for participation in Medicare payments (for skilled nursing care benefits) and Medicaid (for both skilled and intermediate care benefits).

The federal government contracts with each state government to conduct an inspection program at least once a year to determine whether the facility is "in substantial compliance" with federal standards.[4] If the state certifies that the standards have been met, the federal government renews its Medicare-Medicaid contract with the facility. If the state inspection reveals inadequate performance, a "Statement of Deficiencies" must be filed to which the nursing home must respond with a "Plan of Correction."

According to the U.S. Department of Health and Human Services:

> Each report and accompanying statement of deficiencies and written comments are available to the public within 90 days of completion of the survey. Medicare reports are available at any local Social Security Office. The statements of deficiencies and written comments are available at the Social Security District Office and at the public assistance agency servicing the area in which the nursing home is located. The State Welfare Department is responsible for establishing procedures for the disclosure of survey information for facilities participating only in the Medicaid program.[5]

Copies of these reports should be on file in the office of the nursing home itself and be made available to visitors and residents on request.

The federal Office of Standards and Certification of the Health Care Administration under the jurisdiction of the Department of

4. The federal regulatory system is being revised, and as of October 1986, new standards have not been issued.

5. "How to Choose a Nursing Home," published by the Department of HHS, Health Standards and Quality Bureau, Office of Standards and Certification of the Health Care Financing Administration, December 1980. This publication has not yet been superseded.

Health and Human Services also directs that states participating in the federal program must maintain a licensing program for nursing home administrators. Thus every licensed nursing home must be directed by a licensed administrator. In recent years, one of the requirements for this license is participation in continuing education courses monitored by the American College of Health Care Administrators.

The Ombudsman Program

One result of the public hearings conducted by the Subcommittee on Long Term Care of the Senate Special Committee on Aging was the establishment in 1971 of the Office of Nursing Home Affairs at the Department of Health, Education and Welfare (now the Department of Health and Human Services). And at the same time, President Nixon directed that "the Department of HEW assist the states in establishing investigative units which will respond in a responsible and constructive way to complaints made by or on behalf of individual patients. The individual who is confined to an institution and dependent upon it is often powerless to make his voice heard. This new program will help him deal with concerns. . . ."

Each state has fulfilled the federal requirement by appointing a nursing home or *long-term care ombudsman* (the official title) to resolve complaints and investigate allegations of patient abuse. (The name, address, and telephone number of the ombudsman in your state is included in the state-by-state listings in the appendix.)

Patient Abuse Reporting Laws

One of the results of past adverse publicity about patient abuse in the form of physical mistreatment, inappropriate medication, and neglect has been the enactment by several states of a Patient Abuse Reporting Law. The typical way in which such a law is implemented is the posting in all the state's long-term care facilities of a Hot Line phone number that accepts collect calls seven days a week around the clock. Within forty-eight hours after receiving the telephone report, state health care professionals conduct an on-site investigation in such a way as to safeguard the patients and protect the confidentiality of the person who made the report. Such state laws usually require that every residential health care employee, including administrators, operators, and all licensed professionals, must report occurrences of patient abuse. Friends, relatives, visitors, and patients may make reports as well. The law spells out procedures for the conduct of hearings and the imposing of fines.

Watchdog Groups

One of the most productive developments in the regulation of nursing homes is the increase in the number of community-based watchdog organizations and advocacy groups for residents and their families. As a result of their activities, the rights of patients have been extended to include participation in decision making about their own care. In 1983, the National Citizen's Coalition for Nursing Home Reform, with the support of the American Association of Retired Persons (AARP), developed its "Consumer Statement of Principles for the Nursing Home Regulatory System." This document, which received the endorsement of forty-three national organizations and over two hundred state and local citizen groups, was presented to the Secretary of the Department of Health and Human Services, the administrator of the Health Care Financing Administration, the Association of Health Facility Licensure and Certification Directors, the Institute of Medicine of the National Academy of Sciences, the Senate's Special Committee on Aging, and the House of Representatives' Select Committee on Aging.

An extension of the coalition's activities was a research project exploring the residents' viewpoint on the nature of quality care and how it can be measured. With funds provided by the Health Care Financing Administration of the Department of Health and Human Services by the AARP and several foundations, nearly four hundred nursing home residents in fifteen cities were able to meet for discussions of these questions. This was the first time that research was undertaken to ask the residents themselves to describe what constitutes good care and how to achieve it. The study concluded in February 1985 with a national symposium on quality care and the publication of a report offering recommendations to government policymakers and health care professionals. It is hoped that these recommendations will be incorporated into the new federal standards for licensing, inspection, and payment of nursing homes.

For further information about the activities of the National Citizen's Coalition for Nursing Home Reform, write to:

NCCNR
1309 L Street, N.W.
Washington, D.C. 20005

A final word on regulation: In those nursing homes where active resident councils can voice their individual and collective grievances to a responsive administration, conditions are likely not only to conform to official standards, but to improve on them. And it is generally agreed that residents who are visited frequently by attentive friends and relatives are likely to receive good care.

ESSENTIAL SERVICES, EXTRA AMENITIES, AND SPECIAL PROGRAMS

A judgment of geriatric centers that offer both levels of long-term care, ICF and SNF, should be made not only on the basis of their furnishings and equipment, but on the effectiveness with which they restore and/or maintain the residents' highest degree of physical and mental health. To achieve this goal, the following therapeutic services are essential:

Medical Care

A physician who is an official staff member of the facility on a full-time or consulting basis must be responsible for an ongoing assessment of each resident's condition and for prescribing the necessary combination of medication, therapy, diet, and other treatments. The physician may be the resident's own personal doctor rather than the one provided by the nursing home. In a skilled nursing facility, a house physician should be on twenty-four-hour duty.

Nursing Care

Services should include every aspect of professional nursing necessary for the continuing comfort of residents recovering from a stroke, major surgery, a heart attack, or broken bones, as well as of those who are chronically ill. The nursing staff should consist of registered nurses, nurse practitioners, practical nurses, aides, and orderlies.

Pharmaceutical Services

A qualified pharmacist is expected to dispense drugs only under the supervision of the physician and to review drug combinations as necessary.

Rehabilitation Therapy

To the basic physical, speech/language, and occupational therapies, some nursing homes have added "memory" therapy and reality orientation.

Social Services

These services are usually under the direction of a professional social worker whose staff can assess the social and emotional needs of the resident. If the facility isn't equipped to cope with these needs, the proper outside agencies should be petitioned for assistance. The social service director is also responsible for helping the family deal with the emotional stress occasioned by the decision to institutionalize a parent. For temporary residents who are to return home, the staff, in consultation with the physician, is responsible for setting up the ongoing home care program. Social service is also responsible for making arrangements for Medicaid payments when the patient's funds have been exhausted.

Food and Nutrition Services

Meals and snacks should be supervised to meet nutritional standards and to conform to the requirements of each resident as specified by the physician.

Social Activities and Recreational Facilities

Program planning by a professionally qualified activities coordinator is an essential aspect of a properly run nursing home. Such activities should involve the residents as active participants wherever possible and call on the facilities and resources of the community for program enrichment.

In addition to these basics, many nursing homes:

- Schedule regular visits by a chaplain and set a room aside for meditation or religious contemplation.
- Encourage the organization of a residents council to act as a liaison between the administration and the residents, participate in the planning of recreation, and help promote the scope of community activities.
- Provide the amenities of a boutique and coffee shop.
- Maintain a well-stocked library on the premises or have an arrangement with a bookmobile sent by the community library.
- Maintain landscaped terraces and gardens.

These special programs have been developed recently:

Resident Pets

Within the last few years, following the results of research that confirm the therapeutic role of animals (see p. 100), many nursing homes have developed a "pet-handling" program, or have established a regular "visiting pet" relationship with the local SPCA. Some facilities have an officially designated "house mascot" who lives in the nursing home under conditions prescribed by the state's health code. In Vermont, for example, "Animals and birds are prohibited in food storage and preparation areas, except in living quarters of the owner or administrator, or by special permission of the licensing agency." One state official commented, "Many of our nursing homes have cats and dogs, and even ducks. The patients' response is very positive." And in the state of Washington, the legislature in mid-1984 "recognized the need for people in nursing homes to have the companionship of animals by providing that a nursing home licensee shall give each patient a reasonable opportunity to have regular contact with animals by permitting appropriate animals to live in the facilities or to visit when supervised properly."[6]

The Humane Society of the United States recommends that inquiries about current state legislation regarding pets in nursing homes should be addressed to a state branch of the SPCA or the state licensing agency.

Intergenerational Projects

A growing number of communities have been sponsoring programs in which young children as well as teenagers and college students visit nursing homes on a regularly scheduled basis. In the past five years, however, a new and more significant intergenerational concept has taken hold: the establishment of child day care centers in long-term care facilities. Working out the details of this mutually gratifying arrangement involves special grants and careful planning by trained professionals—at both ends of the age spectrum. Where the arrangement has been in place for two or three years, many of the residents have been given a new motivation for looking forward to each day. And the children get the kind of "grandparenting" they might otherwise never experience.

The Child Care Centers in Long-Term Care Facilities Project has been developed almost singlehandedly by Joan Sugarman, librarian at the American College of Health Care Administrators. To find out which facilities in your state are participating in this project, write to:

Ms. Joan Sugarman
Library, ACHCA
P.O. Box 5890
4650 East-West Highway
Bethesda, Maryland 20814

---

6. The Humane Society of the United States, Washington, D.C.

WHAT RIGHTS DO PATIENTS HAVE?

To conform to federal regulations, all nursing homes are required to post a statement of Patients' Rights in a conspicuous place. The fourteen "rights" that follow have been established by the federal government. It is expected that the list will be expanded in the immediate future.

Each resident who is admitted:

1. is fully informed, as evidenced by the resident's written acknowledgement before or at the time of admission, of these rights and of all rules and regulations governing the exercise of these rights;
2. is fully informed, before or at the time of admission and during stay, of services available in the facility, and of related charges, including charges for services not covered under Medicare or Medicaid, or not covered by the facility's basic daily rate;
3. is fully informed of his/her medical condition by a physician, unless the physician notes in a medical record that it is not in the patient's interest to be told, and is afforded the opportunity to participate in the planning of his/her medical treatment and to refuse to participate in experimental research;
4. is transferred or discharged only for medical reasons, or for his/her welfare or that of other residents, and is given reasonable advance notice to ensure orderly transfer or discharge;
5. is encouraged and assisted, throughout his/her period of stay, to exercise his/her rights as a resident and as a free citizen. To this end, he/she may voice grievances and recommend changes in policies and services to facility staff and/or to outside representation of his/her choice without fear of coercion, discrimination, or reprisal;
6. may manage his/her personal financial affairs, or is given at least a quarterly accounting of financial transactions made on his/her behalf if the facility accepts the responsibility to safeguard his/her funds for him/her;
7. is free from mental and physical abuse, and free from chemical and physical restraints except as authorized in writing by a physician for a specified and limited period of time, or when

necessary to protect the patient from injury to himself/herself or to others;

8. is assured confidential treatment of his/her personal and medical records, and may approve or refuse their release to any individual outside the facility;
9. is treated with consideration, respect, and full recognition of his/her dignity and individuality, including privacy in treatment and in care for his/her personal needs;
10. is not required to perform services for the facility that are not included for therapeutic purposes in his/her plan of care;
11. may associate and communicate privately with persons of his/her choice, and send and receive his/her personal mail unopened;
12. may meet with, and participate in activities of social, religious, and community groups at his/her discretion;
13. may retain and use his/her personal clothing and possessions as space permits, unless to do so would infringe on rights of other patients, or constitute a hazard to safety;
14. is assured privacy for visits by his/her spouse; if both are inpatients in the facility, they are permitted to share a room.[7]

Many states have enacted their own Patient's Bill of Rights, or have added other rights to the basic fourteen. In Connecticut, for example, the list continues in the following way:

(The patient)
15. is fully informed of the availability of all current state, local, and federal inspection reports;
16. may organize, maintain, and participate in a patient-run resident council as a means of fostering communication among residents and staff, encouraging resident independence and addressing the basic rights of nursing home patients and residents free from administrative interference or reprisal;
17. is entitled to the opinion of two physicians concerning the need for surgery, except in an emergency situation, prior to such surgery being performed.

And in December 1984, the New York State legislature mandated the following patient's rights, whose range and specificity are in large measure attributable to the lobbying activities of community advocacy groups, especially by the organization known as

7. The source for these fourteen "rights" is "How to Select a Nursing Home" published by the Health Care Financing Administration of the Department of HHS, December 1980.

FRIA (Friends and Relatives of the Institutionally Aged) based at the Brookdale Center for Aging at Hunter College in New York City.

THE STATE REGULATIONS LIST
THE FOLLOWING PATIENT'S RIGHTS:

1. The Resident is to be fully informed (as evidenced by his written acknowledgement), before or at the time of admission and during his stay, about these rights and about all rules and regulations governing his conduct and responsibilities;

2. The Resident is to be fully informed, before or at the time of admission and during his stay, about services available in the facility, and about related charges—including any charges for services not covered by the Medicare or Medicaid provisions of the Social Security Act, or not covered by the facility's basic per diem rate;

3. The Resident is to be informed, verbally and in writing at the time of admission and again at the time of transfer (to a hospital or other facility for any reason) of the State's policies on reserving the Resident's room;

4. The Resident is to be assured of adequate and appropriate medical care, is to be fully informed, by a physician, of his medical condition—unless this is medically inadvisable (as documented by a physician in the Resident's medical record); and is to be given the name of his house physician. In addition, the Resident is to be given the opportunity to participate in his care plan and proposed treatment. The Resident has the right to refuse to participate in experimental research, and to refuse medication and treatment after being fully informed of the consequences;

5. The Resident is to be transferred or discharged only for medical reasons, or for his welfare or that of other Residents, or for nonpayment for his stay (except as prohibited by sources of third party payment); and he is to be given reasonable advance notice to ensure orderly transfer or discharge. He (or his representative) is to be provided an interpretation of the content of his medical records by a physician of his choosing in instances where there is some question about his continued stay. Such actions are to be documented in his medical record;

6. The Resident is to be encouraged and assisted, throughout his

stay, to exercise his rights as a Resident and as a citizen. To this end, he may voice grievances and has a right of action for damages or other relief for infringements of his rights to adequate and proper treatment and care. He may recommend changes in policies and services to facility staff and/or to outside representatives of his choice, free from restraint, interference, coercion, discrimination, or reprisal;

7. The Resident may participate in the Residents' Council;

8. The Resident is to be instructed in both the facility's and the New York State Department of Health's complaint procedures, verbally and in writing, and is to be provided with the name, address and telephone number of the office established by the Department to receive complaints, and of the State Office for the Aging Ombudsmen Program;

9. The Resident may manage his personal financial affairs, or is to be given at least a quarterly accounting of financial transactions made on his behalf (should the facility accept his written delegation to the facility for any period of time in conformance with State law);

10. The Resident is to be free from mental and physical abuse, and free from chemical and (except in emergencies) physical restraints—except as authorized in writing by a physician for a specified and limited period of time or when necessary to protect the patient from injury to himself or to others;

11. The Resident is to be assured security in storing personal possessions and confidential treatment of his personal and medical records, and may approve or refuse their release to any individual outside the facility, except in the case of his transfer to another health care institution, or as required by law or third party payment contract;

12. The Resident is to be treated with consideration, respect, and full recognition of his dignity and individuality, including privacy in treatment and in care for his personal needs;

13. The Resident is not to be required to perform services for the facility that are not included for therapeutic purposes in his plan of care;

14. The Resident may meet with and communicate privately with persons of his choice, may join with other Residents or individuals within or outside the facility to work for improvements in patient care, and may send and receive his personal mail unopened, unless this is medically inadvisable (as documented by his physician in his medical record);

15. The Resident may meet with, and participate in activities of, social, religious and community groups at his discretion, unless this is medically inadvisable (as documented by his physician in his medical record);

16. The Resident is to be informed of the facility's visiting hours policies and the rights and responsibilities of visitors;

17. The Resident may retain and use his personal clothing and possessions as space permits, unless doing so would infringe upon rights of other Residents, and unless this is medically inadvisable (as documented by his physician in his medical record);

18. The Resident, if married, is to be assured privacy for visits by a spouse; and if both reside in the facility, they are to be permitted to share a room, unless this is medically inadvisable (as documented in their medical records);

19. The Resident is to be assured the right to exercise his civil and religious liberties, including the right to independent personal decisions; knowledge of available choices shall not be infringed; and the facility shall encourage and assist in the fullest possible exercise of these rights;

20. The Resident is to be assured the right to receive, upon request, kosher food or food products prepared in accordance with the Hebrew orthodox religious requirements when the Resident, as a matter of religious beliefs, desires to observe Jewish dietary laws.

The State Regulations also specify that the rights listed as 1, 2, 3, 4 and 5 pass to the Resident's guardian, next of kin or sponsoring agency when the patient has been judged incompetent in accordance with State law; or when the patient is found by his physician to be medically incapable of understanding these rights; or when the patient "exhibits a communications barrier" (is blocked from comprehending by irreversible physical, mental, or emotional handicaps).

WHEN AND HOW TO LOCATE THE RIGHT NURSING HOME

If you can anticipate a time in the future when—for whatever combination of reasons—a nursing home will be the inevitable solution for your parent's physical and/or mental condition, you would be wise to begin to research the situation without further delay. The more time you take to examine the possibilities and weigh the alternatives, the more satisfactory the final choice is likely to be. Also, most of the better facilities have a waiting list, and when you locate one that suits your family's requirements and will eventually meet with those of your parent, it's a good idea to be put on the waiting list. If you get a call about an available place at a time when the situation is still manageable by a combination of home care, day care, and family care, you can respond to the call by saying, "We're not ready yet, but give us a preferential place on the waiting list and we'll give you a month's notice." This anticipatory planning prevents last-minute crises and regrettable decisions made out of desperation. And it can't be said too often: Whatever the situation, a parent who is mentally competent should be included in discussions and decisions preceding institutionalization. With a parent whose mental faculties are increasingly impaired, some professional counseling may be helpful in easing the transition for both generations.

When you embark on your preliminary investigations, set up a number of filing folders or a looseleaf notebook with dividers to accommodate the information as you accumulate it: names and phone numbers of community social service organizations, the state's Area Agency on Aging, and the Long-Term Care Ombudsman;[8] information about facilities mentioned in newspaper and magazine articles; recommendations by doctors, visiting nurses, relatives, and family friends who have found a satisfactory facility for a similar problem; notes following a visit to an aunt or uncle or grandparent, or the relative of a close friend already comfortably settled in a nursing home. Above all, during this preliminary period, get in touch with the nearest advocacy organization for current information.

The past decade has seen the proliferation of citizen-run information and advocacy organizations for the upwards of 1.4 million nursing home residents and their families. These organizations, staffed chiefly by volunteers and independent of the government and health care industry, are currently active

8. Telephone numbers for the Area Agency on Aging and the Long-Term Care Ombudsperson are given in the state-by-state directory, pp. 250-363.

in forty-five states. Among the most well-known are Citizens for Better Care in Chicago, Illinois; Nursing Home Residents' Advocates in Minneapolis, Minnesota; Citizens for Improvement of Nursing Homes in Seattle, Washington; and the Friends and Relatives of the Institutionalized Aged in New York City.

For a comparable organization in your parents' area, consult the local chapter of The United Way, The United Hospital Fund, the AARP, the Gray Panthers, or the Long-Term Care Ombudsman.

The August 1985 issue of *Good Housekeeping* magazine contains an article on the best nursing homes in ten major metropolitan areas, together with their costs per day and the approximate waiting time for admission. The final selection was based on interviews with three hundred social workers, nurses, and administrators. If you're interested in referring to this material and can't find the magazine in your library, you can send your request to:

Back Issues Department, *Good Housekeeping*
250 West 55th Street, New York, New York 10019

Enclose a check or money order for $3.75 made out to the magazine to cover all costs, including mailing charges.

The American Association of Homes for the Aging (AAHA) is a national nonprofit organization that represents approximately 2700 nonprofit members: homes, housing, health-related facilities, and community services for the elderly. Members of the association are sponsored by religious, fraternal, labor, private, and government organizations. The association publishes an annual *Directory of Members* arranged by states. Detailed information is provided for each listing: address, phone number, the name of the administrator, the sponsorship, levels of care, and community services offered by the facility to nonresidents. Lists of associate members—state organizations, attorneys, and concerned individuals—are also included. For the most recent directory, send a check or money order for $7.75 (this amount includes postal and handling charges) to:

AAHA Publications
1050 17th Street, N.W., Suite 770
Washington, D.C. 20036

The American Health Care Association, which represents both nonprofit and for-profit nursing homes nationwide, provides single copies of the brochure "Thinking About a Nursing Home?" free to consumers. Send your request to:

AHCA
1200 15th Street, N.W., Washington, D.C. 20005

Taking Account of Specific Needs and Wants

As information accumulates, it would be practical to begin to rule out particular recommendations on the basis of your parent's condition, attitudes, and preferences so that you can narrow down the number of facilities to be considered for closer inspection. It's best to accept at the outset that at almost every step and with practically every choice, a compromise will be involved. For example, would it be best to sacrifice the gorgeous grounds at an establishment in the country in favor of the broad and stimulating recreation program of the establishment in the city? Should quality of care override all other considerations, including a location convenient for frequent visiting? Should a special effort be made to find a facility connected with a first-rate hospital even though your father's condition is chronic but stable? Is a nursing home that provides various levels of care in one large building to be preferred because it offers greater flexibility over a longer period and obviates the need to move your mother from one institution to another as her condition worsens?

And what about rock-bottom requirements? Have you explored the whole question of institutionalization with your parent's doctor and taken his or her recommendations into account? Will you absolutely rule out all facilities that are run for profit?

You can save yourself lots of time by calling the facilities on the list that results from your research and asking them to send you their promotional literature. These brochures make long telephone conversations unnecessary because they usually contain information about the number of beds, levels of care, Medicare/Medicaid participation, range of programs, requirements for patient admission, and so on. On the basis of these facts, you can carry the elimination process one step further.

What to Look For When Making a Visit—Before Making a Choice

Suppose on the basis of your preliminary investigations, you've arrived at the point where you're ready to go and see for yourself. At this stage it makes sense for you and other family members to rule out unsuitable choices on the basis of one or two visits so that you can eventually present the best possible alternatives for your parent's final consideration.

As soon as you're ready to visit a nursing home, make an appointment by phone and indicate that you'd like to schedule a meeting with the administrator and with the director of nursing services and social services. During this initial telephone call, explain that you'd also like to be taken on a tour of therapy sessions, kitchen facilities, meal service, and recreation activities. The consensus is that the best time to visit is about 10 A.M.—when breakfast is over, therapy sessions are beginning, and lunch preparations are under way in the kitchen. During this initial contact, it would be a good sign if you're invited to stay for lunch.

In your first meeting with the administrator, you have a right to see the state license and to check on the date to make sure that it's still in effect. If the Declaration of Patients' Rights isn't posted in a conspicuous place, ask for that too, and find out if there's a residents' council or a similar group whose members you can speak to during your visit. If no such group has been formed, try to find out why not from a few of the more articulate residents. And before you embark on your tour, BE SURE TO ASK THE ADMINISTRATOR FOR A COPY OF THE ADMISSION CONTRACT OR AGREEMENT THAT YOUR PARENT OR YOU MUST SIGN AT THE TIME OF ACCEPTANCE. (If you're planning to visit several facilities, get the contract from each one, compare the terms, and be sure you understand the legally binding responsibilities for both parties to the contract. Before the time comes to sign it, check it out with your lawyer or your parent's lawyer so that no misunderstandings develop later.)

First Impressions. Throughout your visit, maintain a leisurely pace so that you can record your impressions in your notebook. You might want to draw a vertical line down the center of the page and head the columns Good and Bad. It would be a plus, for instance, if the general environment is attractive, and the administration answers all your questions without giving you the brushoff. On the other hand, there's something wrong when the staff of nurses, nurses' aides, and others who communicate with the residents call them "Honey" and "Dear." When adults are treated "with dignity," they are addressed by name, and not by first name either, but as Mr. Miller or Mrs. Gordon.

Trust your senses for first impressions. Is your nose assaulted by unpleasant smells? Are strident voices trying to make themselves heard over the sound of radios and television? Also—have you been invited to participate in a meal with the residents rather than with the staff? Are you discouraged from speaking in private to staff members or to residents?

The Indispensable Checklist. If you plan to visit three different establishments, you can draw up a list of questions, and to the right of each question, set up columns for Yes/No answers. Here's how it might look:

	Parkside	*Lenox Geriatric*	*Lutheran*
Has it been recommended by someone you trust?	yes | no	yes | no	yes | no

The following is a list of suggested questions whose answers will make it easier to compare advantages and disadvantages. While the "Safety" category is more basic than some others, once these requirements are met, many other factors will affect your final choice.

SAFETY CONSIDERATIONS

- Is the building fire-resistant or fireproof?
- Is there an automatic sprinkler system?
- Are smoke detectors installed throughout the building?
- Are there portable fire extinguishers?

- Are all exit doors clearly marked?
- Are they easy to open from inside?
- Are fire drills held on a regular basis?
- Are hallways properly lighted and free of obstructions?
- Are hallways equipped with handrails on both sides?
- Are grab bars installed in all bathing and toilet areas?
- Are call bells installed at all beds and in all bathrooms?
- Are they in good working order?

INSTITUTIONAL MATTERS

- Is the facility run for profit?
- Is it licensed for the current year?
- Is it accredited by the Joint Commission on Accreditation of Hospitals?
- Is a statement of Patients' Rights conspicuously posted?
- Have you been able to examine the most recent state inspection report?
- Does the Admissions Agreement require that a new resident be given a complete medical examination immediately before or immediately after acceptance?
- Does the facility provide special services required by your parent's condition?
- Are the mentally incompetent or mentally disturbed residents housed on a separate floor or in a different wing of the building rather than with the patients whose mental faculties are functioning normally?
- Is it close enough to a good hospital to facilitate emergency transfer to intensive care?
- Is the atmosphere bright and cheerful or drab and underlit?
- Are residents alert and communicative or do most appear to be withdrawn or overtranquilized?
- Are there no more than four beds in a room?
- Do most rooms have two beds?
- Does every bedroom have a window?
- Do all bedrooms open out onto a corridor?
- Are wheelchair ramps provided for easy access to essential areas?

PROFESSIONAL SERVICES

- Are a physician and registered nurse promptly available on a twenty-four-hour basis?

- Are dentists, eye doctors, podiatrists, and other specialists available on a regular schedule?
- Are rehabilitation programs conducted on a full-time basis or only one or two days a week?
- Are these programs supervised by professionally accredited personnel?
- Does the number of nurses and nurses' aides appear to be adequate for the needs of the residents? (Ask them how they feel about the availability of help when they need it.)
- Are all drugs stored in a room set aside for that purpose?
- Does the pharmacist keep a record of each person's drugs?
- Have individual drug records been computerized so that potentially dangerous combinations can promptly be brought to the doctor's attention?

FINDING OUT ABOUT FOOD

- Is the kitchen clean and is all garbage properly contained?
- Is a dietitian in charge of meal preparation for residents with special requirements?
- Are meals nutritious, varied, and attractively presented?
- Are the portions large enough?
- Are the menus prepared a week in advance? Does the meal being served conform to the menu entry?
- Are nourishing snacks available between meals and at bedtime?
- Is there an attractive dining area for ambulatory residents?
- Is it accessible by wheelchair too?
- Are there sufficient staff members to help those who need it at mealtime before the food gets cold?
- Are individual food preferences taken into account?

RECREATION

- Is there a recreation program organized by a paid professional?
- Are the cultural and educational resources of the community an integral part of this program?
- Are residents taken on group outings to special events?
- Are social and recreational activities planned for patients confined to their own room?
- Is there a choice of activities for each day and evening?
- Are attractively equipped rooms set aside for socializing, playing cards or word games, sewing, and the like?
- Is there a library on the premises that is constantly replenished?

- Are the grounds safe and well maintained so that patients can spend time out of doors?
- Is good use made of community volunteers for visiting, intergenerational activities, celebration of religious holidays, and birthdays?
- Does the Residents Council participate in recreational planning?

PERSONAL MATTERS

- Is every resident's room area provided with a comfortable chair, good reading light, chest of drawers, shelf space, and a closet for personal possessions?
- Are residents permitted to bring a favorite piece of furniture from home?
- Are residents assured of privacy in toilet and bathing facilities, and for dressing and undressing?
- May residents wear their own clothes?
- Are there facilities on the premises for keeping these clothes clean?
- Are the services of a barber and hairdresser regularly available?
- Can outgoing calls be made in complete privacy?
- Can visitors be received in complete privacy?

If you plan to make a follow-up visit after the first one, try to do so after dinner, sometime around 7 P.M., so that you can find out about the evening atmosphere and activities.

Spelling Out the Financial Arrangements

To avoid future wrangling about money, take the time to find out everything you can about how the bills are drawn up and what charges are considered "extras." Even though a facility may be reimbursed by Medicare and eventually by Medicaid, the reimbursement is never total. Be sure you know *well in advance* what will be covered by your parent's insurance. Find out what is covered by the basic daily charge. Find out what is *not* included in the basic charge. If these matters are spelled out in the contract, be sure you understand exactly what the relevant clauses say.

Ask to see a few typical bills (with the residents' names masked, of course) in order to have a clear idea of what the billing procedure is like. In most facilities, extra charges vary from patient to patient and from month to month. For example, additional charges are likely to be made for special laboratory tests, medications, speech and/or therapy sessions beyond those covered by insurance, and for professional services by a dentist or podiatrist. In some nursing homes, "special" diets are part of the basic fee; in others, they are "extra."

If at the time of admission, a resident's assets—in the form of Social Security and pension checks as well as cash—are turned over to the facility, what kind of monthly accounting is provided to indicate the administration's withdrawal from these funds? Are they deposited in an account that collects interest? How is the transition to Medicaid handled when these funds are depleted?

The following formulation of financial arrangements prevails in many not-for-profit nursing homes. You should be provided with a similar statement when you request information about how your parent's care will be paid for:

> Residents need to use all their assets (capital) and income towards their care; supplementation via Medicaid is worked out when their resources are gone. Residents may retain $2850.00 as allowable savings as well as an additional $1500.00 specifically earmarked as a burial fund. All financial details are kept confidential.

————————

If the situation in your family is such that one parent will go into a nursing home while the other remains in the community, BE SURE YOU KNOW WHETHER YOUR STATE HAS PASSED A SEPARATION OF ASSETS law that protects a fair portion of joint assets for the *uninstitutionalized* spouse against the requirements of Medicaid eligibility for the payment of nursing home care.

This information can be supplied by your state's Office on Aging, the Long-Term Care Ombudsman, the local Senior Citizen Information and Referral Service, or the local Medicaid office.

————————

๑ 9 ๑

JOINING FORCES
FOR BETTER SOLUTIONS

PROFESSIONAL HELP IS ON THE WAY—AT A PRICE: THE PRIVATE GERIATRIC CARE MANAGER

In the fall of 1985, a new category of health care professionals serving the needs of middle and upper class families with an aging parent convened for a first national meeting in New York City. When the conference was announced under the title, "Private Geriatric Care in the 21st Century: A Call to a New Profession," no more than fifty participants were expected. It turned out that more than a hundred practitioners answered the call—mainly social workers, but a few psychologists and nurses as well. They came to Manhattan from as far as California to share the problems they face in capitalizing on a growing demand for their services.

Private geriatric case workers have been in business in many parts of the country for many years, and their clientele has been steadily increasing, especially because more and more older people live alone and prefer to remain in their own community, often at a considerable distance from their sons and daughters. Even when the adult offspring live nearby, they prefer to pay a private consultant to deal with the daily needs of an aging parent rather than to turn to the many free or less costly services available to them. Also, many feel that on a short-term basis, money is well spent for knowledgeable guidance on how best to proceed on their own. A consultant who lays out a plan of action in a few sessions, especially in an emergency situation, is thought to be well worth the price.

Although many social workers feel that nonprofit agencies offer

similar help and referrals free of charge or on a sliding scale, the
private practitioners point out that families who can afford to pay
for "special" custom-tailored assistance are entitled to get it. But
Representative Claude Pepper warns, "In theory these services
may be a good idea, but if people turn to them instead of to the
public services we have worked so hard to put in place, we may
lose those public services. The public also has to keep in mind that
there is no watchdog for this group."[1]

How These Services Work

Most private case managers function both as short-term consultants and long-term overseers. Some concern themselves mainly
with health and home management, others take on legal tasks and
estate management, and a growing number specialize in establishing a network that connects an aging parent and a concerned son
or daughter living in different states.

In a typical short-term situation, the care manager meets with
the family caregiver—and with the parent—in order to assess the
problems so that available options can be spelled out. Such an
overview may require no more than three sessions at a cost of
about $150 to $200 for the first consultation, during which the
parent may be visited at home, and $50 to $60 per hour thereafter.
Ongoing hourly services can relieve family members of the responsibility of making arrangements for home-care services, of
researching entitlement programs, and of finding qualified legal
and medical advice as the need arises. Short-term services billed at
various rates might involve installing a part-time homemaker for
your father when he returns home from the hospital, or hiring a
weekly companion to accompany your mother to her appointments with the doctor and the hairdresser. Long-term services are
especially helpful not only when children and parents are separated by distance, but also when the son or daughter can't take
time off from work or from other responsibilities to be available
whenever a crisis arises.

Once having established a working relationship with a private
care manager, arrangements can be made—in some cases for a
monthly retainer—for continuing supervision of your parent's
condition. Visits by the social worker in charge can inform you
that more help is needed to enable your father to remain in his

1. New York *Times,* October 15, 1985.

own dwelling, or that the time is approaching when a nursing home should be considered. These consultants also take on the job of finding the right type of institutional care to meet your parent's needs as well as the family's requirements.

If you plan to hire a private geriatric professional to help you deal with the problems of caregiving, be sure that you discuss this decision with your parent in advance. Some older people resent the intrusion of a "stranger" in what they feel should remain a family situation. Or they may interpret this new element in their lives as the first step to total abandonment. However, the greater the extent to which your parent participates in the decisions affecting his or her well-being, the greater the willingness to cooperate with the care manager's recommendations.

Since money is going to change hands—and in some cases, a considerable amount of money—it should be clear at the outset whether *you* are paying for the care manager's services, or whether your parent will be paying for at least a portion of them. If a three-way discussion is needed to clarify financial arrangements, be sure that the discussion takes place *before* misunderstandings occur that can complicate a family situation that may be sufficiently complicated already. Even though private geriatric family *counseling* isn't covered by insurance, some of the recommended services are reimbursable. The counselor will advise you about these entitlements. Also if you are paying for the counseling on behalf of a dependent parent, there are some circumstances under which IRS regulations will permit you to claim part of the cost as a tax deduction.

Private geriatric case managers can be located through hospital social services and community family service organizations. The information and referral services of the local Area Agency on Aging is another source. The classified or yellow pages of your telephone directory also includes these professionals under the heading "Social Services."

MAKING THE MOST OF MUTUAL HELP GROUPS

There's nothing new about seeking practical advice and emotional support among family members and friends in dealing with life's larger problems. But there are times when these informal "networks" are inadequate, or when relationships within the family are part of the problem rather than the source of a solution.

Many reasons account for the proliferation of mutual help or self-help groups during the past decade. One of the most important is that participants offer each other not sympathy, but *empathy*. Whether you're being worn down by the unpredictable behavior of a father functionally impaired by Alzheimer's disease, or you're trying to juggle the demands of a recently widowed mother with the needs of your own children, you can connect with a group of people living through the same experiences. As soon as you arrive and begin to talk about your feelings, the other group members can identify with practically all of them. Especially refreshing to anyone who has felt isolated and helpless is the sense of security that comes from this type of group participation.

The success of the self-help movement can be measured by the fact that there are now about 500,000 groups across the country and more than 30 regional clearinghouses that provide information about them. The National Self-Help Clearinghouse (see page 75 for address) attempts to keep up-to-date with the whereabouts of these regional centers. Hospitals, mental health agencies, and social service organizations are a helpful source too.

Some areas are following the lead of New Jersey, the first state in the United States to create a *computerized* source of information through the clearinghouse toll-free phone number 800-FOR-MASH (Mutual Aid Self Help). Callers who dial this number (translatable as 800-367-6274) will be given information about the whereabouts of particular groups in their immediate vicinity, or if necessary, the service will continue the search to adjacent counties, and it will provide out-of-state group contacts as well. The computerized clearinghouse also offers contacts and guidelines for those who wish to start a new group.

Children of Aging Parents (CAPS)

From its modest beginnings as "rap sessions" in Levittown, Pennsylvania, living rooms during the late 1970s, Children of Aging Parents now has a network of affiliates throughout the state and has helped launch similar groups (with different names) throughout the country. It is currently estimated that about fifteen thousand family caregivers belong to such groups, and their number increases each year.

The original group publishes a newsletter, *The CAPSule,* containing information about issues affecting families with an aging parent. In addition, CAPS continues to help other groups get organized by providing manuals and videotapes. One of its most productive activities is matching people who write for information about starting a group with those who want to join one. This matching is done by pairing the correspondents' zip codes. CAPS also provides information about self-help clearinghouses nationwide.

Children of Aging Parents can be addressed at:

CAPS Office
2761 Trenton Road, Levittown, Pennsylvania 19056
(215) 547-1070

Send a stamped self-addressed envelope with your request for information.

A recent survey by the National Council on the Aging has discovered that more than three hundred groups similar to CAPS are functioning in thirty-eight states. One of the results of the survey is the Council's *Idea Book on Caregiver Support Groups.* To order a copy, send your request together with a check or money order for $5 to:

NCOA Publications Department
600 Maryland Avenue, S.W., West Wing 100
Washington, D.C. 20024

BACK TO THE CAMPUS: COURSES FOR CAREGIVERS

In addition to the informal workshops and self-help seminars that are increasingly common in many communities, colleges and universities with comprehensive "continuing education" and "lifetime learning" programs are scheduling afternoon, evening, and Saturday lecture courses for family caregivers. A typical course offered in 1985 at the University of Southern Maine in Portland was called "You and Your Aging Parent" and was described in part as follows:

> Each of us will be facing adjustments and decisions regarding older family members. How we think about our own aging process and how we relate to older people will be extremely important in maintaining successful family relationships across generations. This course will discuss the aging process, the problems and opportunities associated with old age, and special issues of concern to adults with elderly parents, such as health concerns, Alzheimer's disease, community support programs, handling the decision-making process regarding independent vs. dependent living situations.

The course met on four successive Saturdays; each session ran for two and a half hours, and the tuition was $50. The lecturer was an associate professor of "educational gerontology"—a recent academic discipline.

If you're interested in taking such a course, you can probably locate one by calling the registrar of the extension division of your local city or state college or university. Libraries usually post notices of such courses, which may also be given under the auspices of a church or synagogue or other community institution.

MAKING THE MOST OF THE MEDIA

Are you and your parents aware of the local newspapers, radio programs, and television broadcasts that concern themselves exclusively with issues of interest to older citizens and their caregivers? Not only does this coverage offer useful information and entertainment, but also readers—or listeners or viewers as the case may be—are encouraged to participate with their own questions and comments. Printed matter ranges from substantial newspapers such as *Senior Edition* published in Denver, to *Senior Summary,* a twenty-page bimonthly published as a community service by the New York Junior League, to weekly newsletters that are photocopied and distributed at senior centers. Contents include nutrition and menu suggestions, health notes, news of local and federal bills and community services. Most publications encourage readers to submit reminiscences, short stories, poetry, and other creative contributions—and the contributors do enjoy seeing their names in print!

Older audiences and their families are also well served by daytime radio programs usually aired on public radio stations. This medium continues to be especially popular with the age group that grew up with it, and programs that are built around talks by specialists or debates on important news items followed by telephone participation by listeners always have a loyal following.

A radio project that has served as one of the models for similar projects across the country is WNYC's "Senior Edition," now called "New York and Company," begun in 1980 in cooperation with the New York City Department for the Aging and other social service agencies. It is broadcast daily from 10 A.M. to noon, and includes interviews, documentary features, call-in segments with experts and elected officials, as well as public service announcements of interest to the elderly. Among the topics covered are government entitlements, medical and health problems, legal and financial issues, consumer counseling, and cultural features—all without interruption for commercial messages.

If your parents have access to a public radio station in their area, be sure they know whether a similar program is part of the broadcast schedule. And if it isn't, you might encourage them to start a movement for one. One way to begin is to get a local bank or a group of merchants to underwrite part of the cost.

Public television stations throughout the country are scheduling programs similar to *Gray Matters,* shown every Saturday morning at 6:30 A.M. on WGME-TV Channel 13, based in Augusta, Maine. (If you or your parents have a VCR, you could tape this for viewing at a more convenient hour.) Each week this program, which is presented under the auspices of the Maine Committee on Aging, focuses on an issue of special interest to senior citizens. It also includes a segment called "Maine Faces," featuring an interview with an older resident. The "Health Spot" offers a weekly suggestion about self-care, and letters from viewers are answered in the "Letter Corner." Viewers are invited to comment on the contents of the program and to appear on it when they have a message of particular interest to communicate.

Be sure to check the Public Television channel's listings for similar programs in your parents' area. The relevance of the material presented, the opportunity to identify with those who appear on the screen, and the possibilities for personal appearance are great morale boosters.

As the percentage of people over sixty-five in the population continues to grow, all the media can be expected to play an increasingly active role in advocacy for this group and their families. In this regard, two important presentations were made in 1985: The first was "Who's Taking Care of Our Parents?" the cover feature of the May 6 issue of *Newsweek* magazine. The subtitle for this extensively researched story is a pithy summary of its contents. "As Americans live longer, more and more children face the reality of becoming parents to their aging parents. Most cope well—some heroically—but the emotional and financial toll is high."

And at the year's end, during prime time on Saturday, December 28, the ABC Television Network presented a three-hour special news "closeup" from 8 to 11 P.M. called "Growing Old in America." The program, which was the result of nine months of research and in-depth interviews with a broad spectrum of experts, gave its viewers a close and chillingly accurate look at the harsh realities facing millions of America's aged and their families.

While such presentations don't pretend to offer easy answers, they do zero in on the problems, and it can only be hoped that they increase the determination of young and old alike to combine their voices, their volunteer advocacy, and their votes to force health professionals, policymakers, and all shapers of social change to provide more humane solutions to the problems of aging in America.

MAKING THE RIGHT CONNECTIONS: LEGAL ADVOCACY FOR THE AGED

A hopeful development in caring for the elderly is the combining of previously separate resources in order to improve necessary services. Geriatricians are calling on the expertise of nutritionists, neurologists, and molecular biologists to help them arrive at a clearer understanding of the aging process. Intergenerational projects are flourishing as child development specialists pool their knowledge with specialists in the social needs of the old—and the result is the creation of day care centers that serve the needs of both groups (as mentioned in Chapter 8). And last year, for the first time in the history of the Long-Term Care Ombudsman Program, the District of Columbia Office on Aging contracted with one of its agencies, Legal Counsel for the Elderly, to perform the day-to-day functions of the Ombudsman.

More and more frequently, as an aging population challenges some of the consequences of changing government regulations on the national and state level, as adult children help their parents fight against age discrimination or for pension entitlements, as a spouse needs to know her rights to a share of joint assets preceding her husband's entering a nursing home, legal services are more and more in demand. From one end of the country to the other, social workers and family counselors are combining their experience with the advocacy know-how of lawyers in dealing with such issues as Medicare, Medicaid, Supplemental Security Income, disability insurance, voluntary and involuntary commitment, and elderly exemption from rent increases.

Legal advocates for your parents can also be consulted about such matters as the most effective way to draw a will, how your father can draw up a prenuptial contract if he's marrying again and his new wife has her own grown children and grandchildren, what loopholes to look for when signing a nursing home contract, and when a transfer of assets is a legal option and when it becomes a crime.

Most family service agencies have inaugurated legal advocacy programs for the aged. The Institute on Law and Rights of Older Adults of the Brookdale Center on Aging of Hunter College has developed an internship program for lawyers that has become a model for similar programs elsewhere. In addition to publishing the *Senior Rights Reporter,* which keeps abreast of the relevant developments in government regulations and legal precedents established in the courts, the institute administers a Legal Entitlement and Advocacy Program (LEAP). Begun in 1982 as a partnership between social workers and lawyers concerned with the rights of the elderly poor, it has since that time trained thousands of community advocates to represent claimants' rights at Fair Hearings.

The Fair Hearings system is national in scope. Your parents' access to this system is based on the following concepts: Every American citizen is guaranteed due process of law as spelled out in the Fifth Amendment of the Constitution, which specifies (in part) that no state shall "deprive any person of life, liberty, or property without due process of law. . . ." Because such programs as Social Security, Medicare, and Medicaid are enacted in law, they are therefore property rights and not charity. When the Supreme Court issued a decision in 1970 upholding a welfare recipient's due process rights, and ruled that before a benefit could be terminated by a government agency, the beneficiary was entitled to an impartial hearing, the groundwork was laid for the guaranteed right to a Fair Hearing. Should circumstances arise in which your parent is deprived of government benefits, or should such benefits be curtailed in a manner you consider legally unjustifiable, take the problem to a suitable legal advocate for the prompt preparation of a formal application for a hearing.

The advocate, who may be a lawyer or a social worker, will spell out your parent's rights. These include the right to study the government's file and the material on which the decision has been made to limit or withdraw the benefits; the right to be represented at an administrative hearing by a lawyer and/or social worker, relatives, and friends; the right to submit evidence and subpoena government witnesses and cross-examine them; and the right to a written decision. According to the LEAP Program of the Institute on Law and Rights of Older Adults, their representation at hearings caused the government agency's initial determination to reduce or deny benefits to be reversed or significantly changed in the claimant's favor in 94 percent of the cases.

Legal advocacy for the aged has also been increasingly effective in lobbying state legislatures for the passage of laws that improve programs and services for them. Recent enactments in various parts of the country that may affect the well-being of your parents include special access requirements for the physically handicapped or disabled, appropriation of funds for the establishment of centers for the education of health professionals, abolition of mandatory retirement based on age, and allocation of funds for occupational retraining programs for men and women sixty years of age and older.

Information about lawyers who specialize in problems affecting the aged and their families is available from the Bar Association in your state and from social services in your community. The following sources may also be helpful:

Institute on Law and Rights of Older Adults
425 East 25th Street, New York, N.Y. 10010
(212) 481-4426

National Senior Citizens Law Center
1636 West 8th Street, Suite 201
Los Angeles, California 90017
(213) 388-1381

Legal Counsel for the Elderly
1909 K Street, N.W., Washington, D.C. 20006
(202) 728-4333

This organization offers free legal services to needy D.C. residents over age sixty and conducts training programs on a national basis for legal advocacy in areas such as retirement benefits, medical care, disability entitlements, housing, and the like.

IN THE FOREFRONT OF FAMILY SERVICES:
THE RELIGIOUS PHILANTHROPIES

An unfailing source of support on the local level for young and old alike are the services provided by such organizations as Protestant Welfare Agencies, Catholic Charities, and the Federation of Jewish Philanthropies. Practically everywhere in the United States, these and similar groups offer counseling, referral, and information to individuals in need of guidance. Since the early twentieth century, these organizations have pioneered in the training of volunteers, conducting educational campaigns, and promoting pilot programs that serve as models for the community. For example:

The Division on Aging of the Federation of Protestant Welfare Agencies in New York recently convened an ad hoc committee of

representative agencies to deal with the problem of abuse of the
elderly. The Jewish Association of Services for the Aged (JASA),
a member agency of the Federation of Jewish Philanthropies, includes among its many activities a Joint Public Affairs Committee
(JPAC) that educates older adults to participate in social action
campaigns and to meet with local legislators, thus fostering leadership development among seniors. Based in Boston, the Unitar-
ian Universalist Service Committee has developed a comprehensive program, Creative Living Environments in Old Age, whose
purpose is to help older people make independent choices and act
in their own behalf. This organization is primarily concerned with
providing education for action on the local and national level so
that older members of minority groups who have had less access
to existing services throughout their lives can finally make their
needs known and their political power respected. This committee
works closely with such groups as the National Caucus and Center for the Black Aged, the National Association of Lesbian and
Gay Gerontology, and the *Asociacion Nacional Pro Personas
Mayores.* In its coalition with advocacy groups across the country,
the Service Committee founded the Boston Chapter of the Older
Women's League (OWL), and together, they sponsored a conference on women and aging, with special emphasis on women and
poverty.

The local affiliates of religious philanthropies can be located
through your family's religious affiliation, through the
United Way, or by consulting the Social Services heading in
your area's classified telephone directory.

In addition to the many organizations mentioned throughout
these pages, the following offer information, special resources, and community services to local affiliates:

American Society on Aging
833 Market Street, Suite 516
San Francisco, California 94103   (415) 543-2617

Founded in 1954 as the Western Gerontological Society, the ASA is a broad coalition. In concert with other organizations, it is a watchdog for legislation that affects the elderly and focuses its efforts on influencing public opinion and policy. It has recently established a Training Center on Aging that sponsors low-cost educational programs designed to provide leadership training for elders.

Center for the Study of Aging
706 Madison Avenue
Albany, New York 12208   (518) 465-6927

The center conducts educational and research activities, leads seminars and workshops, and maintains a reference library of five thousand books as well as a circulating library of cassette tapes for community use.

National Alliance of Senior Citizens
101 Park Washington Court
Falls Church, Virginia 22046   (703) 241-1533

This organization claims a membership of about 770,000. In its efforts to affect policymaking, it publishes ratings of members of Congress based on their voting records on matters such as inflation, Social Security, and crime. Its rating standards reflect the views of the right wing of the Republican Party and of the Moral Majority.

National Council of Senior Citizens
925 15th Street, N.W.
Washington, D.C. 20005   (202) 347-8800

The council has about 4 million members who belong to action groups throughout the United States that advocate improvement in all the services, laws, and programs affecting the elderly. It is also the clearinghouse for information on Medicare, housing, and long-term care, and since 1973, has been rating the voting records of members of Congress on issues that affect the aging population. The council was founded in 1958 to promote the election of John F. Kennedy, and it continues to support liberal policies and liberal legislators.

National Caucus & Center on the Black Aged
1424 K Street, N.W., Suite 500
Washington, D.C. 20005   (202) 637-8400

The caucus represents forty-five local groups nationwide. It owns and manages rental housing, and it lobbies for improvement in federal, state, and local laws affecting black senior citizens.

———————————

It wasn't too long ago that children of aging parents could depend only on each other's resources or the availability of family members when there was a crisis or the need for long-term care. The only alternative was a nursing home.

In recent decades, however, some progress has been made in recognizing the special continuum of needs of the elderly. Of particular significance is the increasing awareness that since most of the help for the elderly is provided by their families, there is a critical need for programs that help the *families* take care of their parents as well as for programs that help the elderly themselves.

Throughout the preceding pages, efforts have been made to give you the necessary information about programs, resources, and strategies for caring for your parents as their needs change. In the pages that follow, you'll find the location and phone number of the Office on Aging officially designated to serve your parents' area and to supply specific referrals and additional information.

Many of the services on the federal, state, and local level are the result of ongoing activities of advocacy groups for the elderly and the recognition by policymakers that people over sixty-five are increasingly important as a political force. One of the most effective ways in which you can safeguard the well-being of your parents (as well as your own future) is to protect the rights of older citizens everywhere and to join in the fight for responsible government policies on all levels. Such hard-won programs as Social Security, Medicare, and subsidized housing, and nutrition, transportation, and information and referral services are increasingly under siege by those policymakers who want to turn back the clock and place practically the entire burden of parent care on the backs of family members, friends, and volunteers.

The stance of the Reagan administration vis-à-vis you and your parents is that you and your parents have no right to expect *any* government assistance unless the *entire family* is on the brink of disaster. Many state and local programs have already suffered because of cuts in federal funding.

Be forewarned. Keep an alert and wary eye on the politicians whose power derives from the votes cast by you and your parents. Make sure that they serve your best interests so that your parents can receive the consideration and care they deserve.

Appendix

A STATE-BY-STATE GUIDE
TO SERVICES AND RESOURCES
FOR THE AGING AND
THEIR FAMILIES

It wasn't until thirty years after the passage of the Social Security Act that the federal government acknowledged official responsibility for attending to the special needs of the aging population. In 1965, the Medicare bill was finally passed, and in the same year, Congress passed the Older Americans Act and mandated the establishment of the Administration on Aging as part of the Department of Health, Education and Welfare (now the Department of Health and Human Services).

From that time to this, the act has been amended many times—to extend its provisions and to spell out in detail how programs are to be funded and with what priorities the funds are to be allocated. In 1973, for example, each state agency on aging was required to divide the state into planning and service areas and to designate within each an Area Agency on Aging to carry out their programs. In 1978, one amendment among many others mandated that state agencies establish and operate a long-term care ombudsman program.

The chief responsibility of every state's Area Agency on Aging is to formulate comprehensive areawide plans and programs, including a broad range of social services for the elderly. In addition to serving as the focus for community resources and to attending to health care, housing, and nutrition needs, the Area Agencies must use half the funds allocated by Title III of the Older Americans Act to facilitate transportation, provide information and referral, and pay for essential in-home services and legal counseling.

Eligibility qualifications for some of these programs are established by the state; other programs are available free to all senior citizens regardless of income, and still others expect participants to pay for services with fees based on a sliding scale.

The funds made available by the amended Older Americans Act for the creation on the state level of the Office of Ombudsman nationwide and without exception were to be applied to a program that would "receive, investigate, and act on" *all* complaints about long-term care facilities. (Many states have extended this program to boarding house and congregate living facilities.) The program may include the training and certification of regional ombudsmen to facilitate the investigation and adjudication of complaints on the local level. In many states, regional ombudsmen and their volunteers are responsible for working with the personnel of the facilities, with community organizations, and with the families of the institutionalized to promote awareness of the needs of the residents.

By the end of the 1970s, practically every state legislature mandated the creation of a State Division on Aging or an Office on Aging as part of its Department of Health and Human Services or its equivalent. As required by federal regulations that implement the Older Americans Act, these agencies have two categories of responsibility: (1) advocacy for the aging and aged, and   (2) delivery of services.

The following are some of the requirements that state offices on aging must fulfill in connection with advocacy:

- Review all state plans, budgets, and policies affecting the elderly
- Conduct public hearings on the needs of older persons
- Represent the interests of older persons before legislative, executive, and regulatory agencies of the state
  And among requirements for fulfilling the "service delivery" are the following:
- Develop and administer the state plan
- Divide the state into planning and service areas
- Provide adequate and effective opportunities for older persons to express their views to the state agency on policy development
- Give preference to older persons with the greatest economic or social need for the delivery of services
- Provide administrative and hearing procedures

- Ensure that all older persons have reasonably convenient access to information and referral services
- Establish an advisory council on aging

In connection with this last requirement, state lawmakers have legislated the creation of such advisory bodies—in some states known as the Advisory Council on Aging; in others, the Commission on Aging. These bodies, which have the primary function of developing general policy, consist of from twelve to twenty members, some of whom are appointed by the legislature, some by the governor. A majority must be sixty years old or older and represent the widest possible combination of different social, geographical, and ethnic groups. Members serve for a limited time and are required by federal regulations to meet at least four times a year and to submit to the governor and to the legislature an annual report in cooperation with the state department on aging that evaluates "the level and quality of all programs, services, and facilities provided to the aging by state agencies."

The information that follows is based on material provided by the department (or division or office) on aging located in the capital city of each state (and the District of Columbia). In view of continuing cuts in the federal budget, many programs that depend on funding from Washington may have been curtailed or may no longer exist. It should also be kept in mind that each Area Agency on Aging has a certain amount of autonomy and may differ in its services from similar agencies in other parts of the state.

An abundant amount of useful information is provided by your local telephone directories. If you haven't done so already, take a close look at the blue pages in the back of the regular directory. The detailed listings for city, state, and U.S. government offices are preceded by the "Easy Reference List [of] Government Offices" arranged by the functions provided. This list contains the address and phone number of local offices of Medicare and Medicaid, Social Security and SSI, senior citizen services, the Veterans Benefits Administration, and the like. More detailed information can be found in:

- The blue pages headed "United States Government Offices," under "Health & Human Services, Dept. of"
- The blue pages headed "State Government Offices," under listings such as "Aging," which lists local Area Agencies on Aging; "Health Services," "Housing," "Home Care," and other state-sponsored programs

■ The blue pages headed "City Government Offices," under listings such as "Aging," "Community Services," and "Human Resources"

The separate telephone directory containing the "classified" or yellow pages provides up-to-the-minute information under headings such as "Home Health Services," "Nurses," "Nursing Homes," "Senior Citizen Service Organizations," and "Social Service Organizations."

If you have already begun to explore and make use of some of the support systems available to you and your parents, it is hoped that the material in the following pages will be an additional source of help. Even if your parents are still living healthy independent lives, there's no harm in finding out what resources you could call upon if the need should arise. Keep in mind that even though priority is given to those older people who are in greatest financial need, *many* programs are available to *all* senior citizens, and when charges are involved, they are based on the family's ability to pay. Get to know your way around in the world of social services. Send for the available handbooks and guides offered by your state's department on aging. You may never find yourself in a crisis situation because of your parents' unanticipated needs; however, should problems develop that require speedy assistance, it's comforting that you've found out in advance where to turn for help.

Where a toll-free 800 telephone number is provided for a state agency, it usually operates only within the state. A reliable source of information is Family Service America, a nonprofit organization that will provide the name and phone number of one of its 280 member agencies operating throughout the United States and Canada. The agencies, whose services are available to everyone regardless of religious affiliation or income, offer counseling for all family members. They can arrange for care by home attendants, and nurses will make referrals to hospitals, nursing homes, and local services for the elderly. Fees for the local agencies' services are reasonable and are determined by the client's household income. Questions about financial arrangements and other matters can be discussed in advance by telephone when calling the local agency. Information about the most accessible agency is available from:

Family Service America
11700 West Lake Park Drive
Milwaukee, Wisconsin 53224
(414) 359-2111

Area Agencies on Aging service every community in the United States. If you or your parents have any difficulty in finding the agency that serves their locality, call the official state unit on aging or write to:

The National Association of Area Agencies on Aging
600 Maryland Avenue, S.W., Washington, D.C. 20024

ALABAMA

Commission on Aging
502 Washington Avenue
Montgomery, Alabama 36130
(205) 261-5473

The Alabama Aging Network consists of thirteen Area Agencies on Aging and numerous local programs. Each Agency is unique, and while the availability of services varies from one to another, major and essential services are said to be provided in every community.

FIFTY-TWO SERVICES FOR ALABAMIANS SIXTY AND OLDER
    A. Area Agency on Aging activities in support of ombudsman
    B. Advocacy assistance
    C. Casework
    D. Chore maintenance
    E. Commodities distribution
    F. Community focal points
    G. Complaint and grievance resolution
    H. Congregate nutrition services
    I. Continuing education
    J. Counseling
    K. Daycare
    L. Disaster relief
    M. Emergency services
    N. Emergency response services

    O. Employment services
    P. Escort
    Q. Foster care
    R. Foster grandparents program
    S. Group services for residents of care-providing facilities
    T. Health screening
    U. Health services
    V. Home companions
    W. Home-delivered nutrition services
    X. Home health services
    Y. Homemakers
    Z. Individual needs assessment
  AA. Information and referral
  BB. Legal services
  CC. Mental health services
  DD. Medicaid waiver, home and community-based services
  EE. Multipurpose senior centers
  FF. Nutrition education
  GG. Outreach
  HH. Personal identification
   II. Physical fitness
   JJ. Placement and relocation assistance
  KK. Postal alert
  LL. Pre-institutional evaluation
 MM. Protective services
  NN. Reading services
  OO. Recreation
  PP. Residential location and assistance
  QQ. Retired senior volunteer programs
  RR. Senior companions programs
  SS. Service management
  TT. Shopping
  UU. Special services for the disabled
  VV. Transportation
WW. Telephone reassurance
  XX. Visiting reassurance
  YY. Volunteerism opportunities
  ZZ. Writing services

For detailed information and referral about these and other community programs, contact the Area Agency on Aging that serves your parents' county.

Area Agencies on Aging

1. *Northwest Alabama Council of Local Governments*
   400 West Hamilton Street, P.O. Box L
   Russellville, AL 35653   (205) 332-9173
   > Counties served: Colbert, Franklin, Lauderdale, Marion, Winston

2. *West Alabama Planning & Development Council*
   Tuscaloosa Municipal Airport, Terminal Bldg, 2d floor,
   P.O. Box 749
   Northport, AL 35476   (205) 345-5545
   > Counties served: Bibb, Fayette, Greene, Hale, Lamar, Pickens,
   > Tuscaloosa

3. *Birmingham Regional Planning Commission*
   2112 11th Avenue South, Suite 220
   Birmingham, AL 35256   (205) 251-2125
   > Counties served: Blount, Chilton, Shelby, St. Clair, Walker

3A. *Office of Senior Citizens Activities*
   2601 Highland Avenue
   Birmingham, AL 35205   (205) 251-2992
   > County served: Jefferson

4. *East Alabama Regional Planning & Development Commission*
   P.O. Box 2186, 700 Quintard Avenue
   Anniston, AL 36202   (205) 237-6741
   > Counties served: Calhoun, Chambers, Cherokee, Clay, Cleburne,
   > Coosa, Etowah, Randolph, Talladega, Tallapoosa

5. *South Central Alabama Development Commission*
   2815 East South Boulevard
   Montgomery, AL 36116   (205) 281-2196
   > Counties served: Bullock, Butler, Crenshaw, Lowndes, Macon,
   > Pike

6. *Alabama Tombigbee Regional Commission*
   P.O. Box 269, Courthouse Annex
   Camden, AL 36726   (205) 682-4234
   > Counties served: Choctaw, Clarke, Conecuh, Dallas, Marengo,
   > Monroe, Perry, Sumter, Washington, Wilcox

7. *Southeast Alabama Regional Planning & Development Commission*
   P.O. Box 1406 (205 Plaza 2)
   Dothan, AL 36302   (205) 794-4092
   > Counties served: Barbour, Coffee, Covington, Dale, Geneva,
   > Henry, Houston

8. *South Alabama Regional Planning Commission*
   P.O. Box 1665, 250 North Water Street
   Mobile, AL 36633   (205) 433-6541

9. *Central Alabama Aging Consortium*
   2911 Zelda Road, Suite B
   Montgomery, AL 36106   (205) 271-6761, 6765
   Counties served: Autauga, Elmore, Montgomery

10. *Lee County Area Council of Governments*
    P.O. Box 1072, 118 North Ross Street
    Auburn, AL 36830   (205) 821-3042
    Counties served: Lee, Russell

11. *North Central Alabama Regional Council of Governments*
    P.O. Box C, 402 Lee Street
    Decatur, AL 35602   (205) 355-4515
    Counties served: Cullman, Lawrence, Morgan

12. *Top of Alabama Regional Council of Government*
    115 Washington Street, S.E.
    Huntsville, AL 35801   (205) 533-3330
    Counties served: DeKalb, Jackson, Limestone, Madison, Marshall

ALASKA

Older Alaskans Commission
   Pouch C.M.S. 0209
   Juneau, Alaska 99811   (907) 465-3250
Senior Citizen Ombudsman
   Bill O'Connor
   1317 West Northern Lights Boulevard
   Anchorage, Alaska 99503   (907) 279-2232

The Commission publishes an annual *Directory for Older Alaskan Consumers,* which is a comprehensive guide organized for quick and easy reference. Under the heading "Statewide Services" are listings for such agencies as the Social Security Administration, Veterans Administration, and Ombudsman. Senior centers and local services are listed by city. For example, among the services listed alphabetically for the city of Anchorage are the following:

■ *Alaska Legal Services Corp.*   550 8th Avenue   (907) 272-9431
   Provides legal services to the economically and socially needy and to persons sixty or older.
■ *Alaska Women's Resource Center*   (907) 276-0528
   Offers counseling, support groups, displaced homemaker and housing assistance, medical and legal advocacy, and a substance abuse program.
■ *Anchorage Senior Center*   1300 East 19th Avenue   (907) 338-7823

Conducts health and physical fitness classes, arts and crafts programs, and other recreational and social activities.

The Anchorage listings, typical of those for all other cities, include volunteer opportunities as a senior companion or foster grandparent, a geriatric counseling center, the Older Alaskans Transportation Service, and the Salvation Army Home Care Center. Additional listings for other cities include respite care for family members, counseling for bereaved spouses, health and nutrition clinics, and day care programs.

The directory continues with city-by-city listings of peer and advocacy organizations such as the Alaska Federation of Natives, The American Association of Retired Persons, Retired Teachers Association, and the like. Approximately fifty pages of the directory are devoted to information about special discounts for seniors, including eye care, groceries, hair care, prescription medications, and recreation. The directory concludes with city-by-city listings that cover Senior Housing, Pioneer Homes (retirement housing for those over sixty-five who have lived continuously in the state for fifteen years or more), Residential Care Facilities, Adult Day Care, In-Home Care, Hospice Services, Continuing Education; and Economic Assistance.

The Directory for Older Alaskan Consumers is available for in-state senior citizens on request from:

The Older Alaskans Commission
   or
The Older Persons Action Group
P.O. Box 102240, Anchorage, Alaska 99510   (907) 276-1059

ARIZONA

Aging & Adult Administration
   1400 West Washington Street
   Phoenix, Arizona 85007   (602) 255-4446
Long-Term Care Ombudsman
   Mary Kay at the above address and phone number
The above agency, which is a division of the Arizona Department of Economic Security, does not provide printed information on statewide programs for the aging. It answers questions by phone and refers callers to appropriate resources. Among the services on the community level are:

- *Economic opportunities* for persons fifty-five and over who can work part-time in the community. Following a period of on-the-job training, they are helped to re-enter the labor force.

- *Foster Grandparent Program* provides part-time job opportunities for senior citizens by training them to work with mentally retarded children.

- *Meals* for persons over sixty are served in group settings or are delivered to the homebound when necessary.

- *A Home Care Program* provides the services of a visiting homemaker to assist with chores on a regular basis until self-care can be resumed.

- *Assistance* is available for locating special services to facilitate changes in housing, guardianship, medical care, and legal counseling.

- *Protection services* provide intervention in situations where older adults are unable to care for themselves or are subject to abuse, neglect, or exploitation.

For information about these programs and referral to all agencies and resources on the state, city, and local level concerned with the needs of your parents, call the most conveniently located office listed below. (The area code is 602 throughout.)

Local Offices of the State Aging & Adult Administration:

Bisbee	432-5581	Nogales	287-9416
Casa Grande	836-7435	Parker	669-9293
Coolidge	723-5351	Phoenix	255-4521
Cottonwood	634-7561	Safford	428-2722
Flagstaff	779-3681	Show-Low	537-4261
Globe	425-4459	Tucson	882-5876
Kingman	753-6941	Yuma	783-1231

Information is also available from the following Area Agencies on Aging:

Bisbee	432-5301	Tucson	624-4419
Flagstaff	774-1895	Yuma	782-1886
Phoenix	264-2255		

ARKANSAS

Division of Aging and Adult Services
Donaghey Building, Suite 1428
Seventh and Main Streets
Little Rock, Arkansas 72201   (501) 371-2441
Long-Term Care Advocate
Gary Morgan at the above address and phone number

The Office on Aging issues "Senior Citizens Guides" detailing the programs, services, and resources available in four different parts of the state. The governor's introduction to each brochure says, "One of the most frustrating aspects of a problem can be knowing where to seek help. Some people find this frustration to be especially great when they are dealing with government agencies. This Senior Citizen's Guide was designed to help steer you in the right direction when you have questions about everything from housing to health. . . ."

Among the headings under which detailed information is provided are the following:

- Where do I call for information on all types of services?
- Where can I get medical assistance?
- How can I find out more about Social Security?
- I want more food for my money!
- I want to live in my own home but I need some help!
- Where do I call for housing information?
- Where can I get transportation?
- How can I stay active and involved?
- Could someone call and check up on me?
- Who can counsel or advise me?
- Where can I find a job?
- Where can I get help with consumer problems?
- What is homestead property tax relief?
- Toll-free numbers for twenty-five services and resources
- Fire, police, and ambulance services

The Senior Citizen's Guide to Human Services in Southeast Arkansas is for residents of the following counties:

> Arkansas, Ashley, Bradley, Chicot, Cleveland, Desha, Drew, Grant, Jefferson, and Lincoln.

For a copy of this guide and for additional information about services in this part of the state, contact:

> Area Agency on Aging in Pine Bluff, at 1-800-272-2025

The Senior Citizen's Guide to Human Services in Northcentral Arkansas is for residents of the following counties:

> Cleburne, Fulton, Independence, Izard, Jackson, Sharp, Stone, Van Buren, White, Woodruff.

For a copy of this guide and for additional information about services in this part of the state, contact:

> Area Agency on Aging in Batesville, at 1-800-382-3205

The Senior Citizen's Guide to Human Services in West Central Arkansas is for residents of the following counties:

> Clark, Conway, Hot Springs, Johnson, Perry, Pike, Yell, Garland, Pope, Montgomery.

For a copy of this guide and for additional information about services in this part of the state, contact:

Area Agency on Aging in Hot Springs, at 1-800-272-2138

The Senior Citizen's Guide to Human Services in West Arkansas is for residents of the following counties:

Crawford, Franklin, Logan, Polk, Scott, Sebastian

For a copy of this guide and for additional information about services in this part of the state, contact:

Area Agency on Aging in Fort Smith, at (501) 783-4500

CALIFORNIA

Department of Aging
    1020 19th Street
    Sacramento, California 95814   (916) 322-3887
State Ombudsman
    at the above address   (916) 323-6681

To streamline and coordinate its services to the elderly, the Department of Aging has developed the Seniors' Initiative, a comprehensive program based on demographic surveys and recommendations of such groups as the California Senior Legislature, the State Housing Conference on Aging, the Commission on Aging, and the Area Agency Advisory Council. Under the Seniors' Initiative, the Department of Aging has become responsible for the Multipurpose Senior Service Programs and Adult Day Health Care. It has also increased housing and nutrition services and expanded already existing support for victims of Alzheimer's disease and their families.

To assure access to a continuum of care by the frail or impaired elderly and their families, the department provides a case management system called Linkages. This system connects people with the programs that provide different levels of care so that premature institutionalization can be avoided. To further the well-being of the state's approximately 3¾ million senior citizens, the department focuses on fostering a working relationship among the many agencies and organizations that serve the elderly, supporting community-based long-term care systems, and establishing practical guidelines for the effective use of Title III funds.

By 1980, the Aging Network developed by the department consisted of 33 Area Agencies on Aging which administer 180 nutrition projects at more than 900 sites. The agencies are also in charge of individualized support service programs, including assistance with legal problems, transportation, in-home care, and Social Security and SSI entitlement, as well as health maintenance and screening procedures.

To find out about the services available to your parents on the state and community level, contact the Area Agency on Aging that serves their locality.

Area 1 Agency on Aging
   300 Glenwood Street, Eureka, CA 95501   (707) 442-3763
   Counties served: Del Norte, Humboldt

PSA 2 Area Agency on Aging
   P.O. Box 1400, Yreka, CA 96097   (916) 842-1687
   Counties served: Lassen, Medoc, Shasta, Siskiyou, Trinity

PSA 3 Area on Aging
   University Foundation, California State U., Chico
   Second and Normal Streets, Chico, CA 95929
   Counties served: Butte, Colusa, Glenn, Plumas, Tehama

Area 4 Agency on Aging
   2862 Arden Way, Suite 101, Sacramento, CA 95825
   (916) 486-1876
   Counties served: Nevada, Placet, Sacramento, Sierra, Sutter, Yolo, Yuba

Marin County Agency on Aging
   Marin County Civic Center, Room 279, San Rafael, CA 94903
   (415) 499-7396

San Francisco City & County Commission on Aging
   1360 Mission Street, 4th floor, San Francisco, CA 94013
   (415) 557-5844

Contra Costa County Office on Aging
   2425 Bisso Lane, Suite 110, Concord, CA 94520   (415) 671-4233

San Mateo Area Agency on Aging
   617 Hamilton Street, Redwood City, CA 94063
   (415) 363-4511   363-4221

Alameda County Area Agency on Aging
   1755 Broadway, 5th floor, Oakland, CA 94612   (415) 874-7233

Santa Clara County Council on Aging
   2131 The Alameda, San Jose, CA 95126   (408) 296-8290

San Joaquin County Department of Aging
   222 East Weber Avenue, Room 402, Stockton, CA 95202
   (209) 944-2203

Central Sierra Area Agency on Aging
   56 North Washington Street, Sonora, CA 95370   (209) 532-6272
   Counties served: Alpine, Amador, Calaveras, Mariposa, Tuolumno

Seniors Council of Santa Cruz and San Benito Counties
   234 Santa Cruz Avenue, Aptos, CA 95003
   (408) 688-0400; 476-6033

Fresno-Madera Area Agency on Aging
   1221 Fulton Mall, Suite 553, Fresno, CA 93721   (209) 445-3278

Kings-Tulare Area Agency on Aging
1920 West Princeton, Suite A-B, Visalia, CA 93277
(209) 733-1079

Inyo-Mono Area Agency on Aging
P.O. Box 1799, Bishop, CA 93514 (619) 873-4248

Central Coast Commission for Senior Citizens
122 West El Camino, Santa Maria, CA 93454 (805) 925-9554
Counties served: San Luis Obispo, Santa Barbara

Ventura County Area Agency on Aging
800 South Victoria Avenue, Lower Plaza, Ventura, CA 93009
(805) 654-3560

Los Angeles County Area Agency on Aging
1102 Crenshaw Boulevard, Los Angeles, CA 90019
(213) 857-6401

San Bernadino Office of Aging
686 East Mill Street, San Bernadino, CA 92415 (714) 383-3861

Riverside County Office on Aging
P.O. Box 1480, Riverside, CA 92502 (714) 683-7780

Orange County Area Agency on Aging
801-C North Broadway, Santa Ana, CA 92701 (714) 834-6017

County of San Diego Area Agency on Aging
4161 Marlborough Avenue, San Diego, CA 92105
(619) 236-3467

Imperial County Area Agency on Aging
654 Main Street, El Centro, CA 92243 (619) 352-8521

Los Angeles City Department of Aging
207 South Broadway, 7th floor, Los Angeles, CA 90012
(213) 485-4402

North Coast Area Agency on Aging
101 West Church Street, Ukish, CA 95482 (707) 462-1954
Counties served: Lake, Mendocino

Sonoma County Area Agency on Aging
1488 Guerneville Road, Santa Rosa, CA 95401 (707) 527-3138

Solano-Napa Agency on Aging
1814 Capitol Street, Vallejo, CA 94590 (707) 744-6612

El Dorado County Area Agency on Aging
935-A Spring Street, Placerville, CA 95667 (916) 626-2149

Stanislaus County Area Agency on Aging
1024 J Street, Room 416, Modesto, CA 95354 (209) 571-6700

Merced County Area Agency on Aging
2150 M Street, Suite 3, Merced, CA 95340 (209) 385-7550

Monterey Department of Social Services Area Agency on Aging Division
   P.O. Box 299, Salinas, CA 93902   (408) 449-1877
Kern County Office on Aging
   1415 Truxton Avenue, Bakersfield, CA 93301   (805) 861-2445

A Note on the Ombudsman Program

The program is well publicized in residential care facilities and nursing homes throughout the state. In a recent year, 700 state ombudsmen
and volunteers were trained and certified. Volunteers alone contributed
more than 86,000 hours of service, and the program handled over 20,000
complaints. The program serves about 600 nursing homes (about half of
all such institutions statewide) and about 400 residential care facilities
(approximately 10 percent of those officially designated as such by the
state). If you have any complaints to make on behalf of your parents or
of any elderly person in such a facility, DON'T HESITATE TO FIND OUT
HOW TO GO ABOUT INITIATING AN INVESTIGATION.

COLORADO

Department of Social Services Aging and Adult Services
   1575 Sherman Street
   Denver, Colorado 80203   (303) 294-5905
Long-Term Care Ombudsman
   Virginia Fraser
   1565 Clarkson Street
   Denver, Colorado 80218   (303) 830-7744

The state's Plan on Aging as revised in 1985 takes into account the
continuing increase in the 60+ part of the population and points out
that while the elderly as a group are less poor than they were a decade
ago, "the incidence of poverty remains higher for the elderly than for the
state's population as a whole." The plan also recognizes that people are
now faced with planning for twenty to thirty years of retirement rather
than for only ten, and that married women will have to spend about half
that time as widows. In setting goals, the planners stress the point of
view that "long-term care systems must broaden in focus from the
chronically ill to address the needs of more independent elders for enabling, preventive, and supporting services" and due recognition is given
to the concept that "throughout society the growing emphasis on serving
and empowering older persons across the continuum of need has already
begun to compete with the emphasis on caring for dependent elders."

To inform senior citizens and their families of the services available to
them, the Division of Aging and Adult Services has prepared a guide to

these services, which is available on request. Here is a summary of a typical entry:

TITLE III-B OLDER AMERICANS ACT
SUPPORTIVE SERVICES & SENIOR CENTERS

Services/benefits: Information and referral, legal, transportation, advocacy, coordination, chore, in-home assistance, outreach, senior centers, health screening.

Eligibility: Any individual aged 60 or above. Means test prohibited, but a requirement that services be prioritized for "those of greatest economic or social need," with emphasis on low-income minority elderly.

Access to services: Services provided by private or public agencies under a subgrant or contract from the Area Agency on Aging, or the AAA may be the direct provider.

In addition to the programs described in this publication, each Area Agency on Aging develops additional or substitute programs of its own based on the particular needs of the elderly population in the counties it serves and the network of support resources provided by the local community.

For detailed information about programs available for your parents, contact the Area Agency on Aging that serves their locality.

Area Agencies on Aging

I. *Northeastern Colorado Association of Local Government*
300 Main Street, Fort Horgan, CO 80701   (303) 867-9409
Counties served: Logan, Morgan, Phillips, Sedgwick, Yuma

IIA. *Larimer County Area Agency on Aging*
525 West Oak, Fort Collins, CO 80524   (303) 221-7440

IIB. *Weld County Area Agency on Aging*
Weld County Health Dept Building
1516 Hospital Road, Greeley, CO 80631
(303) 353-0540, ext. 328

III. *Aging Services Division*
2480 West 26th Avenue, Suite 2008, Denver, CO 80211
(303) 455-1000
Counties served: Adams, Arapahoe, Boulder, Clear Creek, Denver, Douglas, Gilpin, Jefferson

IV. *Pikes Peak Area Agency on Aging*
21 East Vermijo, Colorado Springs, CO 80903   (303) 471-7080
Counties served: El Paso, Park, Teller

V. *East Central Council of Government*
P.O. Box 28, Stratton, CO 80836   (303) 348-5562
Counties served: Cheyenne, Ebert, Kit Carson, Lincoln

VI. *Lower Arkansas Valley Area Agency on Aging*
Otero County Courthouse, P.O. Box 494, La Junta, CO 81050
(303) 384-8165
Counties served: Baca, Bent, Crowley, Kiowa, Otero, Pioneers

VIIA. *Pueblo Area Agency on Aging*
228 North Union, Pueblo, CO 81003
(303) 544-4307; 544-7839 (Human Resources Commission)

VIIB. *Huerfana/Las Animas Area Agency on Aging*
Courthouse, Room 201, Trinidad, CO 81082   (303) 846-4401

VIII. *South Central Colorado Seniors Inc.*
P.O. Box 896, Alamosa, CO 81101   (303) 589-4511
Counties served: Alamosa, Conejos, Costilla, Mineral, Rio
Grande, Saguache

IX. *Southwest Community Resources*
572 Sixth Avenue, Durango, CO 81301   (303) 259-1967
Counties served: Archuleta, Dolores, La Plata, Montezuma,
San Juan

X. *District X Regional Planning Commission*
Drawer 849, Montrose, CO 81402   (303) 249-2436
Counties served: Delta, Gunnison, Hinsdale, Montrose Ouray,
San Migu

XI. *Assoc. Governments of Northwest Colorado*
P.O. Box 351, Rifle, CO 81650
(303) 625-1723; 1-800-332-3669

XII. *Skyline Six Area Agency on Aging*
P.O. Box 739, Frisco, CO 80443   (303) 668-5445
Counties served: Chaffee, Eagle, Grand, Jackson, Lake, Pitkin,
Rouff, Summer

XIII. *Upper Arkansas Area Agency on Aging*
1310 East Rainbow Boulevard, #17, Salida, CO 81201
1-800-634-1283
Counties served: Custer, Fremont

If your parents live in Denver, they may already subscribe to the
newspaper called *Senior Edition,* one of the best commercial enterprises of its kind. If they're not receiving it, have a look at a sample
issue, and you may decide to present them with a gift subscription:
$6 for eighteen issues. Call (303) 837-9100 for additional informa-
tion.

A lively source of information and entertainment is the radio program "High Time, the Senior Edition of the Air," presented every Sunday on the following schedule:

KEZW	Denver	1430 AM	9:05 P.M.
KBOL	Boulder	1490 AM	7:00 A.M.
KGIW	Alamosa	1450 AM	10:05 A.M.
KEXO	Grand Junction	1230 AM	7:30 A.M.

CONNECTICUT

Department on Aging
   175 Main Street
   Hartford, Connecticut 06106   (203) 566-7772
Nursing Home Ombudsman
   Jacqueline C. Walker at the above address   (203) 566-7770

A guide to services for the elderly, *When Care Is Needed,* is available on request from the Department on Aging. Whether your parent needs only a few services during recovery from a hospital stay, or a large number of services in order to remain at home instead of being institutionalized, this guide is indispensable, especially if you are the family caregiver. Assistance can include light housekeeping, home-delivered meals, nursing care, home health aid, counseling (for depression, bereavement, isolation), physical therapy, and/or a companion. If you need information about how to obtain these services before your copy of the guide arrives, call the Department on Aging or the Connecticut Department of Health Service at (203) 566-3694. The guide also contains information about the program known as LAMP (Legal Assistance for Medicare Patients) with main offices in Willimantic. LAMP can be reached at (203) 423-2556.

Other programs described in the guide include:

■ *CADAC (Connecticut Alcohol and Drug Abuse Council),* for people whose parents have developed a substance abuse problem in their later years.

■ *"Vial-of-Life,"* which enables your parent to obtain a special container for a list of all medications being taken. This container is then placed in or on the refrigerator so that when medical personnel arrives in an emergency, the situation can be dealt with more efficiently.

If you need information or referrals before you receive your copy of *When Care Is Needed,* call the Area Agency on Aging that serves your parents' part of the state:

Eastern Connecticut	(203) 887-3561
North Central	(203) 278-2044
Northwestern	(203) 566-4810
South Central	(203) 933-5431
Southwestern	(203) 333-9288

DELAWARE

Department of Health and Human Services, Division of Aging
    1901 North DuPont Highway
    New Castle, Delaware 19720   (302) 421-6791
Nursing Home Ombudsman
    Marietta Wooleyhan
    507 West 9th Street
    Wilmington, Delaware 19801   (302) 655-3451

The Division of Aging has prepared a *Guide to Services for Older Delawareans,* which lists all the important agencies, services, and programs of interest to the elderly and their families. Because the guide attempts to be comprehensive, covering an unusual range of services and support groups, it is in a continual state of revision. It also makes every effort to keep abreast of new programs and new community groups. The Division of Aging will send you a free copy of the guide on request.

In addition to providing information about such standard programs as health and medical screening, alternatives to institutional care (foster care, adult family care homes, respite care, in-home assistance), home-delivered meals, lawyer referral services, housing, and transportation, the guide also describes the division's lending library of books, films, and audiovisual equipment. Other special support programs include:

- *Women's Vocational Services,* designed to help women who have lost their main source of income because of separation, divorce, or disability or death of a spouse.
- *Career and educational counseling.*
- *The Golden Eagle Craft Shops* in Wilmington and Dover, which serve as retail outlets for items created by the state's senior citizens.

The division also produces a bimonthly publication, the *Delaware Senior Sentinel,* which focuses on the changes in already existing regulations and laws as well as on recently enacted or proposed laws and court decisions affecting the elderly. The *Sentinel* also contains useful articles on health, safety, nutrition, and items of special interest to senior consumers.

If your parents are unfamiliar with this publication (it is routinely distributed at senior centers), they can be placed on the mailing list by calling the paper's editor at the division's office.

The division has also prepared a list of support groups for victims of Alzheimer's disease and their families. If you would like to receive a copy of the most up-to-date list, contact the division at (302) 421-6791.

DISTRICT OF COLUMBIA

Office on Aging
    1424 K Street, N.W.
    Washington, D.C. 20005 (202) 724-5622
Long-Term Care Ombudsman
    Ann Hart, Legal Counsel for the Elderly
    1331 H Street, N.W., 10th floor
    Washington, D.C. 20005 (202) 234-0970

If you have a parent among the 104,000 persons aged sixty and older who represent more than 16 percent of the District's population, you should know about the many services that can be called on to help in maintaining self-sufficiency, independence, and well-being.

The Information & Referral Service Hotline, (202) 724-5626, which operates Monday through Friday from 8:15 A.M. to 4:45 P.M., links the caller with the specific agency that provides help in the following areas:

Consumer advocacy	Health	Nursing homes
Counseling	Homemakers	Nutrition
Discounts	Housing	Recreation
Education	Legal aid	Social security
Employment	Medicaid	Transportation
Food stamps	Medicare	Volunteers

The Senior Service Network also includes agencies that operate programs such as multipurpose senior centers, geriatric day care, telephone reassurance, and case management. One of the most recent—and most popular—components of the Network is:

Washington Seniors Wellness Center
3857A Pennsylvania Avenue, S.E. (202) 575-6400

It is open Monday through Friday, 9 A.M. to 5 P.M., and its services are free to D.C. residents who are sixty or older. A program for fifty-five-to sixty-year-olds is available for a moderate fee. In addition to promoting good health habits and helping to prevent unnecessary and costly medical problems, the Wellness Center focuses on such issues as accident and injury control, alcoholism, nutrition assessment, physical fitness, safe use of medication, smoking cessation, and stress management. There are support groups for victims of stroke, parkinsonism, and Alzheimer's disease and for their caregivers. Your parent can arrange for the initial health risk assessment by calling the center for an appointment.

The Office on Aging also publishes an attractive and informative bimonthly, *Spotlight on Aging*. A typical issue contained articles on the impact on the elderly of the Reagan tax reform plan; a new look at Social Security; statistics on the status of older women; and news about conferences, workshops, and free booklets. To place your parent's name on the mailing list, call the Office on Aging with your request.

The Office on Aging will also provide you with a brochure containing the most recent information about the programs and resources that are part of the Senior Service Network. The brochure contains useful referral data for which you might otherwise have to phone the referral hotline.

FLORIDA

Department of Health & Rehabilitative Services, Aging and Adult Services
    1317 Winewood Blvd.
    Tallahassee, Florida 32301   (904) 488-8922; 487-2274
Long-Term Care Ombudsman Council Director
    Mrs. Beth Sodec at the above address   (904) 488-4180

Florida's in-home and community-based support systems for the elderly bear a particularly heavy burden. Nationwide, Florida is the state with the largest percentage of over-sixty-five population: 17.5% compared with New York's 12.6%, California's 10%, and a national average of 11.7%.[1] In addition to serving the needs of a large number of aged native Floridians who live at the poverty level or just above it, the state's services are also called upon by many retirees from elsewhere who eventually depend on them because they have distanced themselves from the informal support systems that might otherwise be provided by their families.

Sons and daughters who are geographically separated from aging parents currently healthy and self-reliant and basking in Florida's benign climate may want to know what help can be called upon if and when the need for help should arise. Information in pamphlets and "program profiles" is available on request by phone or letter from the Department's Aging Services. Pamphlets include:

> *Aging & Adult Services,* a comprehensive survey of state and Area Agency on Aging programs
> *Adult Congregate Living Facilities*

1. *Statistical Abstract of the United States,* 1985.

Housing Choices for Older Adults
Adult Foster Care

Data sheets are available for the following programs:

Adult Day Care	Displaced Homemaker
Adult Placement	Program
Adult Protective Services	Domestic Violence Program
Community Care for the	Home Care for the Elderly[2]
Elderly	Hospice Care

GEORGIA

Office of Aging
878 Peachtree Street, N.E.
Atlanta, Georgia 30309   (404) 894-5333
Long-Term Care Ombudsman Program Coordinator
Ms. Ellen Lebowitz at the above address   (404) 894-5833

An annually updated handbook, *Laws and Programs Affecting Senior Citizens in Georgia,* is a collaborative effort prepared by members of the Committee on Legal Services to the Elderly of the Young Lawyers Section of the State Bar of Georgia, with funds provided by the Bar Association and the state's Office of Aging. This handbook is available on request from the Office of Aging.

It is an indispensable source of information about statewide programs, Area Agencies on Aging, and special programs and services for Atlanta residents. The contents are organized under the following headings:

Financial Assistance for the Senior Citizen; Health Care; General Information:
Wills, Estate Planning, Real Estate Transfers, Guardianship, and Alternatives; Age Discrimination; Helpful Legal Information about Landlord-Tenant Relations; Public Housing; Consumer Guide; Funeral Regulations; the Court System
Reference and Referral Information

The Office on Aging has prepared additional source material which is available on request: *Programs, Services, and Resources for Georgia's Elderly; Community Care for Older Georgians; Georgia Long-Term Care Ombudsman Program;* and a list of useful contacts in and around Atlanta. Included are the local AARP chapter, Georgia Association of Realtors, Medical Association of Georgia, Georgia Hospital Association, the Georgia Bureau of Industry and Trade (which supplies information about vacation areas, sports, fishing, and golfing), and the Georgia Ho-

2. See Chapter 7 for details on this program.

tel-Motel Association (which offers a directory of vacation facilities and prices).

Also, if your parents have not yet received one, ask the Office of Aging for the oversize plastic card that serves as a quick and easy reference for essential information. Among the resources listed with their address and phone number are: the eighteen Area Agencies on Aging and the counties they serve; health-related associations and support groups; agencies that handle complaints; agencies that offer advice on matters such as job training and energy costs, and those that provide referral to legal services for elderly Georgians of limited means. (There are seventeen regional Legal Services Programs statewide.)

In 1982, the Atlanta Area Chapter of the Alzheimer's Disease and Related Disorders Association (ADRDA) was organized to offer support and information to families with relatives who are victims of these disorders and to educate the community about the nature of these diseases and their impact on the family.

For information about support groups, the telephone network, education facilities, and special day care and respite programs, contact:

The Atlanta Area Chapter of ADRDA
Wesley Woods Campus
1817 Clifton Road, N.E.
Atlanta, Georgia 30029
(404) 633-8759

HAWAII

Executive Office on Aging
   1149 Bethel Street, Room 307
   Honolulu, Hawaii 96813   (808) 548-2593
State Ombudsman
   Mr. Rodney Kuba at the above address and phone number
Long-Term Care Resources in Hawaii is a 130-page guide to the services and programs that are designed to meet the health and social needs of older residents. It is available on request from the Office on Aging.

Organized for easy reference, the guide is addressed to the elderly, their families, and the agencies that help them and provides essential facts about community and institutional services offered within the continuum of long-term care. There are charts of island locations of services, and for each entry—there are several hundred listings—the following information is given:

WHERE: location and/or mailing address, phone, branch offices, office hours, emergency contact if available.

WHAT: types of services provided, staffing.

WHO: persons eligible to receive the services (age, health, financial status, residence and referral procedure).

COST: what the person can expect to pay; insurance or third party payment, if any.

(This last item is especially useful to know in advance and is rarely included in similar handbooks from other states.)

Here are three sample entries:

Commission on the Handicapped
335 Merchant Street, Room 215
Honolulu, HI 96813
(808) 548-7606

WHAT: Provides technical and legislative information, information and referral on services, programs, and community resources; coordinates interagency communication; assists in planning and service improvement.

WHO: Anyone with a disability or interest in disabled.

COST: None.

Maluhia Hospital

1027 Hala Drive	Hours: 7:00 A.M. to 5:15 P.M.
Honolulu, HI 96817	Monday through Friday
(808) 845-2951, ext. 173	except state holidays

WHAT: Day hospital for the elderly: Medical problems that need monitoring, remedial training, physical and occupational therapists, nursing treatments. Staff: One registered nurse and director, one licensed practical nurse, three nurses' aides, half-time social worker, dietitian consultant.

WHO: Intermediate Care Facility with lower level Skilled Nursing Facility patients. Must have wheelchair or sitting tolerance, able to stand up with assistance. Referral: By doctor, family, or social worker to the director. Must have physician to continue medical care with monitoring.

COST: $30 a day. If Medicaid recipient, form 1147 must be completed before acceptance.

OTHER: Transportation is family's responsibility.

NOTE: Other Day Hospitals are under development. Please check with Department of Health, Facilities Branch, in your county.[3]

3. See Chapter 6, "Adult Day Care," for additional information about other types of day care in Hawaii.

Hawaii Meals on Wheels
3358 Emekena Place   Hours: 7:30 A.M. to 1:30 P.M.
Honolulu, HI 96822
(808) 988-7439

WHAT: Home-delivered meals, five days a week. Staff: Coordinator.
WHO: Home-bound elderly, convalescing and handicapped people of all
  ages who are unable to cook/shop for themselves. Residents between Ward Avenue and Diamond Head. Referral: Hospitals, agencies, individuals; applications accepted by coordinator.
COST: $13.50 to $19.50 per week. Subsidies available.

IDAHO

Office on Aging
  Statehouse, Room 114
  Boise, Idaho 83720   (208) 334-3833
State Ombudsman for the Elderly
  Arlene Davidson at the above address   (208) 334-2220
  Idaho is one of many states that have been relying heavily on funding
from Washington to support programs for the elderly. Idahoans sixty
and over make up almost 14 percent of the state's population, compared
with a national average of 11 percent. A recent annual report issued by
the Office on Aging indicates that of a total of over $4,750,000 spent on
the department's programs, $4,200,000 was supplied by federal funds.
  One of the most important federally funded support systems is the
Advocacy Assistance Program, whose main purpose is to help institutionalized *and* noninstitutionalized older persons to secure all the rights
and benefits to which they are entitled by federal, state, and local laws.
To accomplish this goal, the program has two components: a network of
ombudsmen, and a network of legal services.
  The network of legal services, known as the Idaho State Bar Pro Bono
Program, is made up of more than five hundred lawyers statewide who
provide legal services to the elderly free of charge or on a reduced fee
basis. The volunteer attorneys participate on behalf of their clients in
such matters as probate, preparation of wills, real estate transactions,
guardianships, and Medicare appeals.
  The ombudsmen in each service area are responsible not only for
assuring that the institutionalized elderly are receiving the quality of care
to which they are entitled, but also for investigating and resolving problems encountered by seniors and their families in their dealings with
public agencies that handle entitlements: Medicare, Medicaid, supplemental insurance (SSI), and retirement pensions.
  Information about these services and other programs, including nutri-

tion, job training, homemakers, day care, housing, Alzheimer's support groups, and special minority interests, is available from the Area Agency on Aging that serves your parents' county:

Area I. Association for Intercommunity Development (AID)
3655 North Government Way, No. 6
Coeur d'Alene, ID 83814   (208) 667-4523
Counties served: Boundary, Bonner, Kootenai, Benewah, Shoshone

Area II. Area Agency on Aging
1424 Main Street
Lewiston, ID 83501   (208) 743-5580
Counties served: Latah, Nez Perce, Lewis, Clearwater, Idaho

Area III. Ida-Ore Regional Planning & Development Assoc.
P.O. Box 311
Weiser, ID 83672   (208) 549-2411
Counties served: Adams, Valley, Washington, Payette, Gem, Boise, Canyon, Ada, Elmore, Owyhee

Area IV. College of Southern Idaho
P.O. Box 1238
Twin Falls, ID 83301   (208) 733-9554, ext. 334
Counties served: Camas, Blaine, Gooding, Lincoln, Jerome, Minidoka, Twin Falls, Cassia

Area V. Southeast Idaho Council of Governments
1070 Hiline Road, Box 2170
Pocatello, ID 83206   (208) 233-4032
Counties served: Bingham, Power, Caribou, Bannock, Oneida, Franklin, Bear Lake

Area VI. Eastern Idaho Special Services Agency
P.O. Box 1098
Idaho Falls, ID 83401   (208) 522-5391
Counties served: Lemhi, Custer, Clark, Fremont, Butte, Jefferson, Madison, Teton, Bonneville

ILLINOIS

Department on Aging
421 East Capitol
Springfield, Illinois 62701, and

100 West Randolph
Chicago, Illinois 60601
Statewide toll-free information: 1-800-252-8966

Nursing Home Ombudsman
Marjorie Burnett in the Springfield office

In 1973, when Illinois became one of the first states to create a cabinet-level department devoted entirely to the problems and needs of the elderly, the appropriation for services was $5 million. A dozen years later in 1985, the appropriation was more than twenty times as much: $101.4 million.[4] About one in every nine persons (more than 1¼ million) in Illinois is age sixty-five or older, and of these, more than 54 percent live in families. However, 23 percent of all elderly households are near or below the poverty level.[5]

The 154-page 1986 Plan prepared by the Department on Aging for presentation to the state legislature points out that "the participation of the family is especially crucial to maintaining clients in their homes" and "as much as 80% of the support received by highly impaired clients is provided by relatives." In recognition of these facts, the department ". . . provides services to relieve the stress placed on the family caring for the frail older person; provides training to case management staff on the assessment of family support levels and needs, and promotes family involvement in the design of care plans for their relatives. . . ." (In 1985, the department allocated funds to the state's Association of Family Service Agencies to explore policy options for the support of the family's efforts in caring for a frail older family member.)

With federal and state funds, the Department operates more than three hundred social service projects, of which thirteen are Area Agencies on Aging. These agencies are responsible for reallocating funds to stimulate, develop, and supervise programs on the local level. Among these programs are information and referral, multipurpose senior centers, transportation and escort, home/health aides, telephone reassurance, training for reemployment, lip reading, hearing tests, and cooperation on the Senior Driving Program.

The brochure *Federal & State Programs for the Aging* is available from the department on request. In addition to describing these programs in detail and listing the state's thirteen Area Agencies on Aging, it provides you and your parents with many useful toll-free numbers. Here are a few:

Lieutenant Governor's Senior Action Office   1-800-252-6565
Where to find help with matters involving Medicare, Medicaid, nutrition, transportation, and other programs.
Secretary of State's Office   1-800-252-8980
Assistance for seniors who need information about license plates, driver's licenses, defensive driving insurance discounts, and state libraries.
Legislative Information Hotline (during sessions)   1-800-252-8652

4. *Facts & Figures on Older Persons in Illinois,* Illinois Department on Aging, 1984.
5. *1986 Plan: Phase I,* Illinois Department on Aging, 1984, 1985, 1986.

State Dental Society 1-800-252-2930

Information about two special programs: one that enables low-income citizens to receive dental care at reduced fees; the other that makes available portable dental equipment for the elderly, homebound, and handicapped.

The brochure *Illinois Cares . . . about Its Seniors* is also available from the department on request. Among its useful listings are:

Department of Insurance in Springfield (217) 782-4515
in Chicago (312) 793-2427

Answers questions and investigates complaints about insurance.

Department of Rehabilitation Services (217) 785-3893

For a Directory of Services for the Handicapped.

Governor's Office of Voluntary Action (312) 793-2789

For volunteer opportunities for Seniors, including the RSVP (Retired Senior Volunteer Program) offering part-time positions in schools, hospitals, and community service programs.

Department of Commerce and Community Affairs 1-800-252-8643

For information about the Home Energy Assistance Program and the Home Weatherization Program.

One of the Department's most supportive projects is called Community Care. Its purpose is to provide an individualized combination of services that will enable partially impaired elderly persons to remain in their own home instead of being institutionalized. Three types of services are available:

Homemakers, who are trained and professionally supervised to teach home management, personal care, and support techniques, thereby strengthening the capabilities of individuals and/or family caregivers.

Chore/housekeeper assistants, who help with household tasks and personal care under the supervision of the client or other responsible individual.

Adult day care and supervision in a group setting for part of the twenty-four-hour day to provide personal attention, and promote social, physical, and emotional well-being.

Detailed information about eligibility requirements, cost of services, and other relevant matter is contained in the brochure *Things You Need to Know about the Community Care Program.* You can request your copy by calling the Department on Aging's toll-free number, 1-800-252-8966, Monday through Friday, 8:30 A.M. to 5 P.M.

INDIANA

Department on Aging & Community Services
115 North Pennsylvania Street
Indianapolis, Indiana 46204   (317) 232-7000
Nursing Home Ombudsman
Barbara Coulter at the above address   (317) 232-7115
Nursing Home Complaint Hot Line   1-800-622-4484

Community Services for the Elderly consist of a variety of programs provided to recipients through a case management component. The case manager is responsible for determining eligibility, assessing the need for any combination of the services listed below, monitoring the provision of the services, and reassessing the client's needs on a regular basis:

Service linkage escort to transport a functionally impaired client to essential medical or community services.

Activity visitor, who provides regularly scheduled social, recreational, educational, and/or errand services to the homebound.

Respite care in the client's home during the absence of the unpaid caregiver—usually a family member.

Adult day care, consisting of community-based group services in a protective setting for functionally impaired older adults. Included are a nutritionally balanced meal and transportation to and from the day care site.

Homebound meal delivered to eligible clients.

Transportation to medical appointments, grocery shopping, and activities connected with business matters or with obtaining social service benefits. (This service is not available to those who need physical assistance.)

To request case management assessment for any of these programs and to find out about other support systems, activities, and special community resources that might be of particular interest to you and your parents, contact the Area Agency on Aging that serves their county.

Area Agencies on Aging

Area 1.   Lake County Economic Opportunity Council
5518 Calumet Avenue, Hammond, IN 46320   (219) 937-3500
Counties served: Jasper, Lake, Newton, Porter, Pulaski, Starke

Area 2.   R.E.A.L. Services of St. Joseph County
622 North Michigan Street, P.O. Box 1835

South Bend, IN 46634   (219) 233-8205
Counties served: Marshall, St. Joseph

Elkhart Count Council on Aging
255 Oakland Avenue, Elkhart, IN 46517   (219) 295-1820

LaPorte County Council on Aging
612–614 Indiana Avenue, P.O. Box 443, LaPorte, IN 46350
(219) 326-7889

Area 3.   Northeast Area III Council on Aging
5720 St. Joe Road, Fort Wayne, IN 46815   (219) 485-4206
Counties served: Adams, Allen, DeKalb, Huntington, LaGrange, Noble, Steuben, Wells, Whitley

Area 4.   Area IV Agency on Aging and Community Services
10 North Earl Avenue, P.O. Box 4727, Lafayette, IN 47903
(317) 447-7683; 1-800-382-7556
Counties served: Benton, Carroll, Clinton, Fountain, Montgomery, Tippecanoe, Warren, White

Area 5.   Area V Council on Aging and Community Services
912 East Market Street, Logansport, IN 46947   (219) 722-4451
Counties served: Cass, Fulton, Howard, Miami, Tipton, Wabash

Area 6.   Area 6 Council on Aging
1968 West Main Street, Muncie, IN 47303
(317) 289-1124 or 1121
Counties served: Blackford, Delaware, Grant, Henry, Jay, Madison, Randolph

Area 7.   West Central Indiana Economic Development District
1718 Wabash Avenue, P.O. Box 359, Terre Haute, IN 47808
(812) 238-1561
Counties served: Clay, Parke, Putnam, Sullivan, Vermillion, Vigo

Area 8.   Central Indiana Council on Aging
615 North Alabama Street, Suite 336, Indianapolis, IN 46204
(317) 633-6191
Counties served: Boone, Hamilton, Hancock, Hendricks, Johnson, Morgan, Shelby

Community Centers of Indianapolis
615 North Alabama Street, Suite 312, Indianapolis, IN 46204
(317) 638-3360
County served: Marion

Area 9.   Area 9 Agency on Aging
Indiana University, 303 South A Street, Richmond, IN 47374
(317) 966-1795
Counties served: Fayette, Franklin, Rush, Union, Wayne

Area 10.   Area 10 Council on Aging of Monroe and Owen Counties
924 West 17th Street, Bloomington, IN 47401   (812) 334-3383

Area 11.   Area XI Agency on Aging
   4340 Jonathan Moore Pike, P.O. Box 904, Columbus, IN 47202
   (812) 342-9009
      Counties served: Bartholomew, Brown, Decatur, Jackson, Jennings

Area 12.   Area 12 Council on Aging
   P.O. Box 97, 100 North Street, Dillsboro, IN 47018
   (812) 432-5215
      Counties served: Dearborn, Jefferson, Ohio, Ripley, Switzerland

Area 13A.   Area 13A Agency on Aging
   Vincennes University Oldier Hoosier Programs
   P.O. Box 314, Community Service Building, Room 104
   2nd and Indianapolis, Vincennes, IN 47591   (812) 885-4292
      Counties served: Daviess, Dubois, Greene, Knox, Martin, Pike

Area 13B.   Southwestern Indiana Regional Council on Aging
   7 Southeast Seventh Street, Evansville, IN 47708   (812) 464-7800
      Counties served: Gibson, Perry, Posey, Spencer, Vanderburgh, Warrick

Area 14.   South Central Indiana Council for the Aging and Aged
   134 East Main Street, New Albany, IN 47150   (812) 948-9423
      Counties served: Clark, Floyd, Harrison, Scott

Area 15.   Hoosier Uplands Economic Development Corp.
   521 West Main Street, Mitchell, IN 47446   (812) 849-4457
      Counties served: Crawford, Lawrence, Orange, Washington

The Department of Public Welfare Office in each county can supply information about the following programs: Room and Board Assistance; Assistance to Residents in County Homes; Medicaid; Nursing Home Care for the Aged, Blind, and Disabled.

IOWA

Commission on the Aging
   236 Jewett Building, 914 Grand Avenue
   Des Moines, Iowa 50319   (515) 281-5187
Long-Term Care Resident's Aide
   At the above address   (515) 281-4656
The services available to the elderly are developed, coordinated, and delivered by thirteen Area Agencies on Aging in cooperation with the Commission on the Aging. These services come under four main headings:

Access services—transportation, outreach, information and referral.
Community services—congregate meals, continuing education, legal services, counseling, assessment and case management, and assistance.

In-home services—home health, homemaker, home-delivered meals.

Services to residents of care-providing facilities—casework, placement/relocation, grievance resolution.

Federal funds have been paying for more than 52 percent of the cost of these programs and services.

Information is available from the Area Agency on Aging that serves your parents' county:

Area 1. 808 River Street, Decorah, IA 52101 (319) 382-2941
Counties served: Allamakee, Clayton, Fayette, Howard, Winneshiek

Area 2. North Central Iowa
500 College Drive, Mason City, IA 50401 (515) 424-0678
Counties served: Cerrogordo, Floyd, Franklin, Hancock, Kossuth, Mitchell, Winnebago, Worth

Area 3. Iowa Lakes
2 Grand Avenue, P.O. Box 3010, Spencer, IA 51301
(712) 262-1775
Counties served: Buena Vista, Clay, Dickinson, Lyon, O'Brien, Osceola, Palo Alto, Sioux

Area 4. Simpco
400 Orpheum Electric Building, Sioux City, IA 51102
(712) 279-6286
Counties served: Cherokee, Ida, Monona, Plymouth, Woodbury

Area 5. 330 Avenue "M," Ft. Dodge, IA 50501 (515) 955-5244
Counties served: Calhoun, Hamilton, Humboldt, Pocahontas, Webster, Wright

Areas 6 and 7. Hawkeye Valley
P.O. Box 2576, Waterloo, IA 50704 (319) 233-5214
Counties served in Area 6: Hardin, Marshall, Poweshiek, Tama
Counties served in Area 7: Black Hawk, Bremer, Buchanan, Butler, Chickasaw, Grundy

Area 8. Scenic Valley
810 Davis Avenue, Dubuque, IA 52001 (319) 588-3970
Counties served: Dubuque, Delaware, Jackson

Area 9. Great River Bend
Bi-State Metropolitan Planning Commission
1504 Third Avenue, Rock Island, IL 61201 (309) 793-6334
Counties served: Clinton, Muscatine, Scott

Area 10. Kirkwood Community College—Heritage
6301 Kirkwood Blvd., S.W., Cedar Rapids, IA 52406
(319) 398-5559
Counties served: Benton, Cedar, Iowa, Johnson, Jones, Lynn, Washington

Area 11.   Crossroads of Iowa
    1040 4th Street, Des Moines, IA 50314   (515) 244-4046
        Counties served: Boone, Dallas, Jasper, Madison, Marion, Polk, Story, Warren

Area 12.   527½ N. Adams, P.O. Box 663, Carroll, IA 51401
    (712) 792-3512
        Counties served: Audubon, Carroll, Crawford, Greene, Guthrie, Sac

Area 13.   SW Eight Area XIII
    P.O. Box 368, Council Bluffs, IA 51502   (712) 328-2540
        Counties served: Cass, Fremont, Harrison, Mills, Montgomery, Page, Pottawattamie, Shelby

Area 14.   228 N. Pine, Creston, IA 50801   (515) 782-4040
        Counties served: Adair, Adams, Clarke, Decatur, Ringold, Taylor, Union

Area 15.   Sieda
    P.O. Box 658, 226 W. Main Street, Ottumwa, IA 52501
    (515) 682-8741
        Counties served: Appanoose, Davis, Jefferson, Keokuk, Lucas, Mehaska, Monroe, Van Buren, Wappello, Wayne

Area 16.   Southeast Iowa
    510 Jefferson Street, Burlington, IA 52601   (319) 752-5433
        Counties served: Des Moines, Henry, Lee, Louisa

If your parent is a nursing home resident, you may be interested in knowing more about the Long-Term Care Resident's Aide Program, the statewide network of 685 Care Review Committees with 2773 volunteer advocates for residents of licensed health care facilities. Information about this program is available from the director at the Office on Aging, (515) 281-4656.

KANSAS

Department on Aging
    610 West 10th Street, Topeka, Kansas 66612   (913) 296-4986
Office of the Long-Term Care Ombudsman
    At the above address and phone number or toll-free 1-800-432-3535
Wichita Area Ombudsman
    335 West Lewis, Wichita, Kansas 67202   (316) 267-0302
Kansas City Area Ombudsman
    736 Shawnee Avenue, Kansas City, Kansas 66105   (913) 281-5109

The Older Kansan, a brochure prepared by the Department on Aging, indicates that of a total of more than 412,000 Kansans aged sixty or over, approximately 50,000 were identified as living in poverty by the 1980 Population Census. Other facts that contribute to the shaping of policy by the Department are the following: In the 60+ group, there are 140 women for every 100 men, and in the 85+ age group, there are 228 women for every 100 men. As for living arrangements, in the 60+ age group, 59% live in a family setting, and of the 39% who live alone, 56% are women and 15% are men.

The task of planning, coordinating, and delivering services to all older Kansans is the responsibility of eleven Area Agencies on Aging.

These services can be grouped under the following headings:

Health Insurance and Medicare, nursing homes, homemaker/chore services, day care, nutrition, accident prevention.

Housing Public housing, home repair, weatherization.

Social Recreation, aging advocacy organizations, transportation, volunteer opportunities, continuing education.

Economic Tax assistance, utility assistance, employment, public benefits.

Legal Referral for counseling, representation, negotiation, and drafting of legal documents. Priority is given to persons in social or economic need. Help is provided with the following problems:

  Public benefits: Social Security, SSI, Medicare, Veterans' Benefits, Food Stamps, Medicaid.

  Consumer affairs: Product and service disputes, fraud and deceptive practices, landlord/tenant disagreements, utility payments, medical bills, age discrimination, civil suits.

  Protective services: Guardianship, conservatorship, power of attorney, nursing home disputes.

The Department on Aging makes available on request the following useful brochures:

Legal Assistance for Older Kansans
Nutrition Services Program for Older Kansans
Kansas Long-Term Care Ombudsman
and
Information about Aging Services

For information and referral about all programs and services as well as special community support systems, contact the Area Agency on Aging that serves your parents' county.

Area Agencies on Aging
(officially called Planning & Service Areas)

PSA 1. Wyandotte-Leavenworth Counties Area Agency on Aging
9400 State Avenue, Kansas City, KS 66112   (913) 788-7820

PSA 2. Central Plains Area Agency on Aging
510 North Main, Room 306, Wichita, KS 67203   (316) 268-7298
Counties served: Butler, Harvey, Sedgewick

PSA 3. Northwest Kansas Area Agency on Aging
301 West 13th Street, Sunflower Building, Hays, KS 67601
(913) 628-8204
Counties served: Cheyenne, Decatur, Ellis, Gove, Graham, Logan, Norton, Osborne, Phillips, Rawlins, Rooks, Russell, Sheridan, Sherman, Smith, Thomas, Trego, Wallace

PSA 4. Jayhawk Area Agency on Aging
1195 Buchanan, Suite 103, Topeka, KS 66604   (913) 235-1367
Counties served: Douglas, Jefferson, Shawnee

PSA 5. Southeast Kansas Area Agency on Aging
1500 West 7th Street, P.O. Box 269, Chanute, KS 66720
(316) 431-2980
Counties served: Allen, Bourbon, Cherokee, Crawford, Labette,
Montgomery, Neosho, Wilson, Woodson

PSA 6. Southwest Kansas Area Agency on Aging
P.O. Box 1636, Dodge City, KS 67801   (316) 225-0510
Counties served: Barber, Barton, Clark, Comanche, Edwards,
Finney, Ford, Grant, Gray, Greeley, Hamilton, Haskell,
Hodgeman, Kearney, Kiowa, Lane, Meade, Morton, Ness, Paw-
nee, Pratt, Rush, Scott, Seward, Stafford, Stanton, Stevens, Wich-
ita

PSA 7. Mid-America Council on Aging
1610 South Main, Ottawa, KS 66067   (913) 242-7200
Counties served: Anderson, Coffey, Franklin, Linn, Miami, Osage

PSA 8. North Central Flint Hills Area Agency on Aging
2601 Anderson, Manhattan, KS 66502   (913) 776-9294
Counties served: Chase, Clay, Cloud, Dickinson, Ellsworth,
Gary, Jewell, Lincoln, Lyon, Marion, Mitchell, Morris, Ottawa,
Pottawatomie, Republic, Riley, Saline, Wabaunsee

PSA 9. Northeast Kansas Area Agency on Aging
107 Oregon West, P.O. Box 456, Hiawatha, KS 66434
(913) 742-7152
Counties served: Atchison, Brown, Domiphan, Jackson, Marshall, Nemaka, Washington

PSA 10.   South Central Kansas Area Agency on Aging
   P.O. Box 1122, Arkansas City, KS 67005   (316) 442-0268
      Counties served: Chattauqua, Cowley, Elk, Greenwood, Harper,
      Kingman, McPherson, Reno, Rice, Sumner
PSA 11.   Department of Human Resources & Aging
   130 North Cherry, Olathe, KS 66061   (913) 764-7108
      County served: Johnson

KENTUCKY

Department for Social Services, Division of Aging Services
   275 East Main Street
   Frankfort, Kentucky 40601   (502) 564-6930
Long-Term Care Ombudsman
      Karen O'Connell at the above address and phone number or toll-
      free 1-800-372-2991

A recent survey entitled *Kentucky Elderly Needs Assessment* sponsored by the Division of Aging Services and conducted by the Urban
Studies Center of the University of Louisville has been an important
guide for policy planning and decision making. The survey's in-depth
interviews explored the most effective ways of enabling the elderly to
maintain their own independent living arrangements, thereby giving the
respondents "an opportunity to participate in the decision-making process."

Results indicated that among the statistically representative sampling,
the most important concerns in order of their importance are (1) physical health and home care;[6] (2) family, religion, and social activity;
(3) housing; (4) finances; and (5) transportation.

The services and opportunities available to older Kentuckians are
planned with these concerns in mind. In addition to programs funded by
federal appropriations and those supported by state and local dollars,
additional state money is available to counties on a matching basis for
those support programs that help maintain the elderly in their own
home. Payment for these programs is calculated on the basis of individual circumstances.

Every county contains at least one senior citizen center which is the
source of information about available services for you and your parents.
The centers are also the setting for social activities, informal networking,
and the development of programs particularly suitable for a special
group of people over sixty-five.

In addition to the Office of the Long-Term Care Ombudsman in
Frankfort, the program operates six district offices statewide. The pro-

6. A detailed description of Kentucky's Home Care Program will be found in Chapter 7.

gram also issues on request a brochure entitled *Your Rights as a Resident in a Long-Term Care Facility.*

If you want to know about a particular program in which your parents might participate or you need referral to services to which they are entitled, contact the Area Agency on Aging that serves their county.

Area Agencies on Aging

1. *Purchase Area Agency on Aging in Mayfield*   (502) 247-7171
   Counties served: Ballard, Calloway, Carlisle, Fulton, Graves, Hickman, Marshall, McCracken

2. *Pennyrite Area Agency on Aging in Hopkinsville*   (502) 886-9484
   Counties served: Caldwell, Christian, Crittenden, Hopkins, Livingston, Lyon, Muhlenberg, Todd, Trigg

3. *Green River Area Agency on Aging in Owensboro*   (502) 926-4433
   Counties served: Daviess, Hancock, Henderson, McLean, Ohio, Union, Webster

4. *Barren River Area Agency on Aging,* Bowling Green
   (502) 781-2381
   Counties served: Allen, Barren, Butler, Edmonson, Hart, Logan, Metcalfe, Monroe, Simpson, and Warren

5. *Lincoln Trail Area Agency on Aging,* Elizabethtown   (502) 769-2393
   Counties served: Breckinridge, Grayson, Hardin, Larue, Marion, Meade, Nelson, Washington

6. *Kentuckiana Regional Planning & Development Agency,* Louisville
   (502) 589-4406
   Counties served: Bullitt, Henry, Jefferson, Oldham, Shelby, Spencer, and Trimble

7. *Northern Kentucky Area Agency on Aging,* Florence
   (606) 283-1885
   Counties served: Boone, Campbell, Carroll, Gallatin, Grant, Kenton, Owen, and Pendleton

8. *Buffalo Trace Area Agency on Aging,* Maysville   (606) 564-6894
   Counties served: Bracken, Fleming, Lewis, Mason, Robertson

9. *Gateway Area Agency on Aging,* Owingsville   (606) 674-6355
   Counties served: Bath, Menifee, Montgomery, Morgan, Rowan

10. *Fivco Area Agency on Aging,* Catlettsburg   (606) 739-5191
    Counties served: Boyd, Carter, Elliott, Greenup, Lawrence

11. *Big Sandy Area Agency on Aging,* Prestonsburg   (606) 886-2374
    Counties served: Floyd, Johnson, Magoffin, Martin, Pike

12. *Kentucky River Area Agency on Aging,* Hazard   (606) 436-3158
    Counties served: Breathitt, Knott, Lee, Leslie, Letcher, Owsley, Perry, and Wolfe

13. *Cumberland Valley Area Agency on Aging,* London   (606) 864-7391
     Counties served: Bell, Clay, Harlan, Jackson, Knox, Laurel, Rockcastle, Whitley
14. *Lake Cumberland Area Agency on Aging,* Jamestown (502) 343-3154
     Counties served: Adair, Casey, Clinton, Cumberland, Green, Mc-Creary, Pulaski, Russell, Taylor, Wayne
15. *Bluegrass Area Agency on Aging,* Lexington   (606) 272-6656
     Counties served: Anderson, Bourbon, Boyle, Clark, Estill, Fayette, Franklin, Garrard, Harrison, Jessamine, Madison, Mercer, Nicholas, Powell, Scott, Woodford

LOUISIANA

Office of Elderly Affairs
     4528 Bennington Avenue, P.O. Box 80374
     Baton Rouge, Louisiana 70898-0374   (504) 925-1700
Long-Term Care Ombudsman
     Sara S. Hunt at the above address and phone number
Medicaid Information
     Division of Medical Assistance
     Department of Health & Human Resources
     P.O. Box 44065
     Baton Rouge, Louisiana 70804   (504) 342-4953
Adult Day Care Association
     c/o Associated Catholic Charities
     Division of Elderly Services
     1231 Prytania Street
     New Orleans, Louisiana 70130   (504) 523-3755

Every one of the state's sixty-four parishes has a Council on Aging. The councils, which are listed in local telephone directories, are the best source of information and referral about all matters relating to your parents' concerns and needs: health and physical fitness, employment, transportation, legal assistance, home health aides, housing, and the like. The Office of Elderly Affairs will send you on request the brochure *Services for the Aging,* which provides information about the following programs:

Advocacy	Individual needs assessment
Case management	Information and referral
Chore maintenance	Legal assistance
Counseling	Nutrition services
Day care	Ombudsman
Education and training	Outreach

Employment	Recreation
Escort service	Residential repair and renovation
Health facilitation	Transportation
Homemaker services	Visiting and telephone reassurance

The Councils on Aging also fund the senior centers that serve as local social meeting places for older persons and provide up-to-date information on the community's special educational, recreational, and vocational opportunities.

Two other participants in the Aging Network are the Medigap Insurance Information Service which maintains a toll-free number: 1-800-521-3784. This service is operated by the Louisiana Association of Councils on Aging. The other program is the Louisiana Senior Games Project, an annual event that promotes physical fitness through competitive sports activities for the elderly.

MAINE

Department of Human Services Bureau of Maine's Elderly
    State House Station 11
    Augusta, Maine 04333   (207) 289-2561
Nursing Home & Boarding Home Ombudsman
    Jill Duson at the above address and phone number or toll-free
    1-800-452-1912
Food Stamp Program
    1-800-452-4643

The Bureau of Maine's Elderly has prepared an indispensable purse- or pocket-size *Resource Directory,* available on request, that provides detailed information about all aspects of the state's Aging Network. In addition to the programs federally funded under the Older Americans Act and administered by the five Area Agencies on Aging, the directory lists many services and resources, together with the particular source for information about them. For example:

■ The Cooperative Extension Service of the University of Maine offers courses such as "You and Your Aging Relative," "Nutrition Education," "Cooking for 1 or 2," and "Pre-Retirement Planning."

■ Persons sixty-five and older may register for undergraduate or graduate courses on either a credit or a noncredit basis at any campus of the University of Maine. Information is available through the Admissions Office at Augusta, Farmington, Fort Kent, Machias, Orono, Portland, and Presque Isle.

■ If your mother is trying to adjust to divorce or the disability or death of her spouse, the statewide Displaced Homemakers Project can help her function on her own through such services as one-to-one counseling, support groups, and referrals. For the regional office closest to her, consult:

Displaced Homemakers Project
Stoddard House, University of Maine
Augusta, Maine 04330
(207) 622-7131 or toll-free 1-800-442-2092

■ If the annual income of your parents meets the eligibility requirements, assistance with problems of eyesight is available. The Department of Human Services will authorize and pay for a diagnostic examination by the doctor of your parent's choice, and for ongoing care if the doctor's report indicates the need for it. Contact the

Medical Eye Care Program
Bureau of Health, Department of Human Services
State House Station 11
Augusta, Maine 04333   (207) 289-3886

The *Resource Directory* also contains information about mental health centers, adult foster homes, the Foster Grandparent Program, and regional offices for legal referral services.

Until you receive your copy, you can contact the Area Agency on Aging for information about all state and local services that are available for your parents.

Area Agencies on Aging

Aroostook County Area Agency on Aging
P.O. Box 1288, 493 Main Street, Presque Isle, ME 04769
(207) 764-3396   or   toll-free 1-800-432-1789

Eastern Area Agency on Aging
P.O. Box 8148, 435 Broadway, Bangor, ME 04401
(207) 947-0561   or   toll-free 1-800-432-7812
Counties served: Hancock, Penobscot, Piscataquid, Washington

Central Maine Area Agency on Aging
P.O. Box 510, Augusta, ME 04330
(207) 622-9344   or   toll-free 1-800-452-8703
Counties served: Kennebec, Knox, Lincoln, Sagadahoc, Somerset, Waldo

Western Area Agency on Aging
P.O. Box 659, 65 Central Avenue, Lewiston, ME 04240
(207) 784-8797   or   1-800-482-0976
Counties served: Androscoggin, Franklin, Oxford

Southern Maine Senior Citizens Council
    P.O. Box 10480, 237 Oxford Street, Portland, ME 04104
    (207) 775-6503   or   1-800-482-7411
        Counties served: Cumberland and York

If your parents live in the Portland area, they should know about
The Elder Circle whose activities include discussion groups; outings, excursions, and regular trips to the theater; self-expression
through writing, painting, sculpture, photography, and dramatics;
physical movement in the form of exercise, hiking, and dancing; and
stress relief through massage and meditation. Additional information is available from:

    The Elder Circle
    P.O. Box 93 DTS, Portland, Maine 04112
    (207) 773-4457

MARYLAND

Office on Aging
    301 West Preston Street
    Baltimore, Maryland 21201-2374   (301) 225-1083
Long-Term Care Ombudsman
    Pat Bayliss at the above address and phone number
    In response to a federal initiative known as the National Long-Term
Care Channeling Demonstration Project, an interagency panel composed
of high-level officials from the Office on Aging, the Department of Human Resources, and the Department of Health and Mental Hygiene
evolved a plan for the delivery of essential services to the elderly so that
unnecessary and costly institutionalization can be delayed for as long as
possible or eliminated altogether. The method for achieving this goal is
known as Channeling, a process which establishes a single point of entry
for clients in need of health and social services. The aim of this process is
to provide screening, client assessment, case management, and an appropriate combination of services on an individually determined basis.
Channeling is accomplished through Maryland's Project Gateway II.
    Here's how Gateway II works: When an older person with chronic
health problems needs services from several different public and private
agencies, an evaluation of these needs is made during a home visit by a
qualified staff person or a team from Geriatric Evaluation Service. The
evaluation is part of a program sponsored by the U.S. Public Health
Service Hospital. Following an identification of the individual's needs, a

Gateway II case manager then helps to locate the agencies that provide the necessary services, arranges for their delivery, and ensures that the client receives the right services at the right time. In addition to the state agencies called upon to supply services, the U.S. Veterans Administration offers the following to eligible applicants:

- A nursing home program that provides for placement of patients into a non-VA-administered facility in or near their own environment or close to friends and family.
- Care and a protective environment for those who do not need hospitalization or skilled nursing services.
- A community-based residential care program that arranges with a relative, friend, or neighbor to supply a home and give care and supervision, thus enabling the veteran to enjoy a family environment and remain in the community.
- Day treatment in centers where patients with physical and/or mental disabilities can receive medical aid, meals, and participate in social and educational activities.

Project Gateway II has been operating in nine jurisdictions throughout the state. Referrals may be made by doctors, family members, or friends. Eligibility consists of the following requirements: The applicant must be:

- sixty-five years old or older.
- in need of assistance with daily activities such as bathing, dressing, and meal preparation.
- medically at risk of institutionalization.
- a resident of one of the local areas where Gateway II operates.
- able to meet established financial standards.

Additional information is available from the Gateway II office in your parent's locality:

Anne Arundel County Health Department   1-800-492-2499

Baltimore City Area Agency on Aging   (301) 396-1605

Baltimore County Department on Aging   (301) 494-2594

Hartford County Office on Aging   (301) 838-2552

Howard County Health Department   (301) 992-2333

Montgomery County Department of Social Services
(301) 468-4240

Prince George's County Health Department   (301) 386-0130

Talbot County Health Department   (301) 822-6828

Washington County Commission on Aging/Area Agency on Aging
(301) 790-0275

For information and referrals concerning the many other programs and services for Maryland's senior citizens, including those that are federally funded under the Older Americans Act, contact the Office on Aging at (301) 225-1083.

MASSACHUSETTS

Executive Office of Elder Affairs
  38 Chauncey Street
  Boston, Massachusetts 02111   (617) 727-7750
  Elder Hotline 1-800-882-2003
Long-Term Care Ombudsman
  Susan McDonough at the above address   (617) 727-7273

In 1973, the Massachusetts Executive Office of Elder Affairs was established as one of the first cabinet-level agencies nationwide to assume responsibility for addressing the needs and concerns of senior citizens. Three subsidiary offices are in charge of administration, programs, and planning and policy, and together they coordinate the services of home care, advocacy, legislation, and nutrition activities. Elder Independence is the comprehensive home care program that enables frail elders to remain in the community by providing a continuum of assistance in terms of changing needs. Income thresholds on which eligibility is based are increased each year to keep pace with inflation.[7] Primary services provided through the Elder Independence program include:

Case management	Information and referral	
Companionship	Homemaker and chore	Home-delivered
Emergency shelter	Transportation	meals
Personal care	Social day care	

(Emergency shelter is a service designed to provide temporary housing for elders without a home owing to disaster, eviction, or an unsafe condition in their home.)

INFORMATION AND REFERRAL SERVICES ARE AVAILABLE TO ELDERS AND THEIR FAMILIES OR FRIENDS, *REGARDLESS OF INCOME.* Contact the Elder Hotline or the Area Agency on Aging that serves your parents' community.

Area Agencies on Aging

Baypath Senior Citizens Services
  P.O. Box 2625, Central Station, Framingham, MA 01701
  (617) 620-0840

7. In 1985, services were provided to a single elder whose income did not exceed $9065 and to couples whose income fell below $11,846.

Serving: Ashland, Dover, Framingham, Holliston, Hopkinton, Hudson, Marlborough, Natick, Northborough, Sherborn, Southborough, Sudbury, Wayland, Westborough

Bristol County Home Care for the Elderly
182 North Main Street, Fall River, MA 02720 (617) 675-2101

Coastline Elderly Services
106 Huttleston Avenue, Fairhaven, MA 02719 (617) 999-6400
Serving: Acushnet, Dartmouth, Fairhaven, Gosnold, Marion, Mattapoisett, New Bedford, Rochester

Chelsea/Revere/Winthrop Elder Services
300 Broadway, P.O. Box 189, Revere, MA (617) 286-0550

Commission on Affairs of the Elderly
One City Hall Square, Room 271, Boston, MA 02201
(617) 725-4366; hotline 722-4646

Elder Services of Berkshire County
100 North Street, Pittsfield, MA 01201 (413) 499-1353

Elder Services of Cape Cod & the Islands
68 Route 134, South Dennis, MA 02660 (617) 394-4630;
toll-free 800-352-7178

Elder Services of the Merrimack Valley
420 Common Street, Lawrence, MA 01840 (617) 683-7747;
toll-free 800-892-0890
Serving: Amesbury, Andover, Billerica, Boxford, Chelmsford, Dracut, Dunstable, Georgetown, Groveland, Haverhill, Lawrence, Lowell, Merrimac, Methuen, Newbury, Newburyport, North Andover, Rowley, Salisbury, Tewksbury, Tyngsborough, Westford, West Newbury

Franklin County Home Care Corporation
Central Street, Turners Falls, MA 01376 (413) 863-9565

Greater Lynn Senior Services
90 Exchange Street, Lynn, MA 01901 (617) 599-0110
Serving: Lynn, Lynnfield, Nahant, Saugus, Swampscott

Greater Springfield Senior Services
66 Industry Avenue, Springfield, MA 01104 (413) 781-8800
Serving: Agawam, Brimfield, East Longmeadow, Hampden, Holland, Longmeadow, Monson, Palmer, Springfield, Wales, West Springfield, Wilbraham

Highland Valley Elder Services
320 Riverside Drive, Northampton, MA 01060 (413) 586-200;
toll-free 800-322-0551
Serving: Amherst, Blandford, Chester, Chesterfield, Cumminttton, Easthampton, Goshen, Granville, Hadley, Hatfield, Huntington, Middlefield, Montgomery, Northampton, Pelham, Plain-

field, Russell, Southampton, Southwick, Tolland, Westfield, Westhampton, Williamsburg, Worthington

Holyoke/Chicopee Regional Senior Services
198 High Street, Holyoke, MA 01040   (413) 538-9020

King Philip Elder Services
IGO Building, Carpenter Street, Foxborough, MA 02035
(617) 769-7440
> Serving: Canton, Dedham, Foxborough, Norfolk (toll-free 800-462-5221), Norwood, Plainville, Sharon, Walpole, Westwood, Wrentham

Minutemen Home Care Corporation
83 Hartwell Avenue, Lexington, MA 02173   (617) 862-6200; 263-8720
> Serving: Acton, Arlington, Bedford, Boxborough, Burlington, Carlisle, Concord, Harvard, Lexington, Lincoln, Littleton, Maynard, Stow, Wilmington, Winchester, Woburn

Mystic Valley Elder Services
661 Main Street, Suite 110, Malden, MA 02148   (617) 324-7705
> Serving: Everett, Malden, Medford, Melrose, North Reading, Reading, Stoneham, Wakefield

North Shore Elder Services
484 Lowell Street, Peabody, MA 01960   (617) 535-01960
> Serving: Danvers, Marblehead, Middleton, Peabody, Salem

Old Colony Planning Council
9 Belmont Street, Brockton, MA 02401   (617) 583-1833
> Serving: Abington, Avon, Bridgewater, Brockton, Carver, Duxbury, East Bridgewater, Easton, Halifax, Hanover, Hanson, Kingston, Lakewille, Marshfield, Middleborough, Pembroke, Plymouth, Plympton, Rockland, Stoughton, Wareham, West Bridgewater, Whitman

Region II Area Agency on Aging
1128 Main Street, Holden, MA 01520   (617) 829-5364; toll-free 800-322-3032
> Serving: Worcester, Montachusett, and Tri-Valley.

Senior Home Care Services
2 Main Street, Gloucester, MA 01930   (617) 281-1750
> Serving: Beverly, Essex, Gloucester, Hamilton, Ipswich, Manchester, Rockport, Topsfield, Wenham

Somerville/Cambridge Elder Services
One Davis Square, Somerville, MA 02144   (617) 628-2601

South Shore Elder Services
639 Granite Street, Braintree, MA 02184   (617) 749-6832; 383-9790; 848-3910

Serving: Braintree, Cohassett, Hingham, Holbrook, Hull, Milton, Norwell, Quincy, Randolph, Scituate, Weymouth

West Suburban Elder Services
Parker Office Bldg., 124 Watertown Street, Watertown, MA 02172
(617) 926-4100
Serving: Belmont, Brookline, Needham, Newton, Waltham, Watertown, Wellesley, Weston

The Executive Office on Elderly Affairs has inaugurated training programs for Elder Advocates. The programs consist in participatory workshops in which senior citizens learn how to inform their peers about issues that affect them and to function as advocates on matters of health, consumerism, and legislation.

Another peer-to-peer program funded by the Commonwealth of Massachusetts is the Elder Service Corps. The aim of this program is the creation of job opportunities for older people who are assigned to agencies that serve their contemporaries statewide. For information about how your parents can participate in the Elder Service Corps, contact the Program Manager at the Office of Elder Affairs, (617) 727-5948.

RESPITE CARE

The Office of Elder Affairs has developed a Respite Care Program, defined as "temporary assistance for primary caregivers of frail elders under emergency circumstances, or by prearrangement, for special occasions, or on a regular basis, to allow time away from the stresses and demands of providing ongoing care." The program operates on a "sliding fee" basis, which means that middle-income families are eligible at rates they can afford. Call the Elder Hotline for additional information or to make an arrangement for respite care.

The Office of Elder Affairs has prepared several useful brochures available on request. One that is especially helpful is *Cold Facts on Weatherization, Fuel Assistance, Utilities, Winter Hazards, and Health.*

Be sure that your parents get their monthly copies of the Office of Elder Affairs *Newsletter,* distributed free at all Senior Centers. To receive the newsletter by mail, direct your request to the Office of Elder Affairs by mail or by calling the in-state toll-free hotline, 1-800-882-2003.

MICHIGAN

Office of Services to the Aging
   P.O. Box 30026
   Lansing, Michigan 48909   (517) 373-8230
Long-Term Care Ombudsperson
   Ms. Hollis Turnham
   900 West Ottawa
   Lansing, Michigan 48915   (517) 482-1297   or   toll-free
   1-800-292-7852

The state's Commission on Aging and the Office of Services to the Aging advise the governor and the legislature on special problems of persons aged sixty and older, promote senior citizen interests within the state government and in communities, and administer federal Older Americans Act programs and state-funded programs for older people, including:

Senior Community Services, which provide funds for local community programs focused on transportation, counseling, health screening.

Community Nutrition Services, which offer a hot meal and information on better nutrition to seniors in 660 congregate facilities statewide and provide a limited number of meals to the homebound elderly.

Training and Education Courses conducted for professionals, older people, and those who staff aging programs.

Foster Grandparent Opportunities for volunteers sixty and older who meet income requirements to work on a one-to-one basis with children and young adults who have special needs.

Retired Senior Volunteer Program (RSVP), which gives older people the opportunity to serve in local projects and reimburses them for transportation costs with state funds.

Preventive Services, which inform the public about the abuse of alcohol and the misuse of medications and offer some corrective counseling.

Alternative Care, which provides support services enabling the frail or chronically ill older person to remain at home instead of being institutionalized.

Senior Community Services Employment, which offers part-time job opportunities to people fifty-five and older who meet income guidelines.

Legal Services Development, which provides technical assistance, training, and support to legal service programs for senior citizens.

Alternative Food Delivery, which offers program planning, training, and audiovisual materials to older people interested in organizing and maintaining food-growing and buying alternatives, such as community gardens, co-ops, and solar greenhouses.

Senior Companion Program, which offers volunteer opportunities to persons sixty and older who meet income guidelines to work with elderly persons who have special needs.

Long-Term Care Ombudsman Project, which serves the interests of nursing home residents, their families, and friends. The project is administered by Citizens for Better Care, a private nonprofit consumer organization which maintains local offices throughout the state. For information about Ombudsman services in areas without a local office, as well as for similar services in other states, contact the state office at 1-800-292-7852.

Information about all of the above programs and referrals to the local agencies that administer them can be supplied by the Area Agency on Aging that serves the city or county where your parents live.

Area Agencies on Aging

1-A.   *Detroit Area Agency on Aging*
       3110 Book Building, 1249 Washington Boulevard
       Detroit, MI 48226   (313) 222-5330
           Cities served: Detroit, Hamtramck, Highland Park, Grosse Pointe, Grosse Pointe Park, Grosse Pointe Shores, Grosse Pointe Woods, Grosse Pointe Farms, Harper Woods

1-B.   *Area Agency on Aging*
       29508 Southfield Road, Suite 100, Southfield MI 48076
       (313) 569-0333
           Counties served: Livingston, Macomb, Monroe, Oakland, St. Clair, Washtenaw

1-C.   *The Senior Alliance, Inc.*
       3850 Second Street, Suite 160, Wayne, MI 48184   (313) 722-2830
           Serves all of Wayne County except those communities served by Area Agency 1-A

  2.   *Region II Commission on Aging*
       3221 North Adrian Drive, P.O. Box 915, Adrian, MI 49221
       (517) 265-7881
           Counties served: Hillsdale, Jackson, Lenawee

3. *Southcentral Michigan Commission on Aging*
    2401 East Milham Road, Kalamazoo, MI 49002   (616) 343-4996
    Counties served: Barry, Branch, Calhoun, Kalamazoo, St. Joseph

4. *Region IV Area Agency on Aging*
    2919 Division Street, St. Joseph, MI 49085   (616) 983-0177
    Counties served: Berrien, Cass, VanBuren

5. *Valley Area Agency on Aging*
    708 Root Street, Room 110, Flint, MI 48503   (313) 239-7671
    Counties served: Genesee, Lapeer, Shiawassee

6. *Tri-County Office on Aging*
    500 West Washtenaw, Lansing, MI 48933   (517) 483-4150
    Counties served: Clintonk, Eaton, Ingham

7. *Region VII Area Agency on Aging*
    1200 North Madison Avenue, East Community Center
    Bay City, MI 48706   (517) 893-4506
    Counties served: Bay, Clare, Gladwin, Gratiot, Huron, Isabella, Midland, Saginaw, Sanilac, Tuscola

8. *Area Agency on Aging of Western Michigan*
    540 Keeler Building, 60 North Division, Grand Rapids, MI 49503
    (616) 456-5664
    Counties served: Allegan, Ionia, Kent, Lake, Mason, Mecosta, Montcalm, Newaygo, Osceola

9. *Northeast Michigan Community Services*
    2373 Gordon Road, P.O. Box 1038, Alpena, MI 49707
    (517) 356-3474
    Counties served: Alcona, Arenac, Alpena, Cheboygan, Crawford, Iosco, Montmorency, Ogemaw, Oscoda, Otsego, Presque Isle, Roscommon

10. *Northwest Michigan Agency on Aging*
    521 South Union Street, Traverse City, MI 49684
    (616) 947-8920
    Counties served: Antrim, Benzie, Charlevoix, Emmet, Grand Traverse, Kalkaska, Leelanau, Manistee, Missaukee, Wexford

11. *Region 11 Area Agency on Aging*
    UPCAP Services Inc.
    118 North 22d Street, Escanaba, MI 49829   (906) 786-4701
    Counties served: Alger, Baraga, Chippewa, Delta, Dickinson, Gogebic, Houghton, Iron, Keweenaw, Luce, Mackinac, Marquette, Menominee, Ontonagon, Schoolcraft

12. *Region 14 Council on Aging*
    315 West Webster, Muskegon, MI 49440   (616) 722-7811
    Counties served: Muskegon, Oceana, Ottawa

MINNESOTA

Board on Aging
204 Metro Square, 7th and Robert
St. Paul, Minnesota 55101   (612) 296-2770
Nursing Home Ombudsman
Jim Varpness at the above address and phone number
Because of budget cuts that necessitate frequent changes in the Aging Network, thereby causing guides and information directories to go out of date, the State Board on Aging directs requests for information about state programs and local services to the local Area Agency on Aging or the Community Senior Citizen Information and Referral Service.

Area Agencies on Aging

Northwest Area Agency on Aging
425 Woodland Avenue, Crookston, MN 56716   (218) 281-1396
Headwaters Area Agency on Aging
722 15th Street, P.O. Box 906, Bemidji, MN 56601
(218) 751-3108
Arrowhead Area Agency on Aging
330 South 1st Avenue East, Duluth, MN 55802   (218) 722-5545
West Central Area on Aging
P.O. Box 726, Fergus Falls, MN 56537   (218) 739-4617
Region Five Area Agency on Aging
611 Iowa, Staples, MN 56479   (218) 894-3233
Six East Area Agency on Aging
333 West 6th Street, Lower Level, Wilmar, MN 56201
(612) 235-8504
Upper Minnesota Valley Area Agency on Aging
323 West Schlieman, Appleton, MN 56208   (612) 289-1981
Region Seven Area Agency on Aging
East Central Regional Development Commission
119 South Lake Street, Mora, MN 55051   (612) 679-4065
Central Minnesota Council on Aging
26 North 6th Avenue, #330, St. Cloud, MN 56301
(612) 253-9349
Southwestern Area Agency on Aging
2524 Broadway, Box 265, Slayton, MN 56172   (507) 836-8549
Region Nine Area Agency on Aging
410 South Fifth Street, Box 3367, Mankato, MN 56001
(507) 387-5643; toll-free 1-800-722-9389

Southeastern Minnesota Area Agency on Aging
121 North Broadway, Room 302, Rochester, MN 55904
(507) 288-6944

Region XI Area Agency on Aging
Metropolitan Council
300 Metro Square Building, St. Paul, MN 55101   (612) 291-6497

Minnesota Cheippewa Tribe Area Agency on Aging
P.O. Box 217, Cass Lake, MN 56633   (218) 335-2252

MISSISSIPPI

Council on Aging
301 West Pearl Street
Jackson, Mississippi 39203-2013   (601) 949-2013

Long-Term Care Ombudsman
Billie Marshall at the above address and phone number

Local Area Agencies on Aging are the source for information about current programs and services as well as for referral to the community agencies that provide them. Support systems for the elderly vary widely from one area to another. For example, although there are no licensed adult day care centers, three area agencies (2, 5, and 8) have begun to implement a program of extended community care for adults using their already established senior citizen centers.

Area Agencies on Aging

1. *South Delta Area Agency on Aging*
   P.O. Box 1776, Greenville, MS 38702-1776   (601) 378-3831

2. *Central Mississippi Area Agency on Aging*
   P.O. Box 4935, Jackson, MS 39216   (601) 981-1511

3. *North Delta Area Agency on Aging*
   P.O. Box 1244, Clarksdale, MS 38614   (601) 627-3401

4. *North Central Area Agency on Aging*
   P.O. Box 668, Winona, MS 38967   (601) 283-2675

5. *Northeast Mississippi Area Agency on Aging*
   P.O. Drawer 6D, Booneville, MS 38829   (601) 728-6248

6. *East Central Area Agency on Aging*
   P.O. Box 499, Newton, MS 39345   (601) 683-2401

7. *Southwest Mississippi Area Agency on Aging*
   P.O. Box 429, Meadville, MS 39653   (601) 384-5881

8. *Southern Mississippi Area Agency on Aging*
   1020 32nd Avenue, Gulfport, MS 39501   (601) 868-2311

9. *Golden Triangle Area Agency on Aging*
   P.O. Drawer DN, Mississippi State, MS 39762
   (601) 325-3855

10. *Three Rivers Area Agency on Aging*
   P.O. Drawer B, Pontotoc, MS 38863   (601) 489-2415

A useful source of information about all categories of health care facilities statewide that pass the requirement for participation in Medicare and Medicaid programs is the *Directory of Health Facilities* published by:

Mississippi Health Care Commission
Division of Licensure and Certification
2688 Insurance Center Drive
Jackson, Mississippi 39216
(601) 981-6880

Categories are arranged by city and/or county, and each listing contains essential details. Categories include Hospitals; Ambulatory Surgical Facilities; Institutions for the Aged and Infirm (Skilled, Intermediate, and Personal Care); Home Health Agencies; Hospices; Independent Laboratories; Rural Health Clinics; Rehabilitation Agencies; Physical Therapists in Private Practice; and End Stage Renal Disease Facilities.

Consult the local Area Agency on Aging or your local library if you'd like to use the directory, or call the above agency for a copy of your own.

MISSOURI

Department of Social Services, Division of Aging
   P.O. Box 1337
   Jefferson City, Missouri 65102   (314) 751-3082
Long-Term Care Ombudsman
   Duane McGuire at the above address and   (314) 751-8536

Among the broad range of services available to senior citizens are 230 certified home health agencies and an additional 140 that are Medicaid-certified to supply homemaker/chore and personal care services, especially for individuals sixty-five or over who would have to be placed in a long-term care facility at the intermediate care level if such services were not available. The state has spelled out standards in great detail for how such services must be carried out.[8]

Access to these programs is arranged through the Area Agency on Aging that serves your parents' county. The Area Agencies also administer about 280 nutrition sites statewide which provide both congregate and home-delivered meals. They are also the source of information and referral concerning local networks for transportation and legal services and for access to day care.

In 1985, the Department of Social Services issued new licensing requirements for Adult Day Care Programs. In addition to the fifteen licensed day care centers now in operation statewide, a long list of applications is waiting approval following inspection.

In 1980, the Division of Aging began operation of a statewide toll-free hotline, 1-800-392-0210, to receive reports of abuse, neglect, and exploitation of Missourians age sixty and older who live in the community. These reports were investigated and evaluated within twenty-four hours by field staff members trained not only in social work but also in crisis intervention. In 1982, the Division of Institutional Complaint unit was merged with the Central Registry unit, which is now responsible not only for reports of abuse and neglect, but also for processing reports of violations of long-term care facility standards and patients' rights. In February 1986, a total of 11,400 such reports were received. It appears that Missouri may have the most thorough and largest computerized system nationwide for generating a great deal of information about the reports received, including data about the victims, the perpetrators, and the nature of the reported situation. BE SURE TO MAKE USE OF THIS SYSTEM IF YOU OR SOMEONE YOU KNOW HAS A COMPLAINT ABOUT THE MISTREATMENT OF AN ELDERLY PERSON.

For information about all support systems and services for your parents, including self-help groups for those with particular physical or mental problems, contact the Area Agency on Aging that serves your parents' county.

Area Agencies on Aging

1. *Southwest Missouri Office of Aging*
   317 St. Louis Street, Box 1805 SSS, Springfield, MO 65805
   (417) 862-0762
   Counties served: Barry, Christian, Dade, Dallas, Douglas, Greene, Howell, Lawrence, Oregon, Ozark, Polk, Shannon, Stone, Taney, Texas, Webster, Wright

2. *Southeast Missouri AAA*
   2400 County Park Drive, Cape Girardeau, MO 63701
   (314) 335-3331

8. For a detailed description of Missouri's In-Home Service Standards, see Chapter 7, "Home Care."

Counties served: Bollinger, Butler, Cape Girardeau, Carter, Dunklin, Iron, Madison, Mississippi, New Madrid, Pemiscot, Perry, Reynolds, Ripley, St. Francis, Ste. Genevieve, Scott, Stoddard

3. *District III AAA*
604 North Maguire, P.O. Box 556, Warrensburg, MO 64093
(816) 747-3107
Counties served: Bates, Benton, Carroll, Cedar, Chariton, Henry, Hickory, Johnson, Lafayette, Pettis, St. Clair, Saline, Vernon

4. *Northwest Missouri AAA*
P.O. Drawer G, 401 West Jackson, Albany, MO 64402
(816) 726-3800
Counties served: Andrew, Atchison, Nuchanan, Caldwell, Clinton, Daviess, DeKalb, Gentry, Grundy, Harrison, Holt, Linn, Livingston, Mercer, Nodaway, Putnam, Sullivan, Worth

5. *Northeast Missouri AAA*
705 East LaHarpe, P.O. Box 1067, Kirksville, MO 63501
(816) 665-4682
Counties served: Adair, Clark, Knox, Lewis, Lincoln, Macon, Marion, Monroe, Montgomery, Pike, Ralls, Randolph, Scotland, Schuyler, Shelby, Warren

6. *Central Missouri AAA*
609 Nebraska, Columbia, MO 65201   (314) 443-5823
Counties served: Audrain, Boone, Callaway, Camden, Cole, Cooper, Crawford, Dent, Gasconnade, Howard, Laclede, Maries, Miller, Moniteau, Morgan, Osage, Phelps, Pulaski, Washington

7. *Aging Program, Mid-America Regional Council*
20 West 9th Street, 3d Floor, Kansas City, MO 64105
(816) 474-4240
Counties served: Cass, Clay, Jackson, Kansas City, Platte, Ray

8. *Mid-East Missouri AAA*
Kimberly Building, Suite 315, 2510 South Brentwood Blvd.
Brentwood, MO 63144   (314) 962-0808
Counties served: Franklin, Jefferson, St. Charles, St. Louis

9. *St. Louis AAA*
634 North Grand, 8th floor, St. Louis, MO 63103   (314) 658-1173
City served: St. Louis

10. *Region X AAA*
2008 Sergeant Street, Freeman Building, Room 405
Joplin, MO 64801   (417) 781-7562
Counties served: Barton, Jasper, McDonald, Newton

MONTANA

*Department of Social and Rehabilitation Services, Community Services
Program*
 P.O. Box 4210
 Helena, Montana 59604 (406) 449-3865
Long-Term Care Ombudsman
 Doug Blakley
 Seniors' Office, Legal & Ombudsman Service
 P.O. Box 232, Helena, Montana 59620 (406) 444-4676 or toll-free
 1-800-332-2272

The department has developed a program whose purpose is not only
to promote the health and independence of certain Medicaid-eligible
elderly persons requiring long-term care, but also to make a continuum
of home-based services available for private pay and for the medically
needy ineligible for Medicaid. Among the aspects of this program that
address the needs of recipients as well as the problems of cost containment are the following:

- Offering Medicaid recipients less restrictive options by giving them a
  choice of service systems
- Broadening the use of volunteers and natural family support systems
- Eliminating duplication of services through effective case management
- Ensuring that recipients participate in the development of the plans
  for their care

The plans for home-based services which are developed by a case
management team in conjunction with the attending physician and the
recipient include a suitable combination of the following: homemaker,
personal care, respite, adult day care, medical alert, meals, nonmedical
transportation, physical modifications to the home, as well as occupational therapy, physical therapy, speech therapy, and audiology services.

You can receive additional information about this program and about
other programs of possible interest to your parents by contacting:
 Department of Social and Rehabilitation Services
 Cogswell Building, Capitol Station, Helena, Montana 59620
 (406) 444-2037, and
 The Montana Health Information Center
 235 East Pine, Missoula, Montana 59802
 (406) 728-0975 or toll-free 1-800-332-5759, and
 The Area Agency on Aging that serves your parents' county

Area Agencies on Aging

Area I. Action for Eastern Montana
123 North Merrill, Glendive, MT 59330   (406) 365-3364
Counties served: Carter, Custer, Daniels, Dawson, Fallon, Garfield, McCone, Phillips, Powder River, Prairie, Richland, Roosevelt, Rosebud, Sheridan, Treasure, Valley, Wibaux

Area II. Agency on Aging
236 South Main, Roundup, MT 59072   (406) 323-1320
Counties served: Big Horn, Carbon, Fergus, Golden Valley, Judith Basin, Musselshell, Petroleum, Stillwater, Sweet Grass, Wheatland, Yellowstone

Area III. North Central Agency on Aging
123 South Main, Conrad, MT 59525   (406) 278-5662
Counties served: Blaine, Chouteau, Glacier, Liberty, Pondera, Teton, Toole

Area IV. Agency on Aging
P.O. Box 721, Helena, MT 59624   (406) 442-1552
Counties served: Broadwater, Gallatin, Jefferson, Lewis and Clark, Meagher, Park

Area V. Agency on Aging
115 East Pennsylvania, Anaconda, MT 59711   (406) 563-3110
Counties served: Beaverhead, Deer Lodge, Granite, Madison, Powell, Silver Bow

Area VI. Western Montana Area Agency on Aging
8th and Main, P.O. Box 4027, Polson, MT 59860
(406) 883-6211, ext. 288
Counties served: Lake, Lincoln, Mineral, Ravalli, Sanders

Area VII. Montana Inter-Tribal Policy Board
2303 Grand Avenue, Billings, MT 59101   (405) 652-3113
Serves all Indian reservations

Area VIII. Cascade County Area on Aging
1601 2nd Avenue North, Great Falls, MT 59401   (406) 761-1919

Area IX. Flathead County Council on Aging
723 Fifth Avenue East, Kalispell, MT 59901
(406) 755-5300, ext. 322

Area X. Hill County Council on Aging
2 West 2nd Street, Havre, MT 59501   (406) 265-5464

Area XI. Missoula County Council on Aging
333 North Washington, Missoula, MT 59801   (406) 728-7682

NEBRASKA

Department on Aging
   Box 95044
   Lincoln, Nebraska 68509-5044   (402) 471-2306
Long-Term Care Ombudsman
   Jerry W. Kurth at the above address and phone number

The state's Department on Aging makes available free of charge to older Nebraskans and their families an unusually wide variety of materials describing resources, programs, and the many special projects initiated by the individual Area Agencies on Aging for the benefit of the communities they serve. Other state agencies are also engaged in many enterprises that publicize the needs of the elderly and devise the ways in which these needs can best be met.

The Department has prepared an excellent *Consumer's Guide for Older Nebraskans* which discusses in detail matters such as,

> Age Discrimination, Choosing a Nursing Home, Energy Assistance, Food Stamps, Guardianship, Medicare, Medicaid, Supplementary Security Income, and Weatherization.

The guide concludes with a list of the state's services for its older population. These services include:

Advocacy	Employment referral
Alcoholism program	Family case work
Christmas gifts for older people	Farmers markets
Christmas meals for older people	Food pantries
Community cannery	Gardening program
Community centers	Health screening
Community education	Immunization clinics
Craft sales	In-home services
Domestic violence program	Income tax assistance
Education	Information and referral
Emergency clothes	Limited housing rehabilitation
Emergency food	Nutrition services
Emergency house payments	Telephone Reassurance
Emergency transportation	Volunteer programs and services

The department also publishes *The Older Nebraskans VOICE,* an eight-page quarterly that contains news, feature stories, and consumer information of interest to senior citizens and their families. Contact the department's office if your parents would like to receive this publication in the mail. It can also be picked up at senior centers.

The *VOICE* is available on cassette from the Nebraska Library for the Blind and Physically Handicapped. Call the library's toll-free number, 1-800-742-7691, for information about the regional branches that offer this special service as well as many others to eligible applicants.

Projects sponsored by other state agencies on behalf of older Nebraskans include:

■ The *Abuse/Neglect Hotline*, 1-800-652-1999, maintained by the Department of Public Welfare Division of Social Services. For detailed information, call the above number or write to the Department at:

> 301 Centennial Mall South, 5th floor
> P.O. Box 95026, Lincoln, Nebraska 68509

Complaints about nursing homes can be addressed to the Long-Term Care Ombudsman at the Department on Aging and/or to:

> Division of Licensure and Standards
> Nebraska Department on Health
> P.O. Box 95007, Lincoln, Nebraska 68509   (402) 471-2946

■ The *Elder Law Review*, published jointly by the Department on Aging and the Committee on the Delivery of Legal Service to the Elderly (Nebraska State Bar Association Young Lawyers Section). The review deals with such matters as age discrimination, grandparents' rights, pensions, and health insurance. For information about subscriptions and back issues, contact:

> Nebraska State Bar Association
> *Elder Law Review*
> 635 South 14th Street, Lincoln, Nebraska 68508

■ *Explore Nebraska through Elderhostel*, a publication that describes summer courses for seniors conducted at colleges throughout the state.[9] Further information is available from:

> Nebraska State Elderhostel Director
> Doane College, Crete, Nebraska 68333

Area Agencies on Aging

Each Area Agency on Aging listed below has prepared an individual brochure describing in detail the services and programs for which it is responsible. In addition, addresses, phone numbers, and hours of operation are provided for local community service centers and special support systems. For a brochure (and for essential information that you

9. Details on how the Elderhostel program works can be found in Chapter 2.

might need without delay on behalf of your parents), contact the Area
Agency that serves the county in which they live.

South Central Nebraska AAA
>   124 West 46th Street, Kearney, NE 68847   (308) 234-1851 or
>   1-800-652-1922
>>   Counties served: Blaine, Buffalo, Custer, Franklin, Furnas, Gar-
>>   field, Greeley, Harlan, Kearney, Loup, Phelps, Sherman, Valley,
>>   Wheeler

Lincoln AAA
>   129 North 10th Street, Rm. 241, Lincoln, NE 68508
>   (402) 471-7022
>>   Counties served: Butler, Fillmore, Lancaster, Polk, Saline,
>>   Seward, York

Blue Rivers AAA
>   Gage County Courthouse, Rm. 24, Beatrice, NE 68310
>   (402) 223-3124
>>   Counties served: Gage, Jefferson, Johnson, Nemaha, Otoe, Paw-
>>   nee, Richardson, Thayer

Midland AAA
>   Courthouse Annex, 500 N. Denver, P.O. Box 905
>   Hastings, NE 68901   (402) 463-4565
>>   Counties served: Adams, Clay, Hamilton, Hall, Howard, Mer-
>>   rick, Nuckells, Webster

West Central AAA
>   Craft State Office Building, 200 South Silber
>   North Platte, NE 69101   (308) 534-6780, ext. 195
>>   Counties served: Arthur, Chase, Dawson, Dundy, Frontier,
>>   Gosper, Grant, Hayes, Hitchcock, Hooker, Keith, Lincoln, Lo-
>>   gan, McPherson, Perkins, Red Willow, Thomas

Aging Office of Western Nebraska
>   4502 Avenue I, Scottsbluff, NE 69361   (308) 635-0851 or
>   1-800-682-5140
>>   Counties served: Banner, Box Butte, Cheyenne, Dawes, Neuel,
>>   Garden, Kimball, Morrill, Scotts Bluff, Sheridan, Sioux

Northeast Nebraska AAA
>   P.O. Box 1447, Norfolk, NE 68701   1-800-672-8368
>>   Counties served: Boone, Boyd, Brown, Burt, Cedar, Colfax,
>>   Cuming, Dakota, Dixon, Knox, Madison, Pierce, Platte, Stanton,
>>   Thurston, Wayne, Goldenrod Hills

Eastern Nebraska Office on Aging
>   885 South 72nd Street, Omaha, NE 68114   (402) 444-6444
>>   Counties served: Cass, Dodge, Douglas, Sarpy, Washington

NEVADA

Department of Human Resources, Division for Aging Services
Kinkead Bldg., Rm. 101
505 East King St.
Carson City, Nevada 89710   (702) 885-4210
Long-Term Care Ombudsman
Earl Yamashita at the above address and phone number

The Division for Aging Services is the centralized source of information and referral for all programs and services that make up the support network for Nevadans who are sixty-five and older. There are currently twenty-eight Nutrition Programs statewide providing congregate meals, and in some cases, meals for the homebound. The names and addresses of the providers closest to your parents can be requested from the Division for Aging Services. The division will also supply information about senior housing facilities: thirteen are located in Reno, three in Sparks, and two in Carson City.

The following are some of the Social Service Projects that can also be contacted for information about whether your parents are eligible to participate in the services and programs they administer:

HEALTH
Ambulatory Geriatric Health & Podiatry Program
c/o Washoe County District Health Department
1001 East 9th Street, P.O. Box 11130, Reno, NV 89520
(702) 785-4290

Senior Citizens Health Program
625 Shadow Lane, P.O. Box 4426, Las Vegas, NV 89106
(702) 385-1291

HOME HEALTH AND HOME CARE
Homemaker Home Health Aide Service
651 Shadow Lane, Las Vegas, NV 89106   (702) 386-4137

Nevada Home Health Services
P.O. Box 1359, Elko, NV 89801   (702) 738-7178

Senior Citizen Service Center & Home Care Support Program
1155 East 9th Street, Reno, NV 89512   (702) 785-4024

Mt. Grant General Hospital/Home Health Services
P.O. Box 1516, Hawthorne, NV 89415   (702) 945-2461

TRANSPORTATION (many of the Nutrition Projects also provide transportation)
Senior Transportation Project
330 West Washington, Las Vegas, NV 89106   (702) 646-2062

Lincoln Community Transportation
P.O. Box 549, Caliente, NV 89008 (no phone number available)
Elko Senior Community Services
P.O. Box 657, Elko, NV 89801 (no phone number available)

DAY CARE
Senior Day Care Program, First Christian Church
101 South Rancho, Las Vegas, NV 89106   (702) 385-5929
Senior Day Break
1155 East 9th Street, Reno, NV 89512   (702) 785-5925

LEGAL AID
Senior Citizens Law Project
City Hall Annex, City Hall
400 East Stewart Avenue, Las Vegas, NV 89101   (702) 386-6596
Senior Law Project
P.O. Box 50129, Reno, NV 89513   (702) 785-5913

MISCELLANEOUS
Energy Conservation Project
1100 East William Street, Suite 117, Carson City, NV 89710
(702) 885-4420
Senior Employment Service
275 East 4th Street, P.O. Box 5415, Reno, NV 89513
(702) 329-6644
Senior Citizens Protective Services
651 Shadow Lane, Las Vegas, NV 89106
(702) 386-4291

If you're doing your best to cope with a parent who is a victim of
Alzheimer's disease, you should know about these support groups:

Alzheimer's Resource Center
2898 Highway 50 East, Carson City, Nevada 89701
(702) 882-3301

Alzheimer's Family Support Group of Reno
1155 E. 9th St., Reno, Nevada 89512
(702) 785-5925 weekdays
(702) 825-4853 evenings and weekends

NEW HAMPSHIRE

State Council on Aging
105 Loudon Road
Concord, New Hampshire 03301   (603) 271-2751

Long-Term Care Ombudsman

Ms. Jerilym M. Pelch at the above address and phone number or toll-free 1-800-442-5640

New Hampshire is the only state whose residents pay neither a sales tax nor a state income tax, and the services to senior citizens are therefore paid for almost entirely by federal funds provided under the Older Americans Act. The State Council on Aging is the sole agency authorized to receive these funds and administer these funds. The council is responsible for allocating grants to various local public and private agencies and institutions which in turn plan and carry out the projects and services for the aging population and their families. These agencies also train professional personnel for work with the elderly.

It is anticipated that a reorganization will be mandated by state law in 1987 as a result of which the Council on Aging will become a division of the Department of Health and Human Services, to be known as the Division of Elderly and Adult Services. When this development occurs, New Hampshire will have its first organized and integrated statewide service system for older persons.

In the meantime, the council publishes a *Project Directory*, which is available on request. It contains details and referrals for programs such as adult day care, nutrition, fuel assistance, telephone reassurance, health and health-related services, transportation, reduced legal referral system, and the Foster Grandparent Project.

Information about services for your parents is also available from the regional office in their area:

New Hampshire State Council on Aging

105 Loudon Road, Building 3, Concord, NH 03301

(603) 271-2751

Counties served: Belknap, Carroll, Coos, Grafton, Hillsboro, Merrimack

State Council on Aging Regional Office

600 State Street, Portsmouth, NH 03801   (603) 436-3702

Counties served: Rockingham and Strafford

State Council on Aging Regional Office

National Bank Building, Lebanon, NH 03766   (603) 448-1680

Counties served: Cheshire and Sullivan

New Hampshire has approximately ten thousand people sixty years of age and older in long-term care facilities. To guarantee that the conditions under which they live meet state requirements and to investigate and resolve all complaints, one advocacy program now consolidates legal services, protective services, and ombudsman services. The advocacy program is administered by the Office of the Long-Term Care Ombudsman, which operates within the Council on Aging.

For details about how this program works, call the toll-free number

1-800-442-5640 and request the brochure *We Can Help.* The office can also provide you with a manual describing the rights of nursing home patients.

NEW JERSEY

Department of Community Affairs Division on Aging
    363 W. State Street
    Trenton, New Jersey 08625-0807   (609) 292-4833

    Senior Citizen Information and Referral Service
    Statewide toll-free line: 1-800-792-8820

Office of the Ombudsman for the Institutionalized Elderly
    Jack D'Ambrosio, Jr.
    28 West State Street, CN 808
    Trenton, New Jersey 08625-0808   (609) 292-8016

The Division on Aging has prepared several detailed sources of information that are mailed on request. One of the most useful is the forty-page booklet *Federal Programs for Older Persons.* While the booklet is not exhaustive, it provides details about matters such as employment programs; the federal law protecting people between the ages of forty and seventy against age discrimination in employment; the home energy assistance program; subsidized housing; the food stamp program and nutrition programs; recreation entitlements; volunteer opportunities, including information about how your parents can join the Peace Corps for overseas training and service; tax and veterans benefits; and more. Here's a typical entry:

Private Pensions
    Many persons are covered by a private pension as well as by Social Security. It is important to know what these benefits are and what one may do when problems arise. The Employee Retirement Income Security Act of 1974 (ERISA) and Pension Benefit Guarantee Corporation generally provide certain rights and protections for those with pensions provided by private employers.
    For information on a particular pension plan, to file a complaint, or to learn more about pension plan regulations in general, contact:

    Pension and Welfare Benefit Programs
    Labor-Management Services Administration
    U.S. Department of Labor
    134 Evergreen Place
    East Orange, New Jersey 07018
    (201) 645-3016

Another publication you should request is *Statewide Benefits for Older Persons.* This contains helpful information for your parents about practical matters such as property tax deduction, tenant credit, retirement income exclusions (including exclusion of gain on the sale of a home), and pharmaceutical assistance for the eligible elderly; the reduced fare program for all senior citizens; free enrollment in public colleges; and special recreation entitlements. For example, if your parents are over sixty-two, they can apply for a pass that entitles them to free entry and parking at any New Jersey forest, park, and historic site administered by the Bureau of Parks.

Applications may be obtained by writing to:
Department of Environmental Protection
Bureau of Parks, CN 404, Trenton, NJ 08625
Proof of age must be supplied.

Another brochure that may be of special interest to you and your parents is *Community Care Program for the Elderly & Disabled (CCPED),* which describes the many home services offered by the state's Medicaid program to a limited number of eligible applicants.

Urgently needed information and referral about particular services and programs can be supplied by the Area Agency on Aging that serves your parents' county.

County Agencies on Aging

Atlantic County Division of Aging & Disabled
1333 Atlantic Avenue, 3d floor, Atlantic City, NJ 08401
(609) 345-6700, ext. 2800

Bergen County Office on Aging
355 Main Street, Hackensack, NJ 07601   (201) 646-2625

Burlington County Office on Aging
County Office Building, 49 Rancocas Road, Mt. Holly, NJ 08060
(609) 261-5069

Camden County Office on Aging
County Administration Building, 600 Market Street
Camden, NJ 08101   (609) 757-6753

Cape May County Department of Aging
Social Services Building, Box 222, Rio Grande, NJ 08242
(609) 886-2784

Cumberland County Office on Aging
Administration Building, 790 East Commerce Street
Bridgeton, NJ 08302   (609) 451-8000, ext. 357

Essex County Division on Aging
86 Washington Street, East Orange, NJ 07017   (201) 678-9700

Gloucester County Department on Aging
44 Delaware Street, Woodbury, NJ 08096   (609) 853-3312

Hudson County Office on Aging
   114 Clifton Place, Murdoch Hall, Jersey City, NJ 07304
   (201) 434-6900

Hunterdon County Office on Aging
   Community Service Building, 6 Gaunt Place
   Flemington, NJ 08822   (201) 788-1363

Mercer County Office on Aging
   640 South Broad Street, P.O. Box 8068, Trenton, NJ 08650
   (609) 989-6661

Middlesex County Office on Aging
   County Office Annex, 841 Georges Road
   North Brunswick, NJ 08902   (201) 745-3293 or 3295

Monmouth County Office on Aging
   Hall of Records Annex, East Main Street, Freehold, NJ 07728
   (201) 431-7450

Morris County Office on Aging
   Court House, CN 900, Morristown, NJ 07960-0900
   (201) 829-8539

Ocean County Office on Aging
   CN 2191, Toms River, NJ 08754   (201) 929-2091

Passaic County Office on Aging
   Rea House, 675 Goffle Road, Hawthorne, NJ 07506
   (201) 881-4950 or 1-800-223-0556

Salem County Office on Aging
   c/o Lake View Complex, Salem Woodstown Road, RD 2, Box 348,
   Woodstown, NJ 08098   (609) 769-4150

Somerset County Office on Aging
   Administration Building, North Bridge and High Streets
   P.O. Box 3000, Somerville, NJ 08876   (201) 231-7175

Sussex County Office on Aging
   Newton Memorial Hospital, 175 High Street, Newton, NJ 07860
   (201) 383-5098

Union County Division on Aging
   Administration Building, Elizabeth, NJ 07207
   (201) 527-4866 or 4867

Warren County Office on Aging
   Courthouse, Belvedere, NJ 07823   (201) 457-8000, ext. 591

NEW MEXICO

Human Services Department, Agency on Aging
   La Villa Rivera Building, 4th floor
   222 East Palace Avenue

Santa Fe, New Mexico 87501 (505) 827-7640 or toll-free
1-800-432-6217

Long-Term Care Ombudsman

Dolores LaCalle Bersell at the above address and phone numbers

You can be provided with information about federally funded programs for elder New Mexicans and referral to the most conveniently
located agency that delivers them by calling the toll-free number given
above. You can also request a list prepared by the state's Association of
Home Health Agencies of their member organizations which provide
nursing care and in some instances therapy services in the patient's
home. The agencies are listed geographically by county, and those that
are certified for reimbursement by Medicare and Medicaid are clearly
identified. Special services and professional qualifications of personnel
are also indicated.

If your parent needs many of the services of a nursing home but would
rather remain in familiar surroundings, you can find out about the Coordinated Community In-Home Care Program by calling the toll-free
number given above, or by writing to the Human Services Department.
Participants who meet eligibility requirements receive the following:

- Case management that matches the patient's needs with the right
  support services
- Homemaker and personal care assistance, and help with bathing,
  dressing, shopping, meal preparation, and cleaning house
- Adult day care that includes participation in social and recreational
  activities
- Respite care when you have to leave your parent home alone for a few
  days

There are a growing number of Adult Day Care Centers statewide
with requirements and programs that differ considerably. Call the center
closest to your parents' home to find out about eligibility, hours, activities, types of therapy, payment procedures, Medicare and Medicaid certification, and other relevant matters.

Adult Day Care Centers

BERNALILLO COUNTY

Anne Pickard Convalescent Hospital Adult Day Care
5900 Forest Hills Drive, N.E., Albuquerque, NM 87109
(505) 822-6000

City of Albuquerque Senior Day Care
714 7th Street, S.W., Albuquerque, NM 87102   (505) 766-4832

Cornucopia Adult Day Care
   1734 Isleta Boulevard, S.W., Albuquerque, NM 87105
   (505) 877-1310

Share Your Care
   5301 Ponderosa, N.E.
   Albuquerque, NM 87111   (505) 881-8982

DONA ANA COUNTY
City of Las Cruces Senior Recreation
   P.O. Box CLC, Las Cruces, NM 88004   (505) 526-0291

GRANT COUNTY
Area Citizens Council for Services to Senior Citizens
   P.O. Box 2742, Silver City, NM 88061   (505) 538-2386

HIDALGO COUNTY
Lordsburg Senior Citizens
   313 East 4th Street, P.O. Box 759, Lordsburg, NM 88045
   (505) 542-9414

LOS ALAMOS COUNTY
The Day Out
   P.O. Box 488, Los Alamos, NM 87544   (505) 622-3104

LUNA COUNTY
Deming/Luna County Commission on Aging
   800 South Granite Street, Deming, NM 88030   (505) 546-8823

SAN MIGUEL COUNTY
City of Las Vegas Adult Day Care
   P.O. Box 1250, Las Vegas, NM 87701   (505) 425-7195

SANTE FE COUNTY
Open Hands Adult Day Program
   P.O. Box 1025, Sante Fe, NM 87501   (505) 984-0602

NEW YORK

State Office for the Aging
   2 Empire State Plaza
   Albany, New York 12223   (518) 474-4425

   2 World Trade Center
   New York, New York 10047   (212) 488-6405

   Toll-free hotline 1-800-342-9871

Long-Term Care Ombudsman
   Ida Arbitman at the Albany address   (518) 474-0108

The Office for the Aging administers specific services and programs for the state's more than 3 million senior citizens through local offices in every county and in New York City. In addition to providing information and referral about programs including transportation, home care, home-delivered meals, housing, and special community projects, the local Offices for the Aging also offer assistance with problems relating to Social Security, Medicare, special tax exemptions, and other entitlements for the elderly.

Among the support systems whose purpose it is to help older individuals maintain their independence and delay or eliminate costly institutionalization are the following:

Community services, including day care centers, respite services, home care, hospice services, senior centers, mental health centers, telephone reassurance and friendly visiting, legal services, transportation, and protection against abuse.

Nutrition, including congregate meals, home-delivered meals, and food stamps.

Housing, including affordable housing for the elderly, adult homes for those who require room and board with minimum supervision, group-shared living arrangements, housing assistance payments, and rural housing repair and rehabilitation loans.

Taxes, including real property tax exemption, tax rebates, and real property tax-deferred payment loans.

Energy, including utility rights, Home Energy Assistance Program (HEAP), Home Energy Audit and Loan Program, weatherization assistance, and consumer-utility energy assistance.

Employment, including Job Training Partnership, senior community service employment, and Green Thumb Program.

Recreation, including Senior Olympics, Golden Park Pass, Golden Age Pass, hunting and fishing licenses, and special Recreation for the Elderly programs for which the state provides funds to municipalities statewide.

Education, including adult education courses, not-for-credit auditing of State University courses, and Elderhostel summer classes.

Consumer affairs, including help with resolving complaints, informative free pamphlets, discounts, and photo ID cards for nondrivers from the Department of Motor Vehicles.

Crime, including victims' protection, and prevention.

Volunteer opportunities, including the Foster Grandparent Program, Long-Term Care Ombudsman Program, and Retired Seniors Volunteer Program (RSVP).

Details about these programs as well as other resources for older persons are included in the Office on Aging's *Senior Handbook,* available from the local office that serves your parents' county.

Local Offices for the Aging—Listed by County

Albany County Department for the Aging
112 State Street, Room 710, Albany, NY 12207   (518) 447-7180

Allegany County Office for the Aging
17 Court Street, Belmont, NY 14813   (716) 268-7691

Broome County Office for the Aging
County Office Building, Government Plaza
Binghamton, NY 13902   (607) 772-2411

Cataraugus County Department for the Aging
255 North Union Street, Olean, NY 14760   (716) 375-4114

Cayuga County Office for the Aging
County Office Building, 160 Genesee Street, Auburn, NY 13021
(315) 253-1226

Chautauqua County Office for the Aging
Hall R, Clothier Building, Mayville, NY 14757   (716) 753-4471

Chemung County Office for the Aging
425–447 Pennsylvania Avenue, Elmira, NY 14904   (607) 737-5520

Chenango County Area Agency on Aging
County Office Building, 5 Court Street, Norwich, NY 13815
(607) 335-4624

Clinton County Office for the Aging
137 Margaret Street, Plattsburgh, NY 12901   (607) 335-4624

Columbia County Office for the Aging
71 North Third Street, Hudson, NY 12534   (518) 828-4258

Cortland County Office for the Aging
County Office Building, 60 Central Avenue, P.O. Box 1172
Cortland, NY 13045   (607) 753-5060

Delaware County Office for the Aging
6 Court Street, Delhi, NY 13753   (607) 746-6333

Dutchess County Office for the Aging
488 Main Street, Poughkeepsie, NY 12601   (914) 431-2465

Erie County Department of Senior Services
95 Franklin Street, Erie County Office Building, Buffalo, NY 14202
(716) 846-8522

Essex County Office for the Aging
Elizabethtown, NY 12932   (518) 873-6301, ext. 370

Franklin County Office for the Aging
County Court House, 89 West Main Street, Malone, NY 12953
(518) 483-6767

Fulton County Office for the Aging
19 North William Street, Johnstown, NY 12095 (518) 762-8288

Genesee County Office for the Aging
Batavia-Genesee Senior Center, 2 Bank Street, Batavia, NY 14020
(716) 343-1611

Greene County Department for the Aging
19 South Jefferson Avenue, Catskill, NY 12414 (518) 943-5332

Hamilton County. See Warren/Hamilton.

Herkimer County Office for the Aging
County Office Building, Mary Street, Herkimer, NY 13350
(315) 867-1121

Jefferson County Office for the Aging
175 Arsenal Street, Watertown, NY 13601

Lewis County Office for the Aging
Lewis County Courthouse, Lowville, NY 13367 (315) 376-7553

Livingston County Office for the Aging
Livingston County Campus Building 1, Mt. Morris, NY 14510
(716) 658-2881, ext. 18

Madison County Office for the Aging
Box 250, Route 20, Morrisville, NY 13408 (315) 684-9424

Monroe County Office for the Aging
375 Westfall Road, Rochester, NY 14620 (716) 442-6350

Montgomery County Office for the Aging
21 New Street, Amsterdam, NY 12010 (518) 843-2300

Nassau County Department of Senior Citizen Affairs
222 Willis Avenue, Mineola, NY 11501 (516) 535-5990

Niagara County Office for the Aging
Switzer Building, 100 Davison Road, Lockport, NY 14094
(716) 439-6044

Oneida County Office for the Aging
County Office Building, 800 Park Avenue, Utica, NY 13501
(315) 798-5771

Onondaga Metropolitan Commission on Aging
Civic Center, 10th floor, 421 Montgomery Street
Syracuse, NY 13202 (315) 425-2362

Ontario County Office for the Aging
120 North Main Street, Canandaigua, NY 14424 (716) 394-7070,
ext. 2240

Orange County Office for the Aging
    60 Erie Street, Third floor, Goshen, NY 10924   (914) 294-8801,
    ext. 283, 286

Orleans County Office for the Aging
    Orleans County Administration Building, 14016 Route 31
    Albion, NY 14411   (716) 589-5673, ext. 191

Oswego County Office for the Aging
    County Office Complex, 70 Brunner Street, P.O. Box 3080
    Oswego, NY 13126   (315) 349-3231

Otsego County Office for the Aging
    County Office Building, Cooperstown, NY 13325   (607) 547-4233

Putnam County Office for the Aging
    110 Old Route 6, Building A, Carmel, NY 10512   (914) 225-1034

Rensselaer County Department for the Aging
    1700 7th Avenue, Troy, NY 12180   (518) 270-2730

Rockland County Office for the Aging
    Building B, Health & Social Services Complex, Pomona, NY 10970
    (914) 354-0200, ext. 2100

St. Lawrence County Office for the Aging
    County Office Building, Canton, NY 13617   (315) 379-2204

Saratoga County Office for the Aging
    South Street School, South Street, Ballston Spa, NY 12020
    (518) 885-5381, ext. 270

Schenectady County Office for the Aging
    101 Nott Terrace, Schenectady, NY 12308   (518) 382-8481

Schoharie County Office for the Aging
    12 Lark Street, Cobleskill, NY 12043   (518) 234-4219

Schuyler County Office for the Aging
    336–338 West Main Street, Montour Falls, NY 14865
    (607) 535-7108

Seneca County Office for the Aging
    P.O. Box 480, Seneca Falls, NY 13148   (315) 568-5893

Steuben County Office for the Aging
    21 East Morris Street, Bath, NY 14810   (607) 776-3359

Suffolk County Office for the Aging
    65 Jetson Lane, Central Islip, NY 11722   (615) 348-5313

Sullivan County Office for the Aging
    100 North Street, Monticello, NY 12701   (914) 794-3000

Tioga County Office for the Aging
    231 Main Street, Owego, NY 13827   (607) 687-4120

Tompkins County Office for the Aging
    225 South Fulton Street, Ithaca, NY 14850   (607) 274-5427

Ulster County Office for the Aging
240–244 Fair Street, P.O. Box 1800, Kingston, NY 12401
(914) 331-9300, ext. 598

Warren/Hamilton Counties Offices for the Aging
Warren County Municipal Center, Lake George, NY 12845
(518) 761-6347

Washington County Office for the Aging
P.O. Box 58, Whitehall, NY 12887   (518) 499-2468

Wayne County Office for the Aging
P.O. Box 7336, Route 31 W, Lyons, NY 14489   (315) 946-4163

Westchester County Office for the Aging
148 Martine Avenue, Room 938, White Plains, NY 10610
(914) 285-2966

Wyoming County Office for the Aging
76 North Main Street, Warsaw, NY 14569   (716) 786-3144

Yates County Area Agency on Aging
5 Collins Avenue, Penn Yan, NY 14527   (315) 536-2368

New York City Department for the Aging
2 Lafayette Street, New York, NY 10007   (212) 577-0848; Reduced
Fare Program (212) 577-0821

St. Regis Mohawk Office for the Aging
St. Regis-Mohawk Indian Reservation, Hogansburg, NY 13655
(518) 358-2272

Seneca Nation of Indians Office for the Aging
1490 Route 438, Irving, NY 14081   (716) 532-4900

The State Office on Aging has produced a six-session course, *Practical Help—Caring for an Elderly Person,* including a *Caregiver's Curriculum* and an *Instruction Guide for the Course Leader.* If you or others in your community would like to conduct such a course, you can request the material by contacting:

Susan Malloy Murante
Public Relations Officer
New York State Office for the Aging
Agency Bldg 2, 2 Empire Plaza
Albany, New York 12223-0001
(518) 473-7343

NORTH CAROLINA

Department of Human Resources Division of Aging
    1985 Umstead Drive
    Raleigh, North Carolina 27603   (919) 733-3893
Ombudsman Program Director
    Frances Andrews at the above address and phone number

In the little more than two decades since it was established as a separate entity, the Division on Aging has expanded its services to the point where it now functions as the advocate for nearly a million older North Carolinians. The division administers a comprehensive series of programs under the federal Older Americans Act, and it operates with a budget of about $26 million.

Among the services provided are those described in a recently issued brochure entitled *Long Term Care in North Carolina.* The brochure, which is available on request from the division, spells out the details of a program designed to enable older people to remain in their own homes for as long as possible through reliance on homemaker/home health aides, choreworkers, rehabilitative therapy, and medical screening by trained professionals.

In addition, through the Older Americans Act and various state initiatives, senior citizens are eligible for home repairs, counseling, employment referral, and transportation. Provisions are also made for senior centers, disaster relief, an interfaith coalition between the state and local churches to help needy older people, and the statewide operation of the ombudsman program that protects the rights of the institutionalized elderly in addition to monitoring the conditions under which they live.

The division has also initiated several innovative programs available to all older North Carolinians: The JOY program (Joining Old and Young) promotes intergenerational activities that enrich the lives of all participants; the LIFE project (Living Independently for Elders) encourages a life style that includes continuing education, community involvement, and attention to principles of good nutrition and good health. Another special health education program that promotes physical fitness is AHOY (Add Health to Our Years).

Following the deliberations of the Legislative Study Committees on Health Cost Containment and Aging, the following were among the measures adopted by the General Assembly in 1984:

- An increase in the funds for adult day care
- An appropriation of Alzheimer's Disease Support Funds
- Funds to provide for the expansion of Senior Centers

■ Authorization of a tax deduction for the support of a parent sixty-five years old or older.

For information and referral for all entitlements and programs available to your parents in North Carolina, call or write the Area Agency on Aging that serves the part of the state where they live. If you have doubts about which one is closest, call the Division on Aging for instructions.

Area Agencies on Aging

Southwestern North Carolina Planning & Economic Development Commission
    P.O. Drawer 850, Bryson City, NC 28713   (704) 488-9211

Land of Sky Regional Council
    25 Heritage Drive, Asheville, NC 28802   (704) 254-8131

Isothermal Planning & Economic Development Commission
    P.O. Box 841, Rutherfordton, NC 28139   (704) 287-2281

Region D Council of Governments
    P.O. Box 1820, Boone, NC 28607   (704) 264-5558

Western Piedmont Council of Governments
    Old City Hall Building, 30 Third Street, N.W., Hickory, NC 28601
    (704) 322-9191

Centralina Council of Governments
    P.O. Box 35008, Charlotte, NC 28235   (704) 372-2416

Piedmont Triad Council of Governments
    2120 Pinecroft Road—Four Seasons Offices, Greensboro, NC 27407
    (919) 294-4950

Pee Dee Council of Governments
    P.O. Box 728, Troy, NC 27371   (919) 576-6261

Northwest Piedmont Council of Governments
    280 Liberty Street, Winston-Salem, NC 27101   (919) 722-9346

Triangle J Council of Governments
    P.O. Box 12276, Research Triangle Park, NC 27702
    (919) 549-0551

Region K Council of Governments
    P.O. Box 709, Henderson, NC 27536   (919) 492-8561

Region L Council of Governments
    P.O. Drawer 2748, Rocky Mount, NC 27801   (919) 446-0411

Region M Council of Governments
    P.O. Box 1510, Fayetteville, NC 28302   (919) 323-4191

Lumber River Council of Governments
    P.O. Drawer 1529, Lumberton, NC 28358   (919) 738-8104

Cape Fear Council of Governments
    P.O. Box 1491, Wilmington, NC 28402   (919) 763-0191
Neuse River Council of Governments
    P.O. Box 1717, New Bern, NC 28560   (919) 638-3185
Mid-East Commission
    P.O. Drawer 1787, Washington, NC 27889   (919) 946-8043
Albemarle Regional Planning & Development Commission
    P.O. Box 646, Hertford, NC 27944   (919) 426-5753

In 1985, the Division on Aging issued a newly revised edition of a *Handbook for Nursing Home Community Advisory Committees.* This publication, which can serve as a model of its kind, is a comprehensive training manual for members of the committee whose primary purpose is to maintain the spirit of the nursing home patients Bill of Rights. State law mandates that every county that has a nursing home must have such an ombudsman committee. On the local level, committee members are expected to serve as a nucleus for increased community interaction with nursing homes, to work cooperatively with facility administrators and staff, and above all to monitor nursing home care and resolve the grievances of residents and their families.

NORTH DAKOTA

Department of Human Services, Aging Services Division
    State Capitol
    Bismarck, North Dakota 58505   (701) 224-2310   or
    1-800-472-2622
Long-Term Care Ombudsman
    JoAn Hildebrant at the above address   (701) 224-2577
The Office of Human Services, one of the divisions of the Department of Human Services, is responsible for statewide program development, promulgation of rules and regulations, and interpretation of the federal and state laws that govern the administration of services in six major divisions, one of which is the Aging Services Division. (The other five are Alcohol and Drug Abuse, Children and Family Services, Crippled Children's Services, Developmental Disabilities, and Mental Health.)

Unlike most other states which have Area Agencies on Aging, North Dakota's eight regional Human Service Centers are responsible for the delivery of all services under the jurisdiction of the state office. The regional centers, which are located in the state's primary economic, medical, and business areas, also supervise the programs delivered by the social service office in each county. There are fifty-three local county service boards which deliver supportive services to target populations and provide information and referral about home health agencies, homemaker services, alcohol and drug abuse treatment, and support programs for the mentally ill.

The Aging Services Division can also provide you with a list of licensed homes for the aged and infirm together with their daily and monthly rates.

The Division of Health Facilities of the State Department of Health has prepared three useful directories which are available on request through the Aging Services Division:

- A list of licensed home health agencies, including the services they offer and the areas they serve
- A list of licensed intermediate care facilities
- A list of skilled nursing facilities

Information about programs for senior citizens operated under federal grants and mandated by the Older Americans Act, as well as all other services for which your parents may be eligible, will be provided by the county social service center or one of the following regional centers.

Regional Human Service Centers

Northwest Human Service Center
316 Second Avenue West, Box 1568, Williston, ND 58801
(701) 572-8126
Counties served: Divide, McKenzie, Williams

North Central Human Service Center
400 Twenty-second Avenue, N.W., Minot, ND 58701
(701) 852-1251
Counties served: Bottineau, Burke, McHenry, Mountrain, Pierce, Renville, Ward

Lake Region Human Service Center
Highway 2 West, Devils Lake, ND 58301   (701) 662-7581
Counties served: Benson, Cavalier, Eddy, Ramsey, Rolette, Towner

Northeast Human Service Center
1407 24th Avenue South, Grand Forks, ND 58201   (701) 746-4421
Counties served: Grand Forks, Nelson, Pembina, Walsh

Southeast Human Service Center
15 Broadway, Fargo, ND 58107   (701) 237-4513
Counties served: Cass, Ransom, Richland, Sargent, Steele, Traill

South Central Human Service Center
520 Third Street, N.W., Box 1743, Jamestown, ND 58401
(701) 252-2641
Counties served: Barnes, Dickey, Foster, Griggs, LaMoure, Logan, McIntosh, Stutsman, Wells

West Central Human Service Center
  600 South Second Street, Bismarck, ND 58501   (701) 255-3090
    Counties served: Burleigh, Emmons, Grant, Kidder, McLean,
    Mercer, Morton, Oliver, Sheridan, Sioux

Badlands Human Service Center
  Pulver Hall, Dickinson State College, Dickinson, ND 58601
  (701) 227-2771
    Counties served: Adams, Billings, Bowman, Dunn, Golden Val-
    ley, Hettinger, Slope, Stark

OHIO

Department of Aging
  50 West Broad Street, 9th floor
  Columbus, Ohio 43215   (614) 466-5500   or   466-6191
State Nursing Home Ombudsman
  Mrs. Jean Wood at the above address   (614) 466-9927

In a recent State Plan on Aging submitted to the federal Administration on Aging, the Ohio Council on Aging stressed the fact that since the
amount of federal participation will continue to decrease relative to the
needs of Ohio's elderly, the state itself must compensate for this loss by
stimulating local support from private sources and through volunteerism. The plan also recommended that funding for in-home care be increased from all sources. A major enterprise has been the building and
renovation of 169 multipurpose senior centers at the cost of almost $10
million over the past six years, bringing the current total number of
centers to 398. By the end of the decade, it is hoped that there will be
approximately 500 service centers statewide.

These centers not only provide better access to support systems for the
less impaired elderly, but also can target more services for the frail group
with higher levels of impairment who are at greater risk for institutionalization in the absence of in-home help. The centers are also the focal
points for organizing the skills and experience of those senior citizens
who are well enough to be able to provide volunteer support for community services.

The guidelines of the plan's community-based long-term alternative to
institutionalization include finding effective ways to support informal
care by family and friends and expanding the supply of housing options
for frail and impaired older adults.

The efforts of the Department on Aging are also directed to *postpone*
chronic frailty and impairment by providing easy access to social and
nutritional services through congregate and home-delivered meals, and
by promoting subsidized and unsubsidized employment opportunities, to

support financial independence and security especially for those older persons in greatest economic and social need.

To find out the location of the multipurpose senior center that serves your parents' community, call the Department of Aging or the office of the Area Agency on Aging that serves your parents' county.

(The office is located in the *italicized* county.)

Area 1 serves Butler, Clermont, Clinton, *Hamilton,* and Warren.

Area 2 serves Champaign, Clark, Darke, Logan, Miami, *Montgomery,* Preble, and Shelby.

Area 3 serves *Allen,* Auglaize, Hancock, Hardin, Mercer, Putnam, and Van Wert.

Area 4 serves Defiance, Erie, Fulton, Henry, *Lucas,* Ottawa, Paulding, Sandusky, Williams, and Wood.

Area 5 serves Ashland, Crawford, Huron, Knox, Marion, Morrow, *Richland,* Seneca, and Wyandot.

Area 6 serves Delaware, Fairfield, Fayette, *Franklin,* Licking, Madison, Pickaway, and Union.

Area 7 serves Adams, Brown, *Gallia,* Highland, Jackson, Pike, Ross, Scioto, and Vinton.

Area 8 serves Athens, Hocking, Meigs, Monroe, Morgan, Noble, Perry, and *Washington.*

Area 9 serves Belmont, Carroll, Coshocton, *Guernsey,* Harrison, Holmes, Jefferson, Muskingum, and Tuscarawas.

Area 10a serves *Cuyahoga,* Geauga, Lake, Lorain, and Medina.

Area 10b serves Portage, Stark, *Summit,* and Wayne.

Area 11 serves Ashtabula, Columbiana, *Mahoning,* and Trumbull.

OKLAHOMA

Department of Human Services, Special Unit on Aging
P.O. Box 25352
Oklahoma City, Oklahoma 73125   (405) 521-2281
Long-Term Care Ombudsman
Esther Houser at the above address and phone number

Oklahoma offers its elderly a wide variety of programs enabling them to remain in their own home rather than to be unnecessarily institutionalized: mobile meals, telephone reassurance, chore services, nontechnical medical care by trained providers, and adult day care. Support groups and respite care are also available to ease the burdens of family caregivers. Case management can be called upon to implement a coordinated group of services designed to meet individual needs. The spectrum of these services differs from one part of the state to another.

The Special Unit on Aging has prepared a variety of directories and guides that are indispensable for locating services when your parents need them. Among the materials you can request are:

- *Congregate Meals Programs,* a directory listing exact locations.
- *Long-Term Care Facilities,* a directory that lists these licensed facilities.
- *Retirement Housing for the Elderly.*
- *Nursing Home or Alternative Care in Oklahoma.*
- *Long-Term Care Ombudsman Program,* a leaflet describing the program and how volunteers can participate.
- *Putting the Pieces Together,* which describes the operations of the Special Unit on Aging and the programs it administers.
- A directory of services for the elderly called *Focal Points.* This is probably the most useful information source for you and your parents. It lists service centers statewide, alphabetically by city, and describes in detail the programs provided by each. Here's an example chosen at random:

MARLOW Oklahoma (Stephens County)
Marlow Nutrition Site/Eastside
    Eastside Baptist Church, East Evans, Marlow, OK 73055
    (405) 658-5773
    Mary Sain—Site Manager
        Services provided: Nutrition, home delivered meals, recreation, continuing education, telephone reassurance, information and referral, arts & crafts, health screening.

Marlow Senior Citizen Center
    323 W. Main Street, Marlow, OK 73055   (405) 658-5628
    Joyce Caughran—Coordinator
        Services provided: recreation, games, arts & crafts, health screening, continuing education, telephone reassurance, nutrition.

If you need information and referral in a hurry, call the Area Agency on Aging that serves your parents' county:

Area Agencies on Aging

1. *NECO AAA*
    P.O. Drawer "E," Vinita, OK 74301   (918) 256-6478   or 1-800-482-4594
        Counties served: Craig, Delaware, Mayes, Nowata, Ottawa, Rogers, Washington
2. *EODD AAA*
    P.O. Box 1367, Muskogee, OK 74401   (918) 682-7891
        Counties served: Adair, Cherokee, McIntosh, Muskogee, Okmulgee, Sequoyah, Wagoner

3. *KEDDO AAA*
   P.O. Box 638, Wilburton, OK 74578   (918) 465-2367   or
   1-800-722-8180
   > Counties served: Choctaw, Haskell, Latimer, LeFlore, McCurtain, Pittsburg, Pushmataha

4. *SODA AAA*
   P.O. Box 848, Ardmore, OK 73401   (405) 226-2250   or
   1-800-522-3780
   > Counties served: Atoka, Bryan, Carter, Coal, Garvin, Johnston, Love, Marshall, Murray, Pontotoc

5. *COEDD AAA*
   400 North Bell, Shawnee, OK 74801   (405) 273-6410
   > Counties served: Hughes, Lincoln, Okfuskee, Pawnee, Payne, Pottawatomie, Seminole

6. *Tulsa AAA*
   Room 336, 200 Civic Center, Tulsa, OK 74103   (918) 592-7688
   > Counties served: Creek, Osage, Tulsa

7. *NODA AAA*
   3201 Sante Fe Trail, Enid, OK 73701   (405) 237-4810
   > Counties served: Alfalfa, Blaine, Garfield, Grant, Kay, Kingfisher, Major, Noble

8. *Areawide Aging Agency*
   P.O. Box 1474, Oklahoma City, OK 74101   (405) 236-2426
   > Counties served: Canadian, Cleveland, Logan, Oklahoma

9. *ASCOG AAA*
   P.O. Box 1647, Duncan, OK 73533   (405) 252-0595
   > Counties served: Caddo, Comanche, Cotton, Grady, Jefferson, McClain, Stephens, Tillman

10. *SWODA AAA*
    P.O. Box 569, Burns Flat, OK 73624   (405) 562-4886
    > Counties served: Beckham, Custer, Greer, Harmon, Kiowa, Jackson, Roger Mills, Washita

11. *OEDA AAA*
    P.O. Box 668, Beaver, OK 73932   (405) 625-4531   or
    1-800-522-4344
    > Counties served: Beaver, Cimarron, Dewey, Ellis, Harper, Texas, Woods, Woodward

---

The Daily Living Center is a nonprofit day care program sponsored by The United Way. It provides the following services for the impaired but mobile elderly: transportation, regular nursing and physical therapy evaluations, planned activities, hot lunches including special diet modifications, and special family sessions. The center is staffed by professionals and volunteers and is easy to reach. The daily cost for one participant is about $15, but the actual fee depends on your parents' income. For additional information, call (405) 949-1197, or write to:

> The Daily Living Center, Arts Annex Building
> 3000 Pershing Boulevard, Fair Park
> Oklahoma City, Oklahoma 73107

OREGON

Department of Human Resources Senior Services Division
  313 Public Service Building
  Salem, Oregon 97310   (503) 378-4728
Long-Term Care Ombudsman
  Bert Wroley
  State Capitol, Room 160
  Salem, Oregon 97310   (503) 378-6533

In 1985, the Office of the Governor issued the first of a series of publications prepared by the Citizens' Representative. The 131-page *Seniors Handbook,* available on request from the above address, is a comprehensive guide to the federal, state, and local programs for older Oregonians. The contents have been organized so that they are easy to read and understand. Among the subjects covered in considerable detail are the following:

- Social Security: early retirement, dependents, survivor's insurance, Supplemental Security Income (SSI).
- Medicare, supplemental insurance, Medicaid.
- Oregon *Project Independence:* a program of in-home services financed entirely with state funds for the elderly who are at risk of being institutionalized and who are not receiving Medicaid support. Ability to pay determines the cost of services.
- Tax relief programs: renters' refunds, rental assistance, property tax deferral, veterans' property tax exemption, state income tax.
- Food stamp program.
- Veterans' benefits and special programs.
- Protective services.
- Transportation services statewide.
- Legal services statewide.
- The Long-Term Care Ombudsman Program and how it works.
- Senior centers listed by city.
- Housing Resources and a checklist of what to look for.
- Nutrition sites.

In addition to specific addresses and phone numbers, a toll-free number is provided wherever possible.

If you need information and referral before you receive your copy of the *Seniors Handbook,* call the Area Agency on Aging that serves your parents' county:

For Clatsop and Tillamook counties:
District One Area Agency on Aging
P.O. Box 488, Cannon Beach, OR 97110   (503) 436-1156

For Clackamas County:
Social Services Division, Clackamas Area Agency on Aging
1107 7th Street, Oregon City, OR 97045   (503) 655-8640

For Columbia County:
Columbia Council of Senior Citizens
P.O. Box 141, St. Helens, OR 97051   (503) 397-4000

For Multnomah County:
Portland/Multnomah Area Agency on Aging
426 S.W. Stark Street, 6th floor, Portland, OR 97204
(503) 248-3646

For Marion, Polk, and Yamhill counties:
Mid-Willamette Valley Senior Services Agency
410 Senator Building, 220 High Street, N.E., Salem, OR 97301
(503) 371-1313

For Lane County:
Senior Services, L-COG, Lane County Public Service Building
125 East 8th Avenue, Eugene, OR 97401   (503) 687-4283

For Douglas County:
Douglas County Senior Services
621 West Madrone, Roseburg, OR 97470   (503) 440-3601

For Benton, Lincoln, and Linn counties:
Senior & Disabled Adult Services
155 S.W. Madison, #5, Corvallis, OR 97333   (503) 757-6851

For Coos and Curry counties:
P.O. Box 647, North Bend, OR 97459   (503) 756-2563

For Jackson and Josephine counties:
District 8 Area Agency on Aging
Rogue Valley—COG, P.O. Box 3275, Central Point, OR 97502
(503) 664-6674

For Sherman, Wasco, and Hood River counties:
Mid-Columbia Area Agency on Aging
Wasco County Courthouse, Annex B, 502 East 5th Street
The Dalles, OR 97058   (503) 298-4101

For Crook, Jefferson, and Deschutes counties:
Central Oregon Council on Aging
875 S.E. Third, Bend, OR 97702   (503) 389-3311

For Klamath and Lake counties:
  Klamath Basin Senior Citizens Council
  2045 Arthur Street, Klamath Falls, OR 97601   (503) 882-4098

For Gilliam, Grant, Morrow, Umatilla, and Wheeler counties:
  ECOAC
  P.O. Box 1207, Pendleton, OR 97801   (503) 276-6732

For Baker, Union, and Wallowa counties:
  EOCDC
  104 Elm Street, La Grande, OR 97850   (503) 963-3186

For Harney County:
  Harney County Senior Citizens
  17 South Alder Street, Burns, OR 97720   (503) 573-6024

For Malheur County:
  Malheur Council on Aging
  P.O. Box 937, Ontario, OR 97914   (503) 889-7651

For Washington County:
  Washington County Aging Program
  341 Northeast Lincoln, Hillsboro, OR 97123   (503) 640-3489

PENNSYLVANIA

Department of Aging
  231 State Street
  Harrisburg, Pennsylvania 17101   (717) 783-1550
Long-Term Care Ombudsman
  John Harwood at the above address and phone number

Thanks to the funds made available by the state lottery, Pennsylvania may well be in a position to offer its senior citizens more benefits than practically every other state. In 1983, for example, the legislature signed into law what was then the nation's most generous prescription program for senior citizens. Called PACE (Pharmaceutical Assistance Contract for the Elderly), it enables older people of limited income to have a doctor's prescription filled for no more than $4. Lottery funds pick up the balance of the cost, estimated at $1 million annually for the program.

Other innovative projects operated by Area Agencies on Aging[10] in cooperation with Senior Centers and community organizations, include:

- *Carrier Alert,* a volunteer effort by the U.S. Postal Service which takes note of an unusual accumulation of mail and newspapers in the mailbox, and if the premises (especially of the homebound elderly) are suspiciously quiet, the carrier calls the police or other authorities. (Your parents can register with the local post

10. A complete list appears at the end of this section.

office for this service and get a special sticker that indicates their participation in the program.)

■ *Blizzard boxes* are special food survival kits to be used when weather conditions in rural areas prevent or delay meal deliveries or the prompt arrival of essential groceries. The contents are meant to be stored for emergencies and remain edible for up to one year after the date stamped on the carton.

■ *The Supportive Older Women's Network (SOWN),* which began in Philadelphia and now functions in many other counties, is a program in which displaced homemakers, widows, and older women in general can discuss their personal problems as well as topics of special interest to their age group.

■ *Mobile Services for the Aging* brings health and special services to widely scattered elderly people living in rural areas.

Other projects include intergenerational activities, a Home-Sharing program, and the annual Senior Games festival featuring sixteen different sports events in which Pennsylvanians aged fifty-five to eighty-nine compete for prizes.

The Department on Aging has also expanded its Long-Term Care Assessment and Management Program (LAMP). Various aspects of the program are regularly evaluated in different parts of the state, and each year, better case management and more community participation enable those at risk of institutionalization to remain in their own home. An indispensable part of the continuum of long-term care for the recipient *and* the family caregiver is the expansion of adult day care centers. Fees are based on the ability to pay, and when necessary, costs—which may range from $15 to $25 per day—are covered through arrangements with the Area Agency on Aging.

There are about 550 neighborhood senior centers throughout the state, and they continue to grow in size and scope. Activities vary depending on location, access to public transportation, and the interests of the participants.

The Older Pennsylvanians' Handbook is available on request from the Department on Aging. It is an indispensable guide to federal, state, and local programs and resources available to older people.

If you need information and referral without delay and you don't yet have a copy of the *Older Pennsylvanians' Handbook,* call the Area Agency on Aging that serves your parents' county.

County	Telephone	County	Telephone
Adams	(717) 334-9296	Armstrong	(412) 548-3290
Allegheny	(412) 355-4234	Beaver	(412) 728-7707

County	Telephone	County	Telephone
Bedford	(814) 623-8149	Lawrence	(412) 658-5661
Berks	(215) 378-1635	Lebanon	(717) 273-9262
Blair	(814) 946-1237	Lehigh	(215) 820-3248
Bradford	1-800-982-4346	Luzerne	(717) 822-1158
Bucks	(215) 348-0510	Lycoming	(717) 748-8665
Butler	(412) 282-3008	McKean	1-800-672-7145
Cambria	(814) 472-5580	Mercer	(412) 662-3800
Cameron	(814) 486-3708	Mifflin	(717) 242-0315
Carbon	(717) 325-2726	Monroe	(717) 424-5290
Centre	(814) 355-6712	Montgomery	(215) 278-3601
Chester	(215) 431-6350	Montour	(717) 275-1466
Clarion	(814) 226-4000	Northampton	(215) 759-7970
Clearfield	(814) 765-2696	Northumberland	(717) 648-6828
Clinton	(717) 748-8665	Perry	(717) 582-2131
Columbia	(717) 784-9272	Pike	(717) 296-7813
Crawford	(814) 336-1580	Philadelphia	(215) 496-0520
Cumberland	(717) 243-8442	Potter	(814) 274-8843
Dauphin	(717) 255-2790	Schuylkill	(717) 622-3103
Delaware	(215) 891-4455	Snyder	(717) 837-0675
Elk	1-800-672-7145	Somerset	(814) 443-2681
Erie	(814) 459-4581	Sullivan	1-800-982-4346
Fayette	(412) 437-7677	Susquehanna	1-800-982-4346
Forest	(814) 726-1700	Tioga	1-800-982-4346
Franklin	(717) 263-2153	Union	(717) 524-4460
Fulton	(717) 485-5151	Venango	(814) 437-6871
Greene	(412) 852-1510	Warren	(814) 726-1700
Huntingdon	(814) 643-5115	Washington	(412) 228-7080
Indiana	(412) 349-4500	Wayne	(717) 296-7813
Jefferson	(814) 849-3096	Westmoreland	(412) 836-1111
Juniata	(717) 242-0315	Wyoming	(717) 822-1158
Lackawanna	(717) 961-6707	York	(717) 846-4884
Lancaster	(717) 299-7979		

RHODE ISLAND

Department of Elderly Affairs
    79 Washington Street
    Providence, Rhode Island 02903   (401) 277-2858
Long-Term Care Ombudsman
    Anthony Fontaine at the above address   (401) 277-6880
    Each year, the Information and Referral Service of the Department of
Elderly Affairs prepares a new edition of their *Pocket Manual of Senior*

Services. This publication, available on request, provides you and your parents with essential information about the network of programs and sources for people aged sixty and older and their families. You are also invited to visit the department (or place a *collect* call from outside the Providence area) if you need assistance.

In addition to providing details about such federally mandated activities as the Foster Grandparent Program, Senior Companion Program, transportation assistance, nutrition counseling and congregate meals (as well as meals for the homebound), the Retired Senior Volunteer Program (RSVP), the manual describes other projects sponsored by the Department of Elderly Affairs:

- A "stay fit" program, which conducts aquatic exercise sessions at ten swimming pools statewide
- Forty-three walking clubs operating at senior centers and senior housing
- A "Senior Olympics" track and field meet for athletes forty years of age and older

Mental health clinics that provide group therapy, education, individual psychotherapy, marital and family counseling, as well as treatment for alcohol and drug abuse are available for you and your parents as part of the community services administered by the department. Fees are based on a sliding scale and ability to pay.

Elderly day care is available for convalescing seniors and for relieving family caregivers of some of the responsibilities of daily parent care. The centers provide transportation, lunch, health services, group activities, social rehabilitation, and recreation. They operate five days a week and fees are based on ability to pay. Call the department for information about the program located in your parents' area.

Once your parents reach age sixty, they are entitled to a senior citizen photo ID card issued by the department. The card entitles them to many privileges, including those offered by the Senior Citizen Discount Program and the state-sponsored Extension and Summer Courses.

Other agencies also administer programs of special interest:

State Services for the Blind and Visually Impaired provides vocational rehabilitation, counseling, medical evaluation, home teaching, and other services. For information, contact:
46 Aborn Street, Providence, Rhode Island 02903
(401) 277-2300

The Department of Social Services helps seniors who have vision problems. It offers assistance and some social activities for those with 20-70 vision and up. For information, contact:
INSIGHT, 1058 Broad Street,
Providence, Rhode Island 02905   (401) 941-5421

The Catastrophic Health Insurance Plan (CHIP) is designed to help permanent residents faced with large medical bills who are not eligible for Medicaid. The program is tax-supported; therefore, if your parents qualify, there are no premiums to pay. For additional information, contact:

CHIP, RI Department of Health, Cannon Building, 75 Davis Street, Providence, Rhode Island 02908   (401) 277-2485

The Rhode Island Bar Association helps persons sixty and older to obtain legal services and advice. Seniors receive a free initial consultation of up to thirty minutes. A reduced fee plan is available for those with moderate income. A no-fee program is also available for those who qualify. For additional information, contact:

Local Information and Referral Services for the Elderly, 1804 Fleet Bank Building, Providence, Rhode Island 02903 (401) 521-5040

The Rhode Island Hospital's Outpatient Hearing & Speech Center offers programs in the diagnosis and treatment of hearing, speech, and language problems. Seniors may schedule a complete hearing evaluation, schedule the fitting and testing of hearing aids, and enroll for training in lipreading. Payment for all services is based on a sliding scale. They are located at:

59 Eddy Street, Providence, Rhode Island 02903
(401) 277-5485

The Neighborhood Friendly Visitor Program provides companionship, friendly support, and respite for family caregivers during visits to the homebound elderly. Volunteers read aloud, write letters, and socialize during visits. The program also welcomes senior volunteers who wish to participate in the program. Contact the program at:

Broad and Stewart Streets, Providence, Rhode Island 02903 (401) 421-7833

In addition to the In-Home Services Program, which is administered by the Department on Aging and provides homemaker and medical assistance, here are some additional agencies to call upon for help:

Sources Inc., (401) 421-1213

provides companions who are paid for offering companionship and some in-home care.

Home Health Services of RI, (401) 751-3152

offers light housekeeping, in-home care, chore and errand services, and companionship. In some eligible cases, fees are based on a sliding scale.

Jewish Family Service, (401) 331-1244; Newport County & Child
Family Services, (401) 849-2300; and Woonsocket Child & Family
Services, (401) 766-0900

offer homemaker services to seniors within their jurisdiction
for fees based on ability to pay.

SOUTH CAROLINA

Commission on Aging
915 Main Street
Columbia, South Carolina 29201   (803) 758-2576
Long-Term Care Ombudsman
Ms. Mary Vieth
Office of the Governor
1205 Pendleton Street
Columbia, South Carolina (803) 758-2249 or 758-8016

South Carolina is one of twelve states whose sixty-five and older population have increased by more than 10 percent since 1980, surpassing
even Florida, the "retirement state." There are now about 491,000 people in this age group, with about 150 older women for every 100 older
men. An estimated 75 percent of older South Carolinians remain in
independent living situations, 18 percent live with an adult child, and
about 5 percent live in nursing homes. Of the 20 percent of the state's
elderly who have a spouse, most are men. Slightly half of all elderly
women live alone, while only 20 percent of elderly men live alone. The
major explanation for this disparity is that women live about eight years
longer than men. The state's poverty rate for the elderly is between 20
and 25 percent.

The Commission on Aging is the agency that administers the federal
funds provided to each state in amounts based on the percentage of its
aging population. The funds are allocated to a system of coordinated and
comprehensive services that enable older people to live in their own
homes for as long as possible. In South Carolina, an important aspect of
federally funded services is the Nutrition Program, which not only provides hot nutritious meals five days a week in a group setting (approximately eight thousand older citizens are served daily at 160 nutrition
sites statewide); it also alleviates isolation through fellowship and encourages participation in local project councils that determine menus.
The councils also review existing and desired social programs.

The Older Americans Act also funds the Legal Services for the Aging
Program as well as the Nursing Home Ombudsman Program, whose
objective is to ensure that patients are receiving quality care and that
their rights are respected. Federal funds also support the following additional community-based services (not all of which are available in all

localities): information and referral, escort service, telephone reassurance, friendly visiting, minor home repairs, home chores, day care, housing information, transportation, home-delivered meals, home health services, employment services, and volunteer opportunities.

Block grant funds of the Social Security Act are used to provide many of the services that enable people with special needs to remain in their own home and thereby prevent institutionalization. State funds are used to extend the aging program as a whole, and many projects depend on volunteers.

Workshops, seminars, and the Summer School of Gerontology improve the skills and understanding of those who work with the elderly, and institutions of higher learning offer professional training to those interested in careers in this field.

You and your parents can contact the Commission on Aging for information about the many publications that are available on aging, including a bimonthly newsletter called *Vintage.*

To receive the most up-to-date information and referral for all programs and projects available to your parents, contact the Area Agency on Aging that serves their county.

Area Agencies on Aging

Appalachia
P.O. Drawer 6668, Greenville, SC 29606   (803) 242-9733
Counties served: Anderson, Cherokee, Greenville, Oconee, Pickens, Spartenburg
Abbeville County
P.O. Box 117, Abbeville, SC 29620   (803) 459-4511
Edgefield County
P.O. Box 510, Edgefield, SC 29824   (803) 637-5326
Greenwood County
P.O. Box 997, Greenwood, SC 29646   (803) 223-0164
Laurens County
P.O. Box 777, Laurens, SC 29360   (803) 984-4572
McCormick County
P.O. Box 684, McCormick, SC 29835   (803) 465-2626
Saluda County
P.O. Box 507, Saluda, SC 29138   (803) 445-2175
Catawba
P.O. Box 862, Rock Hill, SC 29730   (803) 327-9041
Counties served: Chester, Lancaster, Union, York
Central Midlands
Suite 155, Dutch Plaza, 800 Dutch Square Blvd.,

Columbia, SC 29210 (803) 798-1243
Counties served: Fairfield, Lexington, Newberry, Richland

Lower Savannah
P.O. Box 850, Aiken, SC 29801 (803) 649-7981
Counties served: Aiken, Allendale, Bamberg, Barnwell, Calhoun, Orangeburg

Santee Lynches
P.O. Box 1837, Sumter, SC 29150 (803) 775-7382
Counties served: Clarendon, Kershaw, Lee, Sumter

Pee Dee
P.O. Box 5719, Florence, SC 29502 (803) 669-3138
Counties served: Chesterfield, Darlington, Dillon, Florence, Marion, Marlboro

Waccamaw
P.O. Box 419, Georgetown, SC 29440 (803) 546-8502
Counties served: Georgetown, Horry, Williamstown

Trident
P.O. Box 2696, Charleston, SC 29403 (803) 723-1676
Counties served: Berkeley, Charleston, Dorchester

Low Country
P.O. Box 98, Yemassee, SC 29945 (803) 726-5536
Counties served: Beaufort, Colleton, Hampton, Jasper

cp11,13]SOUTH DAKOTA

Department of Social Services, Office of Adult Services and Aging
Richard F. Kneip Building
700 North Illinois Street
Pierre, South Dakota 57501 (605) 773-3656
Long-Term Care Ombudsman
Rolland Hostler at the above address and phone number

If your parents need less than twenty-four-hour skilled nursing care, a mix of services and programs that provide a practical and preferred alternative to institutionalization can be worked out by contacting a social worker in the closest Office of Adult Services and Aging. There are twenty-one such offices, and while not all programs are available in every community, the social worker can work out an effective plan of care based on assessments of a physician and a nurse. The purpose of this plan is to help your parent continue to live at home and as independently as possible for as long as possible.

The help that may be provided includes:

- *Homemaker/home health aide services* such as part-time skilled nursing, personal care with bathing and dressing, meal preparation, nutrition and diet counseling, laundry and light housecleaning, and transportation to medical appointments.

- *Home-delivered meals* for the person unable to prepare them— usually one hot meal a day, Monday through Friday, supplemented in some cases by the Meals-on-Wheels weekend delivery.
- *Group (congregate) dining* at noon; meals are served midday in a social setting, usually at a senior center, school, church, or other community facility. Social activities and special programs often take place before and after mealtime.
- *Adult day care,* primarily social in nature, but with some health-related services also available; usually scheduled Monday through Friday for six to nine hours, with transportation offered both ways.
- *Transportation services,* provided through volunteer programs and public conveyances for those older people who are unable to drive or are without a vehicle.
- *Telephone reassurance* providing daily contact for older people who live alone and have chronic health problems or anxiety about safety. When the volunteer who phones gets no response, a check is made in person.
- *Friendly visiting* arranged by volunteers on a regular basis through senior centers, religious groups, or community organizations for people who are isolated or homebound and have no regular contact with relatives or neighbors.
- *Protective services,* providing legal assistance and arranging guardianships for mentally confused persons who cannot manage their own affairs.
- *Adult foster care,* which pays a foster family (or an individual) to provide a home and care for an older person incapable of living alone, usually because of a medical problem.
- *Congregate living,* enabling several older people unable to live totally independently to share a living arrangement in which each can contribute to some of the tasks of running a household.
- *Health screening* conducted at senior centers and community health nursing offices to check up on blood pressure, vision, hearing, and diabetes.
- *Respite care* provided by friends and neighbors, to relieve the family caregiver for brief periods.

For details about these services and others for which your parents may be eligible, contact the most conveniently located Adult Services & Aging Office, listed below, alphabetically by city.

422 South Washington, P.O. Box 1300, *Aberdeen,* SD 57401
(605) 622-2388

629 5th Avenue, *Brookings,* SD 57006   (605) 692-6301

704 N. Main, P.O. Box 430, *Chamberlain,* SD 57325
(605) 734-6581

688 Main Street, P.O. Box 607, *Deadwood,* SD 57732
(605) 578-2402

Courthouse, P.O. Box 570, *Faulkton,* SD 57438   (605) 598-6227

602 Jennings, P.O. Box 830, *Hot Springs,* SD 57747
(605) 745-5100

239 Wisconsin, S.W., P.O. Box 1436, *Huron,* SD   (605) 352-8421,
ext. 358

210 Main Street, P.O. Box 156, *Lake Andes,* SD 57356
(605) 487-7607

P.O. Box 250, *Martin,* SD 57551   (605) 685-6521

North Main, P.O. Box 818, *Mission,* SD 57555   (605) 856-4489

116 East 11th Street, *Mitchell,* SD 57301   (605) 996-7630

920 West 6th, P.O. Box 160, *Mobridge,* SD 57601   (605) 845-2922

804 North Euclid, *Pierre,* SD 57501   (605) 224-3521

Planning Center Building, P.O. Box 279, *Pine Ridge,* SD 57770
(605) 867-5865

2301 East St. Charles, P.O. Box 2440, *Rapid City,* SD 57701
(605) 394-2538

405 South Third Avenue, P.O. Box 1504, *Sioux Falls,* SD 57101
(605) 339-6448

119 East Cherry Street, P.O. Box 230, *Sisseton,* SD 57262
(605) 698-7675

312 9th Avenue, P.O. Box 933, *Watertown,* SD 57201
(605) 886-7000

649 West 2d Street, *Winner,* SD 57580   (605) 842-0400

419 Cherry Street, *Vermillion,* SD 57069   (605) 624-8606

114 East 3d Street, *Yankton,* SD 57078   (605) 665-3671, ext. 242

TENNESSEE

Commission on Aging
715 Tennessee Building, 535 Church Street
Nashville, Tennessee 37219   (615) 741-2058

While the most extensive and innovative services for the elderly are located in the metropolitan areas, basic entitlements under the Older Americans Act Title III such as nutrition, transportation, and in-home services are available in every county. County hospitals are within driving distance from all locations, and regional medical centers, used for referrals, are available throughout the state. Home health care agencies can be called upon to provide essential services when your parents are homebound no matter where they live.

There are about 150 Senior Citizen Centers and satellites in ninety-four of the state's ninety-five counties. These centers provide such services as volunteer opportunities, social and recreational activities, adult education, outreach, transportation, nutrition, and health-related activities. They are also the source of information and referral for local projects and community support programs that vary from county to county.

The Commission on Aging administers the Senior Community Service Employment Program together with five national organizations: Tennessee Green Thumb, National Council on the Aging, National Caucus & Center on Black Aged, National Council of Senior Citizens, and the U.S. Forest Service.

The commission has published a *Senior Citizens Guide to Legal Problems, Rights, and Benefits.* Copies are free to older people while the supply lasts. All others must pay $2. The state also has established a network of legal services projects to serve persons sixty years old and older with problems relating to federal entitlements, eligibility, and benefits. Lawyers and paralegals especially trained in these matters travel to senior centers in order to interview clients.

For information and referral concerning all state and federal programs for senior citizens, contact the Area Agency for Aging that serves your parents' locality.

Area Agencies on Aging

Southeast Tennessee Development District
   2100 Broad Street, Chattanooga, TN 37408   (615) 266-5781

South Central Tennessee Development District
   P.O. Box 1346, 805 Nashville Highway, Columbia, TN 38401
   (615) 381-2040

Upper Cumberland Development District
   1225 Burgess Falls Road, Cookeville, TN 38501   (615) 432-4111

Southwest Tennessee Development District
   416 East Lafayette Street, Jackson, TN 38301   (901) 422-4041

First Tennessee-Virginia Development District
   207 North Boone Street, Johnson City, TN 37601   (615) 928-0224

East Tennessee Human Resource Agency
   P.O. Box 11428, 617 Deane Hill Drive, Knoxville, TN 37919
   (615) 691-2551

Northwest Tennessee Development District
   P.O. Box 63, Martin, TN 38237   (901) 587-4213

Delta Commission on Aging
City Hall, Office of Planning & Development
   115 North Main Street, Room 419, Memphis, TN 38103
   (901) 528-2600

For a description of the benefits and services provided for your parents by local, state, and federal governments, the Commission on Aging suggests that you send for the regularly updated brochure *Government Programs for Senior Citizens* available on request from the senior advocate:

Ed McClain
Golden Rule Insurance Company
Golden Rule Buildings
The Waterfront
Indianapolis, Indiana 46224-4199   (317) 297-4123

TEXAS

Department on Aging
P.O. Box 12786, Capitol Station
Austin, Texas 78711   (512) 475-2717   or   1-800-252-9240
Long-Term Care Ombudsman
John Willis at the above address and phone number

About fifteen years after the establishment of the state's Committee on Aging in 1965 as mandated by the Older Americans Act of the same year, the Texas Legislature abolished the committee and formed the Texas Department on Aging, an independent state agency whose sole responsibility is to serve the state's 2 million older citizens.[11] The department, which is funded primarily with federal appropriations, fulfills its mandate through the Aging Network, consisting of twenty-eight Area Agencies on Aging statewide. The basic task of all these regional organizations is to provide aging Texans with the following:

- *Nutrition services,* including congregate meals in a social setting and home-delivered meals.
- *Social services,* including those that relate to access, such as transportation, outreach, information and referral, assessment and evaluation of needs, and those that relate to in-home support, such as homemaker/home health aide, visiting and telephone reassurance, chore maintenance, personal care, housekeeping, and the like.
- *Community services,* including legal counseling, escort, residential repair, health screening, and physical fitness and recreation programs; guardianship/conservatorship; income support, and advocacy.

11. Texas has the fifth largest sixty-plus population nationwide, exceeded only by California, New York, Pennsylvania, and Florida.

Every Area Agency is required to develop formal written plans to meet the particular needs of the elderly within the region served. To accomplish this, all twenty-eight agencies depend on input from advisory councils composed of community leaders, representatives of senior citizen organizations, and elderly persons representing themselves and their own needs. State funds, special federal grants, donations by community organizations, and money raised through the efforts of local groups have provided the wherewithal for an ongoing expansion of services and the development of innovative programs on the area level. Here are some recent examples:

- *The Alamo AAA* weatherized over five hundred houses, thus enabling seniors to remain in their own homes with reduced utility costs.
- *The Capital AAA* worked with the Bureau of Dental Health of the state's Department of Health to provide denture cleaning and identification marking for seniors.
- *The Central Texas AAA* implemented a program on the wise use of prescription drugs.
- *The Coastal Bend AAA* organized a legal services circuit that goes to the senior centers in the area, providing information and counseling to over seven hundred seniors each year.
- *The Concho Valley AAA* added new vans to its fleet, one of which is now used for long distance trips to pageants, zoos, museums, and parks.
- *The Dallas County AAA* has been instrumental in helping the University of Texas Health Science Center at Dallas receive additional funding as the Southwest Long-Term Care Gerontology Center.
- *The Deep East Texas AAA* has developed an ongoing workshop on Alzheimer's disease.
- *The Panhandle AAA* has expanded its Adult Day Care Center to include a twenty-four-hour respite care program accommodating sixteen people for a maximum stay of two weeks.
- *The Tarrant County AAA* sponsors an annual Senior Information Expo during Older Americans Month to increase the visibility of the community's many services.

To find out about the programs available to you and your parents, contact the Area Agency on Aging that serves their locality.

Area Agencies on Aging

Alamo Area AAA
   118 Broadway, Suite 400, San Antonio, TX 78205   (512) 225-5201

Counties served: Atascosa, Bandera, Comal, Frio, Gillespie, Guadalupe, Karnes, Kendall, Kerr, Medina, Wilson

Ark-Tex AAA

Center West, 911 Loop 151, P.O. Box 5307, Texarkana, TX 75501 (214) 832-8636

Counties served: Bowie, Cass, Delta, Franklin, Hopkins, Lamar, Morris, Red River, Titus

Bexar County AAA

118 Broadway, Suite 400, San Antonio, TX 78205   (512) 225-5201

Brazos Valley AAA

3006 East 29th Street, P.O. Drawer 4128, Bryan, TX 77805 (409) 822-7421   or   800-392-5563

Counties served: Brazos, Burleson, Grimes, Leon, Madison, Robertson, Washington

Capital AAA

2520 Interstate Highway 35 South, Suite 100, Austin, TX 78704 (512) 443-7653   or   800-252-8244

Counties served: Bastrop, Blanco, Burnet, Caldwell, Fayette, Hays, Lee, Llano, Travis, Williamson

Central Texas AAA

302 East Central, P.O. Box 729, Belton, TX 76513 (817) 939-1886   or   800-792-3022

Counties served: Bell, Coryell, Hamilton, Lampasa, Milam, Mills, San Saba

Coastal Bend AAA

2910 Leopard, P.O. Box 9909, Corpus Christi, TX 78469 (512) 883-5743

Counties served: Aransas, Bee, Brooks, Duval, Jim Wells, Kenedy, Kleberg, Live Oak, McMullen, Nueces, Refugio, San Patricio

Concho Valley AAA

5002 Knickerbocker Road, P.O. Box 60050, San Angelo, TX 76906 (915) 944-9666   or   800-592-4719

Counties served: Coke, Concho, Crockett, Irion, Kimble, Mason, McCulloch, Menard, Reagan, Schleicher, Sterling, Sutton, Tom Green

Dallas County AAA

1900 Pacific, Suite 1725, Dallas, TX 75201   (214) 741-5851

Deep East Texas AAA

274 East Lamar Street, Jasper, TX 75951   (409) 384-5704

Counties served: Angelina, Houston, Jasper, Nacogdoches, Newton, Polk, Sabine, San Augustine, San Jacinto, Shelby, Trinity, Tyler

East Texas AAA

3800 Stone Road, Kilgore, TX 75662   (214) 984-8641   or 800-442-8845

Counties served: Anderson, Camp, Cherokee, Gregg, Harrison, Henderson, Marion, Panola, Rains, Rusk, Smith, Upshur, Van Zandt, Wood

Golden Crescent AAA

115 South Main Street, P.O. Box 2028, Victoria, TX 77902 (512) 578-1587   or   800-292-1565

Counties served: Calhoun, DeWitt, Goliad, Conzales, Jackson, Lavaca, Victoria

Harris Count AAA

402 Pierce, Suite 201, P.O. Box 1562, Houston, TX 77251 (713) 757-7822

Heart of Texas AAA

320 Franklin Avenue, Waco, TX 76701   (817) 756-6631   or 800-792-2008

Counties served: Bosque, Falls, Freestone, Hill, Limestone, McLennan

Houston-Galveston AAA

3555 Timmons, Suite 500, P.O. Box 22777, Houston, TX 77227 (713) 627-3200

Counties served: Austin, Brazoria, Chambers, Colorado, Fort Bend, Galveston, Liberty, Matagorda, Montgomery, Walker, Waller, Wharton

Lower Rio Grande Valley AAA

Texas Commerce Bank Building, Suite 707, 1701 West Business Highway 83, McAllen, TX 78501   (512) 682-3481

Counties served: Cameron, Hidalgo, Willacy

Middle Rio Grande Valley AAA

403 East Nopal, P.O. Box 702, Carrizo Springs, TX 78834 (512) 876-3533

Counties served: Dimmit, Edwards, Kinney, La Salle, Maverick, Real, Uvalde, Val Verde, Zavala

North Central Texas AAA

616 Six Flags Drive, Centerpoint Two, 2d floor, P.O. Drawer COG, Arlington, TX 76005   (817) 640-3300

Counties served: Collin, Denton, Ellis, Erath, Hood, Hunt, Johnson, Kaufman, Navarro, Palo Pinto, Parker, Rockwell, Somervell, Wise

North Texas AAA

2101 Kemp Boulevard, P.O. Box 5144, Wichita Falls, TX 76307 (817) 322-5281

Counties served: Archer, Baylor, Childress, Clay, Cottle, Foard, Hardeman, Jack, Montague, Wichita, Wilbarger, Young

Panhandle AAA

801 South Jackson, Briercroft Building, Suite 200, P.O. Box 9257, Amarillo, TX 79105   (806) 372-3381

Counties served: Armstrong, Briscoe, Carson, Castro, Collingsworth, Dallam, Deaf Smith, Donley, Gray, Hall, Hansford, Hartley, Hemphill, Hutchinson, Lipscomb, Moore, Ochiltree, Oldham, Parmer, Potter, Randall, Roberts, Sherman, Swisher, Wheeler

Permian Basin AAA

2514 Pliska Drive, P.O. Box 6391, Midland, TX 79711 (915) 563-1061

Counties served: Andrews, Borden, Crane, Dawson, Ector, Gaines, Glasscock, Howard, Loving, Martin, Midland, Pecos, Reeves, Terrell, Upton, Ward, Winkler

Southeast Texas AAA

3800 Highway 365, Port Arthur, TX 77640   (409) 727-2384 and P.O. Drawer 1387, Nederland, TX 77627

Counties served: Hardin, Jefferson, Orange

South Plains AAA

3424 Avenue H, P.O. Box 2787, Lubbock, TX 79408 (806) 762-8721   or   800-858-1809

Counties served: Baily, Cochran, Crosby, Dickens, Floyd, Garza, Hale, Hockley, King, Lamb, Lubbock, Lynn, Motley, Terry, Yoakum

South Texas AAA

600 South Sandman, Laredo Intl. Airport, P.O. Box 2187 Laredo, TX 78044   (512) 722-3995   or   800-292-5426

Counties served: Jim Hogg, Starr, Webb, Zapata

Tarrant County AAA

210 East 9th Street, Fort Worth, TX 76102   (817) 335-3473

Texoma AAA

10000 Grayson Drive, Denison, TX 75020   (214) 786-2955

Counties served: Cooke, Fannin, Grayson

West Central Texas AAA

1025 East North 10th, P.O. Box 3195, Abilene, TX 79604 (915) 672-8544

Counties served: Brown, Callahan, Coleman, Comanche, Eastland, Fisher, Haskell, Jones, Kent, Knox, Mitchell, Nolan, Runnels, Scurry, Shackelford, Stephens, Stonewall, Taylor, Throckmorton

West Texas AAA
> #2 Civic Center Plaza, 8th Floor, El Paso, TX 79999
> (915) 541-4972
>> Counties served: Brewster, Culberson, El Paso, Hudspeth, Jeff Davis, Presidio

———————————

Every area agency has at least one paid staff person who coordinates the efforts of specially trained and certified volunteers participating in the nursing home ombudsman program. In addition, the Texas Department of Health has established a toll-free line which provides information about nursing home care: 1-800-252-9106.

The Attorney General's Consumer Protection Series called "Know Your Rights" includes the brochure *Selecting a Nursing Home.* Order your copy from:

> Attorney General of Texas
> P.O. Box 12548
> Austin, Texas 78711

———————————

UTAH

Division of Aging and Adult Services
> 150 West North Temple
> P.O. Box 45500
> Salt Lake City, Utah 84145-0500   (801) 533-6422

Long-Term Care Ombudsman
> Marj Drury
> Department of Social Services at the above address and phone number

Information and referral for all services and programs for Senior Citizens is provided by the Area Agency on Aging that serves the county where your parents live. Each community also contains a branch of the Office of Community Operations which is administered by the Department of Social Services. These branch offices are responsible for providing adult protective services, foster care, in-home assistance, and many of the support systems federally funded under the Older Americans Act. Call the local Area Agency on Aging for additional details.

Area Agencies on Aging

Bear River AAA
P.O. Box 567, 236 North 100 East, Logan, UT 84321
(801) 752-9456
Counties served: Box Elder, Cache, Rich

Weber County AAA
Raddison Hotel, Second Mezzanine, 2500 Washington Blvd.,
Ogden, UT 84401 (801) 399-8841
Counties served: Morgan, Weber

Salt Lake County Aging Services
135 East 2100 South #3, Salt Lake City, UT 84115
(801) 488-5454

Davis County Council on Aging
Courthouse Annex, P.O. Box 618, Farmington, UT 84025
(801) 451-3370 or 3377

Tooele AAA
c/o Gary Dalton, 47 South Main, #300, Tooele, UT 84074
(801) 882-2870

Mountainland AAA
160 East Center Street, Provo, UT 84601
(801) 534-0772 or 377-2262
Counties served: Summit, Utah, Wasatch

Central Utah AAA
P.O. Box 788, Richfield, UT 84701 (801) 896-9222-9226
Counties served: Juab, Millard, Piute, Sanpete, Sevier, Wayne

Five County AAA
P.O. Box "O," St. George, UT 84770 (801) 673-3548
Counties served: Beaver, Garfield, Iron, Kane, Washington

Uintah Basin AAA
P.O. Box 1449, Roosevelt, UT 84066 (801) 722-4519
Counties served: Daggett, Duchesne

Uintah County Golden Age Center
155 South 100 West, Vernal, UT 84078 (801) 789-2169

Southeastern Utah AAA
P.O. Drawer 1106, Price, UT 84501 (801) 637-4268
Counties served: Carbon, Emery, Grand

San Juan County AAA
County Courthouse, Monticello, UT 84535 (801) 587-2231

VERMONT

Office on Aging
> 101 South Main Street
> Waterbury, Vermont 05656   (802) 241-2400   or   1-800-642-5119

Long-Term Care Ombudsman
> Patrick Flood at the above address and phone number

The services, programs, and resources available for elderly Vermonters are set forth in handbooks called *Who Cares?* There are five such handbooks, one for each part of the state, and they are among the most informative, well-organized, and attractively presented guides being offered by any state agency nationwide. The services are described in detail, with a name, an address, and a phone number for each one that can be called upon in a particular community. Material is organized under the following headings:

> *Care Away from Home,* including hospitals, skilled and intermediate level nursing homes, community care homes.

> *Care in Your Home,* including home health agencies, visiting nurse associations, hospice care, in-home emergency response systems, homemaker and personal care service providers, sources for medical equipment and supplies, respite care, companionship-visiting services, chore services, meals for seniors, and home repair and reconditioning services.

> *Other Community Services,* including adult day services, community mental health, legal and protective services, ombudsman services, guardianship information, income-related programs (food stamps, fuel assistance, Medicare, Medicaid, Social Security benefits, Supplemental Security Income), housing programs, transportation, and tax assistance.

> *Special Services,* including those for the blind and visually impaired, for the deaf and hearing impaired, for stroke patients and their families, substance abuse programs, veterans services, dental services.

> *Organizations for Special Health Problems,* including fourteen different programs and support services offered by the American Cancer Society; community activities and resources; and counseling and referral offered by local chapters of the American Diabetes Association, American Heart Association, Arthritis Foundation, Epilepsy Association, Muscular Dystrophy Association.

> *Social Service Agencies,* including the Area Agency on Aging, De-

partment of Health, Department of Social Welfare, and Community Action Agencies.

Each handbook contains an unusually detailed index for easy reference.

The specific handbook for your parents' part of Vermont can be requested from the Agency of Human Services, Office on Aging *or* from the Area Agency on Aging or Council on Aging that serves their locality. Staff members of the Area Agency will also visit them in their own home to explain the variety of services available in their community.

Who Cares? in Caledonia, Essex, and Orleans counties:
Area Agency on Aging for Northeastern Vermont
   44 Main Street, St. Johnsbury, VT 05819
   Call collect (802) 748-5182 or
   Branch Office, Home Health Building
   Main Street, Newport, VT 05855 (802) 334-6366

Who Cares? in Bennington and Rutland counties:
Southwestern Vermont Area Agency on Aging
   Bardwell House
   142 Merchants Row, Rutland, VT 05701 (802) 775-0486 or
   124 Pleasant Street, Bennington, VT 05201 (802) 442-5436

Who Cares? in Windham and Windsor counties:
Council on Aging for Southeastern Vermont
   139 Main Street, Brattleboro, VT 05301
   Call Collect (802) 254-4446 or
Central Vermont Council on Aging
   18 South Main Street, Barre, VT 05641
   Call Collect (802) 479-0531
      Towns covered: Bethel, Norwich, Rochester, Royalton, Sharon, Stockbridge

Who Cares? in Addison, Chittenden, Franklin, and Grand Isle counties:
Champlain Valley Area Agency on Aging
   110 East Spring Street, Winooski, VT 05404
   (802) 655-0084 or toll-free 1-800-642-5119

Who Cares? in Lamoille, Orange, and Washington counties:
Central Vermont Council on Aging
   18 South Main Street, Barre, VT 05641 (802) 479-0531 or
   Lamoille County Office
   Morrisville Senior Center, Morrisville, VT 05661
   (802) 888-2288

VIRGINIA

Department for the Aging
    James Monroe Building
    101 North 14th Street, 18th floor
    Richmond, Virginia 23219   (804) 225-2271
Long-Term Care Ombudsman Program
    Cathy Saunders or Virginia Dize at the above address and phone
    number or toll-free 1-800-552-3402

In 1982, the Office on Aging, which had been created in 1974, was renamed the Department for the Aging by an act of the state legislature, thus recognizing the importance of programs serving the elderly and the state's commitment to these programs. The department is the agency responsible for planning, coordinating, funding, and evaluating programs and services for improving and enriching the quality of life of the more than 726,000 Virginians who are age sixty or older and who make up almost 14 percent of the state's population.

While most older Virginians live active and independent lives, many can do so only because they can depend on the help of friends and family. Also, many must eventually turn to services provided by state and local sources.

When you need to explore the aging network available to serve your parents' needs and to help you help them remain in the community for as long as possible instead of being institutionalized, the most comprehensive source for information and referral is the Area Agency on Aging that coordinates and administers these programs in your parents' locality.

There are twenty-five Area Agencies on Aging whose activities are financed by federal funds through the Older Americans Act, by state funds, and by appropriations from local public and private sources.

While each Area Agency may vary its programs to suit local conditions and needs, the following are typical statewide:

- *Nutrition program:* A hot nutritious meal is served in a social setting or delivered to the homebound.
- *Community-based services:* These have the prime purpose of helping older people to remain in their own homes rather than to be at risk of institutionalization. The services include help with household tasks and chores, essential shopping, and minor house repairs; day care as a supplement to family care; escorts to accompany an older person needing help to get to medical appointments or other essential destinations; friendly visiting to provide companionship and social stimulation for those who are other-

wise isolated; home health aid and rehabilitative therapy under a doctor's supervision; legal services; telephone reassurance; and transportation.

- *Economic and related programs:* These services focus on the elderly who need help in managing their finances or improving their economic security. They include continuing education to provide vocational or personal enrichment; a discount ID program; employment assessment, counseling, referral, job development, and where possible, job placement; tax and consumer counseling; and Title V (under the Older Americans Act) Senior Community Service Employment providing part-time jobs in community services for low-income persons age fifty-five or older.

- *Recreation and socialization programs:* These provide the opportunity for leisure time activities and socializing. There are now about 170 senior centers statewide offering lectures, arts and crafts classes, sports and exercise programs, parties, and other activities planned by the participants.

Detailed information about these and other services is available from the Area Agency on Aging that serves your parents' locality.

Area Agencies on Aging

Mountain Empire Older Citizens
330 Norton Road, P.O. Box 1097, Wise, VA 24293   (703) 328-2302

Appalachian Agency for Senior Citizens
Box SVCC, Richlands, VA 23641   (703) 964-4915

District III Governmental Cooperative
305 South Park Street, Marion, VA 24354   (703) 783-8158

New River Valley Agency on Aging
143 Third Street N.W., Pulaski, VA 24301   (703) 980-8888

League of Older Americans
706 Campbell Avenue S.W., Roanoke, VA 24016   (703) 345-0451

Valley Program for Aging Services
P.O. Box 817, Waynesboro, VA 22980   (703) 949-7141

Shenandoah Area Agency on Aging
15 North Royal Avenue, Front Royal, VA 22630   (703) 635-7141

Alexandria Area Agency on Aging
1108 Jefferson Street, Alexandria, VA 22314   (703) 838-4822

Arlington Area Agency on Aging
1800 North Edison, Arlington, VA 22207   (703) 558-2341

Fairfax County Area Agency on Aging
4100 Chain Bridge Road, Fairfax, VA 22030   (703) 691-3384

Aging Services Program
City Hall, 207 Park Avenue, Suite B-4, Falls Church, VA 22047
(703) 241-5005

Loudon County Area Agency on Aging
21 North Harrison Street, Leesburg, VA 22075   (703) 777-0257

Prince William Area Agency on Aging
9256 Mosby Street, Suite 103, Manassas, VA 22110
(703) 369-9285

Rappahannock-Rapidan Area Agency on Aging
401 South Main Street, Culpeper, VA 22701   (703) 825-6494

Jefferson Area Board for Aging
205 Second Street, S.W., Charlottesville, VA 22901
(804) 977-3444

Central Virginia Commission on Aging
Forest Hill Center, 2820 Linkhorne Drive, Lynchburg, VA 24503
(804) 384-0372

Piedmont Seniors of Virginia
29 Broad Street, Martinsville, VA 24112   (703) 632-6442

Lake Country Commission on Aging
1105 West Danville Street, South Hill, VA 23970   (804) 447-7661

Piedmont Senior Resources
P.O. Box 398, Burkeville, VA 23922   (804) 767-5588

Capital Area Agency on Aging
6 North 6th Street, Richmond, VA 23219   (804) 648-8381

Rappahannock Area Agency on Aging
601 Caroline Street, 3rd floor, Fredericksburg, VA 22401
(703) 371-3375

Northern Neck—Middle Peninsula Area Agency on Aging
P.O. Box 387, Saluda, VA 23149   (804) 758-2386

Crater District Area Agency on Aging
120 West Bank Street, Petersburg, VA 23803   (804) 732-7020

Southeastern Virginia Areawide Model Program (SEVAMP)
7 Koger Executive Center, Suite 100, York Bldg.,
Norfolk, VA 23502   (804) 461-9481

Peninsula Agency on Aging
944 Denbigh Boulevard, Newport News, VA 23602
(804) 874-2495

Eastern Shore Community Development Group
P.O. Box 316, Accomac, VA 23301   (804) 787-3532

The Department on Aging will send you or your parents on request
the useful *Guide to Long-Term Care in Virginia.* This ninety-five-
page publication includes detailed information about community

services, how to select the right level of care for a frail or chronically ill parent, various types of nursing homes, the ways in which long-term care can be financed, and a list of the state's geriatric treatment centers.

Another helpful publication prepared by the Department is the *Senior Citizen Directory.*

Information about the location of day care centers statewide is available on request from:

The Virginia Institute on Adult Day Care
Box 14607, Richmond, Virginia 23221

WASHINGTON

Department of Social and Health Services Bureau of Aging and Adult Services
　　Olympia, Washington 98504　(206) 753-2504
Long-Term Care Ombudsman
　　Yong Hall
　　Audit Division OB-33B
　　Olympia, Washington 98504　(206) 754-2258

Washington State has established an aging network consisting of thirteen Area Agencies on Aging which are central sources for information and referral and which contract and work with a wide range of private, nonprofit agencies; public agencies such as departments of health and departments of social welfare; volunteer groups which participate in the ombudsman program and which participate in important activities on the community level; advocacy and planning organizations; senior centers; and others. The function of the network is to plan for and make available to older persons a continuum of services enabling them to lead independent and productive lives for as long as possible, thereby preventing unnecessary or premature placement in nursing institutions.

As described in a recent annual report, the services available to senior citizens include those listed below. Note that not all services are available in every area, and eligibility for some is based on family income.

- *Information and assistance/case management* combine services which aim to find the people who need the services and to connect them with the appropriate resources. Services range from providing information and referral to planning and monitoring a continuum of assistance and care that will keep the older person at home rather than in an institution.
- *Adult family homes* are licensed to provide the least restrictive alternative to independent living for adults who cannot live

alone. Residents may pay privately, or the cost of care may be charged to the Department of Health and Social Services.

- *Chore services* may be provided on an hourly basis and may be temporary or long-term and include help with housekeeping, personal care, meal preparation, and transportation.
- *Day health services* are provided in a group setting to participants who need rehabilitative nursing, occupational therapy, activity therapy, a noon meal, and transportation to and from the day care center.
- *Geriatric health screening* focuses on the early detection of asymptomatic diseases to prevent or decrease eventual complications. Each screening includes a general health assessment, limited physical examination, and laboratory tests. Referral to a suitable specialist is part of the program.
- *Home health services* are provided to elderly persons in their own home on a visiting basis under a plan established and regularly reviewed by a physician.
- *Legal services* help older persons determine their legal rights, represent them in noncriminal proceedings, prepare legal documents, and conduct educational and advocacy campaigns.
- *Minor home repair and maintenance services* undertake repairs and modifications of a dwelling that are essential for the health and safety of the occupants.
- *Mental health services* evaluate an older person's need for professional intervention and make referrals to suitable treatment facilities.

Other programs operating statewide are congregate and/or home-delivered meals, employment opportunities for seniors, transportation assistance, volunteer participation, and senior centers.

Detailed information about these services and programs and how they operate in your parents' locality is available from the Area Agency on Aging in their vicinity.

Area Agencies on Aging

Olympic Area Agency
    2109 Sumner Avenue, Room 203, Aberdeen, WA 98520
        Counties served: Clallam, Jefferson, Grays Harbor, Pacific
Northwest Area Agency
    Forest Street Annex, Whatcom County Courthouse,
    1000 Forest Street, Bellingham, WA 98225
        Counties served: Whatcom, Skagit, San Juan Island
Snohomish County Office on Aging
    4th Floor County Administration Building, Everett, WA 98201

Seattle-King County Area Agency
400 Yesler Building, Seattle, WA 98104

Pierce County Area Agency
2401 South 35th Street, Room 5, Tacoma, WA 98409

Lewis/Thurston/Mason Council of Governments
529 Southwest 4th Street, Olympia, WA 98501

Southwest Area Agency
Health & Welfare Planning Council, P.O. Box 425,
Vancouver, WA 98666
Counties served: Clark, Cowlitz, Klickitat, Skamania (part),
Wahkiakum

Northcentral Area Agency
Wenatchee Valley College, 1300 5th Street, Wenatchee, WA 98801
Counties served: Adams, Chelan, Douglas, Grant, Lincoln, Oka-
nogan

Yakima Southeast Area Agency
Board of Yakima County Commissioners
2011 South 64th Avenue, Yakima, WA 98903
Counties served: Asotin, Benton, Columbia, Franklin, Garfield,
Kittitas, Walla Walla, Yakima (part)

Yakima Indian Nation Area Agency
Yakima Tribal Council, P.O. Box 151, Toppenish, WA 98948

Eastern Area Agency
Spokane Public Health Building, Suite 160
West 1101 College Street, Spokane, WA 99201
Counties served: Ferry (part), Pend Oreille, Spokane, Stevens,
Whitman

Colville Indian Area Agency
Colville Confederated Tribes, P.O. Box 150, Nespelem, WA 99155
Counties served: Ferry (part), Okanogan (part)

Kitsap Area Agency
Board of Kitsap County Commissioners
Kitsap County Courthouse, 614 Division, Port Orchard, WA 98366

WEST VIRGINIA

Commission on Aging
Holly Grove—Capitol Complex
Charleston, West Virginia 25305
(304) 348-3317 or 348-2241 toll-free 1-800-642-3671

Long-Term Care Ombudsman
Bob Bianchinotti at the above address and phone numbers

Programs for the elderly in West Virginia have to take into account several difficult specific circumstances: the state continues to be one of the few nationwide in which more people leave than arrive, but this out-migration does not include large numbers of people who are over sixty and who will increasingly make up a larger portion of the total population. Also, senior West Virginians are far more likely than their national counterparts to live in rural areas—57 percent compared to a little over 25 percent in the rest of the United States. A significant number of their houses lack complete kitchen and plumbing facilities and have no central heating. And according to the 1980 Census, over 39,000 West Virginians age sixty-five and over suffer from a chronic health condition that prevents them from using public transportation. In addition, 6 percent of all seniors have no telephone in their housing unit.

In the state's 116-page Plan on Aging for Fiscal Years 1986–1988 prepared by the state's Commission on Aging and submitted to the Administration on Aging of the U.S. Department of Health and Human Services, details are spelled out for development, administration, and delivery of services and programs. Among the objectives are:

- To expand the responsibilities of the Commission on Aging in developing a comprehensive and coordinated system of social and health related services to the elderly.
- To promote and develop a continuum of care services to provide alternatives to those at risk of institutionalization.
- To work with appropriate federal, state, regional and local social and medical service planners to provide an effective statewide case management system by July 1988.
- To work with suitable public and private agencies for the development of housing alternatives for the elderly.
- To promote the expansion of employment opportunities for older West Virginians who wish to be gainfully employed.
- To promote intergenerational activities and thereby dispel negative stereotyping of the elderly.
- To increase and reinforce the advocacy programs for the elderly by representing their interests to legislative and executive bodies.
- To continue to expand the network of long-term care ombudspersons.
- To continue the statewide Golden Mountaineer Discount Program.
- To expand and improve statewide educational opportunities.
- To promote volunteerism as a community resource for expanding services to the institutionalized and noninstitutionalized elderly.

You and your parents may have attended an Annual Senior Citizens Conference sponsored by the Commission on Aging during May of each year. If you haven't and would like to know more about the details, write to the Commission on Aging for a past program covering this important intergenerational event. The Commission has also prepared a brochure,

Working to Improve the Lives of Older West Virginians, which is available on request.

For details about current programs and services in your parents' locality, contact the nearest Area Agency on Aging.

Area Agencies on Aging

Region I: AAA

East River Office Building, P.O. Box 1442, Princeton, WV 24720 (304) 425-9508

Counties served: McDowell, Mercer, Monroe, Raleigh, Summers, Wyoming

Region II: Southwestern AAA

540 Fifth Avenue, Huntington, WV 25701 (304) 525-5151

Counties served: Cabell, Lincoln, Logan, Mason, Mingo, Wayne

Region III: AAA

Community Council of Kanawha Valley

P.O. Box 2711, Charleston, WV 25330 (304) 342-5107

Counties served: Boone, Kanawha, Putnam

Region IV: Eastern Highlands AAA

500 B Main Street, Summersville, WV 26651 (403) 872-4970

Counties served: Fayette, Greenbrier, Nicholas, Pocahontas, Webster

Region V: AAA

Mid-Ohio Valley Regional Council

925 Market Street, P.O. Box 247, Parkersburg, WV 26101 (304) 422-0522

Counties served: Calhoun, Jackson, Pleasants, Ritchie, Roane, Tyler, Wirt, Wood

Region VI: AAA

200 Adams Street, Fairmont, WV 26554 (304) 366-5693

Counties served: Doddridge, Harrison, Marion, Monongalia, Preston, Taylor

Region VII: Central West Virginia AAA

5 South Florida Street, P.O. Box 186, Buckhannon, WV 26201 (304) 472-0395

Counties served: Barbour, Braxton, Gilmer, Lewis, Randolph, Tucker, Upshur

Regions VIII-IX: Eastern West Virginia AAA

P.O. Box 866, Oetersburg, WV 26847 (304) 257-1221

Counties served: Grant, Hampshire, Hardy, Mineral, Pendleton/ Berkeley, Jefferson, Morgan

Regions X-XI: Northern Panhandle AAA
   Bel-O-Mar Interstate Planning Council
   2177 National Road, P.O. Box 2086, Wheeling, WV 26003
   (304) 242-1800
      Counties served: Brooke, Hancock, Marshall, Ohio, Wetzel

---

If you would like to have a detailed list of licensed nursing homes
and licensed personal care homes statewide, contact the Long-Term
Care Ombudsman at 1-800-642-3671, or if you're calling from out
of state, (304) 348-3317.

WISCONSIN

Department of Health and Social Services, Office on Aging
   1 West Wilson Street, P.O. Box 7851
   Madison, Wisconsin 53707   (608) 266-2536
Nursing Home Ombudsperson
   Board on Aging & Long Term Care
   GEF #3, Room 17
   125 South Webster Street
   Madison, Wisconsin 53702

Wisconsin is one of a few states—New York is another—to have prepared special material to help *caregivers.* Available on request from the
Office on Aging is *Help at a Glance: A Handbook of Caregiver Support
Resources.* It is an indispensable source of inspiration and information
for anyone responsible for the well-being of an aging parent. The support
services discussed in detail are adult day care, respite care, self-help
systems, supplementary services, and relatively new and different services. Here are some typical entries:

In-Home Day Services for the Elderly

LOCATION:	In-Home Satellite Day Care Program (care provided in a family home, an extension of the Adult Day Care Center, 312 Wisconsin Avenue, Madison, Wisconsin)
TYPE:	Social (the sponsoring Center is a health maintenance model)
CAPACITY:	3 to 5
SCHEDULE:	2 days per week
SERVICES:	Individual and group activities, group exercise, music, community activities, rest, noon meal, transportation

Altercare: A Respite Care Resource

PROVIDER AGENCY:	City View Nursing Home 3737 Burke Road, Madison, Wisconsin
TYPE OF ORGANIZATION:	Room and Board, family-oriented facility
SERVICE POPULATION:	Independent functioning elderly; may use ambulation assistance such as walkers and wheelchairs
SERVICE SETTING:	Group facility, capacity of 15
SERVICE FACTORS:	Respite care provided in a residential setting; short-term placement (one week to one month); counseling and therapies available; shared activities with nursing home population (in connected building) as appropriate.

The Office on Aging also administers a wide range of programs for persons who are sixty and older. Many of these programs are funded by grants under the Older Americans Act and include congregate and home delivered meals, in-home services, volunteer opportunities, legal referral, transportation, health screening, protective services, and telephone reassurance.

Federal, state, and local funds contribute to senior centers statewide, special peer publications, ongoing education, and intergenerational activities.

Information and referral for these and other programs of interest to your parents can be requested from the Area Agency on Aging that serves their county.

Area Agencies on Aging

Southern Area Agency on Aging
> 3601 Memorial Drive, Madison, WI 53704   (608) 249-0441
>> Counties served: Columbia, Dane, Dodge, Grant, Green, Iowa, Jefferson, Lafayette, Richland, Rock, Sauk

Milwaukee Area Agency on Aging
> 1442 North Farwell Avenue, Milwaukee, WI 53202
> (414) 272-8606

Southeastern Area Agency on Aging
> W255 N499 Grandview Boulevard, Suite 209, Waukesha, WI 53188
> (414) 521-5420
>> Counties served: Kenosha, Ozaukee, Racine, Walworth, Washington, Waukesha

Lake Michigan-Winnebago Area Agency on Aging
850 C Lombardi Avenue, Green Bay, WI 54304-3768
(414) 432-9235

Counties served: Brown, Calumet, Door, Fond du Lac, Green Lake, Kewaunee, Manitowoc, Marinette, Marquette, Oconto, Outagamie, Shawano, Sheboygan, Waupaca, Waushara, Winnebago

Tribes served: Menominee, Oneida, Stockbridge-Munsee

Western Wisconsin Area Agency on Aging
718 West Clairemont Avenue, Rm. 217, Eau Claire, WI 54701
(715) 836-4105

Counties served: Barren, Buffalo, Burnett, Chippewa, Clark, Crawford, Dunn, Eau Claire, Jackson, La Crosse, Monroe, Pepin, Pierce, Polk, Rusk, St. Croix, Trempealeau, Vernon, Washburn

Tribe served: Winnebago

Northern Area Agency on Aging
1853 North Stevens Street, P.O. Box 1028, Rhinelander, WI 54501
(715) 362-7800

Counties served: Adams, Ashland, Bayfield, Douglas, Florence, Forest, Iron, Juneau, Langlade, Lincoln, Marathon, Oneida, Portage, Price, Sawyer, Taylor, Vilas, Wood

Tribes served: Bad River, Lac Courte Oreilles, Lac du Flambeau, Mole Lake, Red Cliff, St. Croix, Stone Lake

WYOMING

Commission on Aging
Hathaway Building
Cheyenne, Wyoming 82002 (307) 777-7986

Nursing Home Ombudsperson
Mrs. Debra Alden
900 8th Street
Wheatland, Wyoming (307) 322-5553

Information concerning the various support systems for senior citizens and their families in this state is available from the following sources in addition to the two agencies given above:

Statewide Senior Organization
Wyoming Senior Citizen, Inc.
510 East Main Street, Riverton, WY 82501 (307) 856-6880

Adult Day Care Centers
Buffalo Helping Hands Inc.
P.O. Box 941, Buffalo, WY 82834 (307) 684-9552

Legal Services Developer
Mrs. Susan Feinman
2111 Central Avenue, Cheyenne, WY 82001 (307) 632-9067

Public Assistance and Social Service
Hathaway Building, Cheyenne, WY 82002 (307) 777-7656

State Health and Medical Service—same as above

Wyoming Home Health Care
262 South Jackson, Casper, WY (307) 237-4471

In addition, the following is a partial list of agencies and organizations statewide that offer supportive services, including the nutrition program of congregate meals and meals for the homebound:

Buffalo Helping Hands
P.O. Box 941, Buffalo, WY 82834 (307) 684-9552

Campbell County Senior Citizens
701 Stock Trail, Gillette, WY 82716 (307) 686-0804

Cokeville Senior Citizens
Box 355, Cokeville, WY 83114 (307) 279-3226

Douglas Senior Citizens Center
Box 192, Douglas, WY 82633 (307) 358-4348

High Country Senior Citizens
Box 918, Dubois, WY 82513 (307) 455-2990

Kemmerer Senior Citizens Center
Box 669, Kemmerer, WY 83101 (307) 877-3806

Laramie County Senior Citizen
3304 Sheridan Avenue, Cheyenne, WY 82009 (307) 634-0876

Laramie Senior Center
103 Ivinson, Laramie, WY 82070 (307) 745-5116 or 745-7705

Natrona County Senior Service
136 West 8th, Casper, WY 82601 (307) 265-4678

INDEX